RIPPER

RIPPER

THE MAKING OF PIERRE POILIEVRE

MARK BOURRIE

BIBLIOASIS
WINDSOR, ONTARIO

Copyright © Mark Bourrie, 2025

All rights reserved. No part of this publication may be reproduced or transmitted in any form or by any means, electronic or mechanical, including photocopying, recording, or any information storage and retrieval system, without permission in writing from the publisher or a licence from The Canadian Copyright Licensing Agency (Access Copyright). For an Access Copyright licence visit www.accesscopyright.ca or call toll free to 1-800-893-5777.

FIRST EDITION
10 9 8 7 6 5 4 3 2 1

Library and Archives Canada Cataloguing in Publication
Title: Ripper : the making of Pierre Poilievre / Mark Bourrie.
Other titles: Making of Pierre Poilievre
Names: Bourrie, Mark, 1957- author
Description: Includes bibliographical references and index.
Identifiers: Canadiana (print) 20250147351 | Canadiana (ebook) 20250147378
   ISBN 9781771967006 (softcover) | ISBN 9781771967013 (EPUB)
Subjects: LCSH: Poilievre, Pierre, 1979- | LCSH: Politicians—Canada—
   Biography. | CSH: Canada—Politics and government—2015- | LCGFT:
   Biographies.
Classification: LCC FC651.P65 B68 2025 | DDC 324.2092—dc23

Edited by Daniel Wells
Copyedited by Jill Ainsley
Typeset by Vanessa Stauffer
Indexed by Allana Amlin
Cover designed by Ingrid Paulson

 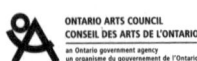 

Biblioasis acknowledges the support of the Canada Council for the Arts and funding support from the Ontario Arts Council and the Government of Ontario, including through the Ontario Book Publishing Tax Credit and Ontario Creates.

PRINTED AND BOUND IN CANADA

For my wife, Marion

CONTENTS

Introduction
Pierre Poilievre and the New Politics / 1

1 A Man of His Time and Place / 25

2 Larval Politician / 43

3 On to Ottawa / 67

4 Newbie / 91

5 Dial-a-Quote / 114

6 Election Skullduggery / 145

7 Contender in the Wilderness / 177

8 Wrecking WE Charity / 197

9   Is Canada Broken? / 221

10   The Convoy / 245

11   Top Dog / 275

12   Trolling (for) the Working Class / 299

13   The Media and the Message / 320

14   On Shifting Ground / 354

Acknowledgements / 377

Notes / 380

Index / 425

*The government you elect
is the government you deserve.*
THOMAS JEFFERSON

INTRODUCTION
PIERRE POILIEVRE
AND THE NEW POLITICS

> *Writing a book is like reading a book, except the book is trying to kill you.*
>
> ANITA ANAND OF THE BBC,
> ON HER *EMPIRE* PODCAST.[1]

SIX WEEKS BEFORE the 2024 American presidential election, CBS Late Night host Stephen Colbert interviewed Prime Minister Justin Trudeau. "Flirtation with fascism has been rising across the globe," Colbert said with impressive seriousness. "The Conservative leader, your opponent there, has been called 'Canada's Trump.' (Sorry about that.) But I am curious why at least some form of nativism or far-right xenophobia might grow even in a country as polite as Canada? Why is it getting a foothold in your country?"

Trudeau started to explain. "We're not a magical place of unicorns and rainbows. We have more than our fair share..."

He went on to dodge the question.

I'm going to try to answer it. This is a book about how Canada made its own version of Donald Trump, albeit with fewer guns and less rioting, but with lots of trucks and lies.

How have we ended up with this Trump-lite? The same way people in the Netherlands, France, Germany, Slovakia, Italy, Austria, Poland, Hungary, and so many other countries got their new extreme-right leaders and contenders. In this updated version of 1930s-style right-wing authoritarianism, there are fewer uniforms, but the message and tactics have not changed. Extreme-right and fascist leaders always see fake threats and vague enemies. They offer easy and simple answers to complicated problems. They say the institutions that protect democracy are run by the enemies of the people.

Since the end of the Second World War, we've had jarring political revolutions in Russia and China and sweeping political change in most other nations.[2] At the same time, technological innovation and freer trade destroyed the financial security of many working-class families. Big outlet stores crushed the commercial class, people who owned small businesses, and killed North American downtowns. A plutocracy of intellectual property owners and tech company shareholders amassed more wealth than anyone in history. (The total GDP of the entire Roman Empire at its height is estimated at $US100 billion. The seven billionaires who stood behind Donald Trump when he was inaugurated in 2025 were estimated to control $1200 billion, enough to pay off Canada's $834 billion national debt and still be among the richest people in the world.)[3]

Even when revolutions aren't happening, people flourish, fail, or just plod along in a world in which they have little real power. Their upbringing, the place they live, who their friends are, what (or if) they read, how they look, the quality of their brains, and their ambition help determine how their life will go. Politics offers aggressive people a chance to change their stars. And it is an easy route to success for sociopaths and demagogues, if the political environment is right.[4]

That's why this book is about Pierre Poilievre's world as much as it is about the man himself. He can't be understood without knowing the story of his childhood, his formative teen years, the almost unique political opportunities that existed in Calgary in the late 1980s, and the loss of effective media scrutiny of any politician. Those changes helped to shift the zeitgeist in a way that benefitted Poilievre after he spent years on the scene as the political equivalent of a hockey goon. In life, doors open and close. For this man, the doors have been huge. Pierre Poilievre was made in Alberta and emerged from the conservative pack in the 2020s, although he's hardly developed intellectually since the 1990s, when he was still a teenager. Poilievre has always been what he currently is. He has not changed to win over voters; they have shifted to where he is, and we need to understand how and why that's happened.

IN THE MOVIE *Dirty Dancing*, the villain is a creep who doesn't help the poor young woman he impregnated. Ignoring this girl's pleas for money for an abortion, he hangs around a Catskills resort and annoys Baby, the movie's heroine. We know he's a douche because he thrusts an Ayn Rand book on her. He tells Baby: "Some people count, some don't." Eventually, he gets his slight comeuppance.[5] When the movie was in theatres in 1987, the heel was an aberration. Today, he's politically in vogue.

For most of us, Covid and the disruptions that came with it were the greatest external challenges of our lives. We were afraid. We lived with travel and socializing restrictions, saw the closed stores and empty streets, watched some of our friends lose jobs and fall into depression. We bought hand sanitizer and baked bread and stayed out of parks. Most of us did our best, trying to live as well and as safely as we could. But some Canadians bought the lie, which had even greater currency in the United States, that Covid was harmless. And a few of these people lashed out and smashed the short-lived consensus that united us. Populists and sociopaths came forward to rewrite history, falsely calling Covid a "flu," claiming it didn't kill many people, insisting any Covid mitigation was overreach, lying that vaccines were not just useless but dangerous. They offered quack cures. The Trumpists in the US and the hard-right in Canada, including Poilievre, sucked the hope and optimism from people who thought political leaders and experts could get us out of the strange and scary pandemic.

Canadians see themselves as rational, generous people. Covid showed that many are not. Lies about the pandemic helped to make people mean, partly because they were struggling to find ways to deal with their own Covid-generated grief and anxiety.[6]

Pierre Poilievre is a creature of this century and a man of this time. He's the Canadian leader of a movement that hasn't got an accurate name. *Neo-conservative* doesn't really work, because that ideology believes in an interventionist foreign policy and free trade. *Libertarian* is also a bad fit. Ayn Rand, the grotesque prophet of that movement, likely would have been horrified by Donald Trump's campaign pledge to arrest and deport undocumented immigrants who live and work peacefully in the United States. *Fascist* perhaps comes closest to defining Trumpism, with its delegitimization of political debate and description of opponents as "the enemy within"; with its gutting of institutions that limit the leader's power, including the media, the courts, legislatures and the civil service; with its "othering" of minorities; its robbing of government to enrich the leaders' supporters; its media control and propaganda.[7] All these things happened in Mussolini's Italy, Hitler's Germany, and smaller countries like Spain, Portugal, Argentina, and pre-war Austria and Poland.[8]

Pierre Poilievre is not really a conservative in the way Canadians understand that ideology. Conservatives are cautious about change. They embrace technology and science. They listen to expertise and embrace as large a swath of the business community as possible. They believe governments should step in when there's an issue the private sector can't handle (Conservative prime minister R.B. Bennett started the CBC) and to build vital infrastructure like railways (as Macdonald did in Canada) and highways (Republican president

Dwight Eisenhower built the interstate system). They are wary of corporate power (Eisenhower warned of the military-industrial complex and Teddy Roosevelt broke oil and railroad monopolies. George Drew, a Conservative premier of Ontario and, later, leader of the federal Tories, bird-dogged and exposed Sir Basil Zaharoff, First World War–era international arms dealer and political manipulator, who was likely Ian Fleming's model for James Bond's nemesis, Ernst Stavro Blofeld). In a normal conservative regime, government works quietly and, hopefully, efficiently, without pestering people. Tradition, social order, and internal peace are very important to them. This is not what the new populists, many of them outright fascists, are pushing.[9]

Critics of this book will say I'm anti-conservative. I'm not. This book is, in part, a warning about radical change and the careless instigation of class warfare. I'm well aware that conservatives were the most determined opponents of Adolf Hitler. More than 4,500 German conservatives, people who believed in rule of law and basic decency, were guillotined, shot, or hanged on thin cords as the price of failing to kill Adolf Hitler on July 20, 1944. Hannah Arendt's writings are, at their core, conservative works advocating freedom, responsibility, civic duty, and suspicion of the kind of bureaucracy that can break down evil acts into simple tasks that members can perform without accepting moral responsibility. Like Eisenhower and Diefenbaker, I'm suspicious of a rapacious military and the corporations that profit from it. In 2024, I published a book about seventeenth-century missionary Jean de Brébeuf, *Crosses in the Sky*, that showed that the Hurons were decent people who should have been left alone. It was hardly a radical left idea. My previous book, *Big Men Fear Me*, celebrated a capitalist who worked his way up from a teenager peddling newspapers on the back roads of southern Ontario to founding the *Globe and Mail*, making it a great newspaper. And my 2019 book about adventurer Pierre Radisson is about a man who defied governments and social class rules to help create a commercial empire that's central to Canadian history and national identity.

I don't believe modern "conservativism" can claim much moral high ground. There's a big difference between real conservatism and the new right's class warfare: attacks on "gatekeepers" and expertise. Trump abuses military power by deploying the army domestically (which, in 1688, triggered England's Glorious Revolution, a conservative coup against James II). He, like Stephen Harper's Tories, cut veterans' benefits. Trump threatened to prosecute General Mark Milley, the chairman of joint chiefs, for calling his Chinese counterpart during the Capitol riots on January 6, 2021, to warn him and his government not to take advantage of the chaos. Then Trump, supposedly the law-and-order candidate, pardoned rioters who had attacked Capitol police with bear spray, baseball bats, cudgels, and their fists. In Canada, Pierre Poilievre backed, and profited from, a "trucker" occupation of downtown Ottawa where parliamentary security officers were assaulted, small businesses were shut down, and residents who had nothing to do with creating government policy were forced to endure sleepless nights and menaced on the streets. Their right to quiet enjoyment of their private property, supposedly a fundamental conservative principle that underlies their demand for law and order, was ignored because Poilievre had his own agenda. Even after leaders of these occupations were convicted of weapons charges (in Coutts, Alberta) and mischief charges in Ottawa, the "law and order" party continued to back the disorder. This new movement is many things: "populist," anti-intellectual, repressive, uncharitable, unkind, classist, racist, opportunistic, and incoherent. But it's not conservative.

Libertarian Karl Hess, the Barry Goldwater strategist who ditched his belief in big government after being targeted by the Internal Revenue Service after Goldwater's defeat in the US presidential election, became a welder, worked with the poor to help make them self-sufficient, and subsisted on barter because the IRS wanted 100 percent of his income to pay off what Hess thought a politically motivated tax assessment. He embraced wind and solar power to cut himself free from the grid. Like Poilievre and Trump, he railed against financial and political elites. Unlike those two modern politicians, he did not hit billionaires up for campaign contributions or try to win elections. When Hess ran a joke campaign for governor of West Virginia, a reporter asked him what he'd do first if he was elected. Hess said, "I'd ask for a recount." Hess's interview in *Playboy* magazine's July 1976 edition, which Hugh Hefner published on the bicentennial of the Declaration of Independence, is one of the best manifestos on liberty that I've ever read.

I believe in careful spending and efficient government. The waste that I saw while working on Parliament Hill disgusted me. I get angry when I see road workers staring into a hole. I think we are better off with fewer rules. I don't want to defund the police. I wanted the "hole" in the Canada–US border at Roxham Road mended, not just because it was a blatant flouting of the law, but because I know so many decent new Canadians who jumped through hoops to be in Canada. The idea that people could fly to New York City, take a bus upstate, get a cab in a town near the border and walk down a path to start the process of becoming Canadian bothered me.

I think unions can be snake pits run by professional staffers who are more interested in their own agendas than in what's going on in the workplace. At the same time, I know that people who work in unionized workplaces are far more likely to have decent wages, pensions, and a grievance system that protects them from crazy and stupid bosses.

I believe in free speech, and I have represented clients in court when politicians tried to stifle them. I've also gone to court to advocate for women who were sued for describing abuse in toxic relationships. I'm prouder of those cases than anything else I've done as a lawyer.

And I know that bad things are happening in our cities, small towns, and countryside, too. I saw factory equipment being loaded onto semis in my hometown in the 1990s. The machinery was headed to the US sunbelt, "right to work" states that made a mockery of workers' rights.[10] A lumber and paper mill where I worked in the 1970s has closed, as have most of the rest of the mills in northwestern Ontario, a part of Canada where I spent my formative years. My job with CP Rail was replaced by technology years ago, and its successor company has far fewer employees. I do understand that, except for people in trades or in union workplaces, economic and social mobility no longer exists for blue-collar workers.

Nor can they take risks and start their own retail businesses. Walmart, Costco, and Amazon have made that very difficult. People across Canada have watched their main streets die, overwhelmed with ground-floor offices, cannabis shops, tattoo joints, cheque-cashing businesses, bars, restaurants, and far too many vacancies. Try to find a pair of shoes.

They struggle to understand why drug addicts and people with no homes panhandle on streets in small towns, where they were never seen, even in the worst economic downturns. Politicians and media who say the economy has never been better lose credibility with people who drive by woodlots and alleys and see homeless people living in tents.

And I know that liberal urban elites gave up on worker issues years ago and embraced issues normally interesting only to people hanging around grad school lounges. Many academics embraced the self-hating anarchy of Michel Foucault and other ideas that most people find patently absurd. I sat through law school in my late fifties and heard a lot of denigration of old, white, cis men and wondered how profs with these beliefs could square them with the fact that they knew they were educating people who would be competing for jobs at the very law firms that enable corporations to do the things they do.

I think there are ways to make government more efficient, focused, and less intrusive without blowing it up altogether or embracing authoritarianism. Unlike modern "conservatives," I dread living through a revolution, because I know how they always end. In that way, I am a staunch, dedicated conservative. As for authoritarians, the idea of fast decision-making has obvious appeal, if you forget that the decision-maker is human and surrounded by people who want things. Vladimir Putin and Xi Jinping make the decisions for their countries, but do they ever get all the information they need to make choices that don't come with nasty surprises? Do you believe there are people in Beijing and Moscow bringing bad news to the "leader," telling him things he doesn't want to hear? In a democracy, facts and policy options flow into the political system from legislators inside and outside government, and from the media. When our system works, the political conversation tells the elected leadership and the bureaucracy what works and what doesn't. They just need to listen.

SIX WEEKS INTO the Covid pandemic, *New York Times* columnist David Brooks argued that America's public sphere is inhabited by what he termed "rippers" and "weavers." Under the headline "How the Trump Ploy Stopped Working," Brooks tagged Donald Trump and his ilk as rippers. Rippers, whether on the left or right, see politics as a war that gives their lives meaning. Weavers are the opposite: they try to fix things by bringing people together and building consensus.

The weavers were winning in March and April of 2020, as people hunkered in their homes, struggling to keep their families calm and to put in a full day's work if they still had a job or business. Trump was still president and spouting absurdities, but the great majority of Americans supported lockdowns and other tough measures to slow the spread of this terrifying new disease. Early in the pandemic, a Yahoo News–YouGov poll found 90 percent of Americans thought a second wave of Covid was likely if lockdowns ended too early. It felt like September 11, 2001, except the damage was in every home and the anxiety didn't let up.

Brooks went on with enduring naivete: "According to a USA Today–Ipsos poll, most of the policies on offer enjoyed tremendous bipartisan support: increasing testing (nearly 90 percent), temporarily halting immigration (79 percent) and continuing the lockdown until the end of April (69 percent). A KFF poll shows that people who have lost their jobs are just as supportive of the lockdowns as people who haven't."

America's polarization industry—the partisans of Fox News and MSNBC, the MAGA crowd, and the rest—was on the ropes. The country was, Brooks said, more united than it had been since the terrorist attacks of September 11, 2001. Decades of division generated by rippers had made Americans hate each other. "The pandemic has been a massive humanizing force—allowing us to see each other on a level much deeper than politics—see the fragility, the fear and the courage."

Politics, Brooks said, had changed. "In normal times, the rippers hog the media spotlight. But now you see regular Americans, hurt in their deepest places and being their best selves.

"Everywhere I hear the same refrain: We're standing at a portal to the future; we're not going back to how it used to be."

That part turned out to be true.

Reading Brooks's column now, it's easy to believe that your cat is smarter than at least one *New York Times* columnist. That's because we've edited our memories of the early days of the pandemic. Don't roll your eyes at Brooks if you hoarded toilet paper and yeast and elbow-bumped your work colleagues. We all watched the bodies coming off the cruise ship at Yokohama and the big machines spraying some kind of chemical fog through downtown Wuhan and wondered when those things would happen on our streets. I believed I would die of Covid if I caught it, and I was likely right. I'm an old, fat man with asthma.[11]

When Brooks wrote this, he seemed right: even Trump tried to look like a weaver, though his mask slipped a few times. Justin

Trudeau, holed up in a house on the grounds of Rideau Hall with his wife, Sophie, who'd caught Covid on a trip to London to talk at a WE Day event, offered news and encouragement every day. Public servants, working from home offices and kitchens, put together relief programs for people who'd lost their jobs and to help business owners who couldn't open. We all watched in horror as the stock market tanked and waited for what was next.[12] Some of us learned to use computer video so we could see family and friends face to face. It was a chance to rekindle marriages and connect with children. For a little while, most rippers were quiet, though it didn't take long for rippers like Poilievre to politicize the pandemic, break the consensus, and turn anxiety into anger.

Brooks's column is an artifact, a still photo from a time when people were more fearful than tired. He was right, that day. More important, he had identified the two forces in Western politics: the rippers and weavers. Pierre Poilievre is a ripper. Donald Trump, who, after he lost the 2020 election and was shown to be a felon and a rapist then came back to win in 2024, will keep ripping until he dies. After he's off the political stage, another ripper, likely J.D. Vance, will replace him. The MAGA movement is too big to be left on the scrap heap of history, at least for awhile.

Ripping makes exciting TV. It's also easier and probably more fun than weaving. Ripping, and the dopamine hits that come from doing it, powers Elon Musk's Twitter. America has barfed up political hairballs before: Huey Long, Joe McCarthy, Roy Cohn, Spiro Agnew. We've never had one who was a national contender in Canada. Our rippers tended to be stuck in provincial legislatures, municipal politics, and student councils. Few made it to the big leagues and those who did didn't last long.

But now we have a Tory front bench full of rippers, led by Pierre Poilievre. Poilievre had most of the advantages that life in Canada offers, but he's still the angriest person on Canada's political stage and the nastiest leader of a major party in this country's history.

Indigenous people, people of colour, Canadians who have genuinely been screwed by governments, victims of corporate negligence—they all have the right to be angry. But none of them are on the road, day after day, flinging rage. The sneering, the incivility, the insults, the over-the-top accusations, the utter meanness sets Poilievre apart from the rest of the people in the national sphere.

YOU BUY A car, hit a curb, and the plastic bumper falls off. You buy some chips, the bag is half full, and you curse the person who sold you air. A ticket from a photo radar camera comes in the mail: you've done fifty kilometres an hour in a forty zone, and you didn't see the speed limit sign or the camera. Roads in some towns look like they've been shelled by heavy artillery and your shocks are shot; there's constant construction where no one seems to be working; your city has money for music and beer festivals and Christmas lights while people sleep in doorways. You aren't sure whether to lock your car at night: leave it unlocked, and an addict will toss it looking for change; lock it, they might break a window, then make a mess as they look for things to steal.

You used to pay off your credit card every month. After the pandemic, you started carrying a balance. Now you're near your limit. You've got a place to live but worry about renewing your mortgage. You've got friends who are looking for a new house, and you're hearing horror stories about crazy prices. Renting seems out of the question. You spent less on your first car than you'd pay every month to rent a two-bedroom apartment, even in some small towns. The adjustable wrench that you just bought loses its grip when you try to loosen a bolt. You're fifty-five years old, your boss makes it clear that you better do what she says or you're out, and you know it's impossible to get a new job. You buy pickles made in India, and you have a friend in Leamington who lost her job when Warren Buffett's holding company, Berkshire Hathaway, bought the Heinz plant and shut it down.

Most of these things have happened to me (the bumper, the wrench, the photo radar ticket, and Leamington friends). It's all part of the shitification of society. Small towns seem to have it the worst. One decision, made far away, can ruin all the lives of a community. Take away the industry from a one-industry town, and it's not just the physical plant that stops having a purpose. This is a story repeating all over Canada.

Canada was founded by foreign corporations like the Company of One Hundred Associates that owned New France and the Hudson's Bay Company. In Southern Ontario, the Canada Company sold nearly 2.5 million acres of land. The Canadian Pacific Railway projected Canadian power into the lands west of Lake Superior. We've long had a small entrepreneurial class, but they've always been undercapitalized. Canadians are usually employees. And that's what they want to be. Within most of our memories, there was a time when skilled and unskilled blue-collar workers could get a steady, secure job and make enough to support a family. Life here was, compared to theirs, so easy and our country so rich that inmates of Auschwitz called the buildings where stolen Jewish property was sorted Kanada. Everyone in the camp wanted to go there to work.[13]

Until the late 1980s, Canadians who had a sense of adventure and no decent job opportunities at home could go to frontier mill and mining towns or the oil patch to make a lot of money. These places might be isolated, but a family could quickly earn what they needed for a middle-class life. There was always a risk the mine would be worked out or the mill might close, but there were other places to go. Whenever the economy was bad, easterners headed west. People found opportunity in Alberta and Saskatchewan before there was an oil patch: in the 1920s and the Great Depression, young men from Ontario went west in the summer to work on the wheat harvest.[14]

After the 1980s, there was nothing but bad news for most small towns. Mills closed, but no new ones opened. Railway companies, once among the biggest employers of men without college degrees, captured their federal regulators and laid off a lot of their workers. Oil was the last frontier industry. Now, Albertans want easterners to stay home and believe the rest of Canada is out to ruin them, whether out of spite, belief in fake climate science, or both.

And none of this was Justin Trudeau's fault.

A lot of these problems result from globalization, an international project that began when Trudeau was a boy and took off after his father left office in 1984. Once the Soviet empire collapsed, the whole world was open for business, hungry for jobs and capital investment. The North American Free Trade Agreement, China's acceptance of most WTO rules, the gutting of Canada's foreign investment laws, the abandonment of serious protection and investment for Canadian mass culture, and the arrival of the American-dominated internet eroded our economic independence and sense of nationhood.

Then there's the issue of demographics, which are remaking Western nations, including Canada. Starting in the 1970s, people in developed countries stopped having as many kids. There was one obvious reason: the shift of population from the country to the city was almost finished. In the country, children are an asset. They work on the farm, and when they're old enough, they look after their parents and grandparents. In the city, children are a big expense: a three-bedroom apartment or house costs a lot of money. A four-bedroom apartment is a mirage. City women are expected to have careers, but they also pay for daycare. Employers might promise maternity leave, but being off for a year is usually a career setback. Contraceptives and abortion gave women the power to decide whether they'd have kids, with all the work and expense that comes with them. Japan became a textbook case of demographic decline. Germany, Italy, Russia, Canada, and China followed. None of those countries have a replacement-level birth rate.

In Quebec, governments tried, in the 1980s, to arrest the baby bust with big payments to encourage large families. They created heavily subsidized daycare. People loved the program, but it did nothing to change the demographic trend. The old-stock (i.e. white) francophone birth rate is still far below the population replacement rate, which explains a lot about modern Quebec politics.

Many of the job losses caused by technology and globalization hit men much harder than women, since the factories that closed tended to be full of men. Women usually work in white-collar jobs, dominating the public service below the executive level, and in places like restaurants and stores.[15] Some middle-aged men see themselves as being trivialized by media, politicians, and public intellectuals. They watch comedy shows where the fathers are humiliated weekly in their own homes by their wives and children and given no respect in the workplace. Radio commercials almost always portray men as idiots who need to be schooled by women and children. And they know that they are the last people anyone wants to hire, especially once they are middle-aged. Men on the shop floor thought diversity, equity, and inclusion policies benched them in the game of life.[16] Canadian men, when they talked about their feelings, expressed their anger as gripes to a friend or two. Even when we can afford it, men aren't keen on therapy.

The anonymity of social media allows men to broadcast this anger. The most extreme "conservatism," which sometimes crosses the line into a new kind of fascism—the stuff espoused by Donald Trump, the Brexiters in Britain, the Alternative für Deutschland in Germany, and Pierre Poilievre's cabal—arrived with Facebook and Twitter. Websites that allow anonymous publishing by angry men and foreign agents are the single most potent force in modern politics.[17]

Pierre Poilievre is a man who's only had jobs that he got through friends or via the ballot box. His work was never at risk of outsourcing. He and his parents have always received a salary, not a wage. Poilievre qualified when he was thirty-one years old for an indexed public pension that could allow him to retire at fifty-five and spend the rest of his life on a beach, unplugged from the internet, writing haiku. The anger he taps into doesn't come from his own economic frustration or feelings of powerlessness. If he truly does feel your pain, it's only in an abstract way.

I READ EVERYTHING I could on the last UK election. So much was familiar: a health system that doesn't work; foreign interference, including London becoming the go-to place for Russian money laundering; and, powering the dissatisfaction, a real decline in working people's standard of living, mostly caused by inflation.[18] Labour won power, but a right-wing party, Reform UK, modelled on and named after Canada's Reform Party, elected five MPs, including Nigel Farage. For years, Farage thrilled the extreme right in the English-speaking world with slogans, insults, and vicious personal attacks. Although he spent years failing to get into Westminster—he'd been a disruptive member of the European Parliament before Brexit but had lost the rest of the elections he fought—he was now seen as an up-and-comer.

Voters, at least in the rural English riding of Clacton, had come around to Farage's way of thinking. Poilievre is a lot like Farage, though not as witty. Poilievre is a man who was an outlier when his intellect and personality formed, the kind of teen who was ignored by smart people and jocks. Poilievre's intellect was locked in when he was a teenager, when he read the sociopathic rants of Ayn Rand and the cruel economic philosophy of Milton Friedman. He was schooled in the mindset of small business by an uncle who ran a struggling vending machine company. It was one of the few interactions he's ever had with real capitalism. If he's grown or changed at all, it's on the issues of gay marriage and gay rights, and that's new: when gay marriage came up for a free vote in Parliament in 2005, Poilievre was against it. He says he supports it now.

—

POILIEVRE'S BEEN LUCKY. He had the good fortune to be accepted into an unpopular but historically important clique at the University of Calgary. Members of this group became a large part of the core of the modern Canadian conservative movement. Jason Kenney, Poilievre, Ezra Levant, Benjamin Perrin, and the rest of the young conservatives at the University of Calgary were connected to some of the Reform MPs elected in 1993. They'd go on to found and run the Conservative Party of Canada. When Poilievre enrolled at the University of Calgary, Reform was a Prairie party with just two MPs elected east of the Saskatchewan–Manitoba border. He was in the right place at the right time. The party expanded quickly and needed as many bright, ambitious young people as it could get.[19]

This is how politics works now. Justin Trudeau and his friends did the same thing and developed a clique at McGill University that included Gerry Butts, Seamus O'Regan, and Marc Miller. These people later connected with a second group of friends, staffers of Ontario's Liberal provincial government, that included Katie Telford, the most powerful person in Ottawa during the Trudeau years. They took over the Liberal Party when conventional wisdom said it might never win power again.

Canadian politics used to be open to bright people who could work their way up through riding associations and become candidates or were recruited because they were local leaders. If they won a seat, they had a chance of making it into cabinet and being listened to. Many became powerful regional ministers like Clifford Sifton, the Laurier cabinet minister who recruited hundreds of thousands of farmers to settle the wheat lands of the West. They may have been brilliant businessmen like C.D. Howe, who brought a level of ruthless efficiency to Canada's effort to defeat Hitler. Even in Brian Mulroney's and Pierre Trudeau's time, indispensable ministers like Don Mazankowski and Allan MacEachen were more powerful than anyone on the prime minister's staff. Over the past thirty years, power has shifted from cabinet to the prime minister's personal staff, which is not part of the federal public service and is accountable to no one except the prime minister. The head of the Prime Minister's Office chooses ministers' chiefs of staff. These "minders" usually come up through the national campaign system or, as is often the case in the Trudeau government, from the party's university clubs. (In Trudeau's PMO, the more prestigious the university, the better.)

These staffers are not making careers in government. Invariably, they end up selling their knowledge of the inner workings of government to lobbying firms or get jobs at large corporations. You'll often see former staffers—now lobbyists—on news network political panels, described as "strategists," without any mention of the people who are paying them.

None of this is good for democracy. The system does not foster real public participation in policy formation, so why would anyone join a riding association? Even if they dominate the local organization and seek a nomination, the party might parachute a famous candidate into the riding. The leader might not sign their nomination papers. If they are elected, what's the job? Most MPs, whether their party is in government or opposition, must do what the leader wants, whether it's voting a certain way on a bill or doing public relations every weekend back in the riding. (Though there are a few free votes on issues of conscience, things like capital punishment, abortion, and same-sex marriage, MPs are usually bound by the policies of the party leader, who can end the career of parliamentarians who insist on independence.) There's little personal satisfaction and the job is hell on families: half of MP marriages break up in the first term. A position isn't very attractive now that the prime minister and his unelected senior staff call the shots. The money might seem impressive to most Canadians—$203,000 for an MP, about $302,000 for a minister in 2024—but an MP's salary is about the same as a mid-level government lawyer. (In Ontario, a member of the legislature makes $116,000, about the typical pay of a police constable or a unionized bus driver who works a bit of overtime, and there's no pension, which explains a lot about the quality of provincial politics.) This is why we get what we get: a mix of people genuinely motivated to serve the public; ambitious people who could never get a job that pays so well, or one as interesting; emotionally damaged people seeking personal power, validation, or revenge; and crooks.

Pierre Poilievre didn't create this system. It created him: a political volunteer and Reform Party campus club member, then a political intern, a leadership race volunteer, a staffer on Parliament Hill, an MP, a cabinet minister, then vocal opposition critic with the skill and luck to create his own leadership team and bring his clique to the verge of power. He didn't change to win the Conservative leadership and dominate federal politics. We, the system and the times, came to him.

The system was partly made by journalists who, mimicking their American colleagues, fixated on leadership and brought presidential politics to Canada. When bureaus were slashed, they stopped covering parliamentary debates on legislation.[20] Most ministers are ignored unless there's a perception that they've screwed up. With the notable exception of Kathryn May, who covered the public service for the *Ottawa Citizen* and Postmedia before ending up at *Policy Options* magazine, no one has expertise on the massive federal bureaucracy, who do most of the work of governing.

Modern journalism is made for Pierre Poilievre. Whether he read about it, got advice from an older person, or just had a gut instinct, Poilievre became a master of the short, sharp soundbite when he was a teenager, and he started doing "newsworthy" political stunts when he was in university. By the time he was elected to the House of Commons in 2004, Poilievre, then the youngest member of the House, knew how to answer the phone and give reporters sharp little quotes. One of the things that impressed me as I researched this book was how many times Poilievre was quoted in media stories when he was still a backbencher. He turns up in stories about issues that had nothing to do with his job because he gave reporters succinct quotes that praised the government or smeared his opponents. Very few, if any, Canadian politicians have ever had this gift for crafting slogans. If Poilievre hadn't gone into politics, he would have cleaned up in advertising.

Contrast his simple, and simplistic, slogans with Justin Trudeau's "empathic dad" style of explaining an issue. Or Chrystia Freeland's interview style, which sounds like she's a frustrated teacher explaining the structure of a chromosome to an eight-year-old. Whether you agree with Poilievre or not, he's far better at delivering a message. Of the people at or near the top of the Liberals, only Mark Carney can lay a glove on him.

There's another important element to his media performance: Poilievre's negativity. Anger is a powerful emotion, and media—traditional and social—seek it. Poilievre is a master of simplicity, exaggeration and smear. He makes common cause with people who fly Fuck Trudeau flags from their trucks. He's almost never denounced anyone on the right as too extreme.[21] His negativity and ruthlessness were useful when he was a rookie MP in opposition. When he was prime minister, Stephen Harper used it against his perceived enemies at Elections Canada. In those years, Poilievre was seen by his colleagues and onlookers as a tool, not the wielder of tools. In the age of Donald Trump and of a social media that values the negative over the positive, Pierre Poilievre fits the times. Poilievre is a ripper in a time when there are cleavages in Western society that are deep enough to generate serious talk of civil war.

He represents the dark side of our nature. He's the feelings and words that spew out when we're cut off on the highway by a careless driver. His slogans resonate when we're broke, when someone steals our kid's bike, when we worry about renewing the mortgage, when we're passed over for a job or a promotion. He taps into the frustration of being a service worker disrespected by an entitled upper-middle-class snob. Pierre Poilievre can't make people better drivers, stop bike thieves, or jail entitled yuppies, but he does send out the message that he will put the screws to people who've had it too good for too long. These people are always somewhere over the horizon, living it up on taxpayer money and laughing at "ordinary people." In fact, pretty much everyone struggles to get by. Whether they are Ottawa bureaucrats, Montreal sophisticates, or climate change activists, they deal with debt, crazy families, troubled friends, health problems, depression and anxiety, usually in combination. Despite what people on the right and the left believe about each other, there is no "them."

MY BOOK *KILL the Messengers*, which came out early in 2015, argued that mainstream media was dying and political partisans were replacing it with online propaganda designed to look like real journalism. Conservatives and extreme-right fanatics are leading the way creating this pseudo-media, but they are not alone. The left has a few of these outlets, too. This fake media—I call it fake because it doesn't try to be fair and has hidden purposes—was, I wrote, fuelling a populism that is a threat to every institution that democracy relies on: the courts, effective legislatures, a professional and non-politicized public service, the sanctity of the ballot box.

My next book, in 2016, *The Killing Game*, was about the use of social media by extremists like ISIS to recruit, spread propaganda, and communicate with each other. This structure is used by all modern movements. I discussed the addictiveness of social media, how governments have tried, and failed, to police it, and how its owners allow it to be used by the most appalling people.

My legal practice focuses on the same problems that I identify in *Kill the Messengers* and *The Killing Game*. I see the collapse of media as being part of a much wider threat to democracy: a new kind of fascism where men and women wear suits instead of uniforms. As was the case with Mussolini and Hitler's fascism, this new fascism "others" minorities, allows corporations free rein in return for support, is contemptuous of democracy, stacks courts, politicizes bureaucracy, humiliates and delegitimizes media, attracts bullies to act as muscle to intimidate opponents and uses propaganda to recruit and to create its own fake version of reality. Modern fascism is not always anti-Semitic, nor does it shelter people who want to engage in genocide (at least, not domestically), but it still relies on "us versus them" scare messages while offering no solutions to real problems. The only goal of the wielders of this new system is to get power and keep it.[22]

I'm not naive about political ruthlessness. People who think politics should be a series of seminars and that all politicians should be gentle public servants should stay away from Canadian politics. Sir John A. Macdonald and his opponents were ruthless. Ontario premier Mitchell Hepburn, a Liberal of sorts, climbed onto a manure spreader and told a crowd that he was speaking from the Tory platform, then ran the province from a hooker- and thug-filled suite in the King Edward Hotel. Hepburn's frenemy and successor, George Drew, had a political spying and dirty tricks operation called Reliable Exterminators run by Montague "Bugsy" Sanderson, whose day job was running a pest-control company. Pierre Trudeau had no qualms with siccing the Mounties on his enemies, and those cops weren't above committing crimes, including arson. Brian Mulroney was a greedy thug and did little to hide that. The famous picture of Jean Chrétien choking a protester reminded one of my aunts of the look on the face of her abusive husband. Chrétien's funnelling of federal money to friends in Quebec ad firms for off-the-books work in the 1995 independence referendum might have saved the country, but once it became public, the scandal kept the Liberals out of power for nine years. Partisan politics in this peaceable kingdom attracts nasty people, but Poilievre and the people around him pushed the boundaries of partisanship and left people wondering if limits even exist anymore. Canadian politics haven't always been clean or polite, but we've seen nothing like this since the brawling days of Confederation, before the days of the secret ballot. Even then, things settled down somewhat between elections.[23]

When *Kill the Messengers* came out, two years before Trump was inaugurated, some critics like Andrew Coyne said its thesis was over the top. I challenge him or anyone else to make that argument today.

So now I spend most of my time defending whistle-blowers, legitimate media outlets, and ordinary people whose right to express themselves is threatened. I am also working on cases that I believe must be litigated to prevent the worst of American-style dirty politics from being normalized in this country.

Critics of this book will say I hate Poilievre. I've got nothing against him as a person. In our few interactions, which started when he was a Stockwell Day organizer at the University of Calgary and ended in about 2017, he was decent and friendly. I also respect his capacity for work, his intelligence, and his political antennae. I was not surprised to discover, while researching the book, that his colleagues voted him the hardest-working MP in the House of Commons and the hardest-working constituency MP in 2005, his first full year in the job. I also want to acknowledge and thank him for his advocacy, with former NDP MP Peter Stoffer, for help for children with autism. This began before his own children were born. As the grandfather of a child on the autism spectrum, I am sincerely grateful to all the people who advocate for this help. As one Hill observer, no friend of the Conservatives or Poilievre, said to me once, "One-on-one, he's a normal, reasonable guy. But when a third person shows up, the circus starts."

Poilievre has lived his adult life in the public eye. I've come at this project as a historian, trained to use the historic record to research and tell a story. This book is not based on interviews with Poilievre, his partisans, and his critics. It's not meant to be a debate between political marketers and strategists. It's a dive into the large documentary record, as well as an analysis of the political and media environment that has propelled Poilievre forward.

Pierre Poilievre is very good at finding and hyping problems: taxes, crime, housing, drugs, inflation, doctor shortages, pandemic management. In more than 150 years of democratic government, no leader of a major party has come close to having Poilievre's skill at whipping up mass anger, in part because no one except John Diefenbaker ever tried, though he at least had boundaries.[24] No one has spoken in slogans the way Poilievre has. No one has been so shameless in his lies about his real and perceived enemies in politics, the media and elsewhere. But real solutions? We haven't heard many of those. They'll come later. Maybe.

Is he a bad person? I'm reluctant to make that claim. I think he's an angry teenager in the body of a grown man. That makes him a stellar opposition politician. It is a bad combination in a prime minister.

1
A MAN OF HIS TIME AND PLACE

When small men begin to cast big shadows, it means the sun is about to set.

CHINESE LINGUIST, NOVELIST,
PHILOSOPHER, TRANSLATOR, AND
INVENTOR LIN YUTANG (1895–1976)

IN HIS CONSERVATIVE leadership victory speech in 2022, Pierre Poilievre described his family as "a complicated and mixed-up bunch … like our country." Conservatives clapped and laughed. Pundits clucked approvingly. One op-ed writer called Poilievre's background "an ace up his sleeve."[1]

"My parents taught me that it didn't matter where I came from, but where I was going," Poilievre told the crowd. "It didn't matter who I knew, but what I could do. That is the hope I want my kids to inherit."

In fact, where you come from has a lot to do with your destination and the path you take to get there.

Poilievre has a French name and has learned to speak the language, but his ancestors were Irish. His biological mother is Jacqueline

Farrell, the daughter of second-generation Irish immigrants. Her father worked for the Canadian Pacific Railway as a young man but spent most of his working life with General Motors. In 1978, while living in Calgary, Jacqueline became pregnant. She was just sixteen, and whoever the father was didn't stick around. Her parents couldn't help: Jacqueline's mother had just died, which must have made things worse for the teenager. An abortion was possible, if Jacqueline jumped through the legal hoops that the law required, but she didn't try. For awhile, she thought about keeping the baby and calling him Jeff.[2] Further along in the pregnancy, she decided on adoption and contacted a Roman Catholic adoption agency. Pierre was born on June 3, 1979, the day before Joe Clark took over from Pierre Trudeau.

Marlene and Donald Poilievre, two Calgary schoolteachers who married in 1971, had not been able to have children, so they had applied to adopt. Although they worked in a profession that many conservatives loathe, with secure jobs and a decent pension negotiated by a union, the Poilievres, especially Marlene, were very conservative. They were Prairie people, born in Saskatchewan and raised in families that had struggled for decades. Marlene and Donald were Roman Catholics, and Marlene embraced the most reactionary tenets of that religion, fitting in with the evangelical Protestants who dominate Prairie society and politics. This is not the Catholicism of people who show up at church at Christmas and are never around the rest of the year. It's a political Catholicism that wants to use government power to impose its social views on people. That's not new: William "Bible Bill" Aberhart, the Social Credit premier of Alberta, hosted his weekly *Back to the Bible* radio show while in office, passing bills to limit press freedom and banning booze, even in passenger planes flying over Alberta. (Aberhart's government also passed a bill allowing the recall of members of the legislature but repealed the law when people in his home riding were on the verge of recalling *him*.)

Ernest Manning was a student in the first class of Aberhart's Calgary Prophetic Bible Institute when it opened in 1927 and started hosting *Back to the Bible* a few years later.[3] His son Preston took the conservative, evangelical Christian populist movement of Aberhart and his father, made it a national movement, and took it to the edge of power.[4]

THE POILIEVRE FAMILY wasn't Quebecois, and Pierre was not raised in a French-speaking home, though his father did speak French and tried to teach Pierre without much success (he learned the language years later in Ottawa, when it became a job requirement). Sir Clifford Sifton, minister of the interior in the Liberal government of Sir Wilfrid Laurier, had scoured Europe for immigrants to farm the land that had so recently been surrendered by (and strong-armed from) the Cree and Blackfoot people. In the first decade of the twentieth century, Sifton brought more than one hundred thousand people a year to Canada. Even though he detested Roman Catholics and opposed government funding of their schools, he recruited anyone who was healthy without regard to their faith, just so long as they were Christians and white.[5]

Donald's grandfather, Joseph, ended up in a small town north of Saskatoon in 1904. Immigrants from France were somewhat rare in these parts. Those who came to Canada found the arable parts of what were then called the Northwest Territories to have more economic opportunities than Quebec, and less anti-Catholic bigotry than Ontario. These newcomers joined a small but interesting community of francophone Metis who, just two decades before, fought under Louis Riel. The year after Joseph Poilievre's arrival, the Laurier government carved Alberta and Saskatchewan out of the southern part of the Northwest Territories and set them up as provinces, with control over their natural resources. Liberals would come to regret that.

The Canadian prairies were opened for agriculture because of government-supported science. Charles Saunders, a botanist working out of Ottawa for the federal department of agriculture, crossed

Red Fife and Red Calcutta strains of wheat to create Marquis, a hardy, high-yield variety that matured more than a week earlier than competing strains. This wheat made farming the prairies a paying proposition. By the beginning of the First World War, this government-bred wheat would be sown all over the northern plains, on both sides of the border. It would feed the people of Britain and France through the war years and be the mainstay of the Prairie economy until the exploitation of oil started after the Second World War.

Joseph had a son, Paul, who bounced between jobs, working as a farm hand, running a garage, and, later, a hotel, in Moose Jaw, Saskatchewan. This was a normal employment pattern for the time as the West suffered terribly during the economic depressions that hit after the First World War and then the 1929 stock market crash. The first depression created radical populist farmers' movements across Canada that briefly took control of the provincial government in Ontario and had more staying power on the Prairies. The second, and far worse, Depression, the one that's capitalized in history books, caused wheat prices to collapse, making wheat more efficient as fuel than a cash crop. After the economy improved, Paul Poilievre became a real estate agent in Saskatoon. Paul's son was the first Poilievre to go to university, where he earned the qualifications to teach high school.

Marlene's mother, Louise Schartner, had her daughter in rural Saskatchewan during the Depression. Her family were farmers. A few months after having her baby, Louise separated from Marlene's father. It must have been tough being a single mother and a fatherless child in that place, at that time. Divorce was not a serious option, even if the couple had agreed to it.[6] Men weren't required by law to pay child support, and financial help from governments was both humiliating and inadequate. Still, Louise was able to raise her daughter and help her get a decent education.

Marlene also became a schoolteacher. She and Donald met and married in Saskatoon and moved to Calgary, which was growing fast as the oil industry expanded, subdivisions spread, and new schools needed teachers. By the time Pierre was born, Donald and Marlene had been married eight years and owned a decent house in Calgary, near Fish Creek Provincial Park. They'd also invested in Calgary's booming real estate market. In 1980, Jacqueline, now eighteen, was pregnant again. This time, she tried to keep and raise the baby but, after a few months, she realized she was unable to cope. She had named the baby Patrick, which wasn't changed when she gave the child up to the same Catholic agency. This half-brother was also adopted by the Poilievres. They had, Pierre said, a "pretty normal upbringing."[7]

ALBERTANS OFTEN CLAIM they hate the federal Liberals because of Pierre Trudeau's National Energy Program (NEP), created by the federal government at a time when Canadians worried about world oil shortages. In fact, Alberta had been hostile to the Liberals for years and rarely sent them to Ottawa as MPs. The province, with some reason, always saw itself as the target of Eastern interests that wanted to loot its resources.[8] Even during the "Trudeaumania" election of 1968, only four of Alberta's nineteen MPs were Liberals. In 1972, they all lost. In the last election before the NEP was created (1980), there were no Alberta Liberals in the House of Commons. In the 1970s, Albertans griped about energy policy and smaller things like the metric system and the flag, which had a leaf from a tree (maple) that wasn't native to Alberta. Some of their complaints had some merit: Trudeau's language policy that required front-line staff and most bureaucrats to be bilingual meant most Albertans had no real chance at a career in public service unless they had been educated in French at one of the rare Prairie French schools or had rich parents who sent them abroad. Albertans saw millions of dollars flow from Ottawa to pay crooks to build Montreal's Olympic venues and received much less to help struggling farmers.

Some Albertans witnessed how Quebec gained autonomy and federal cash by fostering the separatist movement that took power under René Lévesque in 1976 and tried to set up something similar. Trudeau believed Alberta's small group of separatists were bluffing. "The chances of western separatism are absolutely nil," he told reporters. "Canadians are Canadians, and I don't think they'll fall for that kind of thing except as bargaining tools by the premiers." Quebec, said Trudeau, had power in Ottawa because it elected Liberals to Parliament. "Get into governments in Ottawa and scream for more at that level, too, rather than always sit on the opposition benches," he advised. Albertans took him up on that, but not by voting for candidates from his party.[9]

Postwar prosperity ended in 1973 when Arab states in the Organization of the Petroleum Exporting Countries (OPEC) choked the oil supply chain to pressure Western countries into abandoning their support of Israel. This ended the unprecedented postwar prosperity of North America and Europe, but it was a boon to Alberta. Prices fluctuated between 1973 and 1979, but they stayed higher than before the Yom Kippur War. Through the 1970s, Canada was in recession or close to it. Even when the economy recovered a bit, unemployment stayed high despite federal make-work programs, and people in eastern Canada went west to find jobs. That wasn't easy. When I was a university student, I worked for the Canadian Pacific Railway in Northern Ontario. *The Canadian*, CP's transcontinental train, carried optimistic easterners towards Alberta. Many of the passengers on the daily eastbound train were on their way back to Ontario, Quebec, and Atlantic Canada after learning a hard lesson: Alberta needed tradespeople, not unskilled, inexperienced labourers. I wished those trains could have met so people could compare notes.

In the 1970s, all Canadians wanted Alberta's oil industry to succeed. Conventional wisdom, backed up by government and academic statistics, said oil was running out and that the developed world was at the mercy of unstable Middle Eastern countries whose leaders' policies were diverging from Washington's and London's. The idea of alternative energy was new, and it was still focused on hydrocarbons: ethanol, "tar sands," oil shales. Exploiting the sands might be possible. Strip-mining the shales was not. Ethanol was doable, though farmers and consumers were skeptical. Ontario Liberal leader Stuart Smith made "gasohol" a big part of his platform in the province's 1981 election. Farmers, who stood to make money by growing corn for ethanol, rolled their eyes. Consumers weren't interested, even though ethanol boosted octane and helped make up for the power lost when governments ordered refiners to stop adding lead to gasoline.[10] Gasohol was coming, no matter what Ontario voters wanted. By the mid-70s, the US government gave ethanol a forty-cents-per-gallon exemption from federal motor fuel taxes. By 1979, major retailers were selling it. To get people to use it, the industry hired comedian and actor Bob Hope to star in ads promoting the ability of ethanol to "stretch our available supply of gasoline."

The shape of the oil industry would be decided in Washington and Dallas, not in Calgary and Ottawa. Alberta claims to have an entrepreneurial culture, but that's a myth. The oil exists because of geology, not the skills and talents of Albertans. There was little risk in drilling in known oil fields, and new fields were easier to find because of technology invented in the United States that used sound and shock waves to map underground strata. In 1926, Karl Clark, a chemist at the Research Council of Alberta, patented a hot-water separation process to extract oil from the sands, but it was too expensive to use until 1978. The industry and its fans talked about free enterprise, but Alberta's oil patch simply would not exist as we know it without government. Provincial and federal governments gave companies cheap access to public land to extract a public resource and either built, pushed through, or approved pipelines to bring oil and gas to markets.[11] Government provided a lot of the money needed to find and extract the oil and gave oil companies generous tax breaks. Still, it seemed Albertans were blessed by God and protected from the economic troubles that were ravaging the godless outside Alberta's borders.

In 1978, US president Jimmy Carter's scientific advisers warned him that the carbon chemicals that people were adding to the Earth's atmosphere could boost average world temperatures by three degrees Celsius by the end of the twenty-first century. This was a shocking warning that was picked up by some media and academics, but it was overshadowed by the Iranian revolution that would destroy Carter's presidency. In 1979, world oil prices spiked to record highs when Islamic fundamentalists overthrew the pro-Western Iranian monarchy. Now, oil was so expensive that exploitation of the petroleum-rich sands in Alberta and Saskatchewan—oil sands or tar sands, depending on your politics—became economically viable. Canadians were fine with this: progressives who hadn't heard the climate change warning saw the oil sands as an alternative source of energy at a time when many believed that oil wells would run dry in their lifetime. They did, however, worry about pollution from leftover waste.[12] Alberta saw an oil boom that suddenly made Calgary an economically important place. As usual, rather than learn the lesson from history that oil prices are cyclical, people inside and outside Alberta believed this change in the energy market was permanent. When the bottom dropped out of this artificially inflated industry, Albertans blamed Ottawa. When things went well, it was because of Albertans' hard work and free-enterprise values. They never learned from countries like the Netherlands, where the economy was warped and stunted because of the easy money that briefly came from North Sea crude, or from Norway, which tries to prevent oil wealth from wrecking its mixed economy and diverts easy oil money into a massive sovereign-wealth fund worth $US1.75 trillion. It guarantees the country can always pay for its pensions and social programs.

Canada had a ridiculous oil industry. Alberta, Saskatchewan, and, to a much lesser extent, British Columbia and Manitoba, exported their oil. Except for a tiny, rather cute oil patch in southwestern Ontario, the eastern part of the country produced no petroleum.[13] Since Quebec and Ontario still imported much of their oil, the manufacturing regions of the country were open to foreign price manipulation. And, while Ontario and Quebec had some refineries, Alberta didn't (and still does not) make all its own gasoline.[14] Almost all the major oil companies extracting oil and selling gasoline in Canada were foreign corporations.

The National Energy Program, brought in by the newly re-elected Trudeau government in 1980 without the agreement of Alberta, had three pillars. The federal government wanted more Canadian ownership of production, both through the company it owned, Petro-Canada, and from private corporations. (Ontario followed suit when its provincial government, under Tory premier Bill Davis, bought 25 percent of Suncor, a major developer of the oil sands.)[15] Petroleum prices were supposed to be fair for all Canadian consumers, whether they were sitting on a pool of oil in Alberta or living in a small town in rural Quebec. That meant federally imposed price controls without regard to world oil prices. Most important, the program wanted Canada to become energy self-sufficient, no longer dependent on OPEC or any other foreign oil nation. This required a rebuilding of the country's oil extraction and distribution system to feed Alberta oil to eastern Canadian refineries.[16] Two of the three pillars should have been a boon to Albertans, but the idea of missing out on high world prices to help other Canadians enraged Albertans.

Pierre Trudeau's timing was awful. The NEP was imposed when oil was at its peak price of $US37 a barrel (about $US140 in today's money). Alberta was extracting as much oil as it could and selling all of it at world prices. So was everyone else: oil wells all over the world were pumping hard. Even with price controls, Alberta was making money. A few months later, prices started to crash as all the oil-producing countries made up for the missing Iranian oil and added even more to the world's stockpile. At the same time, central banks in most Western countries, including Canada, began to quickly raise interest rates to fight the inflation generated by the previous oil price spike. By 1981, 20 percent mortgage rates were common, and savings bonds issued by the Canadian government paid 19 percent. The 1980 recession, a worldwide downturn that reverberated for years, started in January, the same month that Trudeau's Liberals replaced the Progressive Conservative government of Joe Clark, an Albertan. For about two years, high oil prices cushioned Alberta, but the recession arrived there in 1982, when world prices dropped. In the first years of that decade, power-of-sale signs were common in Canadian neighbourhoods. By 1982, whether they were in the oil patch, like Calgary, or in the manufacturing centre of Canada, like Windsor, people saw boats and recreational vehicles in front of houses with "for sale" signs attached to them. For the first time since the start of the Second World War, soup kitchens opened in some Canadian communities. People became familiar with something they'd never heard of before: food banks. This was a psychic blow to Alberta, which had seen thirty years of growth and prosperity. Albertans couldn't accept the idea that they, like the rest of Canada, were victims of wildly fluctuating oil prices and persistent inflation that governments all over the world struggled with for more than a decade. They would not acknowledge how the "made in Canada" NEP oil prices were often higher than world prices, which effectively insulated Alberta from the price collapse. Instead, Albertans saw it as a policy decision by envious, greedy Quebec Liberals to clip their wings and take their wealth.

There was bound to be a political backlash. The same year that Clark lost and the NEP was created, some right-wing Albertans started the Western Canada Concept Party. It advocated independence from Canada and the creation of a new country, consisting of Manitoba, Saskatchewan, Alberta, and the (then) two northern territories.[17] The party was fronted by screwball lawyer Doug Christie, who shared the opinions of his fascist and Holocaust-denying clients like Ernst Zundel and Wolfgang Droege. In 1982, the party was able to elect Gordon Kesler to the Alberta legislature in a by-election to fill a vacancy in Olds–Didsbury, an oil patch riding just north of Calgary. He was the first separatist provincial politician elected outside Quebec in modern times.[18] That year, under threat by Alberta that it would suspend two oil sands projects and cut production from wells, the Trudeau government and Alberta premier Peter Lougheed worked out a revenue-sharing agreement to divide up resource revenue and compensate for the NEP, and three years after that, Brian Mulroney's government killed the NEP. Still, in Alberta, all the economic pain of the 1980s is blamed on the NEP. Everywhere else in the developed world, the economic downturn was the worst in fifty years. Central banks had decided to use high interest rates to kill inflation, at the expense of working people. About a quarter of US auto workers were out of work. The situation was just as grim in construction and transportation. And because demand for oil sagged, and there was a glut of supply, it fell to $US14.50 a barrel in 1986, a loss of more two-thirds of its 1980 value.[19]

The Trudeau government started Petro-Canada in 1975 to keep some of Alberta's oil profits in the country and provide investment money to the struggling oil sands projects. The company was created at a time when Canadians still cared about who owned the country's industries. It was headed by Maurice Strong, an executive who became the star of right-wing conspiracy theories for the rest of his life. The company went ahead with its plan to build two towers for its new headquarters in Calgary, expecting oil prices to rebound and prosperity to return when the recession was over. Most of the money came from a holding company owned by Erik Engelbert, eleventh Duke of Arenberg, seventeenth Duke of Aarschot, sixth Duke of Meppen, and sixth Prince of Recklinghausen. Petro-Canada's project was one of the few construction opportunities in the city during this time, but Calgary business leaders and politicians blamed it for adding to the local commercial real estate glut. Forty years later, the tower built by Petro-Canada is full, and downtown Calgary commercial real estate is doing as well as anywhere else, but business leaders believed the tower added insult to the injury caused by the NEP.[20]

—

IN 2022, POILIEVRE talked about those days. Like so many Albertans, he remembers the National Energy Program and forgets about the worldwide recession that tanked the price of oil: "I didn't understand politics or anything, I just remember it being a really stressful time for a lot of people," he said. "And as I grew older and I've learned more about how that happened and why, it left a mark on me."[21]

In another interview, he said, "It was kind of a brutal time to be a homeowner or a family because there was [sic] these monstrous interest rates." Some of his earliest memories are of "the financial stress that my folks were going through. And a lot of people were losing their homes and their livelihoods at that time. And I think that made an early impression on my thinking, even though at the time, I didn't really understand what was happening or why. I was able later on to look back at that strain and stress and then try to diagnose it when I was old enough to understand." Those memories of the early 1980s recession, he said, helped form his ideology.[22] He didn't connect those high rates to the inflation-fighting strategies of neo-conservative economist Milton Friedman. It was this economist who advised central banks and governments to use high interest rates to crush inflation. The American and British central banks, as well as the Bank of Canada, have embraced that policy since the early 1980s, often at great pain to workers and businesses.[23]

There was little chance that two schoolteachers with any seniority would be laid off and be forced to choose between hunting for a job in recession-stricken Calgary or moving to some other part of Canada. But they'd made a mistake when they leveraged their savings to speculate in Calgary real estate, and they couldn't hold on to those rental houses.[24] Now in debt, Pierre's parents were forced to sell their home and move to a smaller one near the edge of the city. The move wasn't too disruptive: neither boy was yet in school, and the new neighbourhood had a lot of open space where the kids could play. But it left a mark: "We had moved to a smaller place and we did sell our car... just to kind of keep our heads above water.... And that was a really kind of hellish time, particularly in Alberta because the central government had unleashed a wicked assault on the energy sector called the National Energy Program. And simultaneously the worst of the Trudeau socialist years were coming to bear on the entire national economy....

"But you know, it was a miserable time for a lot of people," he told Jordan Peterson in a 2022 podcast. "Now I was blessed because my folks were teachers, so they ultimately didn't lose their livelihoods. And, you know, we were able to, we had a modest upbringing, but I would never call myself poor. And my folks worked hard to make sure we could play hockey and enjoy life, go on camping trips. So I'm not, I would not cry poor, but it was a modest upbringing."[25]

Poilievre blamed Pierre Trudeau's Liberals and their policies for an Alberta recession that was part of the worst worldwide economic downturn since the 1930s. The US government allowed its dollar to "float" against other currencies, causing a sharp drop in the US–Canada exchange rate. A US dollar cost Canadians about twenty cents more in 1984 than it had in 1979, driving up the price of a lot of imports. Washington imposed credit controls that stifled demand for Canadian lumber, cars, and auto parts. The Americans had even more serious problems: savings and loans companies in the United States collapsed and took with them the life savings of millions of Americans.[26] Latin America was caught in a debt and currency crisis that destabilized governments. In Canada, more than a million people, out of 24.5 million people, were unemployed.[27] In Great Britain, where neo-conservative Margaret Thatcher was elected in 1979 and had begun her austerity campaign, unemployment hit three million by the mid-1980s. By the spring of 1983, two years after Ronald Reagan, a conservative Republican, was sworn in as president, unemployment in thirty states was in the double-digits. In June 1982, the US prime interest rate hit 21.5 percent. In 1983, after the Reagan administration deregulated banking, fifty banks failed. The Federal Deposit Insurance Corporation found that another 540 banks were in such serious trouble that they were on the verge of failure. Yet Poilievre believes Pierre Trudeau caused the downturn in Alberta. And when he was running for leader of the Conservative Party in 2022, he used that recession, and Pierre Trudeau's policies, to attack Justin Trudeau, telling Jordan Peterson, "Here we are with the same policies leading to the same results just as the 'dog returns to his vomit and the sow returns to her mire, and the burnt Fool's bandaged finger goes wabbling back to the fire.'"[28] (Poilievre was quoting Rudyard Kipling's poem "The Gods of the Copy Book Headings," a ferocious attack on socialism written in 1919.)

THERE WAS MORE serious trouble in the Poilievre house, and it had nothing to do with what was decreed in Ottawa. Pierre's father, Donald, was gay, and when Pierre was about twelve his father began a relationship with Ross McWhirter, who became his long-time partner. The Poilievres split up, and Marlene kept the boys. The divorce seems to have been amicable: Donald was a good dad who still played a big role in his sons' lives.[29] After the breakup, Poilievre bounced back and forth between his mom and his dad's place.[30]

This is an intriguing background for a politician who opposed the same-sex marriage bill introduced in Parliament by Prime Minister Paul Martin's Liberal government, which became law in the summer of 2005. "It is my position that this social relationship [marriage between a man and a woman], adhered to throughout the ages, handed down to people from above, is a basic building block of any healthy society," he told the House of Commons on April 15, 2005, when he was a first-term MP.[31] He would later change his opinion on this, stifling attempts by members of the Tory caucus to reopen the issue.

Pierre was an active, athletic child, playing hockey before he started kindergarten, learning to dive, and becoming a competitive wrestler. Donald encouraged the boys to play and to compete against other kids. He built a wrestling ring on the lawn of the family's new suburban home, where his sons took on boys from around the neighbourhood. He took his sons to Hart House, a Victorian mansion and former orphanage owned by Stu Hart, the patriarch of the family of Canada's most famous professional wrestlers. Marlene knew Bruce Hart, brother of professional wrestler Bret Hart, who'd become a teacher when he retired from the ring. Pierre was allowed into the Hart Dungeon, where adult wrestlers, Harts and non-Harts, learned their moves. Sometimes, he'd bring his little corgi. Bruce Hart was still a star in Calgary, and kids knew him when he was a surprise guest at one of Pierre's birthday parties.[32]

Poilievre, despite a setback in his early teens, has kept active all his life, keeping busy in his own homes, renovating and puttering (until he moved into the leader of the opposition's mansion, Stornoway, where that work is done by federal employees). He's also been a regular at Ottawa gyms.

In the summer, when his parents were on holidays, Pierre went on camping trips with his dad or visited his mom's relatives in rural Saskatchewan. He doesn't seem to have been a great student, though he was smart and worked hard on the things that interested him. Although there are Catholic secondary schools in Calgary, Poilievre went to Henry Wise Wood High School, named after one of the populist United Farmers of Alberta premiers. The school calls itself "the home of artists, scholars and champions" and has a reputation for excellence. Poilievre kept up his athletics in grade nine and got by in his courses. He focused on Olympic-style wresting until tendonitis put an end to serious sports competition. This injury may have changed the direction of Canadian history.

"I was a scrappy kid who loved sports, and then I got a terrible tendonitis in my shoulder, which made it impossible for me to do any amateur wrestling or football or any other sports that I enjoyed," Poilievre said years later. "So I'd get home from school and be bored out of my skull. My mom used to go and attend Progressive

Conservative meetings. And so I said, 'Why don't you take me to one of these meetings? Cause I've got nothing to do.' And she took me and I fell in love with it.

"And I just started reading books, all kinds. . . . I started off by reading a lot of left-wing books and commentary, and was very, very briefly persuaded by that. But then I stumbled on a book called *Capitalism and Freedom* by Milton Friedman. And I, you know, I didn't agree with a hundred percent of what he wrote. I still don't. However, the fundamental logic of the free market system to me is inescapable."[33]

Young people tend to start out on the left of the political spectrum then move towards conservatism as they get older (though this trend has started to change). Poilievre's brush with socialism was very, very brief. He says he didn't see the left's claims of "compassion playing itself out in any real way." Their claims of compassion, he says, are just catchphrases. "What we're actually debating is not 'Who's more compassionate?' There's no evidence that people on the socialist left are especially generous with their own money. . . . They like to spend other people's money. And they're hypocrites, living like the pigs in George Orwell's *Animal Farm*."[34]

Marlene was an opinionated Tory who had campaigned for fellow Saskatchewanian John Diefenbaker. In fact, Pierre would later tell a reporter she is "probably the most opinionated member of the family, even more than me." She saw her son's ambition and his drive. "Whatever he did, he wanted to be an achiever and go right to the top," Marlene told an *Ottawa Citizen* reporter in 2012.[35]

She took Pierre to his first Conservative riding association meeting when he was fourteen. Marlene, who remained a devout Catholic despite that church's opposition to divorce, was a frequent protester against women's abortion rights and brought her eldest son to picket lines at abortion clinics and anti-choice rallies.[36]

When he was stuck at home, Poilievre glommed onto Milton Friedman's *Capitalism and Freedom*. Published in 1962, Friedman's argument went against the grain of mainstream academic thought—perhaps best exemplified by ethical socialist R.H. Tawney and sociology pioneer Max Weber—that individual freedom (and capitalism) could not exist in places where learning and creativity are under the thumb of religion.[37] Instead, Friedman argued that personal freedom *follows* economic freedom.[38] Friedman helped create the Chicago School, a clique of conservative economists at the University of Chicago whose main arguments boil down to demands for smaller government. Friedman's ideas influenced Margaret Thatcher, Ronald Reagan, and the small fish that followed them, people like Preston Manning and the pretentiously named Calgary School, a handful of economists at the University of Calgary. At the time, these professors were marginal voices in academia, but some went on to wield tremendous political influence. Poilievre bought Friedman's argument that economic freedom is key to personal freedom and that apart from limited cases where government action is needed for a greater neighbourhood good, government initiatives infringe on personal freedom.[39]

Friedman also helped to create the concept of monetarism, the idea of using tight, expensive credit to kill inflation. This was the policy that caused the recession that cost the Poilievres their first house and the rentals they'd invested in.

There are some holes in the neo-conservative ideology created by the strange alliance that conservative libertarians made with the well-financed and well-organized fundamentalist Christian movement. These people are big on the vengeance in the Old Testament and absent when it comes to Christ's message of charity, while libertarians attracted the support of rich people looking for tax cuts. This alliance results in people who claim to believe in individual autonomy to support state intrusion in private sexual lives. Libertarians are split on the issue of drug use. If individual liberty is the whole point, why can't a person seek self-fulfillment with LSD or heroin? They're inconsistent on property rights and the environment. If governments only exist to prevent individuals from harming other individuals, shouldn't authorities get tough on polluters? Why should the Dene and Cree of the subarctic endure pollution from the tar sands, which devalues their land and the produce from it? And if property rights are sacred and inheritances should pass without government involvement, why wouldn't this apply to the property and inheritance rights of Indigenous people? Neo-liberals, a large part of the Tory party and the media that supports them, want governments to pay the cost of their religious schools but believe people should shut up about the legacy of the "Indian" residential schools.

In his early teens, Poilievre's mother sent him to seminars hosted by the libertarian Fraser Institute, where conservative academics fed him their version of political economy. He was younger than the college and university students who went to those sessions, but he was eager and sharp. It also provided him an opportunity to begin to sharpen his combative debating style. His intellect crystalized in the Reaganite environment of Calgary, a city of both prosperity and grievance, where people believed their hard work and brains, not the oil in the ground, made their province richer than almost all the rest of Canada.

And he took himself outside the mainstream of teenage life. Before he discovered politics, he'd been an athlete and an outdoorsy kid with friends. Now, he says, "there were times when I was interested in hanging out and being part of the club, but there were other times where I just didn't care. . . . Once I got involved in politics, I couldn't care less about the social life at high school anymore. . . . I loved hanging out with my friends and playing sports and stuff, but once I found a new passion, I became more focused on that."[40]

2
LARVAL POLITICIAN

Give me a child until he is seven, and I will give you the man.
ARISTOTLE OR IGNATIUS LOYOLA.
OR BOTH.

POILIEVRE WAS STILL in grade school, playing hockey, wrestling with his friends and picketing abortion clinics with his mom when Canada's political ground shifted. Westerners felt betrayed by Brian Mulroney's Progressive Conservative federal government, which they believed to be dominated by Quebec and Ontario ministers. Don Mazankowski, the pride of Viking, Alberta, was Mulroney's finance minister and deputy prime minister and made many of the most important spending and policy decisions. This did not impress Alberta hardliners. Mulroney quickly killed the National Energy Program, but the oil patch was still moribund because of the international recession and rock-bottom world oil prices. Albertans still fumed about the damage that they blamed on the NEP. The province's political class and most voters hated Mulroney's record budget deficits, which ballooned even while he was selling off Crown corporations like Petro-Canada and Air Canada. Some Westerners weren't happy that immigrants, especially Brown and Black ones, were still welcome. Prairie people were infuriated by the Meech Lake Accord, negotiated by Mulroney and the provincial premiers, which declared Quebec a distinct society and would lock in Quebec's political and judicial power. They believed the country's population centre of gravity was moving westward. The West was growing so fast that it would, in the lifetime of young people like Poilievre, overtake Quebec in population and economic importance.[1] Alberta conservatives wanted their province to have the same power and rights as Quebec, while at the same time, they demanded limits on Quebec's evolution toward an autonomous nation in Canada.

And there was an air of sleaze around the Mulroney government, with a string of scandals—some real, some over-hyped—making the news. The ultimate grift, which combined a suspicious business decision with Quebec favouritism, was Mulroney's decision to award a $C1.4 billion CF-18 military aircraft maintenance contract to Montreal's Canadair despite a stronger bid from Bristol Aerospace in Winnipeg. Bristol offered to do the work for less money and had proven itself by fixing the problems with Canada's earlier jet, the CF-101. The Mulroney government threw the Winnipeg company a bone by giving them a less-valuable contract to maintain an older jet, the CF-5, that was on its way out. There was no clear explanation for who was awarded which contract other than that Mulroney valued the seats his party won in Quebec in 1984 after years of the Tories being shut out. He took the Tories' supposedly safe Western seats for granted. Westerners and others who followed the Mulroney government closely believed something crooked had happened. This was a reasonable conclusion.[2]

Rather than fix the Progressive Conservatives from the inside, Preston Manning, Stan Roberts, and Robert Muir founded the Reform Party in 1987. They were pioneers of modern right-wing populism, anticipating the US Tea Party movement by two decades. In fact, Canada's populist right has been ahead of American conservativism since the 1980s. Stephen Harper's assaults on professional media, his muzzling of public service experts, and attack on elections oversight happened before Donald Trump ran for office. By 1993, the year that the Liberals swept to a massive majority, the federal Progressive Conservatives were dead in Alberta, and the party had just two seats in Parliament: Jean Charest from Quebec and Elsie Wayne from New Brunswick. But Reform's success hurt the overall conservative movement. It won just fifty-two seats while wiping out the PCs but still trailed the separatist Bloc Quebecois, who became the official opposition. Because of the split of the right-wing vote, dozens of Liberals were elected in ridings that their party hadn't won in generations.

Poilievre was fourteen when the first contingent of Reform MPs left for Ottawa, and despite his injury he still had a lot of energy and an urge to compete. Politics, he realized, was the way to blow off his inner rage. Inspired by his mother, he discovered he liked the competitiveness of campaigning. Politics liked him back: Poilievre's boldness impressed his political mentors.[3] In the 1993 election, Poilievre volunteered for the call centre of Calgary Reform candidate Rob Anders. The teenager, who seemed a bit shy in person, was fearless on the phone. He was so good at cold-calling that Anders, who won his seat, took notice and told other Reform politicians about his protege. Preston Manning's people would shortly thereafter block the grade nine student's election to the executive of Manning's Calgary Southwest riding association, but they soon found other things for him to do.

In his teens, Poilievre worked long, hard hours in campaign call centres, phoning potential voters and donors, without asking to be paid. He earned respect and built political connections while still in high school. His social life revolved around provincial Tory and federal Reform meetings, which earned him seats in provincial and national conventions. (The Reform Party was just a federal party. It considered setting up provincial wings but decided not to, so Poilievre still belonged to the provincial Tories under Ralph Klein.

Poilievre abandoned Klein's party when he was in university, claiming Klein was a reckless spender.) Poilievre was making important political connections and learning how to work the press. In 1996, when he was barely seventeen, he was a delegate at a Reform convention in Vancouver where the *Vancouver Sun* reported him saying, "I like what they stand for. I'm very concerned about the financial state of the country and think they're the only ones who can fix it."[4] It's not a great quote. Very quickly, he'd realize what reporters want and give it to them. More important, he reconnected with another young delegate at that meeting. Poilievre had met Jenni Byrne at a Reform Party youth conference the year before. They spent most of the Vancouver conference together, and they'd be romantic partners for many years. Byrne, from a working-class family in the Kawartha Lakes resort town of Fenelon Falls, was a political natural who'd given up a nursing career to become a political strategist. She's been his political ally and chief strategist to this day.

MEANWHILE, AS THE Chrétien government settled into a long hegemony that *Globe and Mail* political columnist Jeffrey Simpson would call the Friendly Dictatorship, Poilievre sat at his high school classroom desks getting into political arguments with teachers. This must have been annoying to everyone in the room except the opinionated teen. He started writing letters to local newspapers, getting more "earned" media: the free coverage that makes and keeps politicians famous and makes them seem relevant.

By 1996, when another federal election was on the horizon, Poilievre volunteered for Reform MP Jason Kenney's election campaign. On the phone with strangers, the adult-sounding high school student described Kenney as a "tax fighter," a description that was new to the chubby candidate. Kenney was elected in 1997, and Poilievre now knew a handful of members of Parliament. By then, Poilievre had won over older Reformers and become a member of Preston

Manning's Calgary Southwest riding association. Manning was now leader of the opposition in the House of Commons, which gave him and his party a much bigger office budget and more political clout. Poilievre was learning from his mother, his friends—who were all young political animals—his girlfriend, and the leaders of a party that had grown in a decade from a Prairie protest movement to a contender for national power. It was the right time and the right place to be an ambitious conservative, an exciting time for ambitious young people, and Poilievre made the most of it.

Poilievre was the kind of high school student who wrote letters to the editor complaining about the national debt. In April 1997, when he was still seventeen, he fired off a zinger-filled attack on government waste targeting something all teens worry about, Canada Pension Plan contributions: "One would expect that the introduction of a $10 billion tax increase over a month ago would cause a storm of opposition. However, when Paul Martin mentioned that contributions to the Canada Pension Plan would leap from 5.85 percent to 9.9 percent, the finance minister felt little more than a gentle breeze."

Poilievre couldn't understand why the country quietly accepted a 70 percent increase—a "gargantuan premium hike"—in CPP deductions when 80 percent of the nation's people believed the pension program was "inefficient and unreliable." Then came the false equivalency, an important part of the way Poilievre tries to score political points. Brian Mulroney, he said, had been hammered on his national sales tax, so why were people putting up with this?

"When it [the Goods and Services Tax] was not removed by the present government, the outrage was almost as vehement.[5] When it comes to the nation's life savings why would the reaction have been so negligible? Well, as a member of the generation who will inherit this fiscal mess, I would contend that there was no significant protest against the premium hike because the age group that the changes would most adversely affect, 30 and below, have little political influence. The vast majority of parliamentarians are well past the age of 40 and, to a great extent, the same situation exists in the media, which is instrumental in assisting a movement develop momentum."

This premium hike, brought in by old Liberals and ignored by their media lickspittles, was "a crushing blow to young Canadians for several reasons. Aside from the fact that young Canadians will receive less from the plan than they contribute (the very definition of a bad investment) the increase in premiums will be a devastating hindrance to those searching for first-time employment." His generation would "pay for the mistakes of our predecessors. A great deal of our future earnings were spent before we were old enough to know what a six-billion-dollar debt was."

After the windup came the pitch: "Jason Kenney, the Reform Party candidate for Calgary Southeast, is the former president of the Canadian Taxpayers Federation and now intends to arrive on Parliament Hill following the coming federal election. He argues that protecting the pensions of current retirees is imperative; however, it would be in the best interest of all Canadians to move toward a mandatory RRSP contribution as an effective replacement for the ailing plan." In other words, get rid of the federal pension system and force people to take money from their earnings and pick their own investments, as though everyone would choose winners and no one would come up short. Poilievre didn't have much of a grasp of risk.

Kenney's idea provided "hope and opportunity where little currently exists and it is incumbent upon today's leaders to embrace them, or the bamboozlement known as the CPP will forever be remembered as just another chapter in the ongoing intergenerational rip-off."[6] The media, Poilievre wrote, was partly to blame. They weren't telling people what was going on. But it's hard to believe the keener learned of the CPP premium hikes by reading Revenue Canada tax bulletins, or from a newspaper or TV story. In fact, any reader of conservative newspapers like the *Herald* or a business paper like the *Globe and Mail* would come across the details of the premium hikes and the business arguments against them.

Kenney, the hero of the piece, had taken a shine to this young conservative. He was so impressed by the quick mind and thick skin that Poilievre displayed as he cold-called voters from the Reform Party boiler room that he asked to meet this bright young man.

Poilievre used the telephone skills he'd learned in Reform's campaign offices to make some money. He got a job in corporate collections at Telus, calling businesses that hadn't paid their bills and helping the financially stressed ones develop payment plans.[7] And in 1997, when he was in grade twelve, Reform MP Art Hanger paid him to work on Hanger's election campaign.[8] Poilievre was good with his money, socking away savings that he later spent on politics and to pay for the damage he caused to a political ally's car.

Poilievre had already developed the political voice that he would use in national politics: the dire, over-the-top claims of a debilitating national problem; the claim he was sharing the grievance of some group of silent-suffering victims; the harsh and cruel blaming of opponents who were too old, out of touch, stupid, or corrupt to understand the issue or care about the damage; the advertisement for his own team; the absurd idea tossed out as a supposed solution but never heard of again. He was also good at finding people who would help him move up. Teenage Poilievre had the same political style that he has now. His over-the-top speeches and even his campaign merchandise are familiar to anyone who was around student politics in the last quarter of the twentieth century. Combined with his mastery of new campaign technology that he embraced as a teenager—especially call centres for identifying potential supporters and raising money—and a talent for turning complex fears, feelings, and gripes into simple phrases that work so well on YouTube and Twitter, the Poilievre of Henry Wise Wood High School and University of Calgary student politics is the same person whose supporters wave "Pierre Poilievre for PM" flags for today.

—

POILIEVRE GRADUATED FROM high school in June 1997, the same month Jean Chrétien won his second majority government. Calgary was back on its feet as oil prices rose, oil sands projects ramped up, and its home-grown populist conservative protest movement continued to grow. When his fellow students were going to proms and graduations, Poilievre was working on Art Hanger's shooting-fish-in-a-barrel campaign. Once nominated in an Alberta riding, Reformers had very little chance of losing in the general election. The real prize for the party was to displace the Bloc Quebecois as the official opposition in the House of Commons and become government-in-waiting.[9]

A couple of months later, Poilievre arrived at the University of Calgary as an undergrad in the school's international relations program, where he found other students, almost all men, who shared his libertarian ideology. He didn't arrive with a career plan: "I don't know that my political ambitions were clearly defined at that point," he said in 2002. "I just knew I was generally interested in politics and that international relations would give me an overview of almost all parts of the [things] that one confronts in a political environment."[10]

A few weeks after Poilievre started classes, Jason Kenney, a University of Calgary alumnus and a first-term MP, started a Reform Party club on campus that soon recruited more than two hundred students. Even in a big school like the University of Calgary, that's an impressive number for a campus political club.

Even though it had a lock on Alberta politics and seats in the national Parliament, Poilievre was part of a movement that identified itself as outside the traditional political system. This is a common theme of populism, whether it be of the right or the left, and a claim always made by wannabe authoritarians from America's Donald Trump to Nigel Farage in the United Kingdom, Jair Bolsonaro in Brazil, Javier Gerardo Milei in Argentina, and Viktor Orbán in Hungary. Ottawa-based national political journalists, who had much more control of the national conversation, made sure people like Poilievre felt like social outsiders, too. Many of the people in the new right-wing populist movement were evangelical Christians who saw themselves as challengers to traditional Christian churches, which they saw as debased and compromised. Some young social and political conservatives, like Reform MPs Rob Anders and Jason Kenney, endured humiliation from the media for their pledge to stay celibate. Their chastity in a town where there's little to do but drink and fornicate was supposedly voluntary.

The new generation of populist conservatives wanted to tear down the wall that "secular humanists," whom they despised, tried to build between church and state. Not all these people were fundamentalist Protestants. Poilievre is a Roman Catholic, as is Jason Kenney, who'd embraced conservatism while studying at a Jesuit college in San Francisco.

In 2016 Preston Manning, the political prophet of this movement, wrote a book called *Faith and Politics: Leadership Lessons from the Life of the Exiles*. In it, he compared the tribulations of modern politically active evangelicals with earlier prophets. These people had believed in the sovereignty of God, which was challenged by foreign powers and people of weak faith.

Manning skipped over the Christian victims of ancient Rome and reached back to some of the heroes of the Old Testament. Joseph, Daniel, and Esther had overcome social and political hostility to become great leaders of the Jews. Ezra and Nehemiah revived a defeated and discouraged Jewish nation living under the Persian Empire. Artaxerxes, king of the Persians, saw the potential in the Jewish eunuch Nehemiah, made him an important officer of his court, then sent him to Jerusalem in 445 BC to govern his people and get the place back on its feet. With the help of Ezra, the chief priest (*kohen*) of the dilapidated Temple, Nehemiah restored Jerusalem and beat back the enemies of Judah: Arabs, Philistines, Ammonites, and Samaritans. Nehemiah governed well for a dozen years before heading back to Artaxerxes' court, but the people failed to keep the laws of their faith. Nehemiah came back, drove the foreigners out of the Temple, made Jewish men divorce their non-Jewish wives, and brought the place under strict Mosaic law.

Manning, using these stories, described the isolation of the right and its potential as both a social and political cleanser. The evidence of decay was everywhere. In 1999, the British Columbia Court of Appeal had rejected a prosecution's moral argument "rooted in the Charter's recognition of the supremacy of God." The judge who wrote the decision said, "I accept that the law of this country is rooted in its religious heritage. But I know of no case on the *Charter* in which the courts of this country have relied on the words [the prosecutor] invokes (i.e. 'principles that recognize the supremacy of God'). They [the words of the phrase 'principles that recognize the supremacy of God'] have become a dead letter and while I might have wished to the contrary, this Court has no authority to breathe life into them for the purpose of interpreting the various provisions of the *Charter* ... ." Manning raged against the judge's rejection of the claim that Christian moral concepts should help define Charter rights. How could a sovereign God allow this to happen?

The "supremacy of God" mentioned in the preamble of the Charter does not give Manning and the rest of the fundamentalists some kind of veto. The Charter's vagueness about the role the "supremacy of God" plays in its interpretation contrasts with the right to freedom of conscience guaranteed by the same document. Manning ignores that, and the fact that Canada is a multicultural country where people have many ideas of what God is.

This interpretation is not a legal cheeseparing. Follow it and ignore the Indigenous traditions that predate the arrival of the "founding" colonists, and you arrive at a place that white, heterosexual Christian men find very comforting. It excludes the ideals of non-Christians, liberal Christians, atheists, and anyone else who does not agree with Manning's interpretation of "founding principles that recognize the supremacy of God."

The point of all this: Manning and his followers believe that they have been wrongly pushed from their place as agents of a supreme God whose fundamental law, as they interpret it, is broken by the people who have control of the country. The new right, he argues, should learn from the Old Testament heroes who rose to power despite the hostility of those around them. They were righteous outsiders who triumphed.

Unless they were rich and part of the country club crowd, which was rare among this group, the young Reformers were on the fringe. They didn't even run the university's student union. The young neo-conservatives of Poilievre's generation were usually outsiders in mainstream culture, the kind of young people who are portrayed as soft sexless geeks and nerds in America's cruel teen movies.[11] They fed on their own social, religious, and regional grievance. As the years went by, they would align with other aggrieved people. Despite being anti-union and opposed to basic workers' rights, they would make common cause with working-class Canadians who believed themselves pushed out of the new economy. They would build bridges to minorities who believed they got nothing more than pandering from the white urban elites who ran the government. Men who believed modern culture degraded and humiliated them by undermining their dominance of the family, politics, and the economy were attracted to their call. So were people who hated Indigenous, Black, and Brown people's challenges to Canada's entrenched racial hierarchy. All these people believed an unworthy group of people profited at their expense. In the 1990s, Poilievre was a pioneer. Like some of the Old Testament prophets, his was a voice in the wilderness. How could he not gain confidence when the movement grew and grew?

AT THE UNIVERSITY of Calgary, Poilievre began filling his political tool chest. He learned how to talk in front of crowds by becoming a regular at the university's Speaker's Corner, modelled on the one in London's Hyde Park. "It was like three floors of balconies where people could look down and someone would stand on a big stool in the middle and shout out a speech." Public speaking is something very few people are comfortable with, and this was a tough crowd. The campus Speaker's Corner met "every Friday, and there'd be lots of heckling," Poilievre said in 2022, when he was running to become leader of the Conservative Party. "And it was just a rowdy affair, but mostly about hilarity and joking around and giving silly, ridiculous addresses. And that was the Friday tradition. We'd go and belt out.

"Sometimes seventy or eighty students would come in and take in these speeches. And I bet that if we had had the phone cameras back then they'd probably be circulating widely on the internet right now."[12]

At the Reform Party club, he met Benjamin Perrin, a devout Christian who went on to become Stephen Harper's adviser on law.[13] He joined a debating club and made the cut to win a seat on the university's United Nations club, which argued against UN clubs in universities throughout the English-speaking world. In his spare time, he read litigation files at the Calgary courthouse for items to print in the *Western Standard*'s "Who's Suing Whom?" column, which ran without a byline.

"I used to go to the courthouse and read the statements of claim. I had to find something interesting to put in this little box on one page. They were just little paragraphs. That was my only job," he says. "It was really human interest more than legal questions."[14]

Reporters who covered Reform events in Alberta and its national conferences in other parts of Canada found Poilievre to be increasingly quotable. He was becoming a master of the short, simple, colourful statement. Poilievre had made an emotional speech advocating school choice, funding for fundamentalist religious schools, and home-schooling, at a provincial Tory meeting that earned him some ink in the local press.[15] He was already doing stunts: at one national Reform conference, Poilievre wore a Jean Chrétien Halloween mask while asking a question from a floor microphone, and that too made the news. The *Calgary Herald*, one of the most conservative broadsheet papers in the country, kept publishing his letters and opinion pieces, even when he denounced the government of right-wing media darling Ralph Klein as spendthrifts.

"Indeed, all Conservatives must understand that the premier's team established lasting principles in the early '90s," Poilievre wrote when he was in third year and was vice-president of the provincial Conservative youth association. "Self-reliance and individual freedom are not fads that went out of fashion, like bellbottoms. They are the cornerstones of conservatism. Rock-solid and unchanging, these principles built our province. Alberta's politicians face a test. Will they forget these lessons in a mad rush to be all things to all people? Or will they defend taxpayers against infinite demands on the public purse? Premier Klein has passed this test. Now, it's time for the 'young Turks' to prove they can, too."[16]

A person starts making their reputation when they're university age, and it's at this time of life that many of their personal connections are formed. "He was there when he was young, and he was always perceived as somebody enthusiastic, charismatic, willing to fight and willing to engage on the level that was maybe abrasive. But they always liked this kind of combativeness in him," Jean-Christophe Boucher, an associate professor of political science at the University of Calgary, told a reporter years later during Poilievre's run for the Conservative leadership.

"He is a kind of unapologetic conservative...and somehow party members have found comfort in this kind of person because he's not somebody that's different. They know what he stands for. They actually respect that. The reason why Conservatives really like Poilievre is that he's never changed since he first ran," Boucher said. "He has values that are clear-cut. He doesn't move between options and he's not [Erin] O'Toole."[17]

Although Poilievre didn't take economics from Barry Cooper, Tom Flanagan, Rainer Knopff, or Ted Morton—the Calgary School professors—he did get to know Morton through the university's Reform Party club. The two really began to work together when Klein's government organized an election for the federal Senate, to put pressure on Chrétien to appoint the winners. Poilievre worked on Morton's campaign, which was hampered by a lack of cash. When the student union tried to keep the university's Reform Party club from campaigning for Morton, Poilievre called local news outlets and led a march across campus and through the university's food court to the replica of the Goddess of Democracy statue erected at Tiananmen Square by student protesters in 1989. It was an absurd comparison, equating neo-con students in Calgary with pro-democracy demonstrators crushed under the treads of the People's Liberation Army's tanks, but Alberta journalists have never been famous for their understanding of proportionality. They covered the photo op as though it were real news.[18]

The local press kept giving coverage of this kind to Poilievre. The *Calgary Herald* published a letter he wrote mocking the provincial Liberal leader for not running against Morton. He made a cheap shot that she expected a seat from Chrétien without having to run for it.[19] (If she did expect an appointment to a soft landing, it never happened.) Morton needed the free publicity. He didn't have much to spend on ads because he'd been dragged into a lawsuit. Strategist Ezra Levant, speaking for Morton's campaign, had been sued for allegedly defaming a Liberal senator. Though Morton and Bert Brown won their elections, neither were given a Senate seat by Chrétien. The Reform Party used this as proof that Chrétien cared more about patronage than voter opinion and took Brown and Morton on the road to drive the point home to people outside Alberta. (Stephen Harper appointed Brown to the Senate in 2007. Morton went on to become Alberta's finance minister for a year, running up a $3.4 billion deficit in 2010–11 before taking a run at the provincial leadership.)[20]

And this was a time when the *Calgary Herald* had enough reporters that it could spare one to cover the visit of a strange actor,

Michael Moriarty. He had left the television show *Law and Order* and the United States after Janet Reno, the attorney general in the Clinton administration, criticized the show's violence. Now he was living in Jean Chrétien's Canada as a self-styled political exile.[21] A *Herald* reporter carefully took notes at the campus Reform meeting as Moriarty shared his political wisdom with Poilievre and his friends. Efforts to unite the national conservative parties were going nowhere. Moriarty offered an alternative to the Reform/Progressive Conservative split: the Republican Party of Canada, which he was starting. As the meeting went on, the speech became more bizarre. He argued that among the first things they should do was elect a woman prime minister, which is a good idea but seemed irrelevant to the issues driving Canadian conservatives. In 1993, the Progressive Conservatives had chosen Kim Campbell as the party leader, and that had not saved them. Socialism, "the triumph of mediocrity," was the alternative to the Republican Party of Canada. Alberta was free of Marxists. "I feel like Churchill on the beaches of Dunkirk," Moriarty told the students.[22] "My England I'll retreat to is Alberta and, out of Alberta, we'll turn this [socialist invasion] back."

Poilievre, vice-president of the Reform Party and Moriarty's host, disagreed with the actor's idea for the Republican Party of Canada, but he praised the "exile's" ideas as "revolutionary."

"Personal freedom is the way of the future," nineteen-year-old Poilievre told the *Herald* reporter after the meeting. The reporter, who did a typical fawning *Herald* story, did not ask Poilievre, head of a political club opposed to the national government, speaking in a public meeting where, to be kind, a foreign actor prattled on with wacky theory, why Poilievre thought he and the rest of Canadians weren't free now. Once again, they simply collected and ran a pithy Poilievre quote.

As for Moriarty's idea of a Canadian arm of the Republicans, it was one of the few, and maybe the only time on the written record, where a right-wing idea was too crazy for Poilievre.[23]

IN 1999, WHEN Poilievre was barely twenty, he entered a contest that changed his life. Frank Stronach, founder and controlling shareholder of Aurora, Ontario–based auto-parts maker Magna International, sponsored an essay contest called "As Prime Minister, I Would . . ." Stronach was an Austrian immigrant who dabbled in Canadian politics and started a right-wing party in 2012 in the country of his birth.[24] The contest was somewhat rigged. Most of the entrants were conservatives. In their book *Rescuing Canada's Right*, Adam Daifallah, a friend of Poilievre and one of the contestants, and co-author Tasha Kheiriddin described the contest as "one of the only outlets for non-liberal voices to be heard and published." The judges were conservative-friendly journalists Joan Crockatt (a future Tory MP), Mike Duffy (for whom the Senate would eventually beckon), and broadcaster Arlene Bynon.[25] If anything, Poilievre's entry shows how much of his ideology has been locked in since he was a teen. Years later, Saskatchewan cabinet minister Jeremy Harrison, who was a Reform Party activist at the University of Calgary with Poilievre, told Campbell Clark of the *Globe and Mail*: "The guy you see giving speeches right now is the same guy that you would have seen giving speeches when he was 19 years old. It's remarkable. Even the content. Phrasing. Pierre's views have not really wavered."[26]

In one night, he put his biggest ideas down on paper. He was inspired by a fat cash prize and the chance to give his thoughts to a big audience on national TV. The 2,500-word essay is only an interesting read because it's part of Poilievre's story. It shows how his modern ideology is still that of a Calgary teenager, edited a bit to get rid of aspects that adversely affect Poilievre himself.

"Although we Canadians seldom recognize it," the young Pierre Poilievre wrote in "Building Canada Through Freedom," "the most important guardian of our living standard is freedom: the freedom to earn a living and share the fruits of our labour with our loved ones, the freedom to build personal prosperity through risk and a strong work ethic, the freedom of thought and speech, the freedom to make personal choices, the collective freedom of citizens to govern their own affairs democratically. The government's real job is constantly to find ways to remove itself from obstructing such freedoms. . . . As prime minister, I would relinquish to citizens as much of my social, political, and economic control as possible, leaving people to cultivate their own personal prosperity and to govern their own affairs as directly as possible."

Poilievre's ideology hasn't changed much since then. The idea of a social contract, that those who do well have an obligation to help less fortunate people, seems to be missing from his thinking. So is the belief that people can disagree about the ways to improve society and still respect each other for trying to make a better country. Poilievre and his followers can't accept the idea that governments provide services, from libraries to art galleries to public transit to hospitals, that make life better. There was a time when governments stayed out of the way of businesses. Conservatives believe capitalism, free of restraint, is still benevolent. In his 2025 inaugural address, Donald Trump fantasized about a return to the gilded age, even though (or maybe because) it was a time of child labour, unrestrained monopolies, quack patent medicines and uninspected—and sometimes poisonous—food. Ripping rules apart, believing libertarian claims of the cleanliness of the invisible hand, means throwing out the lessons of the Great Depression and the reforms of conservatives like Theodore Roosevelt and even Sir John A. Macdonald.[27]

"As prime minister," Poilievre continued, "I would look to find ways to empower citizens, while reducing my own span of control." And, like so many young people of modest means, he had real problems with the idea of capital gains taxes, as though people who make money from investments should not have to pay taxes while wage earners paid *something*, even after he cut taxes.

"As prime minister, I would free the eagle from its cage," he wrote. He ignores, or doesn't understand, that Canada is one of the most pro-business countries on earth. Oil production and other resource industries aren't just heavily subsidized but rely on cheap or free access to publicly owned forests and minerals. The entire economy is full of incentives, subsidies, and tax breaks. Those who get rich off the system can even pass their wealth on to the next generation without the payment of inheritance taxes.[28] "By eliminating the capital gains tax, we could liberate billions of dollars in locked-in investment, allowing Canada's world-class entrepreneurs to cultivate a more prosperous nation. The resulting increase in economic activity would likely make the exercise revenue-positive for the government."

The message is still the same. "This job-killing Trudeau tax will drive billions of dollars of machines, technology, business, and paycheques out of our country," he said at a rally twenty-five years later.

Back in 1999, it was all about liberty. Just, as he claims, the Poilievre message is today.

Poilievre floated some proposals in his contest entry that have somehow lost their appeal over the past quarter-century. Like many in the Reform Party, he wanted MPs to be forced to leave Parliament after serving two terms. The prime minister would also have a two-term limit. He wasn't clear about how this would work, since a prime minister is almost always a member of the House of Commons.[29] Would Canada always elect prime ministers with no parliamentary experience? Would it be two terms as PM after two terms as an MP? Poilievre didn't say, probably because this was simply a cut-and-paste of American conservative dogma. In that country, the president, state governors, and other office holders are not members of a legislature and so would not be caught in these weeds.

"Politics should not be a lifelong career, and elected officials should not be allowed to fix themselves in the halls of power of a nation. . . . I would make a personal commitment. I would resign after serving my second term in office."[30]

Five years after he wrote the essay, he was elected to the House of Commons, and two decades later, he shows no sign of wanting to leave for a career in the harsh, uncaring world of the private sector.

All his life, the business world he glorifies has been an abstract thing, something he's never been a serious part of.

Poilievre also wanted voters to be able to recall politicians when they weren't working out. In his world, MPs could be forced to resign and run again if, within three months, 40 percent of voters in their riding signed a petition. Since few MPs are elected with 60 percent of the vote and some wildly popular MPs can't keep all their followers happy, motivated organizers could make this nut. Although he introduced a no-hoper private member's bill in 2005 that would have allowed recalls if half a riding's voters wanted it, the Canadian right stopped talking about recalls when its political leaders got close to achieving power.[31]

And he had a strange plan for Senate reform. Each province would elect one senator. The three territories would have one.[32] This committee of eleven provincial representatives would have a veto over important legislation. The West would have four of these seats; Atlantic Canada would have four. PEI and Quebec would have the same amount of influence in this bizarrely undemocratic, unrepresentative body.

About five hundred students entered Magna's contest. The judges made a longlist of fifty entries, and Magna paid for their authors to go to Toronto for the finals. Those who made the shortlist, including Poilievre, went to Ottawa to pitch their ideas to Prime Minister Jean Chrétien. Poilievre's essay made the shortlist but didn't win. The prize went to Cory MacDonald, whose ideas made Poilievre's look positively centrist. MacDonald wanted the governor general to be able to fire the entire House of Commons if campaign promises weren't kept. (Why opposition politicians, who rarely have a chance to keep their election promises, would be forced out wasn't explained.) Government account books would be audited accurately so newly elected politicians wouldn't be able to make the usual "the cupboard is bare" excuse to wiggle out of election promises. "What they're doing is barefaced lying to Canadians," he wrote. He also argued for an end to interprovincial trade barriers and more global trade deals.

MacDonald went on to become an executive at the Royal Bank of Canada.[33]

Magna president Frank Stronach and his company were combining political altruism with self-interest. The contest was a tool to recruit bright young minds. The final debates were held in November 1999. Magna spent a lot of money to hype the project. The best essays were published in a book where Poilievre was described as a "self-confessed political junkie with a passion for public debating," and the contest was made into a TV show. Before heading to Toronto for the televised final contest at Roy Thomson Hall, Poilievre was taken to Banff and posed in blue jeans and a red winter jacket.

The finalists got a $10,000 cash prize, but at least as important for both Magna and the students, the winner and runners-up won a four-month internship at Magna. When he made it to the finals, Poilievre told a *Calgary Herald* reporter he could use the money, since he was a "starving student." He said he was looking forward to pitching his ideas to Jean Chrétien, giving his usual amount of deference to a Liberal prime minister.

"It will be an honour to speak to someone who holds an office as respectable as that one," Poilievre said. "I just hope that none of my views are offensive to the prime minister because many of them come into conflict with the outdated system he has run for the past few years. But I guess that's what democracy is all about."[34]

Chrétien, always an amiable man, listened politely and ignored all their ideas.

ALL THE WHILE, conservatives in Canada stayed divided between the Progressive Conservatives and the Reform Party. It didn't help that Manning portrayed himself as a wise Prairie soul while his MPs and party staff performed silly stunts on Parliament Hill. Deborah Grey, a former schoolteacher who was the first Reformer elected to Parliament, brought a truckload of piglets to the door of the House of Commons to mock MPs' pensions (though, eventually, Reform MPs willingly took them). In 1998, while working as Manning's Question Period strategist, Ezra Levant organized several of these photogenic media opportunities, which many in the media ignored. He brought a mariachi band to the foyer of the Senate to mock Liberal senator Andy Thompson, who spent most of the year in Mexico.

"The mariachi band was a very light-hearted thing," he told a reporter from the *Hill Times* newspaper.[35] There's little doubt that these stunts were probably a lot of fun, but they weren't the kind of thing the Progressive Conservatives wanted to be part of.

The split helped revive the federal Liberals and confused everyone else. Poilievre was vice-president of both the Young PCs and the Reform Party club at the University of Calgary. Supposedly, he was a Young PC because the party governed Alberta. But the Progressive Conservatives in Edmonton were not the Progressive Conservatives in Ottawa. Ralph Klein was a Progressive Conservative because Manning would not let Reform start provincial parties. If he had, Klein and Ontario's Mike Harris would probably have pushed Manning to let them run as Reformers. Federal Progressive Conservative national leader Joe Clark, who had no power or influence over the provincial parties, was pushing back against what he saw as the Reformers' extremism and nuttery, telling one Tory gathering, "We believe that no one should have a cross [target] drawn through your face because of where you live, or what religion you practise, or your gender, or the colour of skin, or your sexual orientation."[36] Clark was right, but it left provincial politicians like Klein running as supposed members of Clark's party while it in turn needed the votes of people Clark denounced.

After the 1993 election, Preston Manning had implored Tory survivors Elsie Wayne and Jean Charest to join his caucus so Reform could replace the Bloc Quebecois as official opposition in the House of Commons. They said they would not be the people who killed one of the world's oldest political parties, the one that gave Canada Sir John A. Macdonald, built the CPR and the CBC, and brought in the Bill of Rights. Their electors in Sherbrooke, Quebec, and Saint John, New Brunswick, had voted Progressive Conservative, not Reform.

Three years later, in 1996, law student Ezra Levant and conservative pundit David Frum organized the Winds of Change conference in Calgary to try to unite Canada's right.[37] Wits dubbed the session "Windbags of Change," but Conrad Black and the young conservatives in his orbit seized on the idea. The next year, London hosted the conference, and Poilievre was there as a student delegate. A unite-the-right conference in Toronto two years later that was organized by political fringe player Craig Chandler reminded centrists in the Progressive Conservatives why they were opposed to a merger with Reform and others on the hard right.[38] Chandler and the organizing team invited members of the Social Credit, Christian Heritage, Confederation of Regions, and Family Coalition parties, which were oddball right-wing provincial fringe movements. Chandler and his team were probably trying to do the right thing by building a big tent, but it reminded the Toronto-based national media of the extreme elements in the right and provided a host of yokels to reporters looking for a crazy quote.

The unite-the-right movement got a big boost that fall when Conrad Black started the *National Post*. The main story on its first front page was a plea for the merging of the country's conservative parties, and Black's columnists ground out hundreds of thousands of words pleading for and demanding right-wing unity. Black was at the top of his game. He owned major dailies in the country's largest cities and most of the small ones. He was injecting profits from the smaller papers into the *Post* and the *Ottawa Citizen*, trying to make them the two best political papers in Canada, with big arts and features sections to attract readers. Under his ownership, the *National Post* was, arguably, the best newspaper Canada's ever had. It had full pages for science reporting, interesting long features, book pages that were as good as anything published in the world's best papers, and some superb investigative reporting. *Post* reporters dogged Jean Chrétien's sketchy land dealings in Shawinigan, his rural Quebec hometown. It published columns by people like Ezra Levant, who was on the editorial board, but it also made room for left-wing icons like Linda McQuaig. The paper launched the careers of a new generation of conservative journalists like Paul Wells, Jonathan Kay, and Tasha Kheiriddin.[39] Ken Whyte, the paper's first editor, put together a staff that would stay loyal to him for decades as he moved from the *Post* to *Maclean's* and then, in recent years, to his Sutherland House book publishing company. Black gave him the money to hire big names from other papers, people like Christie Blatchford and Andrew Coyne. The paper did everything right but make money. While the good times lasted, the *Post* gave the Canadian conservative movement the adrenaline it needed to fix its many problems.

JOE CLARK, THE only Albertan ever to be prime minister of Canada, was one of those problems. He knew a reverse takeover when he saw one. His was not the party of Ezra Levant or even Conrad Black. Levant and many of the Reform MPs believed in political stunts. Black wanted a much weaker, smaller federal government. Clark and his colleagues had been in power, they knew how government worked, and they saw through Reform's simplistic answers. While leader of the Progressive Conservative caucus in Parliament, he came through with his promise to veto a United Alternative or whatever a new party would be called. This put Poilievre in a bit of a box. As head of the Young PCs at the University of Calgary and waiting to do an internship at Reform's Ottawa office, Poilievre needed to make a choice. He not only left the Young PCs but killed their club at the University of Calgary. This alienated him from Patrick Brown, who was still a Joe Clark Tory and a heavyweight among the Young PCs. Of course Poilievre went public with his decision to quit. "The direction of the party just seems to be downward," Poilievre told a *Calgary Herald* reporter. Joe Clark was "anti-youth," a failed leader with "a record of attacking young people who are interested in new ideas."[40] In a letter to the paper, Poilievre gushed, "God help Canada if the United Alternative fails!"

Although he had been on the executive of Preston Manning's riding association since grade ten, Poilievre was coming around to the idea that the Alberta warhorse was a national non-starter. Manning fought two national elections, picking up some rural Ontario seats in the second one, but he had failed to resonate with Quebec or Atlantic Canadian conservatives. Alberta's media at the time was enamoured with Stockwell Day, a plain-speaking politician in Ralph Klein's cabinet. Rising oil prices and provincial government penny-pinching had pulled Alberta's finances into shape, and Poilievre's generation of conservatives was orgasmic when Day, now Klein's finance minister, kept his party's promise to bring in a flat-rate provincial income tax that shifted the tax burden from the well-off. Alberta was booming again. Day was taking abstract economic theories embraced by Poilievre and others in the Reform movement and making them real policies. The stale federal Liberals were breaking into Jean Chrétien and Paul Martin factions that hated each other. This internal fight was personal, so it was in a different league from the posturing, marketing, and policy differences of party politics. There are times when people with the right skills, who are in the right place at the right time, have tremendous opportunities: a capable young American officer at the beginning of the Second World War, a cute and capable guitarist in London in 1963. Poilievre, a young conservative in Calgary, was part of a generation and political movement poised to take power when voters wanted a change.

3
ON TO OTTAWA

> *Ottawa was the worst, terrible, miserable hole in the entire universe.*
>
> BOB DYLAN, 1966

I'VE BEEN TO Bob Dylan's hometown of Hibbing, Minnesota, and I can guarantee Dylan's seen worse places than Ottawa. The northern Minnesota landscape is lovely, but Hibbing is a dump. Maybe it's not as bad as International Falls, Minnesota, the birthplace of Bullwinkle the Moose, but there are good reasons why Dylan left. He was tough on Canada's capital, but that's normal: Ottawa gets a rough ride from most writers. Allan Fotheringham called it "the city that fun forgot" and "Disneyland on the Rideau." In the 1990s, the city tried to brand itself "Technically Beautiful," but even the locals got the joke and rebelled against the marketers. Ottawa is really two cities. There's the Ottawa Bubble, made up of the downtown core, New Edinburgh, Rockcliffe, Old Ottawa South, and Westboro, which are the places where the national political actors live. The rest of the city is ugly sprawl and "stroads," big roads that are useless to pedestrians and where big-box stores and mini-malls dominate a flat and ugly landscape. The Ottawa of news backdrops and high school trips is a very small part of a city that, except for the downtown, could easily be mistaken for Dayton, Ohio.

Even people who live there tend to be hard on the place. Local talk-radio star Lowell Green, a fire-breathing right-wing fantasist who, from 1993 to 2016, had the most-listened-to show in the city, called his town "Sucking Central" without getting any argument from his listeners. It's a place that used to float on booze—it was, and still is, easy for anyone in Parliament, on a politician's staff, or in the media, to drink for free pretty much anytime they want at conferences and embassy events.[1] These days the drinking has perhaps died down a bit—many of the old watering holes, including the National Press Club, are gone—but booze still lubricates politics. And, since the city is in the wilderness, it's a fine place for outdoorsy folk. There's not much culture, though a few people try and the feds spend a lot of money on the National Arts Centre. But all in all, it's true, Ottawa's a pretty dull place.

When Ontarians think of Ottawa, they picture a quaint place separated from the rest of the province by a hundred miles of wilderness. Albertans tend to see it as the home of a satanic francophone bureaucracy that exists to steal their wealth and divert it to Quebec. It is the home of the woke and the godless. Members of the Reform Party and its descendants believe, as do Quebec nationalists and some provincial premiers, that the less there is of Ottawa, the better.

Rather than taking the Magna internship in 2000, Poilievre got permission from Stronach's company to wait a year so he could spend the summer of 1999 in Ottawa on a Reform Party internship. It was the first time he'd spent more than a few days in the national capital. Jenni Byrne was also there, working as the party's youth coordinator and the manager of their internship program. It was during this time that they started to seriously date, though they'd known each other for almost a year and a half. Byrne had dabbled in Reform student politics and been recruited by Kory Teneycke for a paid job in the leader's office. She had dropped out of Georgian College's nursing program and moved from Barrie to Ottawa to make politics her career.[2]

Poilievre also met John Baird during this internship. He was running for re-election to the Ontario legislature. Poilievre's internship was with Jason Kenney, who always seemed to create opportunities for Poilievre. Kenney had founded the University of Calgary Reform club just in time for freshman Poilievre to join it. He'd spotted Poilievre's talent in the call centre, and he'd helped Poilievre and his friends fight the University of Calgary student union over Ted Morton's Senate election flyers. The two spent most of the summer on the road on a national tour where Kenney talked about the need to cut taxes, especially the capital-gains levy that Poilievre obsessed over. Kenney also started connecting with leaders of minority communities, recognizing they were as unenthusiastic about paying taxes as the rest of Canadians. Later, Kenney would be Stephen Harper's ambassador to the new Canadians who were filling the growing suburbs of Toronto and Vancouver.

Just before he left for Ottawa, Poilievre fired off a letter to the editor of the *Edmonton Journal* to denounce a faction in Ralph Klein's government that wanted to break the province's *Fiscal Responsibility Act*, which mandates 75 percent of all surpluses go to paying down the provincial debt. Now, according to Poilievre, the money would "finance ribbon-cutting, photo-op friendly spending initiatives." This was wrong, Poilievre wrote. "Indeed, if it needs amending at all, the law needs toughening—100 per cent of all surpluses should go against the debt. Either that or the government should use it to refund Alberta taxpayers. After all, a surplus is really just over-taxation." The Klein government's debt repayment "saved the province $1.2 billion from the black hole of interest payments," and the province would save another $700 million a year when it was debt free. On that happy day "an income-tax-free province could be realized. Under the plan, income from energy royalties, interest from the Heritage Trust Fund and other revenue sources would pay the bills."³ But until then, Alberta would have its flat-income-tax rate, thanks to Stockwell Day. And Poilievre was headed into a political mess that he helped to make.

MANNING TRUSTED JASON Kenney. He appointed the ambitious young MP to be his go-between with the Tories in talks about the United Alternative. At the same time, Kenney and his protege Poilievre were betraying Manning by secretly working to win the party leadership for Stockwell Day. Poilievre, while still at the University of Calgary, set up a "Draft Stock Day" website.⁴ The anti-Manning faction claimed Manning would not be able to pull in the Progressive Conservatives that were needed to unite the right. And yet in picking Stockwell Day they had settled on a man who was more vocal in his religious zeal, more of a social conservative, and an even bigger fiscal hawk than Manning. How this would bring in Conservatives from across the country, and especially from Ontario and Quebec, was hard to fathom. "Day's profile as a man of conviction," Andrew Lawton, a Poilievre biographer who is now a Conservative candidate, wrote in his soft-gloved treatment of his subject, "contrasted favourably with the conciliatory, consensus-building approach Manning employed."⁵ But he never explains how this was this going to build bridges with Joe Clark's Progressive Conservatives or anyone else outside the Reform movement. Manning's critics' real complaint was that the Reform leader's style and voice annoyed voters outside of Alberta, while diehard Reform members thought Ottawa had corrupted their boy. The Reform Party had morphed from a grassroots Western protest movement to a party dominated by young political strategists who smelled power and thought Stockwell Day was the guy who could get it for them.

In January 2000, Reformers met in Calgary for a convention to create the Canadian Conservative Reform Alliance. (Wags quickly added "Party" to its name, and the acronym CCRAP stuck, so the party's leaders started calling it the Canadian Alliance.) Day was one of the main speakers. Tom Long, who ran big-tent campaigns that won Mike Harris two elections by appealing to Reformers and traditional Progressive Conservatives, was the conservative emissary from Ontario. None of the important federal Tories showed up. This was the convention where Poilievre spoke at a floor microphone while wearing a Jean Chrétien mask. A vote against a united right "is a vote for the Liberal Party of Canada," he said from inside the mask. He also worked the hospitality suites and later spoke as himself, saying, "This is not a compromise of our opinions and values, it's a way of bringing our principles and values to reality."[6]

Through the winter and early spring, Reform courted the Progressive Conservatives while continuing to fight over whether the whole united conservative thing was a bad idea. Conrad Black and his newspapers, especially the *Calgary Herald*, *Edmonton Journal*, *National Post*, and *Ottawa Citizen*, campaigned against backsliding. Some Reformers, including most of Poilievre's university-age friends, were suspicious of the United Alterative plan, thinking their movement would simply be rejoining a Progressive Conservative party they'd abandoned. The Tories believed the opposite: Manning and the Reform leadership, they thought, were engineering a reverse takeover of their party. In this, they proved prescient.

In March, Reform Party members voted overwhelmingly to morph their party into the Canadian Alliance. There was no vote in the Progressive Conservative party. This was an "if you build it, they will come" operation, with strategists expecting Tories to give up and surrender under pressure from their constituents and the conservative press. The gambit had one important result: it pressured Manning to call a leadership vote, though he resisted for awhile. The contest began as Poilievre was wrapping up classes before heading to Ottawa.

The anti-Manning people, including Kenney and Poilievre, would have been wise to take a long, cold look at Stockwell Day. To use a baseball analogy, he batted .400 in the minors but couldn't hit a curve ball in the big leagues: a good scouting report would have made this clear quickly. Like Stephen Harper, who would follow him in the movement's leadership, Stockwell Day was a transplant from Ontario to Alberta. Born in the backwater of Barrie, Ontario, (the one town east of Manitoba that sent a Reform MP to Ottawa in 1993), Day's father was an executive with the Zeller's department store chain, so the family moved around a lot: Nova Scotia, New Brunswick, Ottawa, Quebec City, Montreal, Victoria. For a couple of years, Day went to high school at Ashbury College, the best private school in Ottawa, with the children of Ottawa's elites.

Day studied at the University of Victoria and Edmonton's Northwest Bible College, dropping out of both before taking a job as the administrator of a Christian private school in Alberta. In 1986, after about seven years of running that little school, he went into provincial politics. Early in the next decade, Day was Alberta's minister of labour. In a government run by Ralph Klein, a radio news reporter, no one questioned Day's qualifications.

How Day's federal backers thought they could sell their man to voters in urban Ontario and in Quebec, which claims to be performing a laïcité exorcism of its Catholicism, is a mystery. Manning was a devout Christian but was subtle about it except when writing for fellow evangelicals. Day, in comparison, was an enthusiastic fundamentalist, and he let everyone know it. He would not campaign on Sundays, and he talked a lot about his beliefs to journalists. He was locked in a defamation suit with an Alberta lawyer who defended a man charged with possessing child pornography. Day falsely claimed the lawyer sympathized with pedophilia. By the time the lawsuit was settled in the lawyer's favour, Day's big mouth and bad judgment cost Alberta taxpayers nearly $800,000 in legal fees. (Day paid the $60,000 damage award out of his own pocket, and taxpayers covered the lawyers' bills.) The lawsuit didn't hurt his chances with conservatives who cared more about owning the libs than the accused's right to counsel and a lawyer's responsibility to provide that representation.[7]

Day didn't want to look too eager to throw his hat into the leadership race. He wanted to be courted. Poilievre bought dozens of long-stem roses.

First, he set up a "Draft Day" website. He used his carefully cultivated media contacts to publicize DraftStockDay.com. The website also attracted the attention of Parliament Hill reporters. "With the momentum that now exists, it's going to be very difficult for Mr. Day to resist," Poilievre told Norma Greenaway, who covered the conservative parties for Conrad Black's newspaper chain.[8] More than ten thousand people visited the website in the first week, pretty good numbers for a political pitch by a university student. "One more day and we'll have enough to fill the Saddledome," Poilievre told a *Calgary Herald* reporter. The hits came from all over Canada, showing the power of the internet in politics. "We've had tons of comments from areas where the Reform party has not, in the past, been successful breaking in, like Quebec, the Maritimes and Ontario.... In the next federal election, there will be 2.5 million first-time voters, and we want to capitalize on that new political entity," Poilievre said.[9]

Two things fuel politics and politicians: votes and money. Day seemed to have some support, but he needed cash or he risked ending up in debt, especially if he lost. Since Ontario premier Mike Harris and party organizer Tom Long had already signalled they were out of the race, Day was the only person who could stop Manning from being acclaimed if a leadership race was held at all. In February, Manning went on a fundraising tour of Western Canada. Before he left, he threw Randy White out of the Reform caucus in the House of Commons for telling the media there should be a leadership race. "Manning has very deep pockets," one Day supporter on Parliament Hill told me at the time. "He has his MP and opposition leader budget, the money of the Reform Party, and his fundraising network in Calgary that he put together in the 1980s. It's going to be hard to overcome that unless we get a national movement that will put up the money for a campaign." Day's backers figured they'd need $500,000 to $1 million to beat Manning.

Interviewed on Don Newman's CBC Newsworld TV show *Politics* in February 2002, Poilievre said he created the website because Day had the "national background" to win, was fluently bilingual, and had a record of governing. And he claimed Day didn't know about the site, even though it told supporters to send encouraging messages to Day's Alberta legislature email address.[10]

Poilievre and some of Day's other supporters commissioned a poll that showed Manning would win the support of Alberta party members, but that Day would get most Ontario votes.[11] Again, Poilievre was the spokesman for the Draft Day team, which included self-identified "stockaholic" Ezra Levant. The only way any conservatives could break the Liberals' lock on 101 of Ontario's 103 seats in the House of Commons was by forming a single party and, Poilievre said, "Clearly, Stockwell is the candidate who can cement that union."[12]

Day did run and won the leadership in the second round of voting on July 8, 2000, when Poilievre was in Ottawa, working in the leader's office as an intern. There was no leader around the head office, since Day had to win a seat in Parliament and mend fences. While the internship was a bit of a bust, except for some networking opportunities, it seemed Poilievre had picked a winner.

IT'S POSSIBLE THAT even Jean Chrétien thought Stockwell Day had a real chance of winning. Chrétien was a wily old pol so, in October, he called an early election. Day and his party weren't ready. Maybe they never would have been. Day had spent part of the summer running in a by-election for a seat in the Commons. That was the election where he arrived at a news conference on a jet ski. The stunt seemed silly, and things got worse during the fall's national campaign. Day was dogged by claims he would undermine medicare and bring in a two-tier health-care system.

Claims of homophobia always followed Day. In June, while running in the Okanagan by-election that was called to get him into Parliament, Day was interviewed by a reporter at the *Montreal Mirror*, an alternative weekly. He said he'd never referred to homosexuality as a "mental disorder" and didn't pry into the sex lives of his campaign workers. But whatever ground he'd gained with the LGBTQ+ world was killed with a later statement that made headlines in newspapers across the country: Day would consider using the notwithstanding clause to block a Supreme Court decision legalizing same-sex marriage.

Since, unlike in the United States, the press does not usually report on candidates' religions and had rarely mentioned Manning's, Stockwell Day's supporters expected the media to stay quiet about Day's faith. That illusion was shattered when the CBC ran a television documentary by Paul Hunter called *Fundamental Day* that examined Day's belief that the world was created in 4004 BC. Journalists covering the 2001 federal election campaign nicknamed Day's tour bus Prayer Force One and hummed the theme of *The Flintstones* cartoon show. Day responded lamely with, "If you're looking for dinosaur politics, you need to look at the Liberals."[13]

The Liberals did explore dinosaur politics. Some of Chrétien's campaign staffers cooked up the idea of claiming Day believed Barney, the purple dinosaur who was loved by the millions of kids who watched his show, had shared his world with people before Noah's flood. They sent a junior volunteer onto *Canada AM*, CTV's national morning show, with a toy Barney to mock Day's creationist beliefs. It was the lowest point in national politics since, eight years earlier, a Progressive Conservative ad had made fun of Jean Chrétien's speech impediment.

"The campaign itself was notable for the unprecedented negative campaign by a Liberal team that sought not merely to defeat their opponents but also to completely vilify them and destroy any credibility they might have had," conservative journalist Paul Tuns wrote later. "It is one thing to criticize a campaign's reported and proposed agenda—in fact, it can be argued that candidates are obliged to do that as part of the discourse that is an election campaign. But the Liberals raised the spectre of a hidden agenda on the part of Stockwell Day himself. The Liberals did not merely criticize and attack Day; indeed, they demonized him."[14]

In *Report* magazine, Paul Bunner wrote: "It was some of the most vicious, personal and utterly fabricated campaign invective ever seen in Canadian politics." Liberal strategists were, with good reason, accused of bringing the dirty politics of James Carville, Bill Clinton's hatchet man, to Canada.[15] They and the reporters who depended on their material had made this election about personality, not policy.

If any politician ever had a reason to hate the media, it was Stockwell Day. He was accused of making gaffe after gaffe, though some of them were minor at best. CBC comedian Rick Mercer started a petition for Day to change his first name to Doris. Reporters made fun of him for being confused about the direction that the Niagara River flows, as though that was important to the governing of the country.[16] His son Logan, who worked on the campaign, was married to a former beauty queen. He had proposed to her in the foyer of the House of Commons, creating another cringe moment for any sentient Canadian Alliance member. On election night, as Day stood on the podium of his victory party in Penticton, BC, shut-ins in Western Canada watching coverage on the CBC could hear a television producer say, "This is Logan Day's wife. I've never met her, but apparently she's got tits that'd stop a—." A quick-fingered technician cut off the microphone, but the twenty-year-old woman was humiliated.[17] In a campaign where nothing had gone right, this was the final kick in the teeth.

Most Canadians ignored the election. They were happy enough with Jean Chrétien. Day picked up eight more seats, but the Liberals increased their majority at the expense of the Bloc Quebecois. Day was blamed for the Canadian Alliance's failure to break through, though it was impossible for the right to win if it was still divided, as it had been.

Maybe Poilievre hadn't picked a winner after all.

IN THE SUMMER of 2001, Poilievre returned to Ontario to do his four-month internship at Magna. After his job at Telus's collections department, this was the second and last time he drew a salary from a company.[18] Poilievre commuted to Aurora from a shared apartment in downtown Toronto. In his spare time, he volunteered to work with the Tories on a hopeless provincial by-election campaign in the suburban Toronto riding of Vaughan–King–Aurora. If Stronach was trying to recruit Poilievre for a career at Magna, it didn't work out. The highlight of the whole experience was almost certainly meeting Jonathan Denis on one of Magna's buses during the contest and reconnecting with him during the internship. The two men bonded fast. In 2002, Denis, a law student, worked with Poilievre on Ezra Levant's campaign for the Canadian Alliance in Calgary Southwest, and the next year they went into business together.

When Parliament resumed for the fall 2001 session, Day's Canadian Alliance split into different factions. Some old Reform MPs sat as a separate caucus, while a few joined the Progressive Conservatives. At the same time, and likely with some arm-twisting, the old Reformer holdouts on the United Alternative scheme began doing simple math. So did Progressive Conservatives. Neither the Canadian Alliance or the PCs were going anywhere in the present circumstances. They weren't even winning back the old Tory seats in Ontario's boondocks, places like Simcoe North, which had sent just one Liberal to Ottawa since the reign of Queen Victoria. Now, the place was represented by a Liberal lawyer who had been in the House of Commons long enough to qualify for a pension.

Some Tories were also facing the music. Patrick Brown was now on board with the United Alternative concept and had patched things up with Poilievre through their mutual friend, Adam Daifallah. The three of them, with Quebec conservative Audrey Castonguay, started a student organization called Youth for a Conservative Future. They made Joe Clark the villain of the story of Conservative failure, knowing he wouldn't allow a takeover of his 150-year-old party without a fight. Poilievre accused Clark of being a fake conservative and a chronic loser. This kind of attack—Poilievre's only method of speaking publicly about opponents—wasn't the best way to build bridges with the Progressive Conservatives, especially the Red Tories who were at the core of the party. But the Tories were tired of losing, too.

All this was happening as the country was trying to cope with the fallout of the September 11, 2001, terrorism attacks in the United States. Suddenly, Canadians everywhere felt vulnerable. Everyone knew there would be war, certainly in Afghanistan and likely in Iraq, though its regime had nothing to do with the attacks. Jean Chrétien tried to balance Canadian policy, protecting Muslims living in Canada from Islamophobic attacks, while unleashing security agencies to hunt down domestic supporters of Osama bin Laden and other radicals. He was pressured by George W. Bush's administration to join American military campaigns. Canada started by sending a small contingent of elite troops to Afghanistan, with more soldiers to follow once the Taliban was driven out, but Chrétien had no intention of joining Bush's adventures in the Middle East. Chrétien knew Canadians, especially in the East, were suspicious of the Republican administration, but he also had to protect himself against a revived conservative movement that could attack him as weak on terrorism. The Liberals brought in some anti-terror laws. Despite people's fears in the fall of 2001, there wasn't anything like another 9/11, so Reform didn't get much traction with this issue. Instead, they sometimes sounded like anti-Muslim racists when they demanded even tougher laws. Even if they had found a way to use the terrorist threat as a wedge, Reformers were too busy fighting each other to take on Chrétien. For now, the prime minister's real threat was from Paul Martin, his finance minister, who desperately wanted Chrétien's job. Martin's supporters were doing a far better job of ruining Chrétien and demoralizing the Liberal Party than anyone in the opposition parties.

ONCE IT BECAME clear the 9/11 attacks were a one-off thing, not likely to be repeated anytime soon, the threat of terrorism did not unify the country to face an external threat. Nor did "the war on terror" galvanize conservatives to work together to support Chrétien's crisis policies. Instead, they criticized Chrétien's refusal to join the American propaganda and military assault on Iraq.[19] After the 2000 election, the Progressive Conservatives watched as Reform's knives came out. A large faction of the Canadian Alliance and the right-wing press blamed Day for their loss, and he eventually succumbed to this pressure and decided to seek a new leadership mandate. John Reynolds moved into Stornoway while Day, Stephen Harper, Diane Ablonczy, and Grant Hill campaigned for the leadership. The tumbrils were coming for Preston Manning, too. By the fall of 2001, it was clear to Manning that his political career, even his time as a member of Parliament, was over. A new generation of the right was taking over. Understanding the situation, Manning announced his retirement, saying he would leave the House of Commons early the following year.

Manning's political end was very ugly. Ezra Levant, who was practising law in Calgary, joined with riding association board member Poilievre to snatch Manning's constituency. Calgary Southwest, Manning's riding, was probably the safest Canadian Alliance district in Canada. Manning tried to stop Levant by suggesting Canadian Alliance members and the Progressive Conservatives temporarily nominate one candidate to run in the by-election.[20] Poilievre, who wanted Ezra Levant to be the next MP, used Manning's odd suggestion of temporary unity and a joint candidate as a wedge to split the riding association between Manning and Day people. The twenty-two-year-old wanted to purge the board of Manning's supporters. This would strip the party's founder of his last bit of power. About five hundred people showed up at that November's riding association meeting. "We need an open and principled board to defend Alliance values," Poilievre said to a big ovation. Most of Manning's supporters kept quiet, though a few fought against the brash young upstart. Riding association member Jerzy Maslanka took the stage and shouted at opponents, "I don't support political terrorism!"[21] This was a bit extreme, but whatever it was called, the gambit had the majority's support, and the board was purged of anyone Poilievre believed had undermined Day's leadership or who might have supported a challenger to Levant.

Levant, always a genius at raising money, was sitting on a fat war chest of donations and his own cash. He and Poilievre wanted a quick nomination meeting while the federal leadership race was still going on. That way, if Harper won, the new leader would not inherit Manning's seat. Again, Poilievre worked the press, saying he was just doing what the grassroots of the riding association wanted, ignoring the fact that he had purged any opposition to make this so.

But the party's national office forced a six-week delay of the nomination meeting. At the time, this didn't seem to be much of a hurdle for Levant. He was still the only candidate, and it gave him more time to raise money and sign up new party members.

Candidates for a local party nomination don't usually make TV commercials, but Levant had money to burn. Poilievre was tasked with putting together the advertising team. The commercials were developed to drive home the accusations that Levant would use to hammer the Liberals and Progressive Conservatives in the by-election—if he got the chance. This was the first time Poilievre and Levant had control of a real campaign. Levant was only twenty-nine years old, and his new sidekick was eight years younger. They showed the talents they'd exploit in the next century: digging up embarrassing videos of their opponents, making over-the-top claims, and finding new, effective ways of making emotional connections with voters. They found a clip of Chrétien saying Prairie wealth was flowing to eastern Canada. In others, Levant promised to fight anything that looked like the National Energy Program. In one TV commercial, Poilievre, Jenni Byrne, and Stockwell Day's baby granddaughter posed as a typical Alberta family as Poilievre narrated a text attacking the Kyoto Accord on climate change as "another NEP." Joe Clark was tagged as "Kyoto Joe," who was going along with this travesty. Levant was "loyal to Calgary." Jim Prentice, who was running for the Progressive Conservatives, was "GST Jim."[22]

Levant, at that point, was not running against any of these people. He was scaring off any potential challenger in his own party by showing his billfold and his media skills. This was an audition as much as it was a nomination campaign, though in most of Alberta winning an Alliance riding nomination was the ticket to Ottawa. When the nomination vote was held, Levant was unopposed.

If Stephen Harper hadn't won the Canadian Alliance leadership in early 2002, Ezra Levant would have been elected to the House of Commons. But Harper wanted this seat, and a twenty-nine-year-old ex-staffer like Levant wasn't going to stop him. At first, he and his team were polite about it. Reynolds, now leader of the Canadian Alliance caucus in the House of Commons, and Carolyn Stewart-Olsen, who was Harper's press secretary, requested a meeting with Levant.

Poilievre, however, was opposed to any negotiations, saying Levant had won the nomination fairly, spent a lot of money and time, and deserved to be able to run. "This board of directors and the volunteers in Calgary Southwest, along with Ezra, have made a gargantuan investment in volunteer hours and finances to win this byelection," Poilievre told a *Calgary Herald* reporter. "That investment will be taken into careful consideration by the board when it takes a decision on the future of the riding," he said. There would be no meeting.

There was also some confusion about Levant's war chest. He claimed to have raised a lot of money, but now news reports were saying he'd also sunk $150,000 of his own money into the nomination campaign. By Poilievre's count, Levant had already run eighty radio and television ads and rented billboards throughout Calgary. People in the riding were targeted with spam calls and printed fliers in support of his campaign. To be fair to Levant and Poilievre, Calgary Southwest wasn't the only safe seat that Harper could run in,[23] and Levant's campaign was attracting support from other twenty-something Alberta right-wingers like Hamish Marshall and Jonathan Denis.

But there was a lesson to be learned here: you don't screw with Stephen Harper. He was able to use the power and prestige of his job to simply take the nomination. Though Levant was slow to back down, he eventually did so, and Harper easily won the seat. Levant's political career was over, partly because he complained too much. Levant would become one of the big players in the new conservative movement but as a media star, not a politician. It would take years for that to happen, but he'd be a kingmaker (and breaker) by the time Poilievre was ready to try for the party leadership. Poilievre, for his part, would get to stay in Harper's political tent. Though he'd stuck his neck out many times during the nomination fight, the twenty-two-year-old university student hadn't directly criticized Harper, and he still had Day's protection.

When Harper won the Canadian Alliance leadership, Day had taken the loss graciously, unlike Manning, who would soon settle some scores, especially those with Day and his strategists, in an autobiography that no one except party insiders read. Day was given the law-and-order file and became the Canadian Alliance critic responsible for smearing the Liberals as soft on crime, especially terrorism. In the summer of 2002, Day recruited Poilievre for a full-time job on his Ottawa staff. After getting his mother's approval, Poilievre dropped out of the University of Calgary and headed for Ottawa.

Marlene didn't expect the move to be permanent. "I said, 'You better go there and get this out of your system. After the next election, come back here,'" she recalls telling him in 2002. "Well, that just didn't happen."[24]

IN HER 2010 book *The Armageddon Factor: The Rise of Christian Nationalism in Canada,* Marci McDonald accused Stephen Harper of having a secret Christian extremist agenda that he planned to implement if he got a majority. The book sold well and large chunks of it were excerpted in the liberal press.[25] A year after the book came out, Harper won that majority, and he didn't turn Canada into a fundamentalist Christian state.

So imagine being a young fundamentalist Protestant or conservative Catholic man who truly believes in the ideas of Margaret Thatcher, Milton Friedman, and Ayn Rand, raised in a province where the local media affirm many of their beliefs. Your family and friends believe the same stuff. So do most of your neighbours. A lot of them left Ontario and the Maritimes to try to find better jobs, and they see themselves as pioneers and entrepreneurs, even when they're drawing a weekly wage. You and your friends might not get many dates, but you aren't utter freaks. In Ontario, you know you would have been, since you go to national conventions and hear the stories of your Ontario colleagues. They live like the outcasts in John Hughes high school movies.

Your university professors, by and large, support your worldview and have their own gripes with "gatekeeper" peers who decide whether their work is published in the better journals. Even though you and your friends are just out of your teens, you know important people in the provincial government. You volunteer for the campaigns of federal politicians who have had a string of recent election successes. The people who attack your social and economic beliefs are outsiders, easily written off as "Laurentian elites". Your ideology and world view are completely normal in your province.

Then you get to Ottawa. You arrive in the 1990s and depend on Stockwell Day for what you hope will be a career at the centre of power. *Frank* magazine runs stories about you and your friends under the standing headline "Just Off the Turnip Truck" and plays humiliating (though often funny) pranks, such as conning your colleagues into believing the Chrétien government is sending Zambonis to Africa in foreign-aid packages ("Zambonis Up the Zambezi").[26] Media people, strategists, and lobbyists think you're a fringe player, a temporary visitor, uncool and uninteresting. You're not going to impress them with your lifestyle: political staffers are there for the experience, not the money. Your chances of getting a date with one of the beautiful, bright Parliament Hill staffers are slim. So all you have are your friends from your political party. It's easy, and far less frustrating to hang around with them than to try to become part of the downtown Ottawa social scene. How could you not feel like an outsider and hope for a day when you could pay them all back?

PEOPLE WHO LIVE in Toronto and other big cities don't understand the shock and, sometimes, anxiety felt by people who come from the countryside or small towns when they visit or move in. Ottawa, a city of almost a million and a half,[27] is both a depressing, expensive urban wasteland with the noise and vibe of a fairly big city, and a backwater satellite of Montreal. It's a long way from Western Canada, and people are far less friendly, partly because political people are transient. Reform MPs and staffers struggled with loneliness. Marriages broke down because of distance and, quite often, infidelity.[28]

Our Westminster system is *supposed* to allow ordinary people to win the support of their neighbours, go to Parliament, and learn how the mind-numbingly complex legislative and executive systems work. If they're in opposition, they're supposed to ask tough questions. When MPs are new, they'll ask some dumb questions too. Some will make the mistake of believing they can speak their mind any time someone asks their opinion. I come from a small town in central Ontario, not far from or a lot different than Jenni Byrne's hometown of Fenelon Falls. Back in the day, before the place was inundated with Toronto retirees, strangers said hi to each other when they passed on the street. Many members of the Reform caucus were like the people I knew back home: friendly, opinionated, but requiring help to understand the way Ottawa worked.[29]

The Canadian Alliance needed good staffers. Joe Clark had a research team that had found the Liberals' soft spot: corruption, especially in Quebec. The Clark Tories owned Shawinigate, which involved shady land deals by Chrétien himself, and the sponsorship scandal, a kickback scheme to reward Quebec advertising agencies for secret and possibly illegal work they'd done during the 1995 Quebec sovereignty referendum. Even after the 9/11 attacks, which divided Canadians between people who supported American retaliation and those who wanted no part in a war on terror, these corruption accusations were the real threat to the Liberals and to Chrétien's leadership of the party he'd brought back to power eight years before. The Tories' domination of House of Commons debates and the respect that Clark had earned as a sensible statesman among opposition MPs who often acted like brats, made his reputation as a good, solid man. This, however, did not improve his polling numbers, and in 2002, more than two decades after he'd been prime minister, Clark decided it was time to retire. The Progressive Conservative leadership race came down to a fight between Peter MacKay, scion of a stalwart Nova Scotia Tory family that was strongly allied to Brian Mulroney, Jim Prentice, and Scott Brison, with Prairie populist David Orchard as a long-shot candidate who quietly built support. None of the candidates seemed willing to agree to a Canadian Alliance–Progressive Conservative merger. The Tories took their time picking a new leader. The vote wouldn't be held until the spring of 2003.

While the Tories focused on electing a new leader, Stephen Harper and Stockwell Day worked hard to pressure the Chrétien government into joining the United States and the United Kingdom in the "coalition of the willing" against Iraq. Poilievre was in the middle of this campaign, working beside Day when he and Harper wrote a letter to the editor of the *Wall Street Journal* attacking Chrétien for sitting out the war. In late March, Bush launched the invasion, which went well for the allied countries at first but turned into another expensive quagmire that, after it became clear that the *causa belli* was a lie, ruined the reputations of British prime minister Tony Blair and a few other allied leaders who were sucked in. Day could do little more than cheerlead the American war effort while Poilievre worked with right-wing evangelical minister Tristan Emmanuel to organize a Canadians for Bush rally in Niagara that failed to sway Chrétien. This was just part of his job. MP staffers work hard, doing everything from running errands to analyzing legislation. There's a lot of night work and some out-of-town travel. The money's not great. There's absolutely no job security, and MP employers are exempted from some workplace rules by the ancient laws of parliamentary privilege.[30] But for young people who live for politics, it's a great experience.

There were young, ambitious Liberals, New Democrats, and Greens in Ottawa in those years, lined up on the other side of the political divide. Within a couple of years, they would be the leaders of the opposition to Stephen Harper, but they tended to get along with each other because they understood the nature of their colleagues' work in ways outsiders never could. But Poilievre did not make friends among those colleagues. He's not a consensus-builder, a reach-across-the-aisle kind of guy.

Still, Poilievre settled nicely into Ottawa, staying out of the Liberal-dominated trendy downtown watering holes, which were too expensive for a financially prudent staffer, and spending time at home with Jenni Byrne and other conservative friends of his generation. These were very young people, just out of school, and half a generation removed from most of their peers in the other parties. This new group of strategists and young MPs came to an Ottawa where most politicians and people in the media had been on the scene since the early 1990s, and some had come to Parliament Hill long before that. Poilievre's network grew to include John Baird, a very young, up-and-coming member of the Ontario provincial cabinet.

Poilievre helped Baird when he ran for re-election in 2003. Baird had no trouble winning his suburban Ottawa seat, though his party was defeated by the provincial Liberals. Poilievre saw Baird, who was ten years older, as something of a mentor. "He has an incredible political gut," Baird said of Poilievre. "The ability to look at a controversy, a complex controversy, distil all the information down to what's important and make a fast judgment. And that was important to me as a young candidate because I needed a lot of advice and he was always there to provide it."[31] The two quickly became allies and friends.

In 2003, Poilievre founded 3D Contact Inc. with lawyer Jonathan Denis, who became Alberta's justice minister years later. They were already close friends, though Denis was usually two time zones away. "We saw a bit of a niche in the market ... that we could sell our company on the fact we believed in the cause. We were only working for 'small c' conservative candidates," Denis would tell a journalist nearly a decade later. Partnerships are one of the riskiest ways to do business because they rely on personal relationships that tend to break down when money complicates friendships. Poilievre and Denis managed to prevent that, mostly by being direct with each other. "He's not the type of person who will tell you what you want to hear to your face. He's someone who will tell you what he really believes. I think that shows a lot of conviction for someone in public office," Denis said.[32]

They used their national network of political connections to give communications, polling, and research advice to conservative parties and candidates. The two partners were keen students of the newest trends in voter identification and political marketing. Robocall technology and the remaking of the telephone system to end long-distance charges made it easier to connect with voters. Computer technology helped political parties identify and connect with potential supporters and donors and to know which voters would never vote for them. The internet, especially blogs and chat groups, changed politics. Social media (Facebook after 2004, Twitter starting in March 2006) and YouTube (founded in 2005) revolutionized it.[33] Candidates needed strategists who knew how this stuff worked. Since high school, Poilievre learned things that had real value on the political market. They could also be used when Poilievre made his own political move.

AS POILIEVRE FORGED new political alliances and went into business with Denis, Canadian conservatives finally ended their internal fight. They saw an opportunity: Jean Chrétien, who, despite the scandals, was still a beloved old warhorse, was on his way out, giving into pressure from the Martin camp. In Stephen Harper, the Conservatives finally had a candidate, after Day's clown show and Manning's hectoring, who knew how to present himself as a mainstream candidate. Peter MacKay won the Progressive Conservative leadership in May 2003 with a promise not to amalgamate the party with the Canadian Alliance, but by the end of that year he would break that promise and agree to the merger under the name of the Conservative Party of Canada. At least as important, Ontario premier Mike Harris, whose caucus straddled the Progressive Conservative–Reform divide, also signed off on the deal.

Harper was relieved when Harris and the rest of the better-known Tories, including MacKay, decided not to run for the leadership, which meant Harper had it in the bag. Harper beat Belinda Stronach and Tony Clement in March 2004, and MacKay and his caucus were shuffled to the sidelines. They stayed loyal, determined to end the Liberal winning streak. MacKay was given the empty title of deputy leader, but he would come to have important cabinet portfolios in Harper's government. The old Tory party, the movement of Macdonald and Diefenbaker, Bob Stanfield and Joe Clark, was dead. "Progressive conservative" is now understood as something of an insult in the Conservative party.[34] The 2003–04 reshuffling was in fact a reverse takeover. The Canadian Alliance, the most extreme part of the old Reform movement, took the historic Conservative name but stayed true to its Alberta social and economic conservatism, not the Toryism of Bay Street.

Another page in Canadian politics had turned. The Conservatives were now one party, controlled by a leader who came across to voters as somewhat normal. He had a smart, pretty wife, cute kids, and a love of cats. People saw him at hockey rinks and the Cosmic Adventures indoor playground in the Ottawa suburbs. He even had his own band that played pop music.[35] All these things reminded people that Martin and Chrétien were old. Harper also brought much needed discipline to the party. MPs would learn to follow Harper's scripts rather than sounding off whenever a reporter wanted a quote. Stunts, if they happened at all, would be gamed out by "the centre." Harper hired people with Ottawa experience and had every reason to believe it was a matter of time before he could begin to dismantle what journalist John Ibbitson and University of Toronto professor David Cameron had called the Laurentian Elite.

Martin was in no shape to do what Chrétien had done to Day and call a snap election before Harper could put together a political staff and a national campaign team. The organization that won Harper the leadership race wasn't enough. He needed staffers who knew how to connect with people who normally wouldn't vote for a conservative party. Martin had the same problem: his ambition had split the Liberals, and they needed time to rebuild a national campaign organization around Martin's core group of loyal strategists. After the conservative merger, many Liberal MPs, especially in Ontario outside of Toronto, began to do the math in their ridings and decided to leave as winners rather than be turfed out by voters during the next election. Both parties raced to raise money, find talented strategists, and nominate candidates for an election that they knew would be coming within a few months.[36] There were moments of what passed in Canadian politics for drama, such as when Belinda Stronach broke up with her boyfriend Peter MacKay and her party on the same day and crossed the floor of the House of Commons to sit as a Liberal. But there was no big issue, no national referendum question like the 1988 North American free trade deal, that fired up the voters. Harper was a believer in incrementalism, and he'd walk to power with baby steps.

4
NEWBIE

In politics, absurdity is not a handicap.
NAPOLEON BONAPARTE

THE PRATT FAMILY settled in northern Carleton County when George III was king of England and Napoleon was shivering out the last years of his life on the south Atlantic rock of St. Helena. At the time, there were hints of things to come: a few years after the Pratts arrived, the Rideau Canal, one of the British Empire's great white elephants, was dug through the local malarial swamps to connect the Ottawa River with Kingston. This cost the Brits more than £800,000 at a time when a British pound was a coin with just under a quarter of an ounce of gold. The Duke of Richmond, Canada's governor general, died of rabies not far from the Pratt farm while scoping out the canal's route. It seemed the failings of Canadian politics and administration were predestined by the chemistry of the land itself.

As the Pratts brought more land under the plow, the valley lumber trade picked up, Ottawa was chosen as the country's capital because it had cheap real estate, and the city grew until its suburbs covered the farmland where the Pratts first put down roots.

The riding of Carleton has almost exclusively been Conservative since it started sending representatives to the legislature of Upper Canada in 1821.[1] Most of its colonial and post-Confederation representatives were forgettable men—the riding has never had a female MP—but a couple do stand out: Sir John A. Macdonald parachuted himself into the seat for six years in the 1880s, while the Tory leader George Drew, another outsider, took the seat in a nasty by-election in 1948. Carleton was a wasteland for the Liberals: popular local politician Lloyd Francis, who was elected speaker of the House of Commons, could only hold it for one term in the 1970s.[2] With some rejigging of its boundaries, most of the riding was incorporated into Nepean–Carleton for forty-five years. And while it was under that name, David Pratt, the most local of local politicians, won the seat in 1997.

Pratt made his name in municipal politics as a hard-working city councillor who tried to fix the city's transit problems. Ottawa's system connected the city's malls to the downtown but poorly served suburbs like Barrhaven. In a council of mediocrities, Pratt stood out.[3] And people liked him: when he arrived on Parliament Hill as a member of Jean Chrétien's caucus, he made friends with MPs in all the parties. After a stint as chairman of the House of Common's defence committee, Paul Martin made Pratt the minister of defence. That's a big deal in Ottawa, where thousands of people work for the Department of National Defence and many more people's jobs depend on its contracts.

But municipal politics still haunted Pratt. In the early 2000s, Ottawa councillors and residents fought over the route of a new light-rail commuter system. Pratt was one of the politicians who wanted the line to connect the suburb of Barrhaven, in his riding, to the city's downtown. John Baird, who held the seat provincially, also lobbied for that route. It wasn't a popular choice in the rest of Ottawa, where each suburb and satellite city thought the line should serve *them*.[4] The city's surprisingly hard-right local media heaped all the blame on Pratt and Liberal mayor Bob Chiarelli, letting the slippery John Baird off the hook.[5] Still, with his LRT win, his high profile, and his personal charm, local and Parliament Hill conventional wisdom said Pratt was the person to beat.

PIERRE POILIEVRE HAS better political instincts than the journalists and politics watchers who generate conventional wisdom. He understood Carleton's past as a safe Tory seat and could do simple math. Door-to-door canvassing convinced Poilievre the seat was winnable if Martin's minority fell. The Liberals only held the seat because of the Reform–Progressive Conservative split. Now this was behind them. This wasn't clear to local Tories, so the nomination was truly wide open, without risk of the party appointing a star candidate.

Still, five local people went for it. Several were longtime local politicians, and the man who'd run for the Alliance against Pratt, Ed Mahfouz, was something of a hero to the large local Lebanese-Canadian community because of his fundraising work for their community organizations. He was also a good organizer whose supporters would show up to the nomination meeting. (Many people will pay the minimal membership fee to get a candidate to stop pestering them, with no intention of attending.) On the negative side of the ledger, Poilievre was not from the riding, though he lived in it. This probably counted less than it would have before Ottawa's suburban sprawl overwhelmed much of the old farm community.

Even Stockwell Day, still Poilievre's boss, saw the nomination and the general-election campaigns as long shots. But being a newcomer in a suburban riding was less of a problem than it would have been in most rural ridings: many of the voters were new arrivals, too. Along with Poilievre's willingness to work, he had a good team of local people, helped by Jonathan Denis, who had been Poilievre's partner in their campaign management and polling business for more than a year and would soon be Poilievre's partner in a Calgary rental property.[6] They used old election-result data to identify parts of the riding with big conservative majorities and went door to door day and night repeating Poilievre's campaign slogan that declared him a "Rock Solid Conservative." This slogan appealed to party members, who turned up to the nomination meeting, put up lawn signs, and opened their wallets. Poilievre won the nomination on the third ballot and immediately pivoted to running against Pratt.[7]

Pratt couldn't keep up: he still had an important ministry that demanded some of his time. And, it appears, it took a while for him to take the young staffer's campaign seriously. By the time he did, Poilievre had successfully tagged his opponent as "Liberal Pratt," playing off the English insult. And Poilievre had convinced a lot of local conservatives that the riding was winnable, so a large team of volunteers, including John Baird and Lisa MacLeod, put their backs into his campaign.

The nomination campaign should have opened the eyes of Liberals and pundits that Poilievre was a serious candidate. Unlike his opponents, he and his team went through old Progressive Conservative and Reform/Alliance party lists and worked hard to sign up lapsed members. He also went door to door and sold party memberships, which helped him become the Conservative candidate and introduced him to local voters, who'd usually never heard of him. Other candidates, at most, called up some of the old members. They didn't realize the power of face-to-face campaigning.[8]

Ottawa Citizen columnist Ken Gray underestimated Poilievre as just a former Alberta resident "who studied international relations at the University of Calgary."[9] The pride of Fenelon Falls, Jenni Byrne, was now "from Ottawa." She was his "partner." Their message was unfocused: Poilievre said he was running because of cuts to health care, which is a provincial responsibility.[10] (After 2004, Poilievre's concern about health care seems to have been limited to getting a rent break from the federal government for the Queensway Carleton Hospital, in the west end of Ottawa.) There were the rest of the usual Poilievre beefs: the Liberals took too much in taxes, and they'd thrown away millions on the national long-gun registry and the crooked Quebec sponsorship contracts.[11] The government was soft on crime. Poilievre told Gray the parole and bail systems had to be fixed and said repeat offenders over the age of fourteen should be tried in adult court. Although he didn't like capital punishment, he'd vote for it if the voters of Nepean–Carleton wanted him to.

Speaking about Paul Martin and the Liberal regime that had been in power for eleven years, Poilievre said, with some accuracy: "This is a tired old government proving every day that it has got to go. People are looking for new blood on Parliament Hill. . . . Taxes are a big concern to people. They are a burden on any middle-class family." Baird, still a provincial cabinet minister, was going door to door with the twenty-four-year-old federal candidate. "People will have to decide what they want," Baird said. "The community is ready for change."[12]

Although Paul Martin was struggling in the national campaign, pundits believed until election night that Nepean–Carleton was a safe Liberal seat. Even the conservative *Ottawa Citizen* endorsed Pratt (with some praise for Poilievre) and expected him to win. Pratt was more mature, both in age and in attitude. He'd travelled the world on sensitive military and human-rights missions before he was put in charge of Canada's military. He'd started to expand the size and spending of the armed forces, and a lot of that money was supposed to end up in the pockets of the voters of Nepean–Carleton. But other numbers that the pundits hadn't noticed were at work: Pratt won the seat in 2000 with 41.2 percent of the vote. The Canadian Alliance and Progressive Conservatives, who were still running separate candidates, combined for 53.4 percent of the ballots. NDP and Green Party support was minimal. And now, with the right united, Pratt had to win over some small-*c* conservative voters who hadn't supported him before or he'd lose the seat.

In an interview with a *Hill Times* reporter, Poilievre described Nepean–Carleton as a "rock-solid conservative" riding. "I believe that Nepean–Carleton needs a rock-solid Conservative voice in the House of Commons. Yes [the merger influenced my decision to run] in two ways: One, I believe the candidacy is much more attractive now that we have a broader tent and two, it's especially important to me that this new party retain rock-solid conservative values and the only way to do that is to have candidates who are rock-solid conservatives and that's who I am." Using "rock-solid Conservative" three times in one quote showed how he made this slogan an important part of his campaign.[13]

Still, Parliament Hill reporters didn't take Poilievre and his campaign seriously, when they noticed it at all. The Tories, they believed, had picked the wrong candidate. He was one of the odd ducks that hung around with unpopular people like Ezra Levant and Rob Anders. How could an established politician be beaten by a mouthy young political staffer who had just moved to the riding and had never been much more than a student political animal? Pratt was a powerful minister, popular with the Hill crowd, so how could Carleton voters toss him out?

These reporters didn't realize all politics are local. Outside downtown Ottawa, eastern Ontario is very conservative. Local political hero Baird, still a member of the Ontario legislature but now a performative opposition MPP with a mean mouth, was behind Poilievre. Baird's provincial riding matched the federal district. Baird was twenty-four, the same age as Poilievre, when he was first elected to Queen's Park in 1995, and he provided a fine example of how a young politician could succeed by being annoying but well-focused on things his constituents care about.

Both men found issues that worked. Even though he was a provincial politician who had no say in issues of war and peace, Baird staked out the traditional conservative claim of support of the military. Canadian soldiers were being killed in Afghanistan, and Baird had done an end run around Pratt by having a local freeway declared "Veterans Memorial Highway."[14]

Poilievre sought out voter anger and anxiety. Suburban Ottawa federal bureaucrats tend to be unilingual, which hobbles their chances of advancing far in their career. A lot of people in the riding would like a federal job but don't have a chance because most modern job postings require some level of bilingualism. Poilievre explained away his French name and promised to push for job opportunities for anglophones. His political antennae picked up voters' concerns about the O-Train, the LRT commuter system that smelled of a boondoggle.[15] The young candidate was able to convince people that a fast train that would take them from a big suburb of Ottawa to the city's downtown was a bad idea.

Poilievre turned twenty-five during that campaign. He had a motivated and loyal team who helped fix a few of his shortcomings. They threw Poilievre a birthday party at his campaign office in the rich satellite village of Manotick where, Poilievre told an *Ottawa Citizen* reporter, "a bunch of the ladies on the campaign actually bought me some clothes because they thought I was very badly dressed.... I was out of university, and I hadn't really... mastered my wardrobe at all."[16]

Still, though he'd done the Reform–Conservative math, Poilievre tried to manage expectations. He told his parents he expected to lose "because I didn't want them to be disappointed if I did. I thought I had a good chance of winning but I knew there was an equally good chance that I wouldn't."

Near the end of the campaign, Poilievre began to feel much more confident and started telling people that he was going to win. Poilievre had a poll from Hollinshead Research Institute headed by Frank Hall that showed him way ahead. "We are winning. The poll that came out... showed that we have two-to-one margin over our Liberal opponent. We feel very good about that. People in the riding believe that it's time for change," Poilievre told a news reporter. "After a decade of Liberal corruption, mismanagement and waste, people understand that they cannot have a representation from a Liberal MP."[17]

With so many things in his favour—the public desire to hurt the Liberals (who were returned to power with a minority), Baird's help, the "ladies'" sartorial aid, and the inherent conservativism of that part of the country—Poilievre beat Pratt by an impressive 5.6 percentage points. He hadn't captured all the Progressive Conservative and Canadian Alliance votes of the 2000 election, but he'd got enough of them: 3,736 more than Pratt. The NDP and the Greens increased their numbers by 8 percent, suggesting some voters were unthrilled with either of the candidates who stood a serious chance of winning, but their votes didn't matter. Poilievre was the first past the post, and not just by a nose.

NOW THAT POILIEVRE was an MP and his newly united party had become a national contender, he and Jenni Byrne, who had worked on the national campaign for the Conservative party during the election, were a power couple, though people didn't know much about them or even if they lived together.[18] Powerbrokers wanted to meet the new MP and his tough, politically savvy partner. Conrad Black's flunky Peter White hosted a dinner of Toronto Tories for Poilievre at one of Toronto's better private clubs and invited Conservative heavyweights to meet him. Poilievre's bigger paycheque meant he and Byrne could go out in public looking like they'd finally arrived. From behind his orange-tinted glasses, then-New Democrat MP Pat Martin, a snappy dresser with the style of an Ottawa-version of Roxy Music frontman Bryan Ferry, said Poilievre stood out even as a young rookie politician. Although he was just twenty-five, he was ready to work, and he knew how to act and look like an MP. "It was pretty evident he was a keener right from Day One, and somebody to watch," Martin told a local reporter. "He was undeniably talented and very well dressed." While Martin disagreed "profoundly" with Poilievre on most issues, they both understood the value of a good suit. "He was happy one time to find some suit guy who comes to town once a year with a bunch of Hong Kong suits and measures you up," Martin said. "Then you get the suit later in the mail."[19]

It took more than good suits to impress Poilievre's new colleagues on the Hill. Garry Keller is probably the brightest member of that generation of Alberta conservatives. He had tried to win a nomination back home before going to Ottawa as a staffer, usually working for John Baird. Keller believes that Poilievre may have quickly alienated older MPs with his brashness.[20] Poilievre, unlike Keller, led with his fists, rather than sitting quietly for awhile to learn from House and party veterans. The new MP spoke in the House of Commons for the first time on October 6, 2004, making a one-minute statement before Question Period. When MPs make these short speeches under the Standing Orders, they usually make non-political remarks that publicize riding events and praise people back home. Poilievre's little speech was hardly a pat on the head for the local Boy Scouts or an obituary for a deserving constituent. Instead, he attacked, as he would do so often through the rest of his career. Poilievre led off with the same political message he's become known for. The Liberals, he suggested, only showed signs of competence when they were finding new ways to steal. They sought power to get control of patronage. They couldn't care less about the cost to taxpayers. They and their media buddies believed they owned Ottawa and saw everyone else as outsiders who didn't count.

"Mr. Speaker, since taking office the Prime Minister [Paul Martin] has engaged in a smorgasbord of patronage that is so impressive it would make even his predecessor [Jean Chrétien] blush," Poilievre told the House of Commons. "Gun registry bungler Allan Rock becomes UN ambassador; ivory tower Liberals Sophia Leung, Sarkis Assadourian and Yvon Charbonneau get cushy vacations as foreign advisors and ambassadors; Liberal yes man, John Harvard, hit the jackpot as Lieutenant Governor of Manitoba. The revenue minister personally appointed his banking buddy, Gordon Feeney, as the chairman of the ad-scam-plagued Canada Post.

"Why is the Prime Minister turning back on his promise to do politics differently? He promised to condemn to history the practice and politics of cronyism. If this new king of cronyism will not stop the Liberal bonanza, the only thing Canadians will condemn to history is his government."[21]

In sixty seconds, he had managed to attack two prime ministers, a couple of former MPs, and a handful of government appointees. Soon afterwards, he was scolded by the deputy speaker, who was chairing the House, for breaking the rules, albeit a minor one.

He got back on his feet during a debate on a routine piece of legislation. "Madam Chair, I would like to thank the hon. member for her remarks and I would also like to note with delight the presence of five members of the Liberal caucus here, including the—." The speaker reminded Poilievre that "It is inappropriate for members on either side to point out the number of members in the House."[22] Poilievre had a point: most Canadians would be amazed by the thin turnout in the House of Commons after Question Period. "House duty" is one of the minor jobs of MPs, and the House is usually almost empty while important legislation is debated. The actual making of law has become one of the lowest priorities of MPs, which hasn't been good for democracy. But Conservatives are just as guilty as any other party when it comes to House of Commons turnout. Poilievre could have made his point without breaking House rules, but casual breaking of Commons civility would become part of his political toolkit.

On important issues, Poilievre, like Donald Trump, sees politics as a zero-sum game. He often stakes out positions where he shows no concern for people in need, especially women, if he can get in digs against his political opponents. It doesn't matter if Liberal programs helped working families and that, given the chance, Harper's party would have brought in a similar, if watered-down, version. The Martin government tried to create a national daycare program. Poilievre railed against it. "The throne speech promises to further erode provincial jurisdiction with a pledge to assemble a massive, multi-billion-dollar government-led child raising program it calls childcare. This is an area of provincial jurisdiction. It is not part of the competence of the government. However, at the same time it applies a tax burden on the average family that is so burdensome it is inadequate for one parent to go out into the workforce and raise income by him or herself. As such, both parents have to go out to work.

"The overall policy direction of the government is to discriminate against those families who make the sacrifice to keep one parent in the home to raise the children and instead forces upon them a decision that is not their first prerogative, which is a government-led child raising program."[23]

He could have made the same speech in 2021, when Justin Trudeau, under pressure from the New Democrats, tried again to bring in a reasonably priced national childcare plan like the one Quebec's had for years. When the Liberals and NDP pushed the plan through the House of Commons, Poilievre's opponents blamed him for encouraging conservative premiers to delay the rollout of cheap daycare.[24]

VOTERS AND JOURNALISTS were still wary that the new party was just a spit-polished version of Preston Manning's Western evangelical movement, with no real chance of breaking through in the big cities and east of the Ottawa River. The March 2005 national policy meeting, held in Montreal, was an important barometer. Peter MacKay said the conference was "a chance to put the lie to Liberal fear-mongering" about the new party. Potential star candidates in French and English Canada saw the convention as a litmus test. Would it be about saleable policies or just another forum for angry Western rural delegates to spray spittle on floor mics?

Before the delegates arrived in Montreal, Harper made it clear that social conservatives would not dominate the convention. "People are scratching their heads," Ontario Progressive Conservative MPP Tony Clement said before the convention. "They will be watching Montreal very closely." He said even some of the eastern Tories choked on Harper's stifling of debate on moral issues such as abortion and same-sex marriage. They weren't used to Harper's bear-trap lock on the party.[25]

Harper was already saying things that Quebec wanted to hear about being partners in Confederation while being a province with its own unique history and culture. The question remained whether he would be able to connect both with Quebecers, who were the most socially liberal people in Canada, and Ontario voters who, except for urban hipsters, were fine with things as they were.

Harper threw the hard right a bone by saying his government would bring in a bill to define marriage as the union of one man and one woman. Ontario and British Columbia had already legalized same-sex marriage, and Paul Martin's government, which had the real power over marriage laws, was leaning the same way. (Same-sex marriage became legal in Canada in 2005, when Martin's government got the *Civil Marriage Act* through the minority Parliament. Despite Harper's promise to hold up the traditional definition of marriage at the Montreal convention, the Conservatives never repealed it.)

Delegates, under Harper's firm control, passed resolutions promising that the Conservatives would not regulate or ban abortion. They promised that a Conservative government would cut taxes, help stay-at-home parents (which put them in opposition to Martin, who was trying to get his daycare bill through Parliament), and perform a "review" of Canada's commitments under the Kyoto Accord on climate change mitigation. Pet Quebec issues like a new federal policy that would allow "safe" use of asbestos and greater provincial involvement in international treaty-making were kept from the convention floor. People watching the convention saw a party that seemed serious about crafting a platform that appealed to mainstream Canada. Delegates passed a 112-point policy declaration and ratified the party's nineteen founding principles. (Among them:

fiscal accountability; upholding individual rights and freedoms; support for constitutional monarchy, the institutions of Parliament, and Canada's democratic process; a strong military; law and order; respect for Canada's history and traditions; and equal treatment for all Canadians.) Harper's people even managed to rehabilitate Brian Mulroney, the man Manning and his allies had rebelled against in the mid-1980s, filming a Mulroney pep talk and showing it at the convention. This was an important effort to build bridges with Quebec conservatives, who remembered Mulroney differently, as a man who won Quebec and had brought in right-wing Quebecois to be part of a truly national Conservative party.

Poilievre focused on getting back into his fight with Patrick Brown over whether the new "Tories" should start a youth wing. This was really a struggle over the recruitment and mentoring of the university-aged conservatives who could one day put Poilievre or Brown into the party leadership. Harper allowed Poilievre and Rahim Jaffer, another bright young MP, to earn a little ink on the issue. "We envision a strong and vibrant base of young people taking senior positions in the party, not because of quotas or affirmative action programs, but because of their abilities and merit," this faction said in a statement likely written by Poilievre. Their party didn't need a "sandbox-style youth wing" like the Liberals and New Democrats had.[26] Poilievre's side won the vote. It was a small thing, but it showed Poilievre's organization and debating skills.

In his closing speech, Harper said that the new party had a "moderate, mainstream program which reflects Canadian values proudly and faithfully."[27] The convention accomplished what Harper wanted it to do. Afterwards, reluctant "star" candidates from provincial governments and private business began seeking nominations and meeting Harper's staff to talk policy. Media claims of hidden agendas began to lose their sting.

—

BRASH NEW MPS are not particularly rare, especially when change-hungry voters decide it's time to send a new generation of representatives to Ottawa. Poilievre didn't stand out in the class of 2004 because of his pre-political career, which didn't exist. He was just another one of the true-believer professional politicians and staffers who live for the game when so many Canadians find most national debates and internal party fights boring.

One of his skills, however, separated him from the pack of strange, nerdy, socially isolated young conservatives who'd arrived in Ottawa over the previous decade. Poilievre had a knack for giving journalists good quote and great footage from stunts. In high school, he'd earned a lot of ink in the *Calgary Herald*, shared with papers in the rest of the newspaper chain owned by Conrad Black. In university, he had come up with "free speech" stunts in the Senate election and Ezra Levant's nomination campaign. Baird, now a bored member of the Queen's Park opposition who would move up to the big leagues in the next federal election, spotted this talent. The local boy helped Poilievre sharpen his quotes and his jugular-slashing campaign techniques.

Poilievre understood that he had to make his mark as a ruthless critic of the Liberals and all things liberal because he could never gain attention or ascend the party ranks for any other reason. His partisanship would become his primary value, since he had no private sector experience or professional expertise. Poilievre wasn't even a university graduate, though he was grinding his way through correspondence courses to get his last few credits. Nor was he bilingual, but he was taking lessons offered by the House of Commons. And, though he was so very young, his life was glamour-free. Jenni Byrne, seen as his spouse whether or not she was his life partner in any traditional sense, repelled most non-conservatives. As she climbed the ladder in her own party as a staffer in Stephen Harper's office, her ruthlessness began to scare Conservatives. Socially, they were largely marginalized in a city where the small social scene that exists favours people with money, roots in the community, interesting conversation, and the right address. Poilievre and Byrne had none of those things. They weren't poor, but their income didn't impress the Ottawa elite. They were new and from decidedly unhip places like Fenelon Falls and Calgary. Like Poilievre, Byrne lived for the kind of political battles that most people don't want to hear about at parties. And they lived in Barrhaven, a decent place for middle-class couples and young families but the antithesis of New Edinburgh, Ottawa South, and Westboro, where the interesting people lived.

Poilievre knew he lived in a different Ottawa than the one people see on the news and students visit on drunken school trips. "There are two Ottawas, you see," Poilievre wrote in a 2007 piece published by the *Ottawa Citizen*, a paper that appealed more to the suburbs than the downtown. "The first is the one made up of the hoity-toity chattering class of special interest groups and lobbyists who are obsessed with portrait galleries and pleasing the National Capital Commission. While this group has a disproportionately loud voice in the media, they are relatively small. I am the first to admit that Conservatives were out of touch with this bunch. On the other hand, there is the real Ottawa composed of middle-class families. Real people. They are the folks who work hard, pay their taxes, and play by the rules. As a Conservative MP, I work for them."[28]

The young Tories felt that marginalization, and it helped fuel their desire to break Ottawa. Rob Anders, Ezra Levant, Monte Solberg, Jason Kenney, and Rahim Jaffer hung around as the "Snack Pack" and provided plenty of good copy to the mean people at the gossip magazine *Frank*, which was still a thing. Trying to form a similar glamour-free group of young Conservative MPs, Poilievre, Jeremy Harrison, and Andrew Scheer told *National Post* writer John Ivison they called themselves the "Blue Labelers" after Tory blue and Johnny Walker Blue scotch.[29] Scheer's wife, Jill, gave her husband a wedding gift of a bottle of the stuff to open when he had his first child or won his first election.[30] But the Blue Label name never caught on with the media, one of the only times, perhaps, Poilievre's sloganeering failed to catch.[31]

Whatever they were drinking—which likely wasn't a lot, since Poilievre is not a big drinker—these young men were always talking politics. More precisely, they were gaming out political strategy and trying to come up with a workable plan to finish off the tired old Liberal government. They weren't arguing about fundamental ideas of policy and administration or the legislation that was moving towards becoming law. All of them accepted Margaret Thatcher–style ideas of small government, though they didn't think either Thatcher or Ronald Reagan had gone far enough and believed that Brian Mulroney had let the team down utterly.

The young Canadian Alliance strategists did not just view themselves as outliers in a city full of public servants, lawyers, journalists, academics, tech workers, and other professionals who tended to lean left and shun conservatives. The Albertans believed, rather, that they were pioneers. Ottawa's political "elite" might have rolled their eyes if any of them had read a *Calgary Herald* piece that ran a few weeks after Poilievre was elected, but perhaps they should have paid attention. "All of us, I think, are ideological, we try to be consistent within our thinking," Poilievre said of himself and his friends. "I know the presence of a young entrepreneurial class in caucus will keep the party on the free enterprise track. Electorally, I believe the presence of a youth bloc in caucus will enable us to reach out to a new generation of voters."

Straw polls of national voters conducted at the time showed this new generation of doctrinaire young men could very well become the next cadre of leaders. Ambitious millennials rejected the compromise and pragmatism of earlier generations. They also increasingly saw the social democratic left as out of touch and elitist. Soon these people would take over from the baby boomers as the generation that had the votes to make and unmake governments. But millennial attitudes could not be taken for granted:

"What the voters giveth, the voters can also take away," Poilievre wrote.[32]

In so many ways, Poilievre and his inner circle anticipated the changing political dynamics of North America and Europe in the 2020s. Immigrant communities that the left believed it owned often came from socially conservative cultures and would surprise white progressives by supporting candidates who opposed expanded gender rights. Brown and Black people were no more eager than anyone else to pay taxes, and many looked for candidates who would rein in government. Earlier generations of new Canadians might be grateful to the Liberals for Canada's relatively open door, but that gratitude eventually dissipated. The boomer generation, which had once had fond memories of the progressive culture of the 1960s, was increasingly open to a conservative message as its members aged and passed their best earning years. Most important, people seemed to desire change, even if often only in a very vague way.

Most of Poilievre's future Liberal and NDP opponents weren't on the scene yet. In Montreal, Justin Trudeau was studying engineering and still maintained his friendships with his politically active friends.[33] He'd made an impression in 2000 when he gave a eulogy at his father's funeral and became a minor celebrity because of his charm. He'd also been chosen to give Jean Chrétien a send-off at the 2003 Liberal leadership convention. Usually, he was less political: as a panelist on CBC's *Canada Reads* literary contest and a host of the 2006 Giller Prize for Canada's best fiction book. He and his brother started a peace institute at the University of Toronto (it would be, rather ironically, folded into the Munk School for Global Affairs & Public Policy), co-chaired the Katimavik youth program, and spoke out on a few environmental issues. His friend Gerald Butts spent time in Ottawa as a political staffer before moving on to work for Dalton McGuinty's provincial government in Ontario. Katie Telford would arrive at Queen's Park soon. They would return to Ottawa, along with many of McGuinty's staffers, to form the core of Justin Trudeau's inner group. The New

Democrats were growing under Jack Layton, but this proved to be the last brief spark of a party in long-term decline. Tom Mulcair was Quebec's environment minister in the Quebec provincial government led by Jean Charest.[34] Jagmeet Singh was still in law school, Chrystia Freeland was at Thompson Reuters, and Mark Carney was a senior bureaucrat in the federal finance department.

In 2004, Poilievre and his friends were powerless men—almost always men, though there were some bright young conservative women who had their own cliques—who had potential but were a long-shot bet. Most of these men changed very little as the years passed and they took over their party and campaigned to win national power. Some would be important people in Harper's government and early contenders for party leadership. Others, like Poilievre, would have to wait. The country would come to them.

Politicians often have friendships with people in other parties. This is especially true of MPs and provincial legislators who seek elected office because they want a career of public service, to be in the centre of political action, see how government really works, and aren't hamstrung by ideology. They understand the nature of their seven-day-a-week grind, its terrible toll on family life, and the financial insecurity of a political career, which can end abruptly on an election night. The legislative process requires discussion and compromise, even when there's a majority government. Until this generation, there was a sort of Canadian consensus, with some debate over the role of government, but no real desire for much more than incremental change. The Reformers, much more than even the Co-operative Commonwealth Federation and their later incarnation, the New Democratic Party, wanted a revolution, to implement real change between the way governments and citizens interacted and in the way the central government dealt with the provinces. That revolution began under Stephen Harper, was not significantly scaled back by Justin Trudeau, and is what Poilievre has offered voters since the day he won his party's leadership.

Back in 2004, in that more civil time, Newfoundland MP Scott Simms, who was elected at the same time as Poilievre, sized up Poilievre and admired his skills, if not his ideology. Simms went to an orientation session and saw a young MP who stood out among the class of 2004. "Pierre was like every successful politician of the '80s and '90s wrapped into one kid," Simms told *Globe and Mail* reporter Campbell Clark many years later. Simms is one of those people who saw two Poilievres: one who could be low-key, sometimes funny, and friendly when there were no political spoils at stake and no cameras around; and another who would bully bureaucrats when they testified at committees and say the cruellest things in the House of Commons. Even after years of Poilievre's mean talk, Simms still respected Poilievre, who was now leader of the Conservatives and had a good shot at becoming prime minister of Canada. "I think a lot of people who show disgust at Pierre Poilievre, there's a streak of jealousy in it," Simms said.[35]

Anonymously, MPs and staff from all parties recognized Poilievre's potential. In a 2004 *Hill Times* poll, he was runner-up to Rona Ambrose as Parliament Hill's most dynamic up-and-coming MP.[36] The next year, respondents named him best constituency MP and runner-up for hardest-working MP.[37]

There was another quirk about Poilievre that I have experienced in my own interactions with him, and that is so often noted by people who've talked to him: one-on-one, he's friendly and personable, just so long as the conversation doesn't involve politics. When more people are around, the meanness comes out, and the conversation invariably becomes political and superficial.

PAUL MARTIN TRIED to remake the Liberal caucus that he'd inherited from Jean Chrétien into a government that Canadians could see as new and refreshed. It was a difficult task. It's almost impossible for a Canadian prime minister to hand off power to a successor and have voters separate their opinions of the new leader from the old one. Sir John A. Macdonald died in office. He hadn't set up a successor. In the rest of his term, Canada had four PMs, none of whom could hold on to power.[38] Robert Borden, the Conservative who defeated Wilfrid Laurier, tried to hand off to Arthur Meighen, but Meighen was tossed out by voters wanting change after the First World War. William Lyon Mackenzie King did manage to install a successor, Louis St. Laurent, who won two majorities before losing office. Lester Pearson was able to hand off to Pierre Trudeau, but Trudeau's successor, John Turner, was turfed out only months later by voters. The man who beat Turner, Brian Mulroney, was replaced by Kim Campbell, who endured the most crushing political defeat in Canadian history. So, in more than 150 years, there have only been two times when a prime minister's political successor has been able to hold on to power for any serious length of time.[39]

By 2004, when Martin first faced the voters and won a shaky minority, the Liberals were stale. Until then, the post-Mulroney conservatives—divided into Reform, some of the Bloc Quebecois, and the Progressive Conservatives—were a weak, divided opposition that shot spitballs as Chrétien ran a politics-as-usual regime. In 1995, Quebec had an exciting, dramatic sovereignty referendum that ended with Canada surviving by a few thousand votes. That was the most interesting event in Chrétien's time in office. Mostly, there were trade missions and slight changes to laws to pander to interest groups. As justice minister, Allan Rock toughened the Criminal Code after some high-profile crimes in Toronto and Montreal. National security became a big issue after the terrorist attacks in the United States on September 11, 2001. Still, Chrétien was a firm believer in inaction. Most problems, he believed, solved themselves if left alone. He had the good sense to stay out of the Iraq War, though he did agree to send a contingent to Afghanistan.

Poilievre arrived in Ottawa at almost the same moment that Chrétien was pushed out. Paul Martin's government had to deal with the fallout of some of Chrétien's sketchy actions. His government fed more than $100 million to Liberal advertising firms in Quebec to pay them for off-the-books work in the Quebec referendum, and the resulting scandal, especially in Quebec, proved impossible for Martin to shake. Chrétien had looked after himself quite well in a real estate deal in his hometown, involving government money: this, too, stuck to Martin's government. And these were just the larger scandals: there were many more smaller ones. At the same time, as a result of the leadership battles, the Liberals were split between Chrétien and Martin loyalists, and these truly hated each other: as a result, they each took turns leaking dirt to the media.

This was a great time to be an opposition MP or a political staffer with a killer instinct. The Martin government made enough unforced errors to give Poilievre full-time work before and after he was elected to Parliament. When the Martin government intervened in a Supreme Court of Canada case to oppose more medicare-paid therapy for children on the autism spectrum, the new MP chose the right side of the issue. It was an issue that embarrassed the provincial Liberals, led by Ottawa MPP Dalton McGuinty. When he was leader of the provincial opposition, McGuinty promised to increase autistic children's access to intensive behavioural therapy. This treatment is effective, but it's also expensive: at the time, it cost between $50,000 and $70,000 a year for each child. When McGuinty became premier in 2003, he decided to keep defending a lawsuit launched against the previous Conservative provincial government by parents of autistic kids. Like the Conservatives, McGuinty's government argued judges should not set government policy.[40]

Poilievre took on autism advocacy long before he married and became the father of a child on the spectrum. Parents fought the federal and provincial governments for years, but Poilievre singled out Martin's government for the harshest criticism. On this issue, he allied with New Democrat MP Peter Stoffer to demand proper funding for treatment and support. This earned the gratitude of parents who were ignored by politicians.[41]

When a Bloc Quebecois MP refused to give Canadian flags (which are free to MPs) to veterans for a Remembrance Day service in Richmond, Quebec, Poilievre very publicly sent flags to every veteran in the town and made sure the media knew about it. "I am sending flags directly to a list of veterans, so each one we can track down will get a flag in the mail from our office," Poilievre told journalists. "Local legionnaires and veterans are rolling up their sleeves to help veterans in Richmond who have been rebuffed by their separatist MP."[42] Many journalists become super-patriots around Remembrance Day. And a story of an anti-Canada politician denying flags to poor vets, and another politician offering succor, was a winner.

Patriotism has always been an important theme in Poilievre's messages. Patronage is another vein that Poilievre mines. Poilievre was in office for just a few months when he tangled (rather literally) with one of the biggest Liberal MPs in Western Canada. Reg Alcock, from Winnipeg, was stuck with defending the appointment of one of finance minister John McCallum's former colleagues at the Royal Bank to be the chairman of Canada Post. Alcock said all the government's rules had been followed. Poilievre did his homework and found that this wasn't true. Even the man who had been appointed said some of the steps of the normal process had been skipped. When Poilievre gave the old warhorse a hard time in a sitting of the Commons Standing Committee on Government Operations and Estimates, Alcock made the mistake of getting personal.

"You're young; give it a break," said Alcock, adding a few minutes later, "with age comes wisdom."

"Not always," Poilievre responded. Then Poilievre said that he was insulted by Alcock's "personal attacks based on age."[43] In the House a few days later, Poilievre said: "Faced with my questions about the revenue minister's decision to break all the rules and give a cushy job to his banking buddy, the member for Winnipeg South said, 'you are young, give it a break.' Had the minister directed this anti-youth bigotry at a racial or religious minority, he would have been forced to resign, but apparently, my generation is fair game for ridicule and prejudice.... The minister might miss the good old days when young people were only good for polishing his shoes and picking up his drycleaning, but those days are gone. We do not need to run for coffee. We can run for election and win. That is why I am part of the youngest caucus in the history of this country. The minister says, 'with age comes wisdom.' Well, if his crusty attitude represents wisdom, I am happy staying young."[44]

At first, Alcock wouldn't back down, but a few days later the minister apologized in committee, where he promised to release an entirely new list of rules for government appointments. It was a clear win for Poilievre, and he got a lot of press coverage.[45]

Poilievre was great at attack politics. He wasn't intimidated by older, more experienced opponents. Journalists were collecting his clever insults and keeping in touch. So were Stephen Harper and members of his inner circle, who were looking for caucus members who would be willing to take the low road while cabinet ministers tried to look like statesmen.

5
DIAL-A-QUOTE

If a politician found he had cannibals among his constituents, he would promise them missionaries for dinner.

H.L. MENCKEN

AS PIERRE POILIEVRE finished his first year as an MP, the Conservatives had ninety-nine seats in the House of Commons and were the only serious contenders to take power from Paul Martin's Liberals. Martin had learned a lesson in unintended consequences: he and his faction of the Liberal Party hated Jean Chrétien and his thugs more than they feared Stephen Harper and his party, and they worked hard to undermine the Liddle Guy. The sponsorship scandal was the political fallout of a Chrétien-team scheme to funnel money to Quebec advertising agencies. By the time Chrétien quit, the scandal was starting to cool. Martin poured gas on it by keeping a promise to launch a judicial inquiry, which he and his advisers thought would embarrass the Chrétien team.

A not-too-bright Quebec judge, John Gomery, was assigned to run the hearings and write a report. Gomery had his own habit of stepping in political crap. He hired a journalist to document the inquiry and write a book, presumably with Gomery as the hero. He had a pattern of signalling his opinions about witnesses and political actors, doing stupid things like calling Jean Chrétien "small town cheap" for having his name embossed on golf balls. He should have known better than to take on a tough old pol like Chrétien. The former prime minister was still much more popular than Paul Martin, the man who'd pushed him out. During his next appearance at the Gomery inquiry, Chrétien showed the judge a collection of golf balls belonging to various world leaders. All of them had their names embossed on their balls. When it was all over, Chrétien went to court and had all of Gomery's findings thrown out. Before he did that, the Chrétien faction demanded Gomery investigate Martin and his contracting practices, too. With both sides insisting the other was crooked, and frequent leaks that showed these claims were likely true, it was no wonder Canadians were in a mood to "throw the bastards out."

It must be glorious for opposition MPs to watch an old government commit seppuku. The New Democrats were propping up Martin's government, but there was no solid deal. The Conservatives just had to stay united, put together a solid campaign team, nominate credible candidates in Liberal-held ridings, and they'd win. Bureaucrats and journalists still had a hard time believing a group of Western rubes were a threat to Grit hegemony. Just four years before Martin took office, *Globe and Mail* columnist Jeffrey Simpson, a voice of Ottawa's establishment, warned of de facto one-party government in his book *The Friendly Dictator*.

Now, less than a year into Martin's minority government, Poilievre was hearing people in his riding say they wanted another election. So did he. An *Ottawa Citizen* reporter wrote a piece on Poilievre after tagging along to a trade show in Osgoode, a village on the edge of Ottawa where the new MP was glad-handing. Hayley Mick, the journalist, marvelled at how Poilievre had got a jump on campaigning. She didn't realize Poilievre, even more than the average politician, is *always* on the make for support.

Poilievre found a friendly crowd. "'Bring 'em down! Bring 'em down! Bring 'em down!" someone chanted. Local hobby farmer Audrey Jensen, a petite mother of two, pumped her fist and stamped her foot as she spoke to Poilievre. He asked Jensen if she wanted an election that summer, just a year after the last one. That was fine with her. The Liberals had to go. "It's like a toilet. If it keeps running and running you've got to shut it off," she said. Jeffrey Morris, editor of a local newspaper, told the reporter people in the riding were disgusted by the sponsorship scandal, even though Martin's supporters often said he wasn't the robber, just the guy who sounded the alarm. "People have had enough, they're fed up." Poilievre's staff collected the names of volunteers and people willing to take lawn signs. People could buy "Canada, Vote Conservative" bumper stickers at the Conservative table for five dollars apiece. The money went into the campaign kitty: "We just want to be ready to go," Poilievre said.[1]

Like Tories today, Harper's backers in politics and the media knew the best way to dislodge Paul Martin from 24 Sussex Drive was to keep up a constant cry of "Scandal!" Poilievre tried to whip one up in the national capital, accusing the Liberals of wasting $100 million by taking their time moving public servants into a leased office building on the Quebec side of the Ottawa River. Poilievre's math was absurd, but it made good headlines. The entire fifteen-year lease cost $100 million. Library and Archives Canada staff didn't move in for eight months, which even Susan Murray, spokeswoman for public works minister Scott Brison, admitted was remarkably slow. But, she said, the building needed work before the public servants could use it. An internal investigation and maybe a reprimand should have settled the issue, but Poilievre demanded a public inquiry into the "boondoggle."[2] No one took that demand seriously. It had taken years to get an inquiry into the ad sponsorship scheme that sent tens of millions of dollars to Quebec ad agencies for fake contracts. No one was going to hire a judge to probe the reasons for the slow movement of some unglamorous history and book nerds.

When a boy cries wolf, a wolf may really be nearby. A few weeks after Poilievre went after tardy librarians and absent archivists on behalf of an uninterested nation, he blew the whistle on a Liberal senator. Poilievre seized on a months-old *Ottawa Citizen* story that showed Paul Massicotte, who represented Manitoba, owned a real estate company that leased an Ottawa office building to the government. His apparent conflict broke the *Parliament of Canada Act*, which carried a rather pathetic $200 a day fine. Scott Brison, the Liberal cabinet minister in charge of this kind of procurement, kicked the problem over to the Senate's ethics officer to determine if Massicotte should be personally punished. This official probably had lots of time to work on the file. Brison had Public Works lawyers threaten to withhold the $575,000 a month rent that the federal government paid Massicotte's company.[3] This, unlike the personal fine, was serious money. The real estate company's lawyers said the deal was made *before* Massicotte got his Senate seat, so the law didn't apply. Then the government changed the law to close the barn door and paid the rent.

"Is that not handy, Mr. Speaker? After the Liberals got caught breaking the law, they merely cancelled the law," Poilievre said in Question Period. "Only days before section 14 of the *Parliament of Canada Act* forced them to stop paying rent to the Liberal-tied company, the Liberal cabinet just cancelled section 14, meaning taxpayers will continue to pay big bucks."[4]

He was right. A few months later, he scored again when the federal ethics commissioner began investigating a Liberal Quebec MP's possible conflict of interest over $1 million in federal contracts awarded to his family's company. David Smith represented the Ottawa Valley riding of Pontiac.[5] He claimed to have talked to the ethics commissioner about his family's business. The commissioner hired the accounting firm KPMG to investigate the situation and found about $1 million worth of sole-sourced federal contracts were awarded to Abotech Inc., where Smith was president. This ended when he was elected to Parliament. Poilievre put out a press release saying one of the bureaucrats who awarded the contracts became the secretary of the Liberal Association of Pontiac after Smith was elected to the House of Commons. In the release, Poilievre posed a list of questions to the ethics commissioner, including: "Did Mr. Smith disclose to you or your office that Mr. Brazeau, reportedly a member of his local Liberal riding association, held a position as a contracting officer with Consulting and Audit Canada?" Because an investigation was going on, the commissioner could not answer, even if he had been inclined to.[6] And secretary of a riding association is not a plum job. It's unpaid and not high enough on the political pyramid to be worth a paid patronage appointment.[7]

Like so many opposition MPs, Poilievre loudly advocated for more open government. He wanted people working for the armed forces and CSIS to be protected by a new whistle-blower bill, which was a good idea. Government employees should be shielded when they expose corruption and toxic workplaces. New protection for the RCMP was, he said, a fine start. The Harper government would, soon afterwards, develop the cloak of silence that's been thrown over a bureaucracy that was already tight-lipped and fearful. But in opposition, Poilievre argued people who protect the country and its secrets should have the same whistle-blower protection as someone working in an ordinary ministry.

"I'm sure there was a lot of wrongdoing within the RCMP that has gone unreported because people are intimidated," Poilievre told reporters. "This change will allow uniformed RCMP officers to go to a totally independent commissioner and report wrongdoing without fear of revenge. That can only be good for the RCMP and the people that it's meant to serve."[8]

The Harper government would bring in stronger whistle-blower protection in 2007, when Parliament passed the *Public Servants Disclosure Protection Act*, though the system has never worked.[9] In its first fifteen years, the office that investigates whistle-blower complaints found just eighteen cases of wrongdoing, even though it received more than 1,500 whistle-blower claims. One commissioner served a two-year term without finding anything wrong.[10] But at the time, Poilievre and the rest of the Harper team sold themselves as advocates of open government. Sunlight, they claimed, was the best disinfectant.

THERE WERE OTHER ways for the newbie to make headlines. Poilievre was in the local news for raising money to rebuild the burned-out legion building in the village of Manotick, south of Ottawa. And he was in the papers for flip-flopping on the Ottawa's light-rail plan, which he now seemed to support. Poilievre held a rally for Terry Kilrea, a right-wing populist who wanted to run for mayor to pry Liberals out of city hall. Kilrea, who worked in the city's sheriff's office enforcing eviction notices, had a locally famous name because his brother was a popular minor hockey coach. Kilrea started a local ratepayer group called the People's Voice, presumably unaware that a Canadian Communist newspaper had the same name. Although Kilrea claimed to have signed up nine hundred people, only about a quarter of them turned up to a rally with Kilrea, Poilievre, and John Baird. Maybe to prove his Ottawa Valley bona fides, Baird made a flat joke about "goin' huntin'" with Kilrea. Local pundits thought the idea of Baird heading off to the woods with guns and gear to find some meat created a bizarre mental image that was more humorous than masculine.

The rally was supposedly organized to gather support for a campaign to convince the city to abandon a plan to distribute crack pipes to addicts. Kilrea's people also wanted to fight the council's decision to build a community centre for francophones in Ottawa's western suburbs. Kilrea's followers didn't like francophones any more than crack addicts, and they lined up to sign petitions against both proposals.[11] Poilievre was looking to his own future, telling the small crowd, "If you are not with the Conservatives, you are with the ad scammers. It's time to end the rule of the caviar-eating, limousine-riding Liberals," even though the federal government had nothing to do with the free crack pipe program.

There was a lot of talk about "namby-pambies who are soft on crime," presumably the city councillors who backed the pipe program and, again, Liberals everywhere. Poilievre also took a shot at Paul Martin's national daycare plan, which Poilievre said would cost taxpayers $5 billion.[12]

And he thrilled anglos in the suburbs by attacking the public works department for demanding its tenants on the Sparks Street Mall follow the *Official Languages Act* by putting up bilingual signs and making sure customers could get service in French and English. The mall, a bad idea on its best day, bled tenants for years and was evolving from a shopping district to a string of restaurants, dentist and optometrist offices (to cash in on public servants' benefit plans), and empty stores. Merchants complained about the bilingualism rules, even though they were written into their leases. And their customers, whether they were tourists or people working in the government towers along the street, were a mix of anglophones and francophones. Still, Poilievre waded in, echoing callers to the local right-wing AM radio station that the rules were too harsh.

He wrote an open letter to Scott Brison, the minister of public works. Poilievre, who was taking French lessons offered by the House of Commons, denounced the "heavy-handed decision to intrude into the language policies of independent entrepreneurs who lease property from the government of Canada. While this decision may be politically correct and may pacify the political demands of your government, it constitutes direct interference into the commercial affairs of independent businesses," he wrote. Poilievre claimed the merchants of the dying Sparks Street Mall would do business in both official languages if it made them money. This might be true, but the government agencies that own and lease the buildings are governed by the *Official Languages Act*. Brison replied with his own public statement, saying his department would uphold the law.[13]

Then there were the stunts: pretending to paddle down a dry creek bed south of Ottawa to mock a regulation that required a federal fisheries study before a new high school could be built; tabling a private member's bill that would allow unhappy constituents to recall their MPs (an old Reform policy that Poilievre still remembered, though he forgot his promise to retire after two terms); allowing Catherine Clark, daughter of the Tory leader he'd once derided and mocked, into his suburban home to see its "understated and masculine" make-over. He was even able to pull opponents into these performances. Ed Mahfouz, who'd run against him for the Conservative nomination in 2004, ran in 2008 as the Liberal candidate. Strangely for a challenger, Mahfouz refused to show up for the riding's all-candidates' meetings. Poilievre, along with the NDP and Green Party candidates, went to a local police station to pretend to file a missing person's report. A campaign worker also put a lost dog–style ad on Craigslist.

IN 2005, POILIEVRE made a speech in the House of Commons against gay marriage. The core of his argument: Paul Martin was whipping his caucus to vote against their consciences so the prime minister could push through his own pet "woke" project. With his usual hyperbole, Poilievre politicized the issue, saying, "Let us be blunt. Our Prime Minister and his Liberal Party have divided Canadians with their obsession with imposing gay marriage.... The Prime Minister's behaviour on this issue in the House of Commons tells us a lot about his intentions, for he is willing to turn his guns against those in his own party, his Liberal friends, with whom he disagrees. [By forcing his caucus to vote for the bill, rather than making it a free vote.] If he is willing to coerce them with pressure and threats of demotion and force them to vote against their conscience and their constituents, if he is willing to do all of that, if he is willing to attack the independent conscience of his own members of Parliament, how can he as Prime Minister be expected to defend the freedom of conscience of the Canadian people? He will not."

Poilievre said freedom of religion was under attack and made a false claim that marriage commissioners across the country were already being fired for refusing to perform gay marriages. Supposedly, the charitable status of churches was also at risk. "Liberal youth" thought opponents of same sex marriage were just stupid, even though his party's definition of marriage was the same one "held by every civilization on planet earth.

"Perhaps the Liberal youth think that every other civilization is stupid as well. Perhaps they think that every religion in the world is stupid. Perhaps they think that the vast majority of Canadians who would prefer to give spousal rights to non-traditional couples through civil unions [rather than full marriage] are stupid too."

There's a myth that Poilievre's father, who was in a long-term, committed same-sex relationship at the time of this debate, was in the House of Commons gallery when Pierre voted against Paul Martin's marriage bill. He wasn't, and despite Poilievre's posing to his rural constituents and the big born-again faction in his party, he was quite open to something that guaranteed some same-sex couples' rights while denying them some of the rights that come with legal marriage. The fight for marriage rights at that time had a financial aspect to it that's rarely discussed now. Poilievre understood this. He would vote against Paul Martin's changes to the marriage law, though he was open to some kind of change that would give LGBTQ+ people some spousal financial rights that are denied to people who simply live together. This answered gays' and lesbians' argument that their spouses should be entitled to pension survivor rights and for dental and drug benefits from their partners' workplace insurance. Inheritance laws in Canada give important rights to legally married people. Anyone who thinks "common-law" marriage gives people all the rights as married people should sit down for half an hour with a lawyer. Poilievre was willing to deal on these benefit issues without giving committed same-sex relationships the same legal status as marriages.

"That is the Canadian way: respect and tolerance. We should respect people who are in relationships that are non-traditional and we should give them the same rights, but that need not require us to change the meaning of the most quintessential social relationship in the history of civilization. We can have both at once. We can protect rights while at the same time preserving tradition."[14]

By 2020, Poilievre had changed his mind. It's one of the few political issues where Poilievre has shown any self-reflection. Poilievre told the Montreal newspaper *La Presse* he realized gay marriage has been good for LGBTQ+ people and the dire warnings of 2005 were wrong. When fringe Conservative leadership candidate Richard Décarie called homosexuality a choice, Poilievre tweeted: "Being gay is NOT a choice. Being ignorant is." Some of Poilievre's most important allies and mentors are gay or lesbian: when he won the party leadership in 2022 he appointed a gay man and a lesbian to two senior positions on his front bench. He's also regularly spoken about his adoptive family and his affection for his father and his partner. He's never kept that part of his life secret. Shuvaloy Majumdar, one of Poilievre's university buddies who was elected to the House of Commons in 2023, said all his friends knew about Poilievre's father's sexuality. "I've never seen him uncomfortable with his family," he told *Globe and Mail* reporter Campbell Clark. "It was never something he hid or pretended didn't exist or lied about. It was always, 'This is who I am. This is where I come from.'"[15]

THERE IS A surprising amount of class-bashing in Poilievre's campaign style. Business leaders, unless they are unpopular, are exempt, of course, but anyone in a senior government-paid job can be targeted. This is especially true if the targeted "gatekeeper" can't fight back. In 2005, Paul Martin appointed Haiti-born Michaëlle Jean, a television host on the RDI (French CBC) news service, to be governor general. It had initially seemed a bizarre choice. Jean was a competent television presenter and the first Black journalist to reach the top tier of Quebec media, but she had almost no profile outside Quebec. There were some good reasons to appoint her: she was young, attractive, personable, and bilingual, and the job needed new blood to stay (arguably, become) relevant. Adrienne Clarkson, another media-personality-turned governor general, had been haughty and unapproachable in her official position and was finally leaving the job. Her husband, author John Ralston Saul, had a spectacular ego that was mocked in some media and generated party stories in the Ottawa bubble.[16] In the weeks after Jean's appointment, a story went around Ottawa that someone on Martin's staff had pitched Jean as a joke, making fun of the idea that Jean Chrétien chose Clarkson mainly because of her Chinese ethnicity and media profile. However the decision was made, Jean turned out to be an inspired choice. She enchanted everyone who worked with her and raised the profile of the governor general's office with an ambitious program of public events. Even hard-ass military officers adored her, especially when she visited the Canadian contingent in Afghanistan. Since her term ended, she's continued to do important work for the government and the public.

Publicly, the opposition parties supported the Jean appointment. Privately, the Conservatives spread rumours about her. They could finally bring their criticisms out in the open when separatist journalists in Quebec denounced her and the French-born Jean-Daniel Lafond, her filmmaker husband, as sellouts to their cause. Then a video clip surfaced of Jean and Lafond toasting "independence."

Poilievre jumped on this. He called on Martin to force Jean to "overtly renounce separatism or step down" and demanded Jean renounce the French citizenship that she automatically qualified for when she married Lafond. Poilievre also demanded that Jean tell Canadians how she voted in the 1995 Quebec referendum on sovereignty, this despite the facts that tradition and protocol prevent governors general and their spouses from talking about politics and Canada has a secret ballot for a reason. At first glance, Quebec separatism might seem like something that transcends normal politics—it's an assault on the very existence of the nation. In some Canadians' minds, it's treason or something close to it. But in Canada, advocating Quebec (or, for that matter, Albertan) separatism is legal. There are separatist federal and provincial parties in Quebec, and many Quebec political actors want some kind of constitutional change that makes Quebec a sort of autonomous ethnic and linguistic French state, inside or outside a Canadian federation.

First, the Martin government let critics know that the "independence" that Jean and Lafond toasted was for Haiti, not Quebec. So Poilievre went after Lafond. Surely someone who moved in the circles of Montreal's hipster, left-leaning arts community had to be a separatist. Poilievre didn't find much. Years before, Lafond hired Jacques Rose, a former member of the FLQ's Chénier Cell, the group that had kidnapped and murdered Quebec labour minister Pierre Laporte in 1970, to do home renovation work. Rose, a carpenter, was hired long after he served five years for being an accessory after the fact in Laporte's kidnapping.

Lafond had also spoken kindly about Marxist, separatist extremist author Pierre Vallières.[17] Lafond wrote a piece in the Montreal alt-weekly *Voir* after Vallières' death in 1998 that had a line that could be easily twisted to make it seem as if the writer himself supported FLQ terrorism: "There is a subject on which Pierre [Vallières] never changed his opinion with the passing of years: the death of Pierre Laporte. On that one, he was as solid as a rock." That was true. Vallières stayed faithful to his revolutionary beliefs through his adult life. But that didn't mean that Lafond agreed with him.

Besides, people's political opinions often change as they get older, or they do if they're not as partisan as Pierre Poilievre. This was true of Michaëlle Jean and Jean-Daniel Lafond, who, presumably, wouldn't have accepted Paul Martin's offer if they hated Canada.[18] That was the defence used by the prime minister and Jean's supporters outside government.

"This is nothing but a smear campaign by people who are scared out of their wits by the popularity of Madame Jean. We have no intention [of] asking the future governor-general, or her husband, about their former acquaintances or who they might have had dinner with fifteen or twenty years ago," Martin's spokesman Scott Reid said.[19] As the weeks went by, there were no new revelations, and people stopped caring about the occupants of Rideau Hall. It helped that Lafond was very talented at staying out of the public eye through Jean's term.

Whatever the value of this particular episode, there's a question that makes this obscure partisan moment worth examining. Why was Poilievre, of the ninety-nine members of the Tory caucus, the person who led the attack on Jean and Lafond? Why did so many reporters call Poilievre when they wanted a nasty quote about whatever was the talking point of the day? Poilievre was a new opposition backbencher, but he seemed to be everywhere. His snappy quotes, his meanness, got clicks and generated dopamine, and local journalists understood this and were addicted to what he was dealing. So when reporters wanted to attack Jean, they called Poilievre. It's almost unheard of for parliamentarians to attack new governors general. Very few MPs, even opposition members, would do it as loudly and harshly as Poilievre did. There had been some mumblings about patronage when Pierre Trudeau appointed former Manitoba premier Ed Schreyer to the job. He got more heat when he appointed former Liberal MP and House of Commons speaker Jeanne Sauvé. And there was griping when Brian Mulroney appointed his former minister of justice, Ray Hnatyshyn. But the criticism was always about patronage, not an attack on the loyalty of the appointee.

When an anonymous CBC arts reporter wrote about a controversial Lafond film about the American Black activist Dawud Salahuddin (born David Belfield, Salahuddin is known by several other names, including Hassan Abdulrahman), the journalist quoted criticism in the *National Post* and mentioned a *Maclean's* interview with Lafond. Except for part of a sentence lifted from the *National Post*, Poilievre was the only person, other than Lafond, directly quoted in the piece.

"The office of the Governor General includes that of the spouse.... Officially the spouse is part of the office and should respect the fact that Canada has a profound, deep and committed relationship with the United States of America. They are our friends and our neighbours—and the terrorists are not," Poilievre said.

"I think the office of the Governor General—from top to bottom, all of its members included—should be apolitical."[20]

It was succinct, tough, overreaching, and accusatory, with no real substance. But it was normal Poilievrespeak. He was being noticed by critics who saw the inconsistency of his righteousness in opposition, his defence of moral failings when in government, and his childishness. L. Ian MacDonald, a conservative pundit, described Poilievre and Baird as the most unruly MPs on the Conservative side of the House. "Poilievre is annoying because his insults are so juvenile, inappropriate in a schoolyard, let alone the central forum of Canadian democracy," MacDonald told readers of the *Montreal Gazette*.[21] In 2009, the *Globe and Mail* put him on a list of "ten most irritating people on Parliament Hill."[22] Most observers saw him as nothing more than an attack dog, useful for that political work but not ready for anything complicated.

MPS WITH NATIONAL ambitions need to look after their riding and stay in the local news so there's no real threat that they'll end up like David Pratt: big on the Hill and in the Toronto-based media but out of a job when constituents have their say. Poilievre had a knack for making news and showing he was part of the community. When an eighteen-year-old girl, Jennifer Teague, disappeared, reporters interviewed Poilievre, who lived near the scene of Teague's abduction.[23] He was able to make that story about himself and his partner, Jenni Byrne. At the same time, he raised the level of fear in his community, which had also recently been shocked by the unsolved murder of graduate student Ardeth Wood on the other side of the city. Poilievre said Byrne had stopped her late-night dog-walking because she feared that the streets were no longer safe. "Families have got to exercise extraordinary caution, especially at night. I think the community has to be on high alert. I think it will change Barrhaven possibly forever, given what this event says about our safety."[24]

Everything had to be political. The federal government owned the land under the Queensway Carleton Hospital in the Ottawa suburb of Nepean. Conservative Ontario premier Mike Harris, as part of his "common sense revolution," had reduced the number of hospital beds in Canada's capital, despite the city's growth, and ordered the closure of Queensway Carleton.[25] Under pressure, the province eventually backed down from this, and Poilievre demanded the feds drop the rent to save the hospital money.

It's not clear why the Martin government rejected the idea. Possibly it was because a lot of the land under Ottawa buildings, including Queensway Carleton and some housing projects and co-ops, is owned by the federal government's main local landholding agency, the National Capital Commission. The NCC is supposed to be an independent agency, run by an appointed board.[26] Government intransigence might have become entrenched by the mean talk and hyperbole that Poilievre and his provincial counterpart, John Baird, brought to the discussion. The hospital was in a neighbouring riding held by a Liberal, whom Poilievre claimed was ineffective and uncaring.[27] In the fall of 2005, the House of Commons voted down Poilievre's private member motion to cut the rent to $1 a year.

"I'm disappointed," Poilievre told reporters in the foyer of the House of Commons moments after the vote was taken on his motion.

"Paul Martin whipped his Liberal caucus to vote against the hospital. Martin's Liberals joined into an unholy coalition with the separatists [the Bloc Quebecois] to vote in favour of a massive rent increase on our local community hospital." He attacked Ottawa-area Liberal MPs who voted against his motion, singling out David McGuinty, brother of Dalton McGuinty, Ontario's Liberal premier. David McGuinty was a Liberal warhorse who had been raised in a political family. He wasn't intimidated. Poilievre's campaign, he said, had more to do with politics than concern for the hospital. "I've never seen a more disingenuous, more despicable, politically opportunistic game played by a member of Parliament, using health care and the goodwill and good faith of the people who use that hospital," McGuinty said.[28]

But no matter what the Liberals said, Poilievre was portrayed in the local media as a politician who was willing to fight for a hospital that served so many of his constituents. No one who ran against him in the next election could possibly make any mileage by criticizing him for that.

ALTHOUGH POLITICKING NEVER stopped after the 2004 election, the official campaign only started in late November 2005, when NDP leader Jack Layton looked at the polls and decided to withdraw his support of Paul Martin's minority government. Near the end of the campaign, the commissioner of the RCMP, Giuliano Zaccardelli, told an NDP MP that finance minister Ralph Goodale was under investigation for allegedly leaking part of the federal budget to warn business buddies that the government was going to change the rules that made income trusts a sweet investment. The New Democrat went straight to reporters, but it was Poilievre who got the ink and airtime. He claimed the Liberals knew about the investigation and were covering for Goodale, one of the few Prairie Liberals. "The Liberals should have toughened their campaign rules to exclude anyone under police scrutiny," Poilievre told reporters. "I'm surprised they didn't announce a ban on candidates who are under RCMP investigation."[29] For their part, the Liberals said there was nothing to the claim and accused Zaccardelli of playing politics. In the end, while a bureaucrat was charged, there was nothing to the claim that Goodale was crooked.

The rest of the campaign was almost as bad for the incumbents. A national daycare bill died when Jack Layton pulled the plug on Paul Martin's government. Stephen Harper offered parents a small monthly payment to help cover the cost of child care, whether their kids were in daycare or not. Scott Reid, the main spokesman for the campaign, made headlines with an insulting, patronizing, and unfair claim that Harper's daycare subsidy cheques would be spent on "beer and popcorn."[30] Jean Chrétien's supporters in the Liberal Party closed their cheque books and sat on their hands at a time when people wanted a change. As a result, Stephen Harper won a minority government. It was a remarkable comeback for Canada's right, which seemed mortally wounded twelve years before.

Poilievre wasn't appointed to cabinet in the new government. John Baird, who jumped from provincial to federal politics during this election, had cabinet experience, so he got in, and Poilievre became his parliamentary secretary. Jenni Byrne was an important strategist in that campaign, working under Doug Finley in the Tories' war room and enforcing the Harper clique's will in the ridings. During the campaign, she'd even scuttled Toronto-area Conservative candidate Garth Turner's interview on Mike Duffy's national broadcast because Turner had talked to a Tory-friendly *Financial Post* reporter without permission. (In his political autobiography, Turner says Byrne told Duffy the candidate was "simply not available." This was news to Turner.)[31] Now, still in her mid-twenties, she had a powerful job in the Prime Minister's Office, hiring cabinet ministers' political and communications staff, along with the policy experts that the ministers relied on.[32] Each hire was one more person who had a debt to Jenni Byrne. Within a year, she also had the important job of briefing Harper before Question Period. By 2009, she was Harper's director of political operations, described to a *Maclean's* reporter by a Tory insider as a "hard ass with a temper."[33]

In his book *Harperland*, Lawrence Martin, a *Globe and Mail* columnist with decades of experience in Washington and Ottawa, said observers used Watergate parlance to describe the roles of Finley and Byrne. Finley, a gruff Scot who'd worked for political parties in his birth country and Quebec, was like Richard Nixon's hatchet man, H.R. Haldeman. He was a tyrant who scared and intimidated staff and journalists. Byrne was much more subtle, but she was just as dedicated to Harper and the party. Byrne had worked for Tom Flanagan, who had supervised Harper's master's thesis and worked as his chief of staff, and said early in Harper's term, "I was hoping she would develop more self-control as she got older. I don't see any sign of change."[34] Colleagues said she had a nasty temper that came out with very little provocation. Her partner's employees said the same thing about Poilievre. He was a poor and unsympathetic manager of his staff, a difficult boss for anyone who couldn't give the time, effort, and skill that Poilievre brought to his work.[35]

Baird was the minister in charge of the Treasury Board, a department that's unknown to most Canadians but, because it handles a lot of federal spending, is a very big deal in Ottawa. As parliamentary secretary, Poilievre's real job was to attack Liberals, especially on Mondays and Fridays, when ministers are rarely at Question Period and parliamentary secretaries take their place. Many people on the Tory front benches tried to quickly mature into credible ministers, blaming the previous government for things that went wrong but presenting "Canada's New Government" as a positive thing. Poilievre kept up his attacks on the Liberals even though Harper depended on their House of Commons votes to pass legislation and survive confidence votes.

Behind closed doors, Poilievre's capacity for pranks continued unabated. Once, he made a crank call to Baird, claiming to be a foreign leader cashing in on a promise Baird had made during a foreign trip. Another time, he had a woman call his own office to claim that she was pregnant after a one-night stand with Poilievre.[36]

Poilievre sometimes went too far. When he flipped his middle finger to Bloc MPs in the House of Commons, Liberal veteran Ralph Goodale quipped "this little boy needs some potty training." Later, Poilievre refused to wait in his car at Parliament Hill's new security checkpoint while guards checked a delivery truck that was ahead of him. Poilievre pressed the entrance button and drove through the gate without checking in with guards. The guards, who were not cops, reported the incident to the RCMP but dropped their complaint when they learned the security breach was caused by an MP. "Mr. Poilievre's got to go [from his job of parliamentary secretary to the Prime Minister]," Liberal MP David McGuinty told Parliament Hill reporters. The Nepean–Carleton MP had shown a "pattern of conduct" ever since he arrived in the House of Commons more than six years before. But that didn't happen.[37] And when he whispered "Fuck you guys" into an open microphone at a Parliamentary committee, Poilievre got away with that, too. In fact, it probably resonated with many people.

These bad moments, which might interest people in the Ottawa bubble, were small setbacks that voters and the prime minister didn't care about. Poilievre kept up his campaign for stronger whistle-blower laws, something that appealed to federal employees who lived in his riding and to people who believe managers in the public service are corrupt and wasteful. This was an issue Baird's ministry had some control over, but the Tories would need the support of some of the opposition MPs to change the law. Poilievre was given the whistle-blower file as part of Baird's *Accountability Act* project. He went to Washington to talk to members of Congress to learn more about their *False Claims Act*. Under that law, which was passed when Abraham Lincoln was president, whistle-blowers could sue on behalf of the government and keep any money that was recovered from miscreant civil servants.

"In the US, there is a growing sector of entrepreneurial waste-busters who see it in their self-interest to scrutinize all aspects of government spending to root out fraud and waste," Poilievre told reporters in Washington. "That's a very good thing. Anything we can do to give Canadian citizens and public servants the incentive to stop waste and mismanagement before they get out of control."[38]

Liberals and New Democrats also wanted Baird and Poilievre to outlaw floor-crossing by MPs. The Conservatives were stunned and embarrassed when Belinda Stronach had jumped from the new Conservative Party to the Liberals in the lead up to the 2004 election. Since three of the four big parties in the House were now on the record opposing the rather ancient practice (Winston Churchill did it twice; his father did it once), this should have been an easy fix.[39] Poilievre's support in the House of Commons committee that was studying the bill would have been enough to get it into law, but he refused to make common cause with his political opponents on something that the Reform Party had demanded years before. Compromise, even when in support of a long-sought-after reform, simply wasn't in his nature.

Still, Baird, with Poilievre's help, got the *Accountability Act* through the minority parliament. It banned large personal, corporate, and union contributions to political parties and candidates, barring the kind of massive donations that effectively buy politicians in the United States. Former senior public servants, cabinet ministers, and their staffs were barred from lobbying the government for five years after they left their jobs (something that political aides in both parties claim make it hard to get a job in Ottawa with companies that do business with the government), and gave more power to the auditor general. Experts have described this weak whistle-blower protection law as the worst in the developed world. It did help create a myth among the public, however, that real whistle-blowing protection existed. Politicians and media haven't talked much about insider snitching since Poilievre and Baird got their law passed.[40]

NDP MP Pat Martin, last seen in this narrative praising Poilievre's taste in clothes, gave the twenty-nine-year-old Tory credit for his work on the bill, even though Poilievre had been accused of stacking the Commons committee that was supposed to vet the proposed law. "I think Pierre is punching way above his weight," Martin told a Hill reporter. "As a very young MP, the guy's really gifted and has done an incredible job. This is one of the most complex bills in recent history, and to spear this through a hostile political environment [shows] an acumen normally associated with someone well beyond his years."[41]

After working with Baird on the *Accountability Act*, Poilievre was promoted to the job of prime minister's parliamentary secretary. When Harper wasn't around for Question Period, Poilievre took questions from the opposition. Harper, who never liked House of Commons debate, always made himself scarce when it was clear the questions would be embarrassing. This left Poilievre as the face connected with the minor scandals and policy failures that dog every government. He also had to defend the cabinet and the Conservative party when questions were asked about bigger ethical failures, like the "in-and-out" election-financing crookedness and the "robocalls" election crimes. Poilievre always acted on the strategy that attack is the best defence. Make the questioner regret the question; smear the person trying to do the embarrassing. Some people in this job are ruined by it; others seem to have their spirits broken. Though Poilievre seemed to enjoy trying to turn the table on opposition MPs, he privately admitted to friends and colleagues that he hated the job because it made him the face of scandal instead of a friendly dial-a-quote. A former PMO staffer told author Andrew Lawton that Poilievre often had to "eat shit" by having to face the media and opposition to answer for another Harper mini-scandal that would have otherwise passed him by. Among them: Jason Kenney, the immigration minister, sending Conservative fundraising letters out on government letterhead, and federal government ads that, because of the mass purchase of "hits" from an internet broker, appeared on porn sites.[42]

Despite his closeness to the mediaphobic Stephen Harper, Poilievre was still a dial-a-quote who was willing, even eager, to see his words in print. In the 2006 *Hill Times* poll of MPs and staffers to see what people in the Ottawa bubble think of their colleagues, Poilievre was in a three-way tie with Port Moody–Westwood–Port Coquitlam Tory MP James Moore and (then) Liberal MP Belinda Stronach as "biggest gossip" on Parliament Hill.[43]

STILL, POILIEVRE'S MOUTH was his own worst enemy. On June 11, 2008, Harper decided to apologize to Indigenous people for the residential school system that had traumatized and abused so many of them and their ancestors. This was not popular with all Tories and their media buddies. A few hours before Harper rose in the House of Commons to give the apology, Poilievre was in the studio of CFRA, Ottawa's right-wing AM radio station, trying to dig his own political grave.

Indigenous Canadians, he said, needed, at most, a hand up rather than a handout. He wondered aloud whether Canada was "getting value for all of this money," by which he meant the nearly $2 billion that was being spent to compensate the victims of federally financed residential schools.

"My view is that we need to engender the values of hard work and independence and self-reliance. That's the solution in the long run—more money will not solve it," Poilievre said. "That is an exceptional amount of money, and that is on top of all the resource revenue that goes to reserves that sit on top of petroleum products or sit on uranium mines or other things where companies pay them royalties, and that's on top of all that money that they earn on their own reserves." Some do, most do not, and this is irrelevant to the victims' residential school trauma. Rather, it plays into the "lazy Indian" trope. Then he switched to another stereotype, that Indigenous leaders are crooks. The federal government, he said, needed to keep a sharper eye on the people running the country's reserves and clip the wings of First Nations chiefs. "That gets to the heart of the problem on these reserves where there is too much power concentrated in the hands of the leadership, and it makes you wonder where all of this money is going."

The residential school apology was supposed to be a big day for Stephen Harper and a historic moment for the country. Instead, it ended up being about Poilievre and whether he, rather than Harper, reflected the real attitudes of the Conservatives, as so many Liberals and New Democrats suspected. Inside the party, there was—and still is—a split between MPs who believe the residential schools were a disaster for Canada's Indigenous people and those who believe this history is exploited by Indigenous activists.[44]

"Mr. Speaker, I am saddened and hurt by the attitude expressed by this official spokesperson for the government," Todd Russell, Liberal MP for Labrador, told the Commons. A lot of Russell's constituents were Innu and Inuit people, and he stood up for them. "Referring to the residential school settlement, [Poilievre] said, 'Some of us are starting to ask are we really getting value for this money.' But how do you place a value on a stolen child?" Harper was not a man to be crossed, especially by a twenty-eight-year-old buddy of Ezra Levant who'd already pissed him off years before in the Calgary Southwest by-election. Unless one of them writes an honest memoir, no one will ever know what went on in the prime minister's office the next day, but staffers could hear muffled yelling through the thick door. Poilievre came out looking like he'd been crying, and no one made eye contact with Harper for the rest of the day.

That afternoon, Poilievre went to the House of Commons to apologize. "Yesterday, on a day when the House and all Canadians were celebrating a new beginning, I made remarks that were hurtful and wrong," Poilievre said. "I accept responsibility for them and I apologize." This wasn't enough for the Liberals, who wanted Poilievre fired from his parliamentary secretary job. This stuck Harper with the task of defending the man he'd just reamed out.

"As all members of the House know, the parliamentary secretary has apologized for remarks that were wrong. I know that he has also forthwith contacted national aboriginal associations to indicate that," Harper said. "I know that yesterday we had a historic event, something that aboriginal people in this country have been waiting a very long time for. I know that all parties in this House were supportive of that spirit of apology, and I also know the honourable member in question was very supportive of those actions of the government."[45]

This was close to a career-ending experience for Poilievre, and he'd only be redeemed when the prime minister needed his attack skills. He had another brush with cancellation the next year when he compared the Liberals' green energy plan to a "tar baby," but Harper's strategists were able to divert the controversy into a media discussion of the meaning of the phrase: whether it was a sticky black licorice candy sold until the 1960s, things that stick to people, or Black infants.[46]

THE CONSERVATIVES WERE blessed during this period with opponents who were not ready for government. Michael Ignatieff was lured back to Canada, loaded with Liberal baggage and sent into battle. At the same time, Jack Layton was fighting cancer, a fact that would become important in the next election. The Tories did what almost every government does when an election loomed: they spent money. In 2009, they'd come out with a $60-billion package of stimulus and patronage they called Canada's Economic Action Plan. They justified the spending by saying they were fending off the recession that was still vexing the United States and making badly needed fixes to the nation's infrastructure. It was impossible for people to miss the big signs posted at every Canada's Economic Action Plan work site, since there were 8,500 of them across the country. Although Canada had, for the most part, dodged the downturn that Americans called the Great Recession, there was still a lot of unspent public money left in the infrastructure fund by 2011. Just before the election was called, Harper's government dumped $300 million on new projects. One was in Poilievre's riding: a new wheelchair ramp in the small town of Vernon.

Poilievre made the announcement into a very big deal, bringing immigration minster Jason Kenney, a Tory celebrity, out to the library for the photo op. It was a nothing event, but back then things like this made the news. Geoffrey Stevens, a former Parliament Hill columnist for the *Globe and Mail* and now a *Guelph Mercury* pundit, spotted the story and wondered what was going on. Was Stephen Harper afraid his parliamentary secretary would lose his seat? That was unlikely. Other pundits described Carleton as one of the safest Tory seats in Canada. Was Kenney collecting political IOUs for a future leadership race?[47] It's hard to know why the good people of Guelph would care, but Canadian journalists can't help but paw through bird guts, looking for a new hint of the future.

If they were any good at it, they would have seen unicorns and rainbows in Poilievre's political future. He was showing his constituents that he moved in the big leagues. Kenney and Poilievre had known each other for more than a decade by this time, and when Poilievre ran for Conservative leader years later, it would be Kenney, then Alberta's premier, supporting the former backbencher from suburban Ottawa.

BY 2011, THE Liberal Party was in deep, deep trouble. Paul Martin's replacement, Stéphane Dion, a bright, introverted francophone, probably should have stayed in academia. Politics, especially party leadership, was a bad fit. Bob Rae proved to be a solid interim leader, but the political baggage he'd picked up when he was NDP premier of Ontario in the recession of the early 1990s kept him from moving forward with the federal Liberals. Now they had Michael Ignatieff as their party's leader. On paper, he seemed perfect: a famous international intellectual, winner or runner-up of every major non-fiction literary prize in the English-speaking world worth winning, a serious academic who was also a media star in Britain, the United States, and Canada. He has a master's from Cambridge University and a PhD from Harvard. Ignatieff came from a family of counts who were senior officials in Russia's czarist regime before fleeing to Canada after the 1917 revolution. George Ignatieff, Michael's father, gave five decades of life to Canada's public service, rising to the top of the mandarinate. George had married into Canada's elite: Michael was related to the Massey family and descended from political thinker George Monro Grant.

But there were signs of trouble, if the Liberals and Ignatieff's star-struck media boosters could only read them. Ignatieff came back to Canada during the Martin years to start a political career and never had any luck. He had struggled to win a nomination in Liberal-friendly downtown Toronto. At the end of 2006, Ignatieff lost to the politically hapless Stéphane Dion at the Liberal leadership convention, even though he'd led on the first two ballots. Ignatieff's quick mouth was his biggest enemy during that race: he'd said an Israeli strike at Hezbollah that killed civilians in southern Lebanon hadn't cost him any sleep. This may have generated the "anyone but Ignatieff" movement among left-leaning delegates at the convention. Two years later, he walked into the leadership, but by then it wasn't worth much.

Ignatieff and his supporters saw him as a citizen of the world. His opponents painted a picture of an emigrant, a man who saw himself as too good for Canada, who preferred London, Boston, and New York to Calgary or even Toronto. In Canada, as in much of the West, people are wary of politicians who are too well-educated. Canada has had just one prime minister who earned a PhD (Mackenzie King). Pierre Trudeau, who came across to voters and journalists as something of a genius, had dropped out of his doctoral studies after doing a minimal amount of work and never wrote a book worth reading. (He impressed pundits with his knowledge of philosophy, which he'd learned from the Jesuits who taught him in high school.) Dion, who has real skills as an academic, came across as a stereotypical out-of-touch professor, partly because he was.

Canadians are strange: when they hire a prime minister, they're looking for someone to lead the government of one of the oldest democracies in the world and oversee a bureaucracy that could fill a decent-sized city. The successful candidate must work in a federal system that requires diplomacy and a deep understanding of a vast and complicated land mass that's the largest ever to be governed by a democratic government. Because this is, outside of Westmount, Rockcliffe, Rosedale, and British Properties, an egalitarian nation, Canadians look for someone who would make a good fishing buddy, someone they could stand being stuck with on a long car trip. A Cambridge–Harvard education and aristocratic pedigree is a ticket to the top in Oxbridge-dominated Westminster, but not in Canada. The premiership of Canada is a job that a man can easily lose if overqualified. Women, no matter what their skills, have not heretofore seemed a good fit. Stephen Harper knew this. Throughout his political career, he worked to come across as a middle-class guy who took his son to the hockey rink and tried to follow his charming wife's weight-loss plans.

Oddly, Jack Layton, son and grandson of conservative cabinet ministers, holder of a PhD in political philosophy, a man who had bounced between municipal politics and teaching jobs, was also able to pull off the "everyman" schtick.[48] Layton, who'd learned French when he grew up in a nice town outside Montreal, polished it up with a rough Quebecois slang and developed a speaking style that was direct and jargon-free.

The Tories, especially Patrick Muttart, who developed the strategies Harper used to win working-class votes, knew that tarring Ignatieff with the "he's too smart" stuff was a winner. They translated this into claims that Ignatieff was "cerebral" and "arrogant," and these were parroted in conservative newspapers, on talk radio, and in ads. In real life, Ignatieff is remarkably down-to-earth for a man who was raised in Canadian embassies, been a social lion as a boarding student at Upper Canada College, written bestselling books, made BBC documentaries on important international human rights crises, and has a string of degrees that impresses anyone who cares about that kind of thing. But the real killer was the Tory claim that "he didn't come back for you," an attack that encapsulated class antagonism and anxiety about Ignatieff's return to Canada after years overseas.

Then, in a very sad way, Layton earned the respect and concern of millions of Canadians who had ignored him through previous elections.[49] In early February 2010, Layton announced he'd been diagnosed with prostate cancer.[50] At the time, this was not big news. Most prostate cancer is treatable. Unfortunately, Layton's was not. He went into the race looking gaunt but campaigned with style and energy. Layton became "the man with the cane," and people who'd never voted NDP before were impressed by his courage. This was especially true in Quebec, where Layton, who was born in the province, campaigned in French with a "soft separatist" message that pulled the rug out from under the Bloc Quebecois. Once his campaign showed momentum, voters in the Vancouver and Toronto areas began moving from the Liberals to the New Democrats. Even a smear job by Sun News, run by former Manning strategist Kory Teneycke, about Layton being caught in a "happy ending" massage parlour years before, created sympathy for the struggling leader. By the end of the campaign, it was obvious Layton was dying, but he pressed on. He was becoming the political equivalent of Terry Fox.

In the lead up to the election, the NPD had struggled to find people who would allow their names to be put on the ballots of Quebec's ridings. Five members of the executive of the McGill University NDP club filled out their nomination paperwork. So did a single mom who worked at Carleton University's student pub and spent much of the campaign in Las Vegas. When the votes were counted on May 2, all of them were elected.[51] The NDP formed the official opposition for the first time in Canada's history. When Layton died a few months later, there was genuine sadness among his old foes.

POILIEVRE HAD NO problem winning Carleton in 2011. Geography, however, still stood in the way of promotion to cabinet. John Baird, who had run and won a neighbouring riding in 2006, was guaranteed a cabinet seat because of his provincial cabinet experience and his value to the party. Prime ministers must factor regional representation into their cabinet-making plans. There simply wasn't enough room for two ministers from Ottawa.[52] Baird, though a friend and ally, had become an obstacle to Poilievre's ambition, though, eventually, Harper would change his mind and make room for Poilievre in the cabinet.

He was assigned the job of parliamentary secretary to the minister of transport, infrastructure, and communities under Harper's Quebec lieutenant, Denis Lebel, a former advocate for Quebec separatism. Lebel doled out most of the federal government's patronage in Quebec.[53] Poilievre was also loaned out to ministers Gary Goodyear and Steven Fletcher to work on the Federal Economic Development Agency for Southern Ontario (FedDev Ontario), a porktacular outfit that was supposed to stimulate investment in Canada's industrial heartland. It made the government many friends among potential donors, but it also resulted in another Poilievre gaffe that infuriated Harper. Poilievre went off-script in 2012 and joined with Ontario troglodyte Randy Hillier, still a member of Doug Ford's provincial cabinet, to demand an end to the mandatory check-off of union dues from workers' paycheques.[54] (Harper probably agreed with their position but kept a tight lock on the party's messaging and hated surprises.) Poilievre went after the government's largest union, the troubled PSAC, demanding greater transparency. No one cared. The "Rand Formula," created by the Supreme Court generations ago, guarantees unions' rights to collect dues from everyone who qualifies for membership in a union and benefits from a collective agreement in their workplace, no matter what a worker wants. By repeating an old anti-union gripe, Poilievre seemed determined to win his spurs as a warrior of the far right.

He also tried to gain from the Harper government's new determination to give a little bit of help to everyone—farmers, parents, taxpayers. Harper was willing to put the government back into deficit after years of Liberal surpluses by cutting the federal sales tax and income taxes. The government created a plan that gave parents tax breaks when they saved money to support their disabled children and tax-free savings accounts that rewarded thrifty Canadians. It sent out cheques to people who had daycare-aged children and kids who played sports.

The government also kept the promises it made its base of supporters. After the 2011 election, Vic Toews, Harper's public safety minister, killed the long-gun registry created by Jean Chrétien's government and ordered the destruction of its data. Poilievre made himself part of the story by taking Toews and backbencher Candice Hoeppner to a photo op at a farm in Poilievre's riding that featured firearms that no farmer would ever have had trouble keeping.[55]

None of this was exciting work, and it didn't place Poilievre anywhere near the centre of power, where Harper and a few close associates made the decisions that counted. But Poilievre and Harper had one thing in common: a hatred of Elections Canada. After a couple of years of trading digs with Elections Canada's independent-minded commissioners, it was time for Harper to settle accounts.

On July 6, 2013, a train loaded with explosive petroleum broke loose from a siding in southeastern Quebec and crashed into the downtown of Lac-Mégantic. Waves of burning and boiling oil flowed through the streets, killing forty-seven people and destroying the centre of the city. Very quickly, blame fell on Poilievre's minister, Denis Lebel, whose department had done so much to deregulate railways. In the cabinet shuffle nine days after the disaster, Lebel lost the transport portfolio but kept the infrastructure portfolio and was promoted to Harper's Quebec lieutenant. Poilievre, who had often been the public relations face of the transport department, had stayed out of Lebel's clumsy attempt to control the political damage, and was finally sworn into Harper's cabinet.[56]

Harper had the perfect job for Poilievre: attack the elections oversight agency, delegitimize it, and clip its wings.

6
ELECTION SKULLDUGGERY

> *I think there was a kind of malice to Harper that I don't associate with previous Conservative leaders—for example in his administration's attacks on unions, public servants and civil society groups.*
>
> FORMER NDP LEADER ED BROADBENT[1]

IN THE DAYS of Sir John A. Macdonald, when people didn't fly unless they had a hot-air balloon and you could take a train from one Canadian town to another and expect to arrive on time, it wasn't hard for politicians to rig elections. Canada was a small place. Even if they'd had today's rules, there weren't that many voters. Back then, women couldn't vote. "Indians" couldn't vote. Poor people couldn't vote: voters lists were drawn up using municipal tax rolls, so a man had to own property to make the cut. Except in New Brunswick, which had secret ballots before Confederation, "electors" assembled at one place in a riding and publicly told the returning officer whom they supported. A voter who was bought stayed bought.

In 1873, Liberals under now-forgotten one-term prime minister Alexander Mackenzie introduced the secret ballot in federal elections, but women, Indigenous people, poor people, and immigrants still couldn't vote. Within fifty years, the federal franchise was extended to women and people who didn't own property, unless those people were Indigenous.[2] Canada took elections seriously: arguably, the wartime election of 1917 was the only modern election that was probably rigged. The Tory government that brought in the first *Elections Act* after the First World War appointed a respected lawyer with powerful connections in both major parties, Oliver Mowat Biggar, as Canada's first chief electoral officer.[3] For generations, Canadians may have had doubts about various provincial elections, but the department that ran the country's national voting system had a good reputation. All it had to do was make sure ballot boxes weren't stuffed with fake votes, send people door to door to compile voters' lists, and check that voters who showed up on election day, were, in fact, alive and on the list. It combatted frauds like "the telegram," which lasted until the middle of the twentieth century. Crooked strategists got their hands on a real ballot and marked it for their candidate. They bribed a voter to use this ballot. By bringing back a blank ballot—the one given to them by polling clerks—the voter could show they had done their part and should now be paid. In a tight election, this labour-intensive fraud could make a difference.

Election trickery tended to involve the drafting of voters' lists and breaking the rules about the franchise. Many people were "missed" by partisan canvassers. Lists were edited and added to. Dead people stayed on the list long after they made the transition from animate to inanimate. Retirement residences and nursing homes sometimes had 100 percent turnouts even though some residents were long-gone from dementia. And, from time to time, provincial and federal governments attacked the voting rights of minorities, like the "enemy aliens" in World War I and the interned Japanese Canadians who were temporarily stripped of their vote during the Second World War. All adult Canadian citizens finally had the right to vote in federal and provincial elections when Indigenous people were enfranchised in 1960 by John Diefenbaker's Conservative government.[4]

Like everything else in Ottawa, the mandate and staff of Elections Canada, the federal elections agency, grew over time. In 1974, the (Pierre) Trudeau government put limits on election spending. Now, Elections Canada had to watch national and local campaigns to make sure they didn't overspend. Staff also had to handle the paperwork filed after the election to see if receipts matched what the candidates said were raised and used in the campaign. Paul Martin's government tightened some of the donation rules in 2004 and brought in a per-vote subsidy. In 2004, every party received $1.53 a year for each vote it received in the previous election. This subsidy was indexed to inflation. Over the years, there were new rules about investigations of alleged election wrongdoing. Elections Canada was given the job of updating a national voters list, using income tax forms rather than door-to-door canvassing. The agency ran ads to tell people to get out and vote.

During Jean Chrétien's term, Reform Party backbencher Stephen Harper made a reasonable demand: that governments seek consensus from the major federal parties before making important changes to the voting system. Instead, as they often did, the Liberals used their big majority to invoke time limitations on the debate of election rules. Harper glommed onto the idea that this regulator, like so many others in Ottawa, had been captured by the people it's supposed to regulate. It was controlled by the Liberals, enforcing rules made by Liberals, for the advantage of the Liberal Party.

Meanwhile, political strategists were developing modern ways of polling and tracking voters. The Reformers and, in time, the post-Alliance-merger Conservatives adopted voter tracking technology developed by their American allies. These were based on internet technology and the number-crunching power of computers. In 2013, author Susan Delacourt examined such data-driven systems in *Shopping for Votes,* one of the most important books to be published about modern Canadian politics.[5] She showed how campaigns had been transformed in ways that made it hard for election watchdogs to understand whether parties were acting legally and if campaign spending—once mainly used for mainstream advertising but now paying for data crunching and direct marketing to voters—was clean. The laws were drafted before lobbyists were a serious factor in Ottawa. These people didn't just sell their knowledge of the inner workings of government and peddle their connections to decision-makers; they also worked as election strategists. How could this work be evaluated to see if it broke campaign-spending rules? Politics was becoming professionalized: this new reliance on data collection and professional strategists was happening as fewer people across Canada joined political parties. Computerized opinion tracking was used to raise money to pay for ads on TV, radio, and the internet and for strategists who often had one foot in politics and one foot in lucrative lobbying between elections—while still promoting their paymasters by appearing as experts on media panels. This was new and unanticipated by the drafters of a law more concerned with national and local election-period spending paid by cheque.

HOW DO THEY know who's who? That's the point of *Shopping for Votes*, which describes modern voter identification and tracking. The better the parties get at knowing who's likely to vote for whom, the better they are at getting their people out. When Delacourt wrote her book, the Tories were miles ahead of the Liberals at mastering data-gathering and analysis technology. (The Liberals believe they've caught up since, while the focus of all parties has partly shifted to social media, where the Conservatives are still ahead.)

The Liberals and NDP were stuck in their old-fashioned ways, looking at past election results for each neighbourhood to try to figure out where to spend ad money and concentrate their door-to-door canvassers. They also hired professional pollsters. All this took money and bodies. The Tories' closely guarded computer system, the Constituent Information Management System (CIMS, pronounced "sims"), developed by a direct-marketing company called Responsive Marketing Group, cut down on overhead while improving their ability to raise a lot of money from people who could only afford small donations. The developers and the Conservatives carefully guarded CIMS's operating system secrets and access to the data it used and produced.

Data is everything in elections, or at least that's what the bright new strategists said. Every call from a campaign centre to a voter provides data, whether it be that the voter's a supporter, a die-hard opponent, or on the fence. If you cut the friendly call-centre worker off and slam the phone down, you've told them something. And look at how many people ask for your name and email anytime you engage with anything even mildly political. Your phone, your TV, your car, the media you subscribe to, even some of your new appliances, collect information on you and send it to corporations and, sometimes, political parties. Don't get me started about your laptop, even if you're not a social-media addict. Look at the ads that pop up on your computer. Flip through Netflix to see what they think you like.[6]

Early in Stephen Harper's term as leader of the new Conservative Party, his tech wizards bought and adapted the American marketing technology in CIMS to add to the data on the three hundred thousand people who'd recently supported the Canadian Alliance and Progressive Conservatives. From then on, every contact between a Tory campaign worker and a voter, whether in person, on the phone, or in writing, was entered into CIMS and mined for money and votes. In the first decade of this century, the Conservatives were spending as much money on gathering data and loading it into CIMS as they were on national and local ads. Young staffers like Pierre Poilievre, who had also co-owned a political strategy company with Jonathan Denis, were true believers in CIMS and fast adopters. They'd seen how the Ontario Tories benefitted from a similar, if more primitive, system. But money was the real attraction:

in 2009, the Manning Centre would honour CIMS's developers for raising more than $75 million for the federal Tories and right-wing causes across Canada.[7]

Tories would argue publicly that the government had no business asking people how many rifles and shotguns they had (data gathered by the national long-gun registry) or if their homes had more than one bathroom (information collected on the long-form census), but this was exactly the kind of information fed into CIMS. Along with collecting data and observations made by Tory constituency office workers, MPs, and central office staffers, door knockers, and cold callers, the party bought data from marketing companies who knew a lot about the demographics of specific neighbourhoods. Anyone who approached the party, say by calling an MP's office or filling out an online petition, was asked for their email address. A birthday was gold to these people. (Look at how many online outfits ask for those things. It's not just politicians who want this data.) Anything that showed income or voter intention went into the CIMS machine. Conservative staffers, MPs, and volunteers logged everything they could whenever someone opened a door. They even looked to see what kind of kids' toys were in people's yards. If the car in the driveway had a political decal or a sticker with an obvious demographic signal—say, a NASCAR logo or a "Save the Whales" decal—they made a note of that and put it into CIMS. This was sensitive, valuable information, and the Tories guarded it carefully. Very few of their own strategists got access to the whole system.

Anyone who had donated to the Tories, volunteered on a campaign, or had an election sign automatically got all the Conservative email blasts and mass-mailings. CIMS allowed the party to focus its message, using what it knew about voters to ask for money to fight the CBC or get rid of the long-gun registry. It could carve out lists of voters for private marketing companies to use to make spam calls to potential Conservative donors in every riding, including Poilievre's. All this was legal, despite being creepy. Other parties envied the system and played catch-up.[8] All of this was controlled by a small core at the centre of the campaign. Local candidates, even MPs, did not have access to it. The Tory campaign leadership treated CIMS the way the British guarded the secret of the breaking of the Enigma code machine: the data was doled out when a very small group—which did not include Poilievre—decided when and where it was needed.

Local candidates like Poilievre supposedly didn't have access to CIMS, but it's clear that some bad actors did. Justice Mosely of the Federal Court of Canada found that someone with access to CIMS used its data to decide where to make robocalls to trick Liberal, NDP, and Green voters into not voting in the 2011 election.[9] Data mining and usage was combined with old-fashioned dirty politics, using vote-suppression strategies developed in the United States, by both major parties, that had crept into Canada. In 2010, the right-wing group Citizens United had won a lawsuit that effectively gutted American campaign financing laws and gave important political rights to corporations. Canada had tougher election spending laws than the United States had *before* the Citizens United decision. Canada also had strong civil society organizations that were given voice by the CBC. The Harper government (and Canadian conservatives since then) have fought to change that.

HARPER AND HIS strategists understood social justice organizations and trade unions to be part of their political opposition, so they went after them. Groups that had charitable status—the right to issue receipts to donors, so the gifts were tax-deductible—were vulnerable. So were non-government organizations that the government subsidized to do overseas aid work, usually for the Canadian International Development Agency (CIDA). KAIROS is an international aid organization, created by eleven Canadian churches and religious organizations. It's run by the Anglican Church, an organization that operates as a sort of state religion in one corner of Europe. These heirs of Henry VIII and Thomas Cranmer are allied with social justice warriors like the Evangelical Lutheran Church in Canada, the Presbyterian Church in Canada, the United Church of Canada, the Quakers, the Mennonite Central Committee of Canada, and several Roman Catholic bodies, including the Canadian Conference of Catholic Bishops. In the beginning of Harper's term, these radicals flew under the Tory radar. Bureaucrats at the Canadian International Development Agency recommended KAIROS receive $7,098,758 to help pay for its foreign aid work in 2009. The money was supposed to help the Sudan Council of Churches to monitor and help implement a framework peace agreement in that country. KAIROS also planned to help Indonesia's Commission for the Disappeared and Victims of Violence and the Héritiers de la Justice, which supports women raped in war in the Democratic Republic of Congo.

When this recommendation crossed CIDA minister Bev Oda's desk, she signed off after adding the word *not*. A few days later, KAIROS got a letter saying the church group's foreign aid projects would not get federal money. There was no explanation, but word got back to KAIROS that the Tories saw it as anti-Israel. Héritiers de la Justice, called CIDA's decision "a blow from a sword to our hearts."

The decision had been a political one. Immigration and multicultural minister Jason Kenney, Poilievre's friend and mentor, told an Israeli audience in early 2009 that the Harper government would not give any money to anti-Semitic organizations. He named KAIROS, saying it supported the boycott, divestment, and sanctions campaign against Israel. KAIROS denied these accusations. The churches that were members of KAIROS angrily denied they were political. The cutting of KAIROS's funding created a media storm, with journalists quoting officials of other charities who worried they'd be the next target. A few weeks after Oda's exercise in editing, and after the defunding decision had obviously become a political problem for the Tories, Oda blamed her bureaucrats for cutting KAIROS off and denied she'd fiddled with their recommendation. House of Commons speaker Peter Milliken ruled that the document had been deliberately tampered with by mysterious and unknown people. It took another year for Oda to admit she'd made the decision.[10]

Harper unleashed the dogs of the Canada Revenue Agency, giving them an extra $8 million to go after left-leaning organizations that had charitable status. CRA investigators went through the accounts and publications of religious charities. First, they came for the Mennonites. In 2010, these hellraisers were told their magazine was too political. This was not a threat, but a "reminder." "It has come to our attention that recent issues of the Organization's monthly periodical, entitled 'Canadian Mennonite,' have contained editorials and/or articles that appear to promote opposition to a political party, or to candidates for public office," the letter said. It reminded the Mennonites that charities are "prohibited [by the *Income Tax Act*] from engaging in partisan political activities," including "direct or indirect support of, or opposition to, any political party or candidate for public office." The Canadian Mennonite Publishing Service was "reminded" that "partisan political activities" would cost them their charitable status, which would mean the end of the publishing house.

Anyone who has seen the Mennonites working at a natural disaster site knows these are people who should not be messed with.[11] They'd been oppressed by big-league tyrannies like the Holy Roman Empire, Prussia, the Russian czars, and Stalin, so Harper's government was hardly intimidating.[12] Rather than quietly submit to the Canada Revenue Agency threat, church staff posted the tax agency's letter on the newspaper's website. *Canadian Mennonite* editor and publisher Dick Benner told a CBC News reporter that the letter was "a chill on speech." Benner said the letter "tells me that I need to be very careful on what I say about government policy and how I say it. That restricts me as a journalist and as a religious commentator." He denied they'd opposed or supported any Canadian politicians, though he had criticized two Mennonite Tory MPs for supporting the deployment of Canadian troops to fight the Taliban and written an article after Osama bin Laden's death in which he'd warned of the takeover of Canada by "a militaristic Conservative majority government." The CRA also complained about stories profiling church concerns about an omnibus crime bill, an article on how the death of NDP leader Jack Layton inspired some young Mennonites to get involved in politics, and a piece about Mennonite youths who sent paper airplanes to Ottawa to pressure the government to "spend less money on war."[13]

Various Harper ministers stepped up to the microphones to denounce charities that annoyed them. Peter Kent, the environment minister, accused environmental groups of using their charitable status to launder money. Public safety minister Vic Toews, who'd later end up on the Manitoba Court of Appeal, lumped environmentalists with white supremacists, claiming they were all extremists. Secular organizations like Amnesty International, the David Suzuki Foundation, and the Canadian Centre for Policy Alternatives (CCPA) were also targeted for CRA investigations. In 2016, the Federal Court of Appeal sided with the Harper government's claim that the prevention of poverty through education and political action—rather than alleviating poverty by giving material and financial support to the poor—is not a valid charitable purpose.[14] The next year, Justin Trudeau would try to fix the charities' problem, with unintended consequences.

No one should be surprised by Harper's attacks on unions. While strategist Patrick Muttart was coming up with effective ways of prying working-class support from the New Democrats and the left in general, his boss went after unions, the organizations that had organized blue-collar workers and won them a middle-class lifestyle. In 2013, the Harper government amended the *Canadian Labour Code*, the *Parliamentary Employees and Staff Relations Act* and the *Federal Public Sector Labour Relations Act* to make it easier for employees in federally regulated industries like banks and airlines to decertify their unions and more difficult for workers in non-union shops to organize. Poilievre supported these changes. With deregulation and lax regulation, gig work was already undermining job security, even among cab drivers and university professors. Union membership in the private sector fell from an already pathetic 17.1 percent to 15 percent during the Harper years. Unions were on their way to being a spent force in most of the private sector, while public service salaries rose because of the power of big unions like the Canadian Union of Public Employees and the Public Service Alliance of Canada. The right often describes public servants, with their good wages, pensions, and benefits won through unionization and collective bargaining, as a parasitic elite. Decades before, when the union movement was still strong, most of the country's workers were on their way to having the same thing.

Defanging unions with legislation that weakened their ability to organize, going after social justice charities by stripping them of charitable status, and cutting the financial support that some received from the government were part of a plan to change the political landscape by defunding and casting aspersions on important parts of civil society. Freezing out mainstream media, which Harper started at the beginning of his term by cutting reporters' access to him, his minister, and government experts, helped make this project work.[15] The next step was to change the way elections were run.

IN THE 2000 federal election campaign, Jean-Paul Marchand, the Bloc Quebecois MP for Quebec Est, was accidentally caught in the middle of something that would later be called "in-and-out" campaign financing.[16] The Bloc's central office thought Quebec Est was a safe riding.[17] It transferred federal election subsidy money to Marchand's team that Marchand was supposed to quietly give back to head office as individual donations. The Bloc hive mind would spend the money on its main all-Quebec TV ad campaign. (A big legal cheque comes *in* to a campaign that doesn't need it. "Donations" to the leader's campaign go *out*. The money would be docketed as spent on the campaign, and the "donors" got fat tax refunds.) This scheme is illegal. The plot was exposed when Marchand's people held onto the money, and the Bloc brain trust stupidly sued to get it back. The Martin government, seeing how the scheme worked, tried to tighten the law against it, but the bill died when the Liberal government fell in 2005.

When senior Tories tried something similar in the 2006 campaign, Chief Electoral Officer Marc Mayrand said his agency would not pay almost $800,000 in refunds that their riding associations had billed for. In that campaign, the central campaign office transferred a lot of money to the individual riding associations that ran local candidates' campaigns. The money went to no-hope ridings in places like Quebec, Vancouver, and Toronto that hadn't raised a lot of money and had donation room to spare. They didn't raise or plan to spend the $80,000 that the election law allowed. The local campaigns "paid" their volunteers' expenses. The volunteers donated that money back to the party's central office, which spent the money on national ads. Two things happened: the party was able to claim these local "expenses" from Elections Canada, and the volunteers got a fat tax rebate on their personal income tax, since donors to political parties get bigger tax breaks than people who give money to any other cause.

After Elections Canada caught on and refused to pay the fake expenses, the Tories filed a lawsuit for the money against the election oversight agency. During this litigation, Elections Canada put a lot of sensitive information into the court record, naming candidates and campaign strategists involved in several ridings. This evidence was "privileged," meaning journalists could name the bad actors and describe their roles in the scam without risking a lawsuit.

Some former Tory MPs gave interviews to the media, admitting they'd seen the scam up close. Garth Turner, a financial adviser and journalist who had been a Tory MP but had left to join the Liberals when Harper attempted to muzzle him and shut down his blog, described what he'd seen when he was on the road as a featured speaker at Conservative events. "I was asked to be the guest speaker [at a constituency event]...but before I gave my speech the treasurer gave their report for the annual meeting and they had more than $40,000, which was transferred into their bank account and then the same day they wrote a cheque back to the central party. And by transferring $40,000 into their bank account during the campaign they got a 60 per cent rebate [from Elections Canada]."[18]

Once the story was out, Poilievre became the face of the scandal, even though he wasn't the scheme's mastermind. He was a good choice: Poilievre is the master of simple statements, and the details of the fraud were so mind-bendingly complex that they were impossible to explain in TV-news soundbites. As parliamentary secretary, he was one of the Press Gallery's favourite dial-a-quotes. After Liberal MP Dominic LeBlanc called the Tories out on the "in and out scandal," Poilievre held a press conference in a basement studio in the Parliament Building. It was "a simple matter of freedom of speech," Poilievre said. "Conservative candidates ran Conservative ads with Conservative money. They followed all of the rules and they came in under all of the [spending] limits."[19] Most of this was true, but that wasn't the point. The party's leading strategists had illegally moved money around to break spending rules, and it was for that reason that they were in trouble.

So were campaign staff in dozens of ridings where Elections Canada believed Tory candidates improperly filed expenses that should have been declared by the national party. This sounds like arcane, inside-baseball stuff, but it gave the Tories far more money for national television and radio ads in a close campaign, enough to blow past their spending limit of $1 million for national advertising.[20] "We are in the right, we are going to defend our freedom of speech to determine what kind of ads we're going to run," Poilievre told reporters.[21] Again, that was a straw-man argument. Elections Canada wasn't after the Tories for what was said in the ads. The agency believed the Tories illegally spent money to buy them. It also believed some of the campaign receipts submitted to Elections Canada auditors were altered or forged.

"We're taking Elections Canada to court to prove it's a matter of free speech," Poilievre told reporters who came to the press conference or, more likely, watched it on closed-circuit TV. This deflection became the headline of the media's stories.

Poilievre argued that all of the parties had transferred subsidy money from no-hope and safe election candidates to their main campaigns "for generations," though Elections Canada's beef was that the Conservatives had falsely reported this as money to pay "volunteers" whose "donations" earned tax rebates. This money was effectively laundered, flowing back to the national campaign to pay for ads that stressed the party leader and his platform rather than that of local candidates.

Poilievre said he would welcome an inquiry by a House of Commons committee and challenged all parties to open their books from the past two election campaigns.[22] But this was an attempt at distraction. Hearings by politicians would have hobbled Elections Canada's investigation. The implication that other parties couldn't stand scrutiny was a smear of the election agency, which, by inference, had only investigated the Conservatives, and Poilievre falsely accused his opponents of committing the same crimes as the Tories.

The Conservatives also tried to divert attention from their campaign financing schemes by picking over the bones of the sponsorship scandal, the Quebec advertising kickback racket that finished off the Martin Liberals. Poilievre was given that assignment. He cross-examined sponsorship architect Chuck Guité and Chrétien chief of staff Jean Pelletier, central actors in that affair, when they testified at a parliamentary committee in June 2007. He harangued Pelletier, a thuggish man who exuded sleaze: "You have a chance here sir, to just let it all out. Can you tell us where the $40 million that's still missing from the sponsorship program has gone?"[23] Pelletier declined to do so.

A few months later, Poilievre was able to get a twofer: a shot at Elections Canada and the marginalization of Muslims. He quarterbacked a non-binding but mischievous House of Commons motion that forced people—really, Muslim women—to show their faces when they vote. Elections Canada had already decided they didn't need to. It had already created safeguards: asking women politely to briefly unveil or have someone vouch for them.

"I have asked election personnel to invite anyone whose face is concealed to uncover it in a manner that is respectful to their beliefs," Maynard told a House of Commons committee.[24]

Poilievre's motion passed. Even so, Poilievre engineered a parliamentary committee hearing into the non-issue. A few days before, while scrumming with Hill reporters, Poilievre had attacked Chief Electoral Officer Marc Mayrand. Now he would get him on the record, and under oath, with lots of TV cameras.

In the September 9, 2007, hearing, Mayrand said he would be breaking the law if he obeyed MPs by forcing veiled citizens to uncover their faces when they voted in by-elections that were underway. Even though the *Elections Act* had been tinkered with recently, not one MP or senator who spoke about the law said anything about a "problem" of veiled voters. There weren't very many of them, and arguably, they had *Charter of Rights* protection, so they weren't a thing that Mayrand, a cautious bureaucrat, was willing to regulate. "That would be a requirement for me to offend the [Elections] Act and not uphold the law as stated on the books," Mayrand told MPs on the Commons Procedure and House Affairs Committee. MPs from all the parties were offended. They wanted Mayrand to obey them. Poilievre spoke for the MPs who had voted to make veiled women show their faces.

"As parliamentarians, we're democratically elected, he's not. The law is clear; he should follow it," Poilievre said. That quote went out on TV and was printed in the papers. But the resolution was not law and Maynard was not bound by it. In Canada, laws are made when legislation passes in the House of Commons and the Senate, then gets royal assent, is published in the *Canada Gazette*, and officially proclaimed. Poilievre knew this. Most people don't. It was part of his pattern of using citizens' (and some journalists') ignorance of basic civics to bamboozle them.

Sensibly, Mayrand told the committee that in 140 years of Canadian history there had never been a problem with veiled women voting. And, he noted, Parliament hadn't really changed the law.

"You do not agree that the will of this committee is the will of Parliament?" queried another Tory MP, Tom Lukiwski.

Mayrand responded accurately: "Again, with all due respect, I cannot accept the position that a committee can adapt or amend an act of Parliament."

The MPs on the committee passed a motion by Poilievre that asked Mayrand to use his so called "powers of adaptation" to overrule the *Elections Act* and require veiled women to show their faces when they vote. Mayrand ignored them.[25]

In April 2008, the RCMP and Elections Canada investigators raided Conservative Party headquarters in Ottawa. Someone, likely an Elections Canada staffer, tipped reporters about the raid. Tories were horrified to see it on the television news networks. Poilievre told journalists Elections Canada investigators "stormed into the party's office." He called the raid "a very critical, very serious breach of its own laws."[26]

In the House of Commons, Poilievre said the Liberals, NDP, and Bloc did the same thing as the Tories. Conservative backbenchers chanted "In and out, in and out" as Poilievre repeatedly chanted back, "Where's Elections Canada?"[27]

In response, MPs in the minority parliament ordered the House of Commons committee to begin an investigation of the "in-and-out" scandal, but the Tories used a lot of bogus procedure and other stall tactics to turn the hearings into a circus. The committee chair, Tory Gary Goodyear (a future Harper minister), was so dedicated to not getting to the bottom of the scandal that his fellow MPs passed a vote of non-confidence against him and kicked him out. Conservatives were enraged and said it was unfair when opposition MPs who made up the majority on the Commons ethics committee drew up a list of seventy-eight potential witnesses but turned down everyone the Tories proposed. Most of the witnesses on the Tory list were Liberal, NDP, and Bloc Quebecois campaign strategists who would have had to testify under oath and who, as Poilievre had claimed, might have their own in-and-out secrets.

Poilievre called his committee opponents the "Liberals, separatists, and socialists." Outside the committee room, Poilievre told reporters Elections Canada was so biased in favour of the Liberals that the agency didn't follow up when Judge Gomery, running his sloppy investigation into the sponsorship scandal, found that $1.3 million of federal advertising money had been illegally diverted. It ended up in the bank accounts of the Liberals' Quebec wing to secretly pay campaign organizers and ad agencies in the 1995 separatism referendum. "Elections Canada never thought to investigate that," Poilievre said.[28]

This was a story arc that might resonate with readers of George Orwell's *Animal Farm*. Back in the day, the right claimed to practise a different kind of politics. They sold voters on the idea that they went to Parliament with clean hands and pure hearts. Joe Clark's Progressive Conservatives and the Canadian Alliance/Conservatives under Day and Harper had pecked away at the previous government by denouncing a string of Liberal scandals. Now, Harper had a scandal of his own, driven home when police laid charges in February 2011 against some of his top campaign strategists for playing fast and loose with campaign financing. The Tories knew this scandal was popular with reporters but confusing and uninteresting to voters. Poilievre was sent out again to try to downplay this mess.

Poilievre falsely implied a court had already decided that there was nothing to the accusations. The Federal Court had awarded some money held back by Elections Canada, but hadn't said the scheme was legal. He used words that made the story seem boring before attacking the agency that was investigating the Tories. "This is a five-year-old accounting dispute," Poilievre told reporters. "For Elections Canada to ignore a federal court decision and lay administrative charges is puzzling at best and unfair at worst."[29] The Liberals, who were propping up the Harper minority, and the other parties in the House of Commons didn't see a campaign financing shell game as something worth forcing an election over.

In-and-out dragged on. In 2010, some former Tory MPs, including Helena Guergis of Ontario and Inky Mark of Manitoba, came forward to say they had been punished for not funnelling money back to the Tory head office in the 2006 campaign. But this was a bloodless scandal. At most, people had seen more national ads than they should have, and the Tories might have got some extra votes. Martin didn't really have a chance in an election that had been all about change. There was no way to rid the party of the stink of the sponsorship scandal, and people didn't care that this was a Chrétien, not a Martin, project. The RCMP leak about the investigation into Goodale drove home the idea that the Liberals were unethical and needed some time in opposition.

On February 24, 2011, four Conservative national strategists were charged with overspending over $1 million in the 2006 election. They were also accused of submitting "false or misleading" documents to Elections Canada. Just over a year later, they made a plea deal. The Tories agreed to repay $230,000 in taxpayer money and pay $55,000 in fines in return for the dropping of charges against individual party strategists. To the Tories, this was "vindication," even though Elections Canada had proved the party cheated in the election that brought it to power. The fact that Elections Canada had investigated the scheme added yet one more reason for Harper to hold a grudge against the agency and its head, Mayrand. Eventually, accounts would be settled.

HARPER FAILED TO win his majority in the October 2008 election, even though his opponent, Stéphane Dion, had trouble speaking English and almost every media outlet in the country did what it could to help Harper. Poilievre easily won re-election in his riding. It was becoming a safe seat. There was a slight jolt after the election when the opposition parties tried to form a coalition government and kill Harper's plan to get rid of the subsidies the government paid to political parties after big donations from businesses, unions, and rich people were banned years before. This fell apart when the governor general accepted Harper's request to shut down Parliament. By the time the House of Commons was recalled, the plan was forgotten.

It's not clear if Harper and Poilievre started gunning for Elections Canada because it wouldn't let go of the in-and-out scandal or for other reasons. Republican and Democratic Party strategists in the United States were already analyzing voting patterns and coming up with ways to dodge spending laws and suppress their opponents' turnout. Harper and Poilievre would have known by then that Elections Canada's ads that encouraged young people to vote were good for the Liberals and the NDP. In the Tories' world, nothing that adversely affected them happened by accident. Elections Canada became an enemy.

When Stéphane Dion was unable to raise the money to pay his leadership campaign debts, Poilievre went after him. "If [Dion] does not repay these debts by the June 3, 2008, deadline, they become illegal donations over the donation limit," Poilievre told the House of Commons. "The only escape is if Elections Canada steps in to protect the Liberal leader with preferential treatment and an extension."[30] A few days later, MPs of all parties, including the Tories, voted to amend the *Elections Act* to take some of the financial pressure off leadership candidates of all federal parties.

Donald Trump and his minions were not the first people to attack the credibility of election officials. The Harper government, which came and went before Trump entered his first primary, had been doing it for years. And it was Pierre Poilievre who was given the job of taking down Canada's election oversight agencies.

Political parties want their voters to show up on election day and their opponents' supporters to stay home. Usually, in both Canada and the United States, big turnouts favour centrist and leftist parties. Conservatives want the urban poor, the downtown hipsters, the racialized, and the young to give up on making change through the democratic process. Radical right-wing strategist Paul Weyrich told fifteen thousand American and Canadian conservative ministers and preachers in 1980, "I don't want everyone to vote. Elections are not run by a majority of the people. They never have been from the beginning of our country and they aren't now. As a matter of fact, our leverage in the elections quite candidly goes up as the voting populace goes down."[31] The usual forms of campaigning, things like door-knocking, email blasts, and phone calls to supporters, are tactics used to make sure your supporters get out. But if you can get one of *your* voters out and convince one of *theirs* to stay home, you've doubled the power of that vote. "Sometimes," one California Republican strategist said, "vote suppression is as important to this business as vote-getting."[32] In 2003, the ultra-conservative Koch brothers started cutting cheques for something called Americans for Prosperity. Its president, Tim Phillips, said AFP would try to get more people to vote, but it actually worked to scare or trick potential voters into staying home.[33] Other Koch-funded organizations lobbied for mandatory photo ID, which a lot of poor people don't have.

For decades, politicians in the US and Canada have used false or exaggerated claims of voter fraud to justify new rules that make voting annoying. And, after elections, the people who run the voting apparatus in various states cull voters lists. They're supposed to get rid of the names of people who've moved or died, but sometimes a lot of other names disappear.

A party needs to be elected to do these things. (Unlike Canada, where Elections Canada runs federal elections, laws and policies in the US are set by elected state officials. In places where campaigns don't have advantages that are baked into the voting system, party activists must do the work themselves.)[34]

Spam calls—robot calls or robocalls—are the cheapest way to cheat. In 2020, people in Detroit, Philadelphia, and Pittsburgh got automated calls telling them that personal information would be turned over to cops and debt collectors if they voted by mail.[35] Many robocalls show signs of twisted humour: people being told by automated voices that an election has been postponed, or that it's being held on a Thursday when the election is really on a Tuesday. (Voters in British Columbia got calls like this in the 2024 provincial election.)

In November 2010, more than a hundred thousand people in predominantly Democratic and African American areas of Maryland got calls telling them not to bother voting in mid-term congressional and local elections because the Democrats were going to win anyway. A soothing voice told them to "relax."[36] (The ringleader behind the calls was convicted of vote fraud, but the more surprising fact is that the calls cost just $2,000.)

STARTING IN THE 1990s, a lot of Reform/Canadian Alliance/Conservative staffers began to travel to the United States to learn the latest election magic. They got advice from Republican strategists, lobbyists, and members of the right-wing International Democratic Union, which has a standing committee on election campaigns. Much of that advice was about ways of getting people *not* to vote. Two employees of Front Porch Strategies, an American company that works on right-wing campaigns, worked in the 2011 campaign to get Tory voters to show up at polls and keep Liberals away. Campaign workers deliberately slowed lines at polling places and challenged voters. This caused some would-be voters to give up. (Some academics have called the practice of using ID rules to monkey-wrench the system "vote caging." Its roots go back at least as far as the 2004 US presidential and congressional elections.) Polls were set up in inconvenient places, like the back of big supermarkets or in churches, which discouraged voting by Muslims. Polling places were shuffled around, with fewer overall and fewer still in parts of communities with high turnouts of young people.

During the 2011 election, a few local media outlets carried short articles about people who'd received strange automated phone calls in close ridings. Hundreds of voters in Guelph, where the Liberal incumbent had won by just 1,800 votes in 2008, and other Ontario ridings got calls that the robot voice said were from Elections Canada, telling them their polling station had been moved to some inconvenient location. Somehow, the scammers knew which voters to target: they were people who weren't likely to vote Conservative. (Still, Liberal Frank Valeriote won re-election with a wider voter margin than in the previous election.) Elections Canada investigators linked the calls to a pay-as-you-go cell phone belonging to a non-existent subscriber, identified only as "Pierre Poutine." The Green Party complained about vote-suppression calls, but big newspapers and TV networks ignored them. (After the election, a Tory call centre targeted Montreal voters with a lie that human rights scholar Irwin Cotler, who had been Paul Martin's justice minister, was quitting politics. This caused a ruckus in the House of Commons, but because the calls weren't made during an election, they were not illegal.)

Before the campaign ended, the Green Party and some local media complained about the automated calls. After the election, reporters Stephen Maher and Glen McGregor, working for the

Ottawa Citizen, put the 2011 robocalls scandal onto the national agenda. Their stories, printed in Postmedia papers across Canada, flushed out more victims of this vote-suppression scheme. An affidavit filed by Elections Canada to get a search warrant showed 7,760 calls were made using the Pierre Poutine burner phone number.[37] Very quickly, there was some speculation that Pierre Poilievre, who'd been a master of call-centre campaign strategies, was Pierre Poutine, but the name likely came from a popular fast-food joint in Guelph.[38] Owners of the place said they had nothing to do with politics.

Stephen Harper and Pierre Poilievre saw the vote-suppression stories as just another public relations problem to deal with. They took no moral or political responsibility for this attack on democracy. In the first months of the robocalls scandal, Poilievre was sent out to defuse the stories written by McGregor and Maher.[39] The fruits of their investigations were raised almost every day by opposition MPs in the House of Commons. Since he was seen as Harper's attack dog, no one was surprised when Poilievre became the face of the government when the scandal broke in 2012. CBC reporter Terry Milewski told *The National* anchor Peter Mansbridge, "Poilievre [is] parliamentary secretary to [the] minister of transport, so this was not his responsibility and he's being a dial-a-quote here."[40]

The reporters tried to trace the calls—which, they found, were made in eighteen ridings—to a direct marketing company and then connect that company to the federal Tories. The supposed links are still open to debate and were never proven. Harper flat-out denied any personal involvement, saying, "I have absolutely no knowledge on anything about these calls, but obviously if there's anything wrong, we will expect they will face the full consequences of the law." Jenni Byrne, part of the inner circle of the Tories' 2011 election team, was, with campaign manager Doug Finley, one of the targets of the investigative reporters.[41] They were never able to connect her to the scandal. Byrne laid down the ice that would be used to push a minor campaign staffer under the bus. Speaking to the CBC, she said: "The party was not involved with these calls and if anyone on a local campaign was involved, they will not play a role in a future campaign." Vote-suppression accusations were "extremely serious" and something the Tories would never do. "We spent the entire campaign identifying supporters and we worked hard to get out the vote. Our job is to get votes out. We do not engage in voter suppression."[42]

In the end, one minor Guelph campaign staffer, Michael Sona, went to jail. If there was a Conservative cabal secretly running a vote-suppression campaign, they got away with it. Conservatives claimed the robocalls stories were overhyped, but some, including Preston Manning, were appalled at what they saw as an attack on democracy. In a CBC interview, he condemned the use of vote-suppression tactics and said Canadian political parties should think twice about sending their young staffers to the United States for training. Instead, they needed better ethical training, and campaign managers should keep them on shorter leashes.[43]

Through the summer and fall of 2012, Poilievre kept reminding journalists and fellow MPs that the Liberals had been the only party punished for breaking the rules. (A Liberal campaign staffer had been caught making spam calls saying a Guelph-area Conservative MP supported an abortion ban).[44] In March, the Harper government promised changes to the *Elections Act*. Anyone who hoped for reform should have been careful what they wished for.

On October 15, 2013, Chief Electoral Officer Marc Mayrand established an advisory board to advise him "on matters relating to Canada's electoral system, its voting processes, and support for a vigorous democracy that reflects our constitution, deeply held values, and the evolving needs and circumstances of Canadians." He appointed Bob Rae, the former NDP premier of Ontario, who had also been a Liberal MP and interim federal Liberal leader; former NDP Saskatchewan premier Roy Romanow; Preston

Manning; and Progressive Conservative Senator Hugh Segal and gave them a budget of about $450,000 to come up with fixes to the system.

The report that Mayrand later tabled in Parliament asked for greater investigative powers and the right to issue subpoenas, better protection of voter data, and a requirement that parties submit documents to back up their expense claims. All of this was ignored, even though these were reasonable suggestions.

MAYBE IT WAS Harper's idea of a joke. Maybe a majority government made him bold. But of all the people in his party, Poilievre was chosen in 2013 to be Canada's first "minister of democratic reform." His real job: whack Elections Canada. Poilievre's new law, introduced early in 2014, was a direct attack on Elections Canada and the man in charge of the agency.

The *Fair Elections Act* limited the topics on which the chief electoral officer, who believed getting people to vote was part of his job, could speak. The law allowed only five topics:

- How to become a candidate.
- How voters can add their names to the voters list or have it corrected.
- How voters can cast ballots.
- How voters can prove their identity and address.
- How voters with disabilities can get into polling stations and mark their ballots.

Elections Canada couldn't work on any new voting system, like voting machines, without the approval of Parliament. The chief elections officer no longer had a permanent job. Under the old law, the chief officer stayed in place until they either quit or hit the mandatory retirement age of sixty-five. (Maynard had been in the job for less than seven years.) Now, they were to work under ten-year non-renewable contracts.[45]

Local candidates had to turn in election expense receipts before getting reimbursements from the government. National political parties, however, did not. The headquarters of the country's political parties submitted campaign expense claims for $66 million after the 2011 election. They were reimbursed for 50 percent, so taxpayers paid $33 million in refunds without any receipts to show for that money. The *Fair Elections Act* didn't change that, even though Mayrand had asked for tighter rules. It was an interesting take on accounting, considering the lather being worked up in the media and Parliament over comparatively minor expenses of some senators.

Poilievre's *Fair Elections Act* did, mildly, crack down on robocalls. Anyone who wanted to make them had to register with the Canadian Radio-Television and Telecommunications Commission. And the new law increased the maximum amount that people could donate to political parties and candidates. At the same time, it tackled the non-issue of voter fraud by getting rid of vouching—where a voter with proper identification could tell poll workers that a friend, neighbour, someone they knew without ID, was entitled to vote. The law also banned the use of voter information cards as legal identification, citing stories written by wannabe journalists who had used the cards to cheat, then wrote about it.[46]

The commissioner of Canada's elections, who investigated possible irregularities, would no longer work for Elections Canada, a stand-alone agency. They would now be working under the supervision of the minister of justice for a seven-year term.

Speaking in the House of Commons on February 5, 2014, Poilievre said, "The bill would make it harder to break the law and easier to vote. It would close loopholes to big money and would impose new penalties on political impostors who make rogue calls. It would empower law enforcement with sharper teeth, a longer reach, and a freer hand.

"The fair elections act would make our laws tough, predictable, and easy to follow. Life would be harder for election lawbreakers and easier for honest citizens taking part in democracy," Poilievre said. This was partly true, but it wasn't what critics complained about. Overall, the law limited Elections Canada's investigative powers and made voting more difficult.

Poilievre struggled to explain why he wanted to prevent Elections Canada from encouraging people to vote. Turnout had plummeted from nearly 80 percent in 1972 to 59 percent in 2006, with a slight bounce in 2011. The voting rate for young people was dismal: the 2011 turnout of thirty-two-year-olds, people who'd been able to vote since the 1997 election—five elections before—was just 44 percent.[47]

"Voting is to democracy what free speech is to liberty," he said. "Unfortunately, Canadians are doing less voting these days. Since Elections Canada began promotional voter participation campaigns, turnout has plummeted, from 75% in 1988, to 61% in 2001. A Library of Parliament analysis shows that between 1984 and 2000, right in the middle of which Elections Canada began mounting its promotional campaigns, voter turnout among youth plummeted by 20 percentage points. Somehow this is not working." Poilievre had cherry-picked the Library of Parliament study: after the 2000 election, voter turnout started trending back up.[48]

He used similarly flawed statistics and logic in a *Globe and Mail* op-ed piece, where he confused correlation and causation: "Voter turnout is another point of debate," he wrote. "There are two things that drive people to vote: motivation and information. Motivation results from parties or candidates inspiring people to vote. Information (the "where, when and how") is the responsibility of Elections Canada. The agency's own data suggests it has done a poor job of it.

"After the last election, young non-voters reported that not knowing where (25 per cent), when (26 per cent) or how (19 per cent) to vote played a role in their decision not to vote. Half of Canada's youths (and three quarters of Aboriginal youths) are unaware that they can vote early if they are not available on Election Day. 'The most important access barrier [to youth voting] was lack of knowledge about the electoral process, including not knowing about different ways to vote,' the agency has reported." That argument was based on the unrealistic assumption that every young person had been reached by Elections Canada's ads and other outreach work. It could just have easily been used to justify *more* resources for Elections Canada's get-out-the-vote campaign.[49]

It didn't take long for Poilievre to make things personal. In a news conference that afternoon, Poilievre used one of his more common slogans of the time, saying, "the referee should not be wearing a team jersey." On a CBC News show, he claimed he wasn't talking about Mayrand, but he had used the cliché so often when talking about Mayrand and Elections Canada that Mayrand had little choice but to take it personally.

Mayrand had his own feelings about the new law. "My reading of the act is that I can no longer speak about democracy in this country," he said in an interview on CBC Radio's *The House*. Coming out of a committee meeting, Mayrand told Parliament Hill reporters, "Listen, the only team jersey that I think I'm wearing—if we have to carry the analogy—I believe is the one with the stripes, white and black." Mayrand was shaking when he said, "What I note from this bill is that no longer will the referee be on the ice."

At the same time, the Harper government shut down debate in the House of Commons and sent the legislation to committee.

Jean-Pierre Kingsley, a former chief electoral officer, described to reporter Stephen Maher how he watched with alarm as Poilievre risked eroding the public trust needed to maintain confidence in the electoral process. "We are the oldest independent electoral management body in the world," Kingsley said of Elections Canada, which started running the country's election system on Dominion Day, 1920. "The credibility of that institution is worldwide. And, therefore, I don't see the advantage of attacking it."[50]

On March 6, 2014, Mayrand addressed Parliament, showing MPs how the *Fair Elections Act* threatened the country's democracy. He told the House of Commons that election day "may be the only time, when all Canadians can claim to be perfectly equal in power and influence, regardless of their income, health or social circumstances." On the Tory mouthpiece Sun News Network, Ezra Levant said he'd never seen a supposedly neutral public servant wage such an aggressive campaign against a government initiative.

The bill, however, had more critics than supporters. Former auditor general Sheila Fraser said she hadn't met anyone who supported Poilievre's changes to the law. Activist Maude Barlow and student leader Jessica McCormick wrote a newspaper piece saying: "Bill C-23, the 'Fair' Elections Act, is one of the most destructive things the Harper government has ever tried to do. It is far more serious than proroguing Parliament at whim, curbing the rights of MPs, or centralizing power in the Prime Minister's Office. It's even more serious than muzzling scientists, statisticians and others who disagree with the government. That's because the Act is an attack on the most fundamental right of all citizens in a democracy—the right to cast a ballot in an election that is fair and free from corruption and dirty tricks.

"The Unfair Elections Act is also a way to cover up the electoral fraud that took place during the last election," they continued, referring to the robocall scandal of 2011. "The Federal Court found that there was widespread fraudulent activity, that it was targeted at non-Conservative voters, and that it reduced voter turnout. And, most damning of all, the judge stated in his verdict that "the most likely source of the information used to make the misleading calls was the CIMS database maintained and controlled by the CPC [Conservative Party of Canada]."

One hundred and sixty professors from some of the best universities in the world signed a *National Post* op-ed piece saying the bill was an assault on democracy. They criticized changes to fundraising rules and the structure of Elections Canada and smacked Poilievre for killing Elections Canada's voter outreach.

"Bizarrely, the Bill forbids Elections Canada from promoting democratic participation and voting through 'get out the vote' campaigns. Elections Canada would even be prevented from publishing its research reports on the electoral process. This gag on Elections Canada would make Canada an outlier among liberal democracies, instead of the global leader it now is," they wrote.

Canada's Postmedia newspapers carried editorials criticizing the act, as did the *Globe and Mail*. That paper carried five editorials debunking Poilievre's claims about Elections Canada. Jeffrey Simpson, the *Globe*'s political columnist, was harsh: "The so-called *Fair Elections Act*, however it eventually turns out, will have shown again the hard face of Prime Minister Stephen Harper's government.

"Everything about the bill was wrong, from the way it was conceived to the method of presentation to the scorn for expert evidence. From conception to eventual adoption, even if amended by the Senate (a move obviously orchestrated by the government), the bill will have demonstrated a government determined to wring political gain from every measure, a fierce partisanship for something that ought to have been non-partisan, a dismissal of experts who, by virtue of dissent, were deemed enemies of the party."[51]

Poilievre responded that there was no pleasing Mayrand and the rest of his critics.

"The reality is that regardless of amendments and improvements that the bill potentially will have included, the CEO will not ultimately approve it," Poilievre said. "[Mayrand's] recommendations really boil down to three broad requirements for him: he wants more power, a bigger budget, and less accountability." The chief electoral officer, he said, was "grasping at straws" and making "astounding" claims about the *Fair Elections Act*.

With a bit of minor tinkering, the *Fair Elections Act* became law before the 2015 election that saw Justin Trudeau's Liberals win power.

IT TOOK NEARLY three years for the Liberals to fix some of the worst aspects of Poilievre's election law. Poilievre stayed away from the House of Commons debate on the *Elections Modernization Act*. That law restored Elections Canada's mandate to encourage people to vote. It allowed people to use voter information cards that arrive in the mail as identification.

The law gave Elections Canada something Mayrand had wanted for years: the power to subpoena people and documents, if a court approved. It also increased the fines for third parties using foreign money for campaigns. They can be fined five times the amount of foreign money that was used illegally. There were new spending limits on political party and third-parties spending in the weeks before the official campaign (the "pre-writ period"). And they'd have to tell Elections Canada what they were spending money on. There were rules to make voting places more accessible to disabled people and to make voting easier for members of the Canadian Forces who were posted away from home.

But Poilievre hasn't let this go. He still believes Elections Canada is in thrall to the Liberals. "Elections Canada will never enforce the law on Liberals," Poilievre tweeted on May 29, 2019, when news broke of a settlement between regulators and SNC-Lavalin, which broke the law by giving $110,000 to the Liberals and $8,000 to the Conservatives between 2004 and 2009. The settlement wasn't made by Elections Canada. It was made by the commissioner that Poilievre had moved to the Justice Department's prosecution office. That's arcane to most of us, but it was Poilievre who made the law.

And he became very angry when Elections Canada hired thirteen social-media "influencers"—well-known athletes, musicians, TV personalities, and YouTube celebrities—for a get-out-and-vote campaign to encourage young people to vote in that fall's election. He and other Conservatives claimed that it was part of a campaign to "rig" the election for the Liberals. Young people, they said, were more likely to vote Liberal than Tory.[52]

The *Fair Elections Act* was the peak of Poilievre's career as a cabinet minister. In February 2015, Harper made Poilievre minister of employment and social development (he kept the now-moribund "democratic reform" portfolio). By then, the Harper government was in pre-election mode. Their campaign ads targeted Liberal leader Justin Trudeau with the claim "He's not ready." Harper had been in office nine years, which voters felt was enough. They wanted a smiling leader, someone charismatic and empathetic, and they wanted change.

7
CONTENDER IN THE WILDERNESS

One of the penalties for refusing to participate in politics is that you end up being governed by your inferiors.

PLATO

DESPITE THE OPPORTUNITIES that were to come, the 2015 election was a shock to Pierre Poilievre and his party. The Tories went into that campaign slightly trailing the New Democrats, with Justin Trudeau's Liberals in third place. By the time it was over, Harper's team was trying to save "safe" seats like Poilievre's. And that was a close-run thing.

While Harper and his team had luck, most of it was bad. Their messages about Tory policy were overshadowed, early in the race, by a story that anyone could understand. Kevin Bosch, whose research skills and "war room" tactics helped put Jean Chrétien into office and keep him there, found a clip from a 2012 CBC *Marketplace* investigation of sleazy and creepy contractors. Jerry Bance, a Scarborough appliance technician, did a good job fixing a Scarborough family's dishwasher. He got slightly famous for doing something else: urinating in a cup and dumping the contents down the kitchen sink. Bance was now a Tory candidate in Scarborough.

Bosch gave the video to the major TV networks just after Labour Day. Jenni Byrne was supposed to have vetted candidates for this kind of embarrassing stuff. Bance hadn't told her about the three-year-old clip, and she hadn't found it on the internet. The people closest to Stephen Harper started looking at her as the person who'd be blamed if the Tories lost their majority.

The campaign was already a month old when Bance's moment of personal relief made the news. Harper had decided on a seventy-eight-day campaign, a long one that allowed the Conservatives to spend more of their big war chest. (The 1997, 2000, and 2004 elections were just thirty-six days long.[1] The 2006 election ran over Christmas and was sixty-six days. Only the election campaign of 1871 was longer.) The vote was held October 19.

People tend to tune out of politics during the summer, but Harper's people campaigned hard against the NDP after the election was called on August 2 and had pushed them out of the lead by the time the first leaders' debate was held. Although the Tories had quickly burned through the budget surplus left by Paul Martin within two years and had only eked out a balanced budget in the 2014–15 fiscal year, the Tories warned voters that a Trudeau government would put the country's finances back into the red, and the NDP would be even worse. NDP leader Tom Mulcair, who'd once been a Quebec Liberal cabinet minister who was tight with a buck, derailed his own party's campaign in late August by promising to balance the federal budget. People on the left of the political spectrum knew he'd have to cut programs and federal jobs to do that. People on the centre-right who worry about government debt—many Liberals and Red Tories—didn't believe Mulcair or, if they did, weren't going to switch their vote. His party's numbers started to tank. In Quebec, the Liberals were ready to pick up the lost NDP votes.

The Tories, who, since their Reform days, had claimed to be above the sleazy dealings of Liberal Ottawa, had an image problem. The campaign coincided with the trial of suspended Conservative senator Mike Duffy on charges of expense fraud. Duffy would be acquitted almost a year after this election, but media reports were still full of the embarrassing evidence presented at the trial. People had a hard time believing that Nigel Wright, Harper's chief of staff had, out of charity, used $90,000 of his own money to pay off expenses that the court later found Duffy had never owed. (Charges were expected to be laid against other Liberal and Tory senators for their expense claims, but that didn't happen.) Duffy's legal problems were becoming old news, but they undermined the holier-than-thou Tories who claimed to be political outsiders who'd come to Ottawa to muck out corruption.

The NDP and the Tories also lost votes because of their policies on minorities, especially Muslims. In the later summer of 2015, thousands of people, fleeing the Syrian civil war, travelled through Turkey to central Europe. This caused a political crisis in Germany, which accepted hundreds of thousands of refugees. Many other countries barred the door, including Greece, which tried to prevent Syrians from entering. In late August, Abdullah and Rehana Kurdi loaded their little sons Ghalib and Alan into a small boat to try to make the four-kilometre crossing from mainland Turkey to the Greek island of Kos. Soon afterwards, the boat fell apart. Rehana and the two boys drowned. It was just one of the many tragedies on the Mediterranean that summer, but a photo of three-year-old Alan lying dead on a Turkish beach became iconic. Usually, a story like this would have little effect on Canadian politics, but the Kurdis were trying to get to Canada, where Abdullah's sister Tima lived. Hours after the photo was posted on the internet, Tima called a press conference and told reporters her relatives turned to human smugglers and lost their lives because Canada's government refused to let them come to Canada legally. The opposition parties jumped on that, and it took the Conservatives a week to show the Kurdis had never applied.[2] Journalists didn't let that fact get in the way of a good story. Abdullah Kurdi was under fire for human smuggling, and he fought back, blaming Canada. The Tories' defence was buried deep in a Canadian Press story headlined: "Drowned Syrian migrant boy's father says he blames Canada for tragedy." And, by the end of the campaign, voters who were still interested in the Kurdi family knew that it didn't really matter whether the Kurdis had applied: the Harper government had effectively blocked all immigration from Syria. The immigration department had stopped processing applications from Syria, and any that might have been approved had to be greenlit by the Prime Minister's Office.[3]

The furor over little Alan Kurdi's death was just starting to cool when another racially charged issue came up. Zunera Ishaq, an immigrant from Pakistan, wanted to take the citizenship oath wearing a niqab, a garment that covers all of a woman's face except her eyes. Immigration minister Jason Kenney refused, and Ishaq sued. She won in the Federal Court of Canada, and Kenney's department appealed. On September 15, Ishaq won. This fired up bigots in Quebec and English Canada. The Bloc Quebecois loudly condemned the court's decision and the wearing of niqabs, burkas, and hijabs. Mulcair defended the rights of the country's Muslims to wear what they wanted. This cost him support in Quebec, especially in NDP ridings outside of Montreal that were already shaky. Trudeau—as he would be through most of his time in office—was quiet about the issue.[4]

Harper, Byrne, and the rest of the campaign team thought they had found a winning issue, one that would appeal to patriotic Canadians. "When someone joins the Canadian family, there are times in our open, tolerant, pluralistic society, that as part of our interactions with each other, we reveal our identity through revealing our face," Harper said at a campaign event. "And when you join the Canadian family in a public citizenship ceremony, it is essential that that is a time when you reveal yourselves to Canadians, and that is something widely supported by Canadians." The Conservatives also bought ads telling Quebec voters, "Justin Trudeau is totally disconnected from the values of Quebecers. Justin says 'Oui' to the niqab."[5]

The Conservatives' poll numbers started to rise, showing their campaign had hurt the NDP, but the Liberals were rising as well. By the middle of the campaign, the fifty-nine (out of seventy-five) NDP seats that Layton won in Quebec in the 2011 "Orange Crush" election were in play. But it was the Liberals, not Harper's Tories, who were favoured to win these seats. Still, the Conservatives seemed likely to come back with a minority government.

But, from the start, they'd underestimated Trudeau. He was as close as the country came since his father's retirement in 1984 to a political celebrity. Trudeau packed in big crowds on college campuses. American media ran cheesecake shots of him. A note he wrote that read "Just watch me!" in response to a kid's letter asking if Trudeau could beat Harper sold for $12,000 in a charity auction.[6] The *New York Times* ran a story about the political value of Justin Trudeau's hair, which even had its own Twitter account.[7]

The Tories tried to use Trudeau's youth against him by running a series of ads saying "Justin Trudeau: He's just not ready."[8] The ads sent a strange message: presumably, someday, Trudeau would be ready. Some voters wondered if the Tories would let the country know when that happened. Trudeau did well in a leaders' debate, but it was held in the first week of the campaign, when many voters were on vacation. On September 17, Trudeau went to Calgary, the belly of the Tory beast, to debate Harper and Mulcair on economic issues in a debate moderated by David Walmsley, editor of the *Globe and Mail*. Trudeau needed to beat expectations, and he did. All that money spent on the "He's just not ready" campaign was wasted. This was also the debate where Harper spoke of "old-stock Canadians," which his opponents claimed was a racist dog whistle.[9]

As the chance of a second majority melted away, Canadians, already used to seeing a cold Stephen Harper, started seeing a desperate one. Realizing the NDP bled votes in Quebec on the niqab issue, the Tories tried to make Muslim religious and cultural practices an election issue in English Canada. Earlier that year, it had passed the *Zero Tolerance for Barbaric Cultural Practices Act* with very little blowback from the media. This law banned forced marriages. It also targeted honour killings and child marriages, even though both were already illegal. (Criminal law never gave a break to people who commit "honour killings" and underage marriage, like underage sex, has always been illegal. The minimum marriage age in Canada is sixteen, but people between sixteen and eighteen years old need written consent from a judge.) The Tories also talked tough about female genital mutilation. Polygamists were barred from immigrating to Canada, and clerics who married underaged couples could be charged.[10]

On October 2, a little more than two weeks before Canadians went to the polls, the Tories dropped a bomb. Immigration minister Chris Alexander, who'd been Canada's ambassador to Afghanistan at the end of a career in the foreign service then stayed in Afghanistan for five years working for the United Nations, and Labour minister Kellie Leitch held a weird press conference. They announced plans for a "barbaric cultural practices" tip line to the RCMP that would allow people to report violations of the *Zero Tolerance for Barbaric Cultural Practices Act*, things like forced marriage and polygamy. Why this tip line was needed was left unexplained: there was nothing preventing snitches from calling the police. The Tories, if re-elected, would create an integrated RCMP task force with units in Vancouver, Calgary, Winnipeg, Toronto, and Montreal to step up enforcement of the act. While Britain's left-wing *Guardian* newspaper believed Canadians were a bigoted lot who would reinstall the Tories in gratitude, fair-minded Canadians saw the hotline for what it was: a desperate, last-minute gambit to save the Harper government.[11] The tip-line news conference ended the political careers of Leitch and Alexander, though it took them a couple of years to realize it. Alexander was crushed by Liberal Mark Holland in his home riding of Ajax. Leitch held on to her seat in central Ontario but quit politics before the 2019 election when local municipal politicians challenged her for the Conservative nomination in her riding. Both ran in the 2017 Tory leadership race: Leitch placed sixth, Alexander was tenth in a field of thirteen.

Canadian voters, like those in most other democracies, like to be on the side of a winner. By late September, Trudeau had the momentum. In the days leading up to the election, it was just a matter of whether Trudeau would win a majority or be kept to a minority. Trudeau dazzled progressive voters with the promise that 2015 would be the last "first past the post" campaign. But in the end, the system worked for Trudeau: because of the NDP collapse in Quebec and the very uneven distribution of Conservative votes—where Conservatives win, they tend to win big—Trudeau's Liberals formed a majority government with less than 40 percent of the vote. On election night, Harper announced he was finished as Tory leader.

WHETHER THERE'S AN official election campaign or not, Poilievre is always looking for votes. An election allows him to do it full time. In July 2015, just before Harper asked the governor general to dissolve Parliament, Poilievre went to Halifax to announce an expansion of the federal child-care-benefit program. Poilievre made the announcement as social development minister but wore a Conservative Party of Canada shirt. He told the Haligonians the money was from "our Conservative government." Then he warned, "If the Liberals and NDP were to take office they would take the benefits away and raise taxes." The Liberals and New Democrats called the $4 billion announcement a blatant attempt to buy votes.

Trudeau told a reporter for the online news site iPolitics that the Harper government constantly conflated the interests of the government of Canada with the interests of his own political party. It wasn't a novel claim: it's been made about ruling parties for generations, usually with some accuracy. Still, this was treated as news.

"It's something they just do, they're just getting more and more blatant about it, and it's a way of enhancing cynicism that drives

Canadians away from politics. For me, it's just an extension of a culture that's focused on winning rather than focused on actually serving Canadians," Trudeau said.[12]

To rub salt in the wound, the Liberals complained to Elections Canada that Poilievre was using federal government travel money, rather than Conservative Party funds, to pay for a partisan event. (It took Elections Canada two years to decide Poilievre's critics had been right.)[13]

In his own riding, some interesting candidates challenged Poilievre. Deborah Coyne, mother of Trudeau's half-sister, quit the Liberals and ran for the Greens. (Coyne got a lot of press coverage but a paltry 3.2 percent of the vote.) The NDP candidate Kc Larocque ran a weak campaign, which helped Liberal Chris Rodgers, a public servant at Public Safety Canada who took a leave of absence to run.[14] "I know it sounds idealistic," Rodgers told a local reporter, "but I want our son to know that ordinary people run for office."[15]

The campaign began with a lot of Poilievre signs on roadsides and lawns, but for the first time since 2004, he was feeling the heat. After all he'd done for the riding—landing federal funding for a badly needed bridge on a commuter route, trying to get a better rent deal for a local hospital, raising money for community organizations like the Royal Canadian Legion, which needed to replace a hall that burned down—he was getting a rough ride. In the affluent Ottawa satellite community of Manotick, where the local paper had praised Poilievre for years and gave him a lot of coverage for anything he said or did, people who turned up at an all-candidates' meeting targeted Poilievre. They badgered him on his *Fair Elections Act* and the Harper government's muzzling of federal scientists.[16]

Poilievre started picking up more signs that his party was in trouble. National polls were bad, but local surveys, admittedly far less accurate, also showed a big voter shift, even in the Tory-dominated Ottawa suburbs. Boundary changes took away some of the built-up area of Nepean–Carleton and added a chunk of farm country, which helped Poilievre and might have even saved his career.[17] Still, he believed he was in trouble. The Professional Institute of the Public Service of Canada (PIPSC), a union that represented skilled government workers, targeted him. The union was angry that the Harper government had pushed through a law that allowed the government to impose a collective agreement on its workers, ending the unions' ability to negotiate contracts and strike. Trudeau jumped on this, issuing a statement to Ottawa-area public servants.

"Respect and trust for our public servants by the federal government has never been so low, and I want to take this opportunity to assure you that I have a fundamentally different view than Stephen Harper of our public service," Trudeau wrote in the open letter. Harper answered with a letter of his own, promising to listen to federal workers.

Debi Daviau, president of the PIPSC, said Harper's letter showed Ottawa Tories, who held almost all the ridings outside of the downtown, were "quite desperate. You can bet that these guys have had a lot of doors slammed in their faces, at this point," she said. "I'm thinking that they're facing a lot of opposition, when they're going door to door in this region."

She could have pointed to Poilievre, who suddenly embraced public servants and promised to protect their pay and benefits. During this campaign he wasn't calling them fat cats and gatekeepers. Now, he was promising to protect their sick leave and pensions. Pundits and writers like Michael Harris, author of the bestseller *Party of One*, wrote about the friction, even open warfare, between the Tories and the bureaucracy.[18] Now, Poilievre was saying things he never said before 2015 and hasn't said since: "We have a good relationship, and we're very lucky to have the best civil servants in the world, who have helped us balance the budget, cut taxes and protect Canadians from terrorism." Public servants, he said, "have worked with integrity and professionalism to make this government a success. Canadians are well-served by our world-class public servants, and our Prime Minister has seen their work and appreciates it first-hand. Our government is thankful for the hard work of public servants in upholding the interests of Canadians."

It was Poilievre, not Tony Clement, the minister who was supposed to be in charge of the public service, who was invited to downtown Ottawa to read Harper's response to Trudeau's open letter. This was a sign that the campaign thought the Ottawa seats were in trouble and that the only way to save them was by winning some votes from the 127,000 federal workers who lived in the region. (Clement was also losing support, but his riding didn't have many federal workers.)[19]

Poilievre, who tried to run on local issues and his record as a hard-working constituency MP, also latched onto the Muslim-bashing that the Tories (and Bloc Quebecois) used to win the bigot vote. Poilievre made it clear he supported his party's opposition to the niqabs. "We are not going to succumb to political correctness in order to accommodate a practice that is not in line with Canadian values," he told reporters.[20]

In the end, Poilievre took 46.9 percent of the vote with just 1,949 more votes than Liberal candidate Chris Rodgers. It was much closer than in 2011, when he won by more than 20,000 votes, with the caveat that the riding boundaries had changed a bit.

And not only had Poilievre praised the bureaucracy during the campaign, but he was still generous when he gave his election night victory speech. He was "deeply grateful" to voters, Poilievre told the Tories at his victory party. "I want them to know that I have never taken this honour for granted," he said. "It has never belonged to me, it has been lent to me, and the people have the right to give and they have the right to take away because this is their country."

People at the celebration expected to hear that. The surprise came when Poilievre congratulated the seven Liberals who won seats in Ottawa. And he praised Justin Trudeau for "stirring a lot of passion and interest in our democracy."[21] As for the accusation that Harper and Poilievre wanted to suppress the vote, the results of their fight with Elections Canada are hard to quantify. Their $6 million cuts to Elections Canada's budget stopped the agency from rolling out an online voting experiment. (It hasn't tried to revive the idea.) Probably because this was obviously a "change" election, voter interest was high. Trudeau's campaign targeted new voters, and voter turnout rose by more than 10 percent.[22]

THE 2015 ELECTION changed Poilievre's life. He was out of cabinet, which meant he took a pay cut and lost key perks: a car and chauffeur, access to the fleet of Challenger private jets, the VIP treatment when he stayed in hotels and visited provincial capitals. Lobbyists weren't as interested in speaking with him. But, unlike sixty of his Tory colleagues—more than a third of Harper's caucus—Poilievre still had a job. He was now the senior Tory in the Ottawa area. Baird had bailed before the election, and the Liberals took his riding. Poilievre's party was looking for a new leader, which opened opportunities for him to try to identify the winner and help in the campaign.

The Tories had expected to win, even if they lost their majority. Someone had to be blamed. Jenni Byrne, who was no longer Poilievre's partner but was still a friend and political ally, had the title of campaign manager, even if Harper and a few men around him made many of the big decisions. When the party brought in an Australian political strategist to analyze the campaign, he put a lot of the blame on Byrne. People who understood Harper's controlling personality knew that the loss wasn't her fault. The leader himself and his chief adviser, Guy Giorno, made some of the decisions that had ruined the campaign.

Byrne was in the wilderness while Andrew Scheer led the party, though Erin O'Toole and Poilievre stood by her. Byrne's career revived in 2018, when she played a key role on Doug Ford's winning campaign team in Ontario. She stayed in Toronto to help Ford run the provincial government.

By 2013, when Poilievre was working on the *Fair Elections Act*, he had a new girlfriend, Anaida Galindo, a twenty-five-year-old Senate staffer. Poilievre asked her out when he met her on Parliament Hill and took the reluctant young woman out on long dates. The attraction, at least from his side, is obvious: Anaida is pretty, smart, dynamic, and strong. Poilievre's charms are a little more difficult to identify. He is smart, extremely ambitious, and he had a cabinet job. He was good with money, owning his own home and investing in real estate in Ottawa and Calgary. Poilievre can be funny, and he'd been spending long hours doing brutal workouts at Tony Greco's downtown gym. Poilievre was a love-him-or-hate-him kind of guy, and Anaida went into the relationship unsure which way it would go.

Their first date was at a new downtown coffee shop that was empty. Cabinet ministers, being famous in Ottawa, need to be discreet to prevent their romantic lives from ending up in the media. They were let in before the shop opened for the day. Poilievre pushed aside Anaida's concerns that he was moving too fast. He sent her poetry. Within a couple of weeks of their first evening out, Pierre told Anaida he loved her. These things are usually buzzkills that are fatal to relationships, but Pierre won Anaida over.[23] They found they had some things in common: Catholicism, a conservative world view, belief in the power of cryptocurrencies, ambition, and a strong work ethic. Fairly quickly, the couple moved in together in Poilievre's new house in the Ottawa satellite village of Greely, an even less fashionable part of the National Capital Region but inside the new boundaries of Poilievre's riding.

Anaida worked on Poilievre's campaign in Carleton in 2015 and has been an important ally ever since. A tough political fighter who's written some nasty posts on social media and is fanatically dedicated to her husband's political career, she is often the focus of speculation and invented "facts" spread by the couple's political enemies. Fantastic and bizarre rumours about political leaders' spouses are normal in the Ottawa bubble, which is another reason why so many bright and talented people avoid politics.[24]

These nasty stories, none of which have a speck of evidence of truth, tend to focus on her family. The Galindos immigrated to the Montreal area from Venezuela in 1995. Anaida's father fled Caracas during the political instability that later brought Hugo Chávez to power. He'd been a bank manager in Venezuela, but the best job he could get in Montreal was unloading fruit and vegetables from trucks. "That's what he had to do to feed his family," Anaida told delegates to the 2022 Tory leadership convention. "There is no greater dignity than to provide for your own family." Even with her father's work ethic, the family lived "paycheque to paycheque," where a tank of gasoline was a luxury. The poverty eased after the family started a small business.

Anaida finished high school and enrolled in communications at the University of Ottawa. It wasn't long before the twenty-year-old Anaida was on Parliament Hill, working for a senator. By 2013, she was foreign affairs adviser to the government leader in the Senate and dating Poilievre.

The couple was married in 2017 in a two-person wedding ceremony in southern Portugal. They'd never been there before: the wedding was organized by a local wedding planner and no parents, siblings, or friends were invited. "It was the best decision we could have made. We wanted to make sure that our special day was truly just about us and our commitment to each other," Anaida wrote in *Pretty and Smart*, an online magazine she'd founded.[25]

The couple has two children. Their oldest child, Valentina, has been diagnosed with autism and is non-verbal. Pierre, who had advocated for parents of autistic children many years before Valentina's birth, would have known what services and treatments were available to his daughter.[26] In September 2021 the Poilievres had a son they named Cruz. Even though they have young children, Anaida has been on the road with Pierre since he made his move for the party leadership.

—

JUSTIN TRUDEAU'S GOVERNMENT enjoyed a short honeymoon with voters who liked his "sunny ways" (a phrase swiped from Sir Wilfrid Laurier) and with media who were sick of Stephen Harper's lock on information. In 2016, Donald Trump won the US presidential election, and politics started getting much meaner on both sides of the border. Conservatives chose Andrew Scheer to lead them.

This was good news for Poilievre. Interim leader Rona Ambrose had given Poilievre the glamour-free job of critic for the Treasury Board, a good fit for an Ottawa MP and a chance to win support from public servants in his riding, but Andrew Scheer, who'd been speaker of the House of Commons in the previous Parliament, was named finance critic. When Scheer began his campaign to lead the party, Ambrose made Poilievre the shadow minister of finance. This was the second-best job in opposition, and Poilievre was in the news a lot, bashing finance minister Bill Morneau for conflicts of interest and making digs about his family's vast fortune. He was an effective if somewhat annoying critic.

In 2017, Poilievre introduced a private member's bill to amend the *Federal-Provincial Arrangements Act* to eliminate personal income taxes and payroll taxes paid by people with disabilities. Now, disabled people get a tax deduction, about the same as those seniors are entitled to, after they jump through a lot of Canada Revenue Agency hoops. This bill was a sensible way to deal with clawbacks on the incomes of disabled people, who often have to work because provincial support payments are ridiculously low. Some high earners might have made serious money off this tax break, but mostly it would have helped the poor. Poilievre told the House of Commons, "Work is a basic human need. Its wages feed, clothe, and shelter us. It offers the pride and purpose of doing something valuable for others. Work makes us a living. It also helps us to make a life. That is why almost a million Canadians with disabilities work—including about 300,000 with severe disabilities, according to Statistics Canada—but the system effectively bans many more from working. It is called the 'welfare wall,' and here is how it works. When people with disabilities earn a paycheque, governments sharply claw back supports for income, housing, medications, and other help. These clawbacks, plus taxes, mean that often people are poorer when they work more. They are stuck behind the welfare wall.

"For example, if a person with disabilities who is earning the minimum wage in Saskatchewan goes from working part time to working full time, he would see his take-home pay drop from $21,600 to $21,500 on an annual basis. That is right: he is working double the hours and making less money at the end of the year."

The bill won NDP support, but it was voted down by the majority Liberals and the Bloc Quebecois on second reading, before a Commons committee could hold hearings that would have put Poilievre and his law in the news.[27]

An academic study published by Laval University in the summer of 2019 found the Trudeau government had kept 92 percent of its 2015 campaign promises, but it had reneged on a big one: electoral reform. Trudeau, on the hustings, promised the 2015 campaign would be the last first-past-the-post election where candidates with the most votes win each riding. Usually, with three or four serious contenders in most ridings, MPs are elected with somewhere between 30 and 50 percent of the vote. That means people are often represented by an MP whom most people voted *against*. Political parties often form large majority governments while only winning well under half of the country's vote. In 2015, Trudeau ended Stephen Harper's political career and brought the Liberals back to power with a large majority in Parliament by winning just 39.47 percent of the popular vote.

For awhile, Trudeau's government seemed serious about electoral reform. Karina Gould, one of the brightest of the young ministers in Trudeau's government, was given the file. But she had no backing: Trudeau opposed proportional representation, even though 80 percent of developed nations have systems of proportional representation using multi-member representation. At most, he supported ranked ballots, which are used by most Canadian political parties to choose their leaders. Gould became one of the high-profile women cabinet ministers whom Trudeau tossed under the bus. She took the blame when Trudeau abandoned the idea of changing the first-past-the-post system.[28]

In February 2019, Jody Wilson-Raybould, an Indigenous lawyer who was leadership material, resigned from her cabinet position and claimed she had been pressured to cut a deal for SNC-Lavalin. This Quebec-based engineering firm had a lot of clout in its home province and was a big Liberal donor. The breakup between Wilson-Raybould and the Liberals was messy: she took the health minister, Jane Philpott with her, and the controversy cost Gerry Butts, Trudeau's best friend and closest adviser, his job as head of the Prime Minister's Office. Voters went into the 2019 election with reminders of the Quebec-based scandals that destroyed Paul Martin's government.

Some locally important Liberal MPs like Stéphane Dion and Denis Coderre had left federal politics for better jobs, which weakened Trudeau in Quebec.[29] The election was an opportunity for Scheer, but his campaign went poorly, and it ended with headline-grabbing news that the Tories had paid a political operative to attack People's Party leader Maxime Bernier on social media.[30] Scheer still won more votes than Trudeau, but they weren't cast where the Tories needed them. Tory votes tended to increase in ridings they already held rather than put Conservative candidates ahead in close ridings. Scheer picked up just twenty-six new seats. The Liberals took seats away from the NDP, now led by Jagmeet Singh, and the Bloc Quebecois. Elizabeth May's Green Party got over a million votes for the first time, an achievement that showed the failings of the first-past-the post system, since her party won just two seats. Scheer could only reduce Trudeau's Liberals to a minority in Parliament. It was a decent showing, considering the scandals that embroiled Scheer's campaign in the last days, but the Tories wanted a winner, and it didn't take long for them to begin pushing their leader out. Poilievre, who beat Chris Rodgers, running again for the Liberals, by 5,500 votes, saw this winner every time he looked in a mirror.

THE LAST YEAR before the Covid pandemic was a lousy year for a lot of people: Trump mayhem in American federal politics; Brexit; big fires in North America, Australia, and the Amazon; a hurricane in the Bahamas; a lethal attack on a New Zealand mosque; an Ebola outbreak in East Africa that killed a thousand people. People were miserable, and pundits writing their year-end columns asked if 2019 was the worst year in recent memory. Poilievre seemed to be spinning his wheels: in May 2019, House of Commons speaker Geoff Regan scolded him for calling Trudeau "Little Potato" three days in a row, reaching back to a pet name the prime minister was given during a trip to China.[31] This could hardly be a fulfilling way to make a living. But the new year would make 2019 seem like the good old days. Somehow, a new coronavirus was loose in the Chinese city of Wuhan, home to the Wuhan Laboratory of Virology.

A few items about Covid-19 were buried in the year-end news, but people knew by the end of January that this was a serious health threat. Canadians remembered the Severe Acute Respiratory Syndrome (SARS) outbreak that killed forty-four people in Toronto in 2003. In China, SARS killed nearly 10 percent of the people who caught it. In Toronto, it spread through hospitals and sometimes got out into the community. Thousands of people were quarantined, tourism collapsed, the federal government issued travel advisories, and people were screened for SARS at the country's airports. When it was clear the SARS outbreak was over, the city celebrated with a self-congratulatory outdoor concert headlined by the Rolling Stones. People thought Canada's public health workers had done a good job. In fact, the system, with its three levels of bureaucracy—municipal, provincial and federal—hadn't been able to explain SARS and its threat to the public. The country's main media outlets, headquartered in the city, overhyped the outbreak.

It didn't help that this new virus was of the same genus as the 2002–04 outbreak. People saw the scary stories from Wuhan, where the disease killed the young doctor who'd blown the whistle on China's cover-up of it. The infection of people on a cruise ship stuck in Yokohama harbour showed public health doctors were wrong when they insisted the disease was spread by droplets that came from coughing and sneezing people: people who stayed in their cabins were getting sick and dying. Later, scientists would say the lethality rate of Covid-19 was about .05 percent of infections, still thirteen times worse than seasonal flu but much less than the disease that terrified Toronto seventeen years before. (The overall fatality numbers may be misleading, as most people caught Covid after the roll-out of vaccines. The infection numbers peaked in 2022, as "truckers" frolicked in front of Parliament Hill.)

In the early months, northern Italy was hit hard, and 2.5 percent of the people who caught Covid in that country died of the disease. Mass graves were dug on an island in the East River to handle New York City's dead. Covid was more lethal to the elderly and the obese. When it arrived in Canada in late February 2020, it killed hundreds of people in nursing homes, including one in Montreal where staff abandoned residents to their fate. An inquest found that forty-seven of them died of Covid, starved to death, or died of thirst.[32]

By the beginning of April, nearly ten thousand Canadians had caught the disease, and it had spread all over the world. Cruel kids called it "boomer remover" while newspapers and television newscasts frightened people with graphic accounts of death on respirators. By mid-March, the country was shutting down. Although most students were relatively safe, the universities and colleges closed, then the high schools and elementary schools. Stores and restaurants were next. Government employees worked from home, trying to maintain public services and come up with ways to save the economy as world stock markets tanked.

This was when David Brooks wrote his "rippers and weavers" column. Canadians and Americans insisted they pulled together in a crisis, a claim that doesn't bear scrutiny. In the Second World War, Canada was a divided nation. Quebec's media opposed participation in the war. Recruitment was tough, and it was politically impossible to bring in a draft (conscription) law without a promise from the government that draftees would not be sent overseas. At Christmas 1944, generals were threatening to resign en masse and draftee mutinies were being put down in British Columbia, Ontario, and New Brunswick. Families broke up. (There's a famous picture of a little boy reaching for his dad as hundreds of soldiers marched down a New Westminster street. The boy's mom, who's chasing the boy, sent her husband a "Dear John" letter when he was overseas.) In 2020, the Canadian consensus lasted while federal public servants came up with new programs that saved many families' finances. There were quick cash payments to people who'd lost their jobs, money to bail out small businesses and organizations, and rent subsidies for businesses that rented their stores or offices. It was a spectacular pivot, made more impressive by the fact that public servants were coming up with these things at their kitchen tables or in their home offices.

This was not a good environment for opposition politicians. There was some bitching early in the pandemic about government overreach, especially when municipalities put police tape on playground equipment and bylaw officers wrote fat tickets to people jogging by themselves. The Conservatives were absorbed in a leadership race that Poilievre seriously considered joining in the late fall of 2019. He'd even talked about a campaign team, with Jenni Byrne as a key member. In the end, he decided it wasn't his time yet.

Instead, as finance critic, Poilievre was the Tory point man on the Trudeau government's response to Covid. For once, the party had not appointed an interim leader, so Scheer, still smarting from being pushed out, remained the public face of the party. He left the big decisions on the Covid file to Poilievre. The Liberals, believing Covid was the greatest test of a government since the Second World War, wanted unanimous support in the House of Commons for its major relief programs. Poilievre often stood in the way, claiming Covid spending was just a Liberal excuse to funnel money to favourite causes like climate change and enrich Liberal friends. Yet Poilievre did not offer any alternatives. The prime minister wanted to be able to bail out big industries like airlines and hotel chains, which had completely shut down. Poilievre tried to block them until he was reminded that, during the 2008 American financial crisis, Stephen Harper had bailed out companies that built cars and light trucks in Canada and had given this country's banks $25 billion in government credit. (Trudeau's government ended owning up more than 6 percent of Air Canada. Its share price had fallen from about $50 at the beginning of 2020 to $12.40 on March 22, 2020. At the end of November 2024, the shares were worth about $25.)

Still, during the early weeks of the crisis, political strategists hadn't found ways to use the pandemic as a wedge issue. That would change.

8
WRECKING WE CHARITY

For as much as [Poilievre] is always putting the elbow in your face, he can be likeable and charming.

CHARLIE ANGUS, NDP MP
FOR TIMMINS-JAMES BAY, 2021.

CRAIG KIELBURGER, SON of two schoolteachers living in the Toronto suburb of Thornhill, was twelve years old in 1995 when he came across a *Toronto Star* story about Iqbal Masih, a Pakistani child labourer who was murdered for speaking out against abuses in his country's carpet factories. The Kielburgers are the kind of people whose adolescent children kept up with current events. It's a family built on hard work: rather than take summers off, Craig's parents bought houses, fixed them up, and sold them. The Toronto real estate market has been one of the hottest in the world in the past fifty years, so this turned out to be a wise investment in money and time.

Iqbal Masih's parents sold him to the owner of a Pakistani carpet factory. Masih's parents were no Kielburgers: they offered their four-year-old as collateral for a loan to pay for their eldest son's wedding. His enslaver worked the boy twelve hours a day tying the tiny knots on carpets. He got barely enough to eat, and the cost of his food was added to the loan. When Masih's parents paid the loan down a bit, the carpet maker topped it up by charging for "mistakes" made by the child. Masih was beaten whenever his enslaver felt like it. A non-government organization rescued Masih and sent him to school when he was ten. Two years later, after his story went public, Masih was murdered. The killer was never caught, but everyone knew who was behind it.

After reading the story, Craig Kielburger wanted to do something about child labour. He learned there were some 250 million children working in factories, mines, and other often-dangerous places, mostly in the developing world.[1] Craig, with the help of his mom, Theresa, started organizing small fundraising events in Thornhill.

With a small group of friends and his brother, Craig started a small children's charity, Free the Children. In addition to their small fundraising events in Thornhill, they collected three thousand signatures on a petition to the Indian government calling for the release of Kailash Satyarthi, an activist jailed for advocating for the freedom of child workers.

Satyarthi, who would later win the Nobel Peace Prize, was eventually released and, at the end of 1995, he invited Craig to meet child labourers in South Asia. Kielburger was staying with Satyarthi when Jean Chrétien led a trade-boosting visit to Asia, including Bangladesh. Kielburger caught up to the prime minister in Dacca in February 1996 and again confronted him about the problem with child labour. Canadian journalists again covered the exchange, cementing Kielburger's celebrity status.

Free the Children grew fast, recruiting one hundred thousand supporters in Canada and abroad and raising $150,000 in its first few months. Through 1996, money flowed in, and journalists asked for interviews. The Ontario Federation of Labour provided organizational and managerial help. Free the Children seemed to be saving a lot of kids from exploitation, but follow-up checks showed many of them had been forced back to work. Free the Children's leaders realized the need for systemic change. Rather than disrupt sweatshops, Free the Children began building schools in Nicaragua, Kenya, Ecuador, and India, some of the places where the worst abuses happened. When Oprah Winfrey had Craig on her show in 1999, the movement really took off.

Marc Kielburger, Craig's older brother, was studying international relations at Harvard when the Free the Children movement started. Marc worked with Craig on the project in his spare time. He went to Oxford on a Rhodes Scholarship in 2000 and earned a law degree, specializing in international law. When he graduated, he joined the Free the Children project.

Just before Craig went on Oprah, the brothers organized a party to celebrate thousands of high school students who volunteered for Free the Children. This WE Day was so successful that it became a main part of the engine of Free the Children's branding and fundraising. These events spread to seventeen cities across Canada, the United States, and Britain. Students earned tickets to WE Days by volunteering for community work. World leaders and celebrities like Prince Harry, Lewis Hamilton, Idris Elba, Gord Downie, Kate Winslet, Sarah McLachlan, Lilly Singh, Selena Gomez, Demi Lovato, Jennifer Hudson, Nelly Furtado, and Chloe Wilde attracted them to WE Days. Justin Trudeau, who hadn't yet been elected to Parliament, spoke at one of the early WE Days. The next year, Ben Mulroney, another prime minister's son, became a recurring WE Day host for primetime broadcasts on CTV.

WE Days were part concert, part TED Talk. Kids packed Madison Square Gardens, London's Wembley Arena, Toronto's Scotiabank Arena, and the Los Angeles Forum. Big corporations started to make big donations. International development charities, especially those in Canada, had never done anything as successful. This explains some of the negative blowback the Kielburgers felt in their home country.

Free the Children (WE Charity after 2016) mixed corporate concepts with progressive causes. It created alliances and partnerships with anyone who could help. To help pay for the charity's work, WE started a "social enterprise," a profit-making business, ME to WE, to sell fair-trade products from the developing world. The charity arm got those profits. This wasn't anything new—the Salvation Army has done this for decades with their thrift stores, and the Mennonite Central Committee has its Ten Thousand Villages chain—but for some reason, Canadian journalists and politicians could never get their heads around this.[2] Tapping financial and construction company donors, WE Charity developed a headquarters in a seedy corner of the edge of downtown Toronto. By 2020, it had bought up distressed neighbouring properties and planned to turn this real estate into a nursery for social enterprises run by other charities.

The Kielburgers were celebrities, but they were not part of Toronto's incestuous in-crowd. They didn't try to join it. And they seemed a little *off* to Canada's rather cynical trend-setters. They were too nice, too upbeat, always positive. Their public personas came from their jobs. Media people saw their master of ceremonies work at WE Days, read their inspirational books, and came up with stereotypes of these two young men that had little to do with reality. Left-wing critics claimed the Kielburgers and their charity were cover for corporations that should be taxed somehow to pay to solve poverty issues and undo the damage of colonialism.[3]

In early March 2020, I visited Marc Kielburger at WE's headquarters. I was in the city for a literary event just as Covid was spreading into North America, Europe, South America, and Asian countries outside China. Marc had just come back from the last WE Day in London, not knowing Covid had spread backstage at Wembley Stadium. The rest of the year's WE Day events were cancelled. Schools were closing, so WE's educational programs were on hold, and almost all the staff was laid off or working from home. Marc believed Covid would spread through Africa quickly and that continent, with its frail medical infrastructure, would be the hardest-hit part of the world. Since WE created Baraka Hospital and Kishon

Health Centre in the Masai country and trained nurses in its Kenyan college, the organization could help mitigate Covid's damage in that country. Marc expected 2020 to be a year of challenge and transition.

He had no idea.

JUSTIN TRUDEAU WAS a teacher before he went into politics. His father, with his friends Senator Jacques Hébert and defence minister Barney Danson, created Katimavik, a national youth service program, in 1977. Tory prime ministers Brian Mulroney and Stephen Harper had tried to shut it down as a waste of money, but it survived because Senator Hébert and other friends of Pierre Trudeau fought to save it. Justin Trudeau was also a vocal backer of the program before he went into politics. When he made the jump into politics, Trudeau was made the Liberal youth issues critic. In 2015, he became prime minister and, a few weeks after the election, was on stage at a WE Day in Ottawa's NHL arena.

Before Covid, Trudeau's poll numbers were tanking. Indigenous activists had blocked rail lines to support the Wet'suwet'en First Nation, who opposed the construction of the Coast GasLink pipeline in its territory. This dispute cost Trudeau support on the left side of the political spectrum. The federal government's cancellation of Teck Resource's $20 billion Frontier Oilsands Mine added to his unpopularity among people in Alberta and Saskatchewan. But in the first weeks of the pandemic, Trudeau's approval rating peaked at 55 percent, its highest since 2016.[4] Trudeau reassured Canadians that the country could get through this. The Canadian government's quick transition into a work-from-home bureaucracy and its quick creation and rollout of relief programs during the Covid outbreak is one of the great untold stories of recent Canadian history. Nothing like this happened in Canadian history, even in wartime.[5]

As successful as the pandemic-response rollouts were, none of these popular new programs were aimed at helping students, who were on the verge of missing out on key summer jobs. Finance minister Bill Morneau's adviser Amitpal Singh suggested the development of a youth volunteer program through the Canada Service Corps, which ran Katimavik. Morneau greenlit the exploration of options. On April 18, Morneau's officials briefed him on the limitations of the Canada Service Corps and discussed the possibility of using a non-government organization instead. On April 19, senior assistant deputy minister Rachel Wernick sent an email to Craig Kielburger. "I wondered if you would have a bit of time today to indulge me [in] a quick conversation on something we are working on that might be of interest to WE," she wrote. "There is a window of opportunity today to influence thinking and I would greatly benefit from your thoughts."

Three days later, WE Charity submitted a proposal for a $44.5 million youth program, $30 million of which would be paid in grants to students, $12 million spent on administration, and $2.5 million given to participating charities. That same day, without giving the charity advance warning, the government announced the Canada Student Service Grant (CSSG) program.

Within two weeks, the program ballooned in size at the urging of the government. On May 19, cabinet voted to approve the CSSG program. Finance minister Bill Morneau's wife, Nancy, a member of the wealthy McCain family, was a big donor to WE, and his daughter, whom the couple adopted from Uganda, worked for the social enterprise. Trudeau had similar problems that weren't legally conflicts of interest but looked bad. Trudeau's wife, Sophie, had spoken at WE events—she was recovering from Covid caught while in London for the last WE Day—and the charity had covered some of her expenses when she was on the road. Trudeau's mother, Margaret, a mental health advocate, and his brother Alexandre, a filmmaker, were paid to speak at fundraising events around WE Days. Neither Morneau nor Trudeau sat out the cabinet discussion.

The contract awarded to WE Charity was arranged as a contribution agreement between WE Charity and the federal government. This allowed for a much faster turnaround than putting it out to tender or asking for requests for proposals: most university students had finished their classes, which were taught over video, and high schools were a few weeks from the end of their academic year. Though WE didn't know it, there had been no competitive process. For its efforts, WE Charity would receive $43.5 million for administering the up to $543 million program for a maximum of one hundred thousand students. This was about 8 percent of the money to be spent. The normal rate for private oversight of a program like this is about 13 percent. Participating non-profits would receive up to $8.7 million of WE Charity's administration fee, bringing WE's total potential revenue, to cover all costs of administering the program, to just over 6 percent.

Under the CSSG, students between the ages of fifteen and thirty would receive a grant of $1,000 for every one hundred hours of volunteer service, up to a cap of $5,000 for five hundred volunteer hours (this was less than adults received from CERB). WE Charity quickly built and launched the program, with thirty-five thousand students signing up within the first week to assist eighty-four partner non-profits with programs such as contact tracing, virtual tutoring, and peer-to-peer mental health support. A few days later, the program was dead.

YOU ONLY HAVE to do a bit of digging to see similarities between Pierre Poilievre and the Kielburgers. Both of Poilievre's parents are schoolteachers; so are the Kielburgers'.[6] Poilievre's parents invested heavily in real estate; so did Craig and Marc's. Poilievre and the rest of the people who tried to destroy WE Charity attacked the elder Kielburgers for their real estate holdings. Pierre Poilievre started buying real estate as soon as he was elected to Parliament. There was, however, one serious difference: while the Kielburger brothers and Poilievre are brilliant showmen, WE Charity's founders aren't attack dogs.

Poilievre, who had decided not to run for his party's leadership in late 2019 but was still the Tories' finance critic, first went after the federal youth volunteer program on June 28, 2020. On Twitter, he posted "Dear Auditor General, WE may have a problem," with a letter he'd written, asking for an investigation. This was the first of more than seventy Poilievre tweets about WE over the next five months.

Soon, the story broke that Margaret and Alexandre Trudeau had been paid to speak at WE events.

Poilievre immediately became the media's dial-a-quote on this issue. He accused Prime Minister Trudeau of "personally intervening to direct a dubious sole-sourced $900 million contract to an organization that we now learn paid his family members $300,000. This is the conduct of a corrupt tin-pot dictator. . . . The issue is that his family was paid $300,000 by this organization and that he subsequently, knowing that, presumably, went to a cabinet meeting and helped direct a billion-dollar exclusive contract for this one organization." This came during a weird nine minutes of television, with a CTV News host lobbing open-ended softball questions to Poilievre while a split-screen showed an image of Margaret Trudeau hopping gleefully on a WE Day stage, then a clip of Justin Trudeau high-fiving young people.[7]

In that interview, and from then on, Poilievre pushed the claim that the charity needed to be investigated, as though it had created the CSSG and made the contracting decision. He insisted Trudeau forced the contract on the government to reward WE for paying his mother and brother. The first claim was absurd. The federal independent ethics commissioner later ruled the second accusation was false.

"We must recall Parliament immediately to get answers and bring accountability," Poilievre said on social media. "The Prime Minister personally intervened to direct a billion-dollar program to a group that had paid his family almost $300k. Not in Venezuela. Not in Zimbabwe. In Canada," he tweeted. It was such a gross overstatement, but the media bought into this line. Covid-relief program development, which public servants had worked on with impressive speed, stopped dead. From now on, the Trudeau government was on the defensive. The "weavers" had been driven from the public sphere and were sidelined in the bureaucracy as the minority government fought to save itself.

Soon, Poilievre and the Canadian public knew of Morneau's daughter's job at WE and that he had just paid WE $41,000 in travel costs for a trip with his wealthy wife to see WE's schools in Ecuador. (They had made two $50,000 donations to WE Charity at the end of the trip. Part of the $41,000 covered "rent" for lodging with the charity during their trip to the Amazon.)

By then, the CSSG was under investigation by the House of Commons finance committee, with Liberal Wayne Easter as chair of that committee and Poilievre as vice-chair. The opposition majority hauled in some very strange witnesses. They included controversial podcaster Jesse Brown, who had a vendetta against the Kielburgers and would later be sued by Theresa Kielburger, and former Tory staffer Vivian Krause.[8] In the July 22, 2020, session, Krause, who had never worked on anything to do with WE Charity or the Trudeau government, went off-script and started talking about politics.

"There's one issue that we haven't talked about yet and that's the elections activism of WE," Krause said. "In the 2015 election, for example, they authored an op-ed in the *Globe and Mail* urging youth to get out and vote. If you watch their videos, you'll see, for example, a little button which says, 'I voted today,' inserting the imagery of young people voting as part of being a good person. It's part of the brand of the WE movement: 'We're people who vote.' Even last fall in the 2019 election, WE hosted a federal election debate viewing party. This organization very clearly is about getting out the youth vote." This was an interesting claim, since WE was not targeted by the Harper government as a charity that was too involved in politics. In fact, the Harper family hosted the Kielburger brothers at 24 Sussex Drive after one of their Ottawa WE Days.

While Poilievre and the rest of the Tories on the committee nodded knowingly, no one bothered to ask what was wrong with a youth activism charity encouraging young people to vote. No one in the media did, either. By then, no journalist in Canada was willing to challenge the consensus of their peers and take a cold, hard look at what was really happening to WE Charity. For years, journalists had built up the Kielburger brothers. Now they were cutting the heads off the tall poppies.

But Krause couldn't prove WE had encouraged young people to vote Liberal. So Easter shut her down, saying "Ms. Krause, there is no question that we need to get to the bottom of this, but some of the speculation injures parties, injures reputations. At this committee hearing, I want us to stick as close to fact..."

The real show came later that day when Poilievre cross-examined Morneau on live TV. The news had just come out that Morneau had sent a cheque to WE to cover the cost of his stay in Ecuador, where he and his wife had visited to see how their family's large donations were spent. While American media was fixated with the police murder of George Floyd and the violence that followed, Canadian media was in a news drought. Other than stories on the pandemic, there wasn't much for housebound journalists to cover, so everyone in the media pack gave Poilievre their attention. The hearing, done remotely, was the biggest platform he'd had since his trashing of the residential school settlement and his days defending his *Fair Elections Act*. It wasn't exactly Clarence Darrow's infamous cross-examination of William Jennings Bryan during the 1925 Scopes Monkey Trial, but any port in a storm for a depleted media looking for a sensational story that they could cover in their pajamas.

Poilievre delivered. People could be forgiven if they thought they were tuning into a war-crimes case. "Canadians will find it impossible to believe that this organization showered you with $41,000 worth of luxury accommodations and that you didn't know about it, that somehow you were enjoying all of these benefits and expenses paid for you while you were on an exotic vacation to Ecuador, and that somehow you didn't even know the expenses occurred," he sneered at Morneau. "Who did you think was paying for all of the wine and the food and the luxury travel that you were consuming? Did you think that it was just falling out of the sky, Minister? Who did you think was paying for these tens of thousands of dollars of luxurious expenses that you were enjoying? Where did you think it was coming from?"

Morneau answered that he had paid all the hotel and travel costs but had not been billed by WE for the nights he had spent in their volunteer lodge in the Amazon. "It was absolutely in error," he said. "In looking through my records, I was completely surprised at this situation. That's not an excuse; that's just what happened."9

Poilievre went in for the kill: "We know that this is illegal. We know that you ought to have recused yourself.... Minister, you've lost the moral authority to hold your office."

In fact, Morneau had made the mistake of believing the big donations from his wallet and the fat cheques from his super-rich McCain in-laws entitled him to VIP treatment and to be careless.

Morneau clung to his job for another month. The Prime Minister's Office floated the rumour that Morneau might become head of the Organisation for Economic Cooperation and Development (OECD). At the press conference where he announced his resignation, Morneau told reporters he never planned to run in more than two federal elections. He picked up on the PMO line that he was in the running for the job at the OECD.[10] Morneau and Trudeau had regularly argued over pandemic-relief spending. Trudeau wanted him out, and the bad publicity over the CSSG made it much easier to push him. Poilievre took credit for Morneau's political destruction, but it probably would have happened anyway.[11]

On July 28, 2020, Poilievre got his shot at the Kielburger brothers. They testified from their lawyer's offices, and they looked awful.

Poilievre made outrageous claims and accused the brothers of not answering his questions, then interrupted them repeatedly before they could.

Tag-teaming with NDP MP Charlie Angus, Poilievre sneered and called the thirty-something brothers "boys" in a sort of gangster tone of voice. Both MPs interrupted the session with ludicrous points of order whenever the Kielburgers started giving an answer they didn't like or in the rare times that committee chair Wayne Easter tried to keep order.

"We will let the witness answer the question," Easter, trying to be jovial, told the badgering Tory and NDP MPs. Easter chided Poilievre five times in his first round of questioning and then warned he'd end the proceedings because of Poilievre's behaviour. But it was an empty threat.

Poilievre tried to portray WE as a scam, funnelling government money through a shell company set up for WE's real estate arm.[12] He had picked up on inaccurate reporting, which was hardly rare when journalists were talking about WE. By the end of July 2020, there was a media frenzy over the charity and the two men who created it.

Craig Kielburger told CBC reporters in a break in the hearings that he was surprised the real estate holdings "exploded" as an issue. "We were building a series of buildings ... to create a shared space for youth to launch their own social enterprises and run youth-led charities," he said. "Somehow that's been attacked in the press, when only a few months ago we were being praised."[13]

Sometimes, things seemed to become sexual. "Justin Trudeau appeared in a 'WE are Canada' video," Poilievre said to the Kielburger brothers. "Did he come to a studio to pose so that the cameras could circle him and beam those very impressive light, high-tech images on his forehead and across his body?"

It all made for emotional TV news soundbites and TikTok videos. The Kielburgers seemed small and defensive. And in the four hours—among the longest testimony ever before a Commons committee—Poilievre and Angus bullied them from telling their story.[14]

Toronto Star columnist Judith Timson watched the session. She said she had questions about Trudeau and Morneau's judgment and WE's political connections. "But what struck me during the Kielburgers' lengthy testimony was the savage and unnecessarily rude behaviour of lead questioner Conservative MP Pierre Poilievre who interrupted each Kielburger many times as they sought to explain their relationship with the government and who sounded as if he was prosecuting them for murder one.

"It was more of an obnoxious overreach than the squishy obsequiousness of the Brothers K."[15]

JUSTIN TRUDEAU TESTIFIED from his study at his temporary home on the grounds of the governor general's residence.[16] The prime minister started by saying, "I was not in a position of conflict of interest. I apologized because of the perception [over] ties with my family. I should have recused myself."

Poilievre peppered Trudeau with demands for yes or no answers on complicated questions.

"You're telling me you don't know how much immediate family members have been paid in expense reimbursements by this organization?" Poilievre demanded.

Trudeau replied, "My mother and my brother are professionals in their own right who have engagements, and have for many years, with many different—"

Poilievre talked over him. "Do you know?"

Trudeau kept going: "—organizations across the country. I don't have the details of their work experiences or their expenses."

"How much were those expenses?" Poilievre asked.

"I don't have that number in front of me," the prime minister replied.

"Mr. Prime Minister, it's very hard to believe you don't have that number," Poilievre shot back. "You've been embroiled in this scandal for over a month now and these kinds of questions have been asked repeatedly."

Poilievre piled the CSSG fiasco onto the list of Trudeau "scandals."

"You were found guilty of taking a free vacation from someone who sought a $50-million grant from you, strike one. You were found guilty of interfering with the criminal prosecution of a Liberal-linked corporation, strike two.... You were twice found guilty of breaking the ethics act before, strikes one and two. Now you admit a third strike by your failure to recuse yourself, and in the process you broke the ethics act a third time. What happens in baseball when you have three strikes?"

Later, Poilievre used one of his favourite rhetorical tricks, demanding a witness cite law, chapter and verse.

"I have a yes-or-no question. Prime Minister, you twice were found guilty of breaking the ethics act. After those two convictions, did you decide to read the [Conflict of Interest] act?"

Trudeau said he had read it several times.

"Are you aware of section twenty-one?" Poilievre asked.

"Yes. Since I've read the act, I'm aware of section twenty-one," the prime minister answered.

"What does it say?" Poilievre demanded.

Trudeau hadn't memorized the law. He didn't know.

Poilievre had the floor back.

"It says, 'A public office holder'—and you are one—'shall recuse himself or herself from any discussion, decision, debate or vote on any matter in respect of which he or she would be in a conflict of interest." What you've admitted today is not just that you were in a conflict of interest, but that you consciously recognized in your May cabinet meeting that such a conflict might exist. It didn't just slide by your desk. You were consciously aware that there was an inappropriate link to your family that would put you in a conflict.

"Why did you, at that moment, not call the Ethics Commissioner and recuse yourself?"

Trudeau had a more accurate grasp of the law. He said it prohibited him from advancing the interests of his family. The CSSG had nothing to do with Trudeau's relatives. The situation might have looked bad, but he hadn't broken the law. And a prime minister or bureaucrat explaining the fine points of conflict-of-interest law hardly makes for a short, interesting soundbite. Some print media outlets did quote experts who explained the rules, then went back to describing the situation as a scandal.

As Trudeau kept trying to answer, Poilievre spoke over him, saying a couple of times, "Your sixteen seconds are up." As Trudeau spoke, Poilievre talked over him, again and again, saying, "I want a dollar figure."

IF THE HEARINGS were about getting answers, they failed. Trudeau prorogued Parliament, shutting the committee down. Then he went on holidays while media outlets turned all their guns on WE Charity to try to keep the story alive. At about the same time, bureaucrats released redacted documents about the CSSG.

"This page blacked out," Poilievre complained to the reporters as he flipped documents off the stack. "This page blacked out. This page blacked out. It's clear Justin Trudeau has something to hide," Poilievre said. "He does not want Canadians to know what's in these documents, and that's why he shut down this parliamentary investigation."[17]

Poilievre could have read an April 20, 2020, email from assistant deputy minister for finance Michelle Kovacevic. Despite Poilievre's drama over a bit of profanity, the email bolstered the prime minister and his staff's claims that the program was crafted by the public service.

"The Canada Student Service Grant—bit of a shit show and the way it is positioned right now is not exactly how we will go forward, there is positive communication with WE to be a partner here and discussions are encouraging on that front. (but just discussions, no agreement)," Kovacevic wrote.

The day before, Kovacevic said the mission of WE was "congruent" with national service. The charity had a "massive following" on social media. "An existing payment mechanism could save a lot of work," she wrote.[18]

Poilievre thought Trudeau would call a snap election before opposition MPs could force the government to cough up all the details of the creation of the CSSG contract.[19] In fact, the Canadian arm of the charity would be dead and the media busy with other things when the federal campaign began in 2021.

Although government contracting was the real scandal—if there was one at all—the media's shorthand of "WE Charity scandal" stuck. It would be a devastating blow to any charity. "It wasn't the 'failure to recuse scandal.' It wasn't the 'prime minister scandal.' It wasn't the 'government scandal.' It ended up being the 'WE Charity scandal,'" Marc Kielburger said.

Later, he tried to explain what had happened. WE Charity, Marc said, was destroyed by two men, Poilievre and Trudeau, who had never been able to deal with the trauma of their childhoods and now needed affirmation from the people. It didn't matter that other people suffered, or that perspective, proportionality, and truth were ignored.[20]

IN SEPTEMBER 2020, the Kielburgers shut down WE's Canadian operation and put the proceeds of the sale of its buildings into a foundation. Their volunteer work at seven thousand schools in Canada ended. In seventy-nine days, Poilievre, Angus, and the media destroyed a charity that had taken twenty-three years to build, whose only mistake had been answering the phone when the government called to ask for help in an emergency.

No one, especially in the media, saw the irony of the company that owns the *Toronto Star*, which had run a series of articles with often-dubious allegations about WE Charity, making a lowball offer to buy WE's headquarters and some of the real estate assembled for their social enterprise training centre. That newspaper's founder, Joseph Atkinson, had tried to make the *Star* a social enterprise by leaving the company to the Atkinson Charitable Foundation in 1948, but was thwarted by the provincial government.[21] In December 2020, Torstar offered $27 million for three of WE's properties. WE came back with a counter-offer. That went nowhere. Torstar then submitted a second offer of $30 million for four properties. WE turned that down. Another company described in the *Star* as "associated with Torstar's ownership" offered WE Charity and its business arm ME to WE $41.5 million for twelve properties. Instead, ten of the properties were sold in August 2021 for $41 million.[22] There was a time when a newspaper did not try to buy the distressed assets of a charity that it had helped destroy. That would have been a scandal. Their competitors would have jumped on the story. But not now.

Poilievre had no sympathy for the hundreds of staff who would be out of work. Nor did he mourn the millions of hours of volunteer work that teens performed to earn their WE Day tickets, nor the hundreds of thousands of pounds of food the charity annually collected for local food banks as part of one of its school-based service campaigns. Instead, Poilievre created a false narrative that the organization was shutting down to hide something. "WE closure changes nothing. Finance Committee will resume investigations once Parliament opens. You can run but you can't hide," he tweeted. In six months, he would take another run at the Kielburger brothers.

THE NEXT ROUND opened in March 2021. Poilievre was not a member of the House of Commons ethics committee, but a Tory was willing to give up a seat. Poilievre publicly threatened the Kielburgers with arrest if they refused to appear before the ethics committee.[23] The brothers hadn't refused to testify. They hadn't even been subpoenaed.

"I've got news for the Kielburgers: you will testify," Poilievre tweeted. "If not, Parliament can have the Sergeant pay you a visit—and you don't want that."

In the hearings, he had a creepy habit of calling Craig "my friend." Poilievre accused Craig of perjury. "You're in a lot of trouble here, my friend," he said. "You're under oath. Perjury is a crime." That clip was replayed constantly in the media, even though there had been no perjury.

Marc Kielburger tried to fight back. "Partisan politicians can use their powers irresponsibly and they can do it to any organization or business. This is a political scandal for the government, not WE Charity. The government hid behind a children's charity by letting it take the fall for their political decisions and the opposition allowed them. We've lost sight of what this should have been all about. It should have been about Canadian kids being helped during a pandemic," said Marc.

"On a personal note, my youngest isn't even one year old, and he's already received death threats directed at him," Craig said. "We've had police come multiple times to our home. My three-and-a-half-year-old can't play outside anymore."

Poilievre wasn't interested in police visits if they were just about threats to kids. He wanted to know if the federal cops were investigating the CSSG contract.

"Have you spoken to the RCMP?" Poilievre asked. The Kielburgers didn't want to answer the question, but Craig finally answered no.

Poilievre asked if WE's people had been contacted by the ethics commissioner. Craig Kielburger refused to answer.

"Apparently we are not allowed to answer by statute of the government," Craig explained, after Will McDowell, WE's lawyer, said something that couldn't be picked up by the microphones.

"Which section?" Poilievre demanded.

Craig turned to McDowell, but he couldn't cite the law.

"He should know," Poilievre said.

When McDowell started explaining, Poilievre jumped on him.

"No, no, no! I'm not asking him to speak," Poilievre said as he interrupted McDowell.[24]

When Craig said the advice of McDowell, a former associate minister of justice, should be accepted, Poilievre deadpanned, "Let's assume you're hiding that," and moved on.

Poilievre insisted the brothers calculate the money and expenses paid to Trudeau's family. "You're going to get this number on the record," he barked, "and you're going to testify it into the record under oath because I want the total."

When the brothers and their lawyer started adding up the money paid for forty-two events, Poilievre said, "It's so much money, you can't even keep track of it all."

IN THE END, the federal ethics commissioner, Mario Dion, cleared Prime Minister Trudeau of any wrongdoing in the so-called WE Charity affair. Bill Morneau did breach the *Conflict of Interest Act* when he failed to recuse himself from the cabinet decision the previous spring to have WE Charity administer the CSSG.

A statement from WE Charity said Dion confirmed the choice to give the contract to the organization "was subject to extensive scrutiny and that WE Charity was the only organization equipped" to manage the program. "Through this procurement process, WE Charity did not determine the value of the contract, or the decision to sole-source. WE Charity did not have any input into the government's procurement process, including the decision whether to recuse."[25]

Poilievre ignored Dion's findings. Instead, he told reporters he'd won. The Tories would not force an election over the "scandal" that turned out be what journalists call a "nothingburger," a story with only minimal substance or importance. "We don't have to," he said. "We already got what we asked for, which was for the government to cancel the program and redirect the funds through the professional public service and make it open and transparent for all organizations."

Which, of course, never happened. The summer of 2020 was long past, and the students never got anything.

The Kielburger brothers' lives changed forever. Speaking to Mark Kelley of CBC's news magazine show *The Fifth Estate*, Marc said, "We were politically mugged." The brothers reminded the CBC crew that they had invited politicians of all stripes onto the WE Day stage. "And frankly, in hindsight, let me be very candid, I wish we hadn't," said Craig.

They believed Trudeau and his team were trying to shift blame to them. As early as July 3, 2021, Trudeau shocked the Kielburgers with: "I think the organization is going to take some time to reflect on its next steps and how it exactly responds to this situation."

Marc Kielburger told Kelley, "We had no idea what he was talking about."

"It was really unfortunate that there wasn't a moment when a politician, of any party, chose to stand up and say, you know what, we shouldn't use a children's charity's name as a political football," said Craig.

Marc said testifying in front of Poilievre and the other members of the parliamentary committees was like having a root canal.

"The politicians are allowed to say literally whatever they want [because Parliamentary privilege protects them from lawsuits]. And so it was this surreal political boxing match where they could hit but we couldn't defend ourselves," said Craig.

"I don't think...some of the opposition members care at all, other than serving their parties and scoring political points, figuring out who's going to be the next leader," said Marc. "It all comes down to what TV shows can I be on and how many tweets can I get retweeted, as opposed to how many people am I actually helping? You start to really understand how Ottawa works. It's pretty sad."

These days, some people connected to WE are convinced the Liberals' communications team manipulated search engine algorithms to latch onto "WE Charity Scandal" rather than any other potential names that might bring the affair into the prime minister's orbit.

TRUDEAU CAME OUT of this affair with bruises. The Kielburger brothers' reputation in Canada was destroyed. Reporters kept digging into WE, hanging sensational stories on the word of one or two anonymous sources, usually from a small pool of unhappy former employees. None of that coverage amounted to much, at least in terms of politics. It did ruin WE Charity in Canada. In the end, WE Charity sued *The Fifth Estate* for a bizarre story on WE Charity's schools in Kenya. The charity filed its action in the same federal court in Washington where the Dominion Voting Systems defamation suit against Fox News case was litigated. The CBC tried to have the lawsuit thrown out, saying it should be heard in Canada, but the case was allowed to move forward.

Canadaland, its owner Jesse Brown, and some staff got statements of claim from Theresa Kielburger. They had repeated an old libel, first published in *Saturday Night* magazine in the 1990s, about Craig and Marc's mother. The magazine had paid a hefty settlement for publishing the lie, but Jesse Brown tried to make his listeners believe it was true. In 2024, Canadaland failed to have the lawsuit thrown out under Ontario's law preventing strategic lawsuits against public participation (SLAPPs). Canadaland had to pay $110,000 in costs to Mrs. Kielburger.[26]

CONSERVATIVES ADOPTED THE line that Covid restrictions and federal relief programs weren't needed. Tasha Kheiriddin, a lobbyist and Conservative strategist, said in a 2024 *National Post* article that Trudeau's policies were hardest on working people. White-collar workers, including most government employees, got off easy. She left a few things out, including the innovative relief programs for individuals and businesses that Trudeau's government, working long hours at home and dealing with their own stress, rolled out in the first weeks of the pandemic. Pandemic hardships and the restrictions on movement, many of them ordered by the provinces and municipalities, affected everyone.[27] She also dodged the question of whether any government, struggling with what little was known about Covid in the late winter of 2020, should have let stores, offices, and factories stay open.[28] The rest of the developed world shut down, often with tighter restrictions than those in Canada, while people waited to see how bad Covid would be. And for months, most of the news was terrifying.[29]

The federal government was in a no-win situation: if it tried to "flatten the curve" with some lockdown measures so that Covid gradually moved through the population without overwhelming hospitals, it could save lives, or it could give into demands to allow healthy people to be exposed so they'd develop "herd immunity," which was based on the false assumption that people who caught Covid develop life-long immunity from the disease. The provinces, which have constitutional responsibility for health care, were in agreement on the issue. Quebec and the Maritime provinces closed their borders. Quebec imposed an 8 p.m. to 5 a.m. curfew and police issued tickets to anyone caught outside their homes. The government of Ontario ordered the shutdown of businesses during two Covid waves and limited the number of people, outside of members of their family, individuals could visit. Some municipalities, especially in cottage regions, told seasonal residents to stay away, but could not stop them from using their rural properties. Alberta placed limits on gatherings in the spring of 2020 and banned them altogether in the fall of 2021.

But if mitigation worked, the country's hard-right would say that they'd been correct all along: Covid was just a flu. If, however, the government had allowed Covid to tear through the country, the already frail health care system would have been overwhelmed, and many more people would have died. Governments would be blamed. In the end, restrictions kept most people from getting the disease until vaccinations of seniors and others who were most vulnerable started in the early winter of 2021. The vaccines didn't prevent Covid, but they did tend to reduce its severity. Canada had one of the lowest death rates of any major developed country: 1,424 fatalities per million. In the United States, there were 3,535 fatalities for every million Americans.[30] More than a million people died of Covid in the US in the last year of Donald Trump's first presidency and the first two years of Joe Biden's. If Covid lockdown mythology helped ruin Justin Trudeau's reputation, he can at least take comfort that the policies adopted by the federal government and the provinces saved a minimum of fifty thousand lives.

Charlie Angus announced his retirement from politics, and the antics of the rest of the Opposition MPs were forgotten. Poilievre was the only winner. The media found him so very quotable. He was on television and in the newspapers through the pandemic, scowling and badgering and talking tough.

A dispute over the way the government hires contractors became a frenzy of political and media excess engineered by Poilievre and supported by Angus that cost children in developing countries the chance of an education and killed a huge volunteer program in Canada. WE Charity and its affiliated organizations were never charged with anything, never sued, never criticized by the lobbying commissioner or any other federal watchdog. If there was a police investigation, it amounted to nothing. Innuendo in the *Globe and Mail* and on the CBC that WE was about to be forced out of Kenya turned out to be false. Hundreds of charity staff engaged in youth motivation and volunteer coordination in Canada lost their jobs. There were no more WE Days. Social entrepreneur work, based on the idea that charities could fund themselves with their own businesses, became a lost cause in this country.

Politically, nothing changed. Trudeau won re-election with another minority in 2021. All the fire and brimstone about WE Charity hadn't changed voters' minds. The WE Charity scandal became part of the list of "scandals" recited like a spell by Conservatives.

"I did my job. I'm proud of what I did," Poilievre said to a CBC reporter who asked about his role in taking down WE Charity.[31] Poilievre, who torqued the issue, misrepresented the facts, and bullied witnesses at committee meetings, was now the face of the Conservative Party of Canada, poised for a leadership run. His big chance rolled into Ottawa less than a year later, when disinformation and simple selfishness convinced a small, loud group of Canadians that Covid wasn't a big deal after all.[32]

9.
IS CANADA BROKEN?

Poverty is not an accident. Like slavery and apartheid, it is man-made and can be removed by the actions of human beings.

NELSON MANDELA

RICHARD LIVES IN a pup tent in downtown Ottawa, next to the Bank of Canada and about a block from the temporary home of the House of Commons. He's a thin, tough man in his sixties. Or he could be in his fifties. When you've worked outside for years as a roofer and then end up on the street, your face has seen a lot of sun. Carrying a heavy load of trauma and anxiety is also a great way to look older than you are. He's got a couple of homemade tattoos, some problems with his bladder, and he needs glasses, but that doesn't stop Richard from seeing the rapists. Those rapists are the reason he's been camped on the side of Bank Street for more than two years, long enough for the tent to become so worn that he's using duct tape to fix the rips in it. Richard is not partisan. Unlike the dozen or so people who hang around the entrances to Parliament every day to protest various real and imagined problems, Richard doesn't think a change of government will do anything to solve his problems. Everyone on the Hill knows about the rapists and many cops and politicians are part of the plot, which is run by evildoers and bad thinkers from their headquarters in the nearby town of Carleton Place.

Richard gets by on $789 a month from the Ontario Disability Support Program. That's what everyone gets, whether they're paying for a home or not. As a "benefit unit" of "1," Richard qualifies for a housing allowance of about $500 a month. If he had a dependent spouse, they'd be a benefit unit of 2 and get a little more. If they had a child living at home, the family would be a benefit unit of 3 and would get $850. If they lived in a place that's so isolated it's not connected to the provincial road grid, they'd get an extra $272 a month. To get the housing allowance, Richard would have to do two things. One of them is possible: show ODSP's bureaucrats receipts proving he really does pay rent and doesn't pocket the money while living in a tent next to the Bank of Canada. The other is impossible: find a place in Ontario that costs less than $500 a month and live on the $789 and the odd GST and carbon-tax rebate, plus the vote-buying cheques that provincial and federal politicians send out from time to time.[1]

A few years ago, he might have been able to afford to share a small apartment, but that wouldn't work now: in 2023, the last year that solid numbers were available, the average rent for an apartment or condo in Ottawa was about $2,000 a month. Rentals.ca, a company that advertises homes for rent, reported average rents in Ottawa ranged from $1,699 for a bachelor apartment to $1,892 for a one-bedroom in April 2023. A two-bedroom apartment typically went for $2,075, and that rarest of rental unicorns, a three-bedroom apartment, cost $2,530.[2] So even if local media are right when they say rents have come down a bit, to have a roof, Richard would have to find five roommates, all of them willing to hear non-stop talk about the rapists, and a landlord who would rent to Richard and the rest of them.[3] This math leaves Richard and many of the other three thousand unsheltered people in downtown Ottawa living in pup tents. They're all over the place. And a lot of homeless people spend cold nights lying in sleeping bags in doorways or on ventilation grates that blow hot air.

Richard doesn't panhandle. Not that it would make a difference: no one comes near him. He rarely stops talking. At the core of this one-way conversation is a sad, awful story of addiction, injury, family loss, and the struggle to live in a Canadian city in the 2020s. You have to pick through a lot of crazy to piece it together.

Richard uses a washroom at a nearby McDonald's, but when his bladder acts up or just gets too full, he pees into a cup and flings it onto Bank Street, the city's rundown main street.[4] He offered this cup to me when I asked where the nearest washroom was. Since it was broad daylight and this was downtown Ottawa, I declined with thanks. The McDonald's is beside a building that houses an abortion clinic, and just up the block there really is a sex club, one of two that I know of in the downtown core. (The idea of a sex club within shouting range of Parliament Hill boggles my mind as much as it repulses the reader's, but there really are, or were, at least two in Ottawa's core.) These grotesque passion pits, where bureaucrats, lobbyists, and lawyers go to rut, fit into Richard's delusions. The women who protest the abortion clinic are really the mothers of the women who use its services. The sex club is part of the conspiracy of rapists. They're everywhere: in trucks going by, in white cars, in cop cars. People riding around on rental scooters are delivering drugs. A woman in a nearby store has some kind of cigarette racket going, with the help of the Ottawa and Parliament Hill cops. All of them are connected to the rapists who took Richard's wife and two daughters, and Richard wants them back.

All of this started after Richard had a concussion in a car accident. He grew up in small towns in eastern Ontario, where his dad made a decent living as a barber because he still offered old-fashioned straight-razor shaves and barbering is a cash business. Richard played hockey as a kid. He was never very big, but he was fast and strong. He was so good that Hall of Famer Johnny Bower, who'd retired from the Toronto Maple Leafs after they won the Stanley Cup in 1967 but stayed with the team as a scout and assistant coach, checked him out a few times.[5] Eventually, he ended up out West, re-shingling roofs. This is tough, hard work, but Richard said he was usually paid well. He was hurt a few times in falls.[6] Some of these were liquor-related, but Richard's been home and off the booze for a while. There were some stints in jails, but probably no prison time. Somewhere along the way, Richard lost his wife and two daughters. It's not clear what happened. They might have left him, he might have left them, they might be dead. In his mind, they are in the hands of the rapists who run Ottawa, and he's there to get them back.

Richard is a good man. In his mind, he fights people who are doing terrible things to him and his kin. In the real world, he gets some medical help and support from a downtown community health centre. Someone must be doing a good job: Richard needed help applying for ODSP, which turns down half of the people who ask for benefits. He also needs a mailing address, and "pup tent by the Bank of Canada" will not do.[7] Richard gets most of his food at McDonald's and buys coffee from shops on the Sparks Street Mall. His basics are pretty much covered, though a pup tent is a poor shelter in Ottawa's cold winters and hot, humid summers.[8]

There have always been homeless and addicted men in Ottawa. Thirty years ago, when I first moved to the city, I saw a couple of guys split a bottle of Scope on a weekday morning just a few feet from where Richard's tent is now while public servants and Hill staffers walked by on their way to work. Within a year or so, I saw a man eating out of a garbage can in front of the West Block of the parliamentary complex. From time to time, I came across poor people trying to grab change from the shallow pool around the Centennial Flame and using its fire to get warm.[9] But in this century, homelessness in Ottawa's downtown core has become the city's biggest crisis. Local people, most of them addicted to something, compete with

Indigenous panhandlers for spots on Elgin and Bank streets and in the Byward Market. The market area was once a big tourist draw. In summer, it's still busy, but the rest of the year, it's a wasteland. Ottawa tourism has been on the ropes for years. Some downtown hotels have become dorms for university students. In 2024, the City of Ottawa tried to breathe some life into the core by hiring a "night mayor," a hip-looking Montrealer whose main job seems to be convincing young Ottawans not to go to Montreal for a good time. This is unlikely to work.[10] Three privately owned pubs on the University of Ottawa campus have gone out of business in this decade. A homeless shelter just off campus has more business than it can handle, while broken people lurk near the University of Ottawa's law school entrance, hoping to find a big cigarette butt thrown away by students who grab a few fast drags between classes.

Homeless people wander into downtown Ottawa streets to ask drivers for change.[11] The city capitalized on this by installing red-light and speed cameras on King Edward Avenue. They're the busiest in the city. The one at King Edward and St. Patrick Street, right by the big Shepherds of Good Hope and Salvation Army shelters, issued 623 tickets in the first two months of 2024 at $325 a pop.[12] Maybe the red-light cameras (and new photo-radar cameras) will help protect the troubled people who wander into King Edward Avenue, but so far all they seem to have done is raise millions of dollars that gets spent on "traffic calming" Ottawa streets. None of the money helps the people suffering on King Edward.

There's no simple, clear, non-partisan explanation for why homelessness in Ottawa and almost all of Canada's towns has become a medical and urban crisis. There are some hints: relatively cheap, insanely addictive street drugs; a lack of realistic housing choices for the very poor, who used to find cheap apartments over downtown stores and in poorer parts of towns but can't afford these anymore; the closure of rooming houses; regulation and gentrification that has caused many big Victorian houses that were divided into small apartments to be restored to single-family use.[13] And Canada's psychiatric hospitals were emptied out long ago. Most of the biggest institutions in the country were closed while Canada's population expanded. Mental health care in Canada barely exists, especially in small communities.

So Richard, a man who suffers—truly suffers—from frightening delusions, is left with very few options. He has basic medical support, but not the care he needs. He has a place to live, of sorts. No one seems to be in a hurry to make him move. But that's it. That's all he's got. One infection, one new health condition, and Richard might not be there anymore. More than half of Canadian men live to be seventy-five. Less than a third of homeless men make it that far. It helps that Richard's quit drinking. He couldn't afford not to, and it would certainly have hastened his death. He's proud to have beaten that addiction, and he should be. There aren't many ways for people like him to deal with the pain of mental illness and with trauma, and most of the options open to Richard would kill him. If he wants to see how, he just has to visit the other people living on Ottawa's streets. Almost all of them are addicted.

Richard performs a valuable service to his country. He reminds its leaders, its would-be leaders (like Poilievre), public servants, and visitors to Parliament Hill that we have more and more Richards. So do American and British cities: it's normal to see people living in cheap tents. There are seven square kilometres of tent-covered sidewalks in Los Angeles. More than four thousand people "sleep rough" on the damp streets of England, mostly in London. People have set up tent camps in that city's core and in rich neighbourhoods like Mayfair.[14] No politicians have come up with workable plans to help the homeless and prevent city cores from becoming wastelands like Los Angeles' skid row and Vancouver's Downtown Eastside.

A "housing first" strategy is the proven way to help the mentally ill and addicted people who need shelter and treatment. Slogans won't do it. What part of "axe the tax, build the homes, fix the budget, and stop the crime," the promises made by Pierre Poilievre in the motion he made to try to topple the government in late September 2024, would fix Richard's problems? Or does Poilievre see Richard as a problem, rather than a Canadian in dire need of help?

In the fall of 2024, Richard wasn't sure who he'd vote for. Pollsters would put him down as "undecided." If the drama of 2025 has caused him to make a choice, he'll probably apply the same sort of logic as the pundits and strategists who walk by him every day. Like Richard, they live in a world shaped by their own delusions and myths, reinforced by talks with themselves.

JUSTIN TRUDEAU DID not put Richard onto the street. He's there because he lives on a ridiculously and cruelly low allowance from the provincial government, without proper social and medical support. Many of Canada's mental health supports were cut in the last century. The number of hospital beds in psychiatric hospitals has been slashed: when the provincial government built a replacement for the Royal Ottawa, the local mental health centre, it reduced the institution's capacity even though the city is growing. Deinstitutionalization, which was supposed to give patients more dignity and freedom, was a big idea in the 1980s. It was supposed to put people into community group homes, not into pup tents on downtown sidewalks. Rights too often clash with well-being: if Richard isn't a threat to the public or himself—and choosing to live on Bank Street talking non-stop about imaginary rapists doesn't meet that threshold—no one can make him get psychiatric help, even if it is available. And that's a big if, as so many families of mentally ill people are finding out. Richard will be in that tent until he moves on, gets too sick to function, or dies. No level of government seriously tries to help him get a home and provide the social and financial support he'd need to keep it. This wouldn't change under a Poilievre government: all of Richard's money comes from Ontario, which has jurisdiction over social welfare and health. Poilievre has never promised to build federal housing for the homeless, even though "housing first" strategies are the most effective way to deal with long-term homelessness.[15]

There's some good news: Richard escapes the Ontario government's tender mercies when he turns sixty-five. Then, he'll qualify for $1,742.05 a month from the federal Old Age Pension and the Guaranteed Income Supplement. He might get a small monthly payment from the Canada Pension Plan, if he ever paid into it. Now the math gets a little better for Richard, but it's still not enough to live on. He'll also collect small federal HST and carbon-tax rebates. But he'll still be desperately poor.

The Richards of this country are broken, but when Poilievre says the country's broken, he's not talking about the man in the pup tent near Parliament Hill. He's trying to connect with a generation of slightly younger men who have shelter, some kind of job, and, usually, a family. They almost always have poor career prospects. These men believe they're doing worse than their baby boomer parents and think their kids will have it even worse than them.

Most boomers were much better off than their parents, who grew up in the Depression. Things usually worked out for them: the boomers who entered the job market in the 1960s could expect to make a decent living, own a house, and buy toys like cottages and boats. They usually had it easy and didn't have to learn how to recover from failure. The boomers never taught their kids how to cope with big challenges or setbacks because the idea of wrenching change was so foreign to them. It's been forty-five years since the last mass unemployment "recession," eighty years since the end of the Second World War, and eight-five years since the Great Depression.[16] People in their sixties grew up with their parents and grandparents' nonstop stories about the Great Depression. That public memory is gone.

Starting in the 1980s, every kid got a participation ribbon. No one failed grades anymore. Students were pushed through to graduation—even though many of them lacked basic math and literacy skills or an understanding of basic science, geography, or history—while being raised on American movies that portrayed high schools as social settings where diligent students were ostracized. Why study when teachers would hand out honours for ordinary work? In 2022, Toronto high school students typically left grade twelve with averages of 77 percent.[17] With so much grade inflation, some in-demand university programs turned away students with 99 percent averages.[18] Eventually, though, reality hits: people unprepared for the workplace and ignorant of basic civics learn the grim realities of the job market, leaving them vulnerable to politicians who tell them their challenges are caused by someone else. The left blames the billionaires, and the right blames unions, immigrants, and mythical "Laurentian elites" who have no knowledge of the real world.

Even before Trump started waging economic war on Canada, a lot of Canadians were simply exhausted. The disruption and anxiety of the pandemic took a lot out of them. A report by Canada Life released in the autumn of 2024 found 24 percent of Canadian workers felt burned out in 2023. And that was the good news: this was down from 35 percent in December 2021. But Canadian household debt was creeping upward. Parents believed their children might not "launch" into adulthood with decent jobs, a home of their own, and the ability to start a family. Young people felt the same way, for good reason: a 2024 survey by the Vanier Institute of the Family found 64.6 percent of men and 59.3 percent of women aged twenty to twenty-four lived with their parents. There were many reasons for that, including a change in young people's attitudes about going into debt to attend out-of-town colleges and universities. The living-at-home numbers for people aged twenty-five to twenty-nine were even more surprising. Most of these people had finished their education, yet 35.2 percent of men and 26.7 percent of women were still living at home. The rates varied across the country. Places where houses and apartments are expensive or scarce saw more young adults living with their parents: for example, 54.7 percent of people in their twenties in Nunavut and 53.3 percent of twenty-somethings in Ontario were not living on their own. While this shift has been happening, support among young people for federal and provincial conservative parties has grown.[19]

Standards of living declined through the 1980s and 1990s. Canada, for the most part, was spared from the worst of the 2008 recession, but our house prices kept rising while those in the United States collapsed. This made millionaires of baby boomers who'd bought in the last century but shut most other people out of the market. At the same time, most provinces shredded their rent-control rules.

During and after Covid, prices for many ordinary things like cars and lumber went out of whack. Groceries were more expensive and fast-food prices followed the trend upwards. Canada's central bank, like others in developed countries, fought this inflation with higher interest rates. Unless they were well into their fifties, Canadians could not remember a time when a spike in interest rates posed a danger to people who were renewing their mortgages. In the last interest-rate crisis, the one that kicked off the early 1980s recessions, mortgage rates closed in on 20 percent and For Sale signs sprouted like mushrooms on lawns of Canadian homes.[20] This time, people who needed to renew their mortgages were usually able to find the money for higher payments, sometimes only by going deeper into credit card debt. Still, it stung: for years, financial writers, politicians, and some financial advisers had been saying that low rates were permanent, and people acted on that advice. These higher carrying costs came as people were trying to adjust to the lifestyle and social changes that came with the Covid pandemic.[21]

BUT AGAIN, WHO is to blame? There's only one guy protesting at the Bank of Canada, and Richard doesn't seem to have a beef with its interest-rate decisions. Poilievre has taken anger and frustration that should be directed at the chartered banks that earn billions, grocery chains that earn the same, and the rest of the gougers, and redirected it at Trudeau, his successor, and at Liberals in general. Hardcore right-wingers in Canada's regions, unfamiliar with the realities of life in Ontario and Quebec, echo Poilievre's prattle about "Laurentian elites" as though everyone in central Canada lives a sheltered life in Walkerville, Rosedale, Rockcliffe, and Westmount. These elites are, in the new conservative discourse, unfamiliar with hard work and oblivious to the lives of people who, as Poilievre has said, shower after work instead of before it. The irony and falseness of a lifelong politician denigrating capitalists and professionals who made their money through skill and risk seems lost on most people.

Some frustrated Canadians loathe urban professionals, especially those who work in government and cultural industries. They see people in white-collar jobs and the arts as net losses to the economy, even though Canada's cultural industries added $61 billion to the country's GDP in 2023.[22] And that's not counting the benefits to our quality of life. North Americans differ from Europeans in this regard: even the most conservative Europeans see the arts as something that makes life better and take pride in cities.

Then came mass immigration of Black and Brown people, which coincided with campaigns by Indigenous Canadians, women, gender-diverse people, disabled people, and people of colour for fair treatment. Workers are often exposed to a few hours of "diversity training," another punching bag of the right. The right blames diversity, equity, and inclusion activism for things ranging from the 2025 Los Angeles wildfires to the difficulty of some white students to get into good colleges to the vicious attack on New Years partiers on New Orleans' Bourbon Street.[23] The implication: "diverse" people in the workplace don't have "merit." After Donald Trump's re-election, Amazon, Meta (owner of Facebook and Instagram), and McDonald's started rolling back their DEI policies, seemingly vindicating the right. Those that realized the value of DEI, companies like Costco, were accused of breaking the law, as through Trump, on his own, could declare an anti-discrimination workplace policy illegal.[24]

Pierre Poilievre has always been clear about his position on diversity, equity, and inclusion. In the summer of 2023, he called DEI "garbage" and added, for bad measure, that environmentalism, social, and governance (ESG) is "a fake industry designed to make interest groups, corporate executives and insiders filthy rich." ESG advocates don't really care about the planet, he said. "They're a bunch of hypocrites and phonies."[25]

Poilievre has promised to kill DEI in the federal government. He said he'll go after policies like DEI requirements for university research funding, which means a Poilievre government would interfere in the policies of arm's length agencies like the Social Sciences and Humanities Research Council and the Natural Science and Research Council of Canada.[26] He's falsely accused the Canadian Human Rights Commission, a long-time punching bag of the Canadian right, of trying to cancel Christmas.[27]

Some of this anger is targeted at Indigenous people, who, the right claims, never had it so good in the decades since their land was stolen outright or their chiefs were arm-twisted into signing it away.[28] Poilievre's supporters hate the commemoration of the residential schools tragedy, despise Indigenous and non-Indigenous people who wear orange shirts, bitch about land acknowledgements, and think the police and courts are too easy on Indigenous offenders. The fact that Indigenous people don't live as long as everyone else and are poorer and more likely to end up in jail doesn't seem to register as an injustice. This racism is especially prevalent in Northern Ontario and Western Canada.

There was always a gulf—two solitudes—between French and English Canada. Poilievre, like many Westerners, has claimed federal bilingualism policies discriminate against people who can only speak English. While Poilievre has told anglophones in his riding he sympathizes with their concerns, he worked hard to learn French to further his political career. Still, right-wing provincial governments have proven it's possible to roll back French rights without serious blowback, while Quebec's nationalist conservative government has been attacking anglophone (and other minority) rights in Quebec for years without serious objection from any federal party.[29] Serving Canada in interesting, well-paying jobs with great benefits and pensions was no longer understood to be a career option for people from outside the "bilingual belt" of the eastern edge of Ontario and Montreal.

The fight over bilingualism has dogged Canada from the beginning. The first question asked in the House of Commons when Canada was created in 1867 was about whether the speaker needed to be bilingual. The Liberal Party sent a clear message that the leader they chose in 2025 had to be bilingual.[30] The Trudeau government also made bilingualism mandatory for all Supreme Court of Canada judges, angering ambitious lawyers and lower court judges in the Maritimes and Western Canada who said the court's translation system was effective. Only about 17 percent of Canadians claim to be fluently French-English bilingual.[31]

Change can be mistaken for breakage. Demographics will make Canada a very different place this century, and that change has already started. Canada's birth rate has been below population replacement level for decades. Without immigration, the nation would have fewer people than it did ten years ago. And even with immigration, we have a far higher percentage of older, retired people than we used to. In some towns that have lost their industries— mill towns in British Columbia, mining towns in Ontario—older people have bought cheap houses, and there are hardly any people who aren't retired. The same thing has happened in communities in Ontario's farming regions. Most immigrants to Canada are people of colour. Their presence feeds into the extreme right's great replacement theory, which claims the left wants to use immigration to replace white people. (How white people, including the perpetrators of this atrocity, will be disposed of remains a mystery.)[32]

In 1998, the prestigious academic publisher McGill–Queen's University Press published Martin Loney's analysis of equity efforts in hiring. Loney, a left-wing activist in the 1960s, had by the 1990s concluded that Canada was divided by class, not race. Jean Chrétien was still prime minister. Mike Harris was premier of Ontario, winning office by going after "welfare queens," using the stereotype of Black, single mothers who had kids only to get bigger welfare cheques. Loney, like Harris and his supporters, accused Bob Rae, the most socially left premier in Canada, of putting skin colour ahead of any other criteria.[33] "Identity politics serve not to diminish the accident of race and ethnicity but to endlessly proclaim its importance in asserting the putative oppression experienced by those who are thus identified," he wrote. Loney condemned "the rapidly spreading diversity cult." Academic pretense aside, Loney's message of more than a generation ago was that white men were getting screwed. Their chances of getting hired for a publicly funded job were minimal. If there were layoffs, employers would use equity law to keep people of colour, disabled people, LGBTQ+ people, and women and let the men go. When the City of Toronto restricted its staff, 49.3 percent of affected designated group members were found permanent jobs, while just 28.6 percent of able-bodied men got to stay. To add to the injury, 94.4 percent of retrained men lost their jobs.[34]

Politicians have had no desire to address the real problems of middle-aged workers, or of working people period, in English Canada. Instead, they emphasize equity hiring, a solution to just one of several urgent workplace problems. It helps certain groups, which is a good thing, but it's a lightning rod for people who don't believe the government does anything to help them. People do have problems that need to be fixed. If you don't already have a house, saving for a downpayment is now impossible for most people, and rents are far too high. Provinces haven't trained enough doctors and haven't built enough hospitals to meet the needs of people living in this country.

The challenge, which is a big one these days, is to separate real problems from hyped ones and fix the things that are broken. If you've been robbed, you might be justified in believing the country has an out-of-control crime problem. If you're on a months-long waiting list for an MRI or can't find a doctor, the health system has failed you, and it's logical to assume it's failed the whole country. If you feel left out of the workforce—say you're a middle-aged man who's been fired or laid off and you can't get a job because of ageism or some employers' preference for temporary foreign workers—you might have every reason to feel slighted. It's a horrible feeling to realize your days of making more money every year are over.[35] But it's not the fault of drag queens reading books at some library a thousand miles away, no matter what right-wing media say or the algorithm feeds you. It's just as hard for a middle-aged government worker or lawyer to find work as it is for a fifty-year-old factory labourer. Myths that "elites" somehow escape discrimination have taken over politics. A recent Canadian survey found 63 percent of all older people in Canada feel they had been treated unfairly because of their age by governments, employers, and young people.[36] Our leaders have a responsibility to tell voters the truth about social and workplace issues, rather than use unfocused anger to divide the country so they can win power and fail to deliver solutions.

Some of the private-sector disruption many Canadians are experiencing is caused by demographics, some by worldwide economic and technological change, and some by federal and provincial government policies. Right-wing politicians in Canada, the United States, Britain, France, Germany, Poland, Hungary, Italy, and Australia have tried to leverage the anxiety and anger created by economic and social change to catapult them into power.

If you're a guy like Richard, a young person starting out, or a middle-aged worker trying to hang onto a job, you're standing outside as hurricanes loom over the horizon. The Covid pandemic was one of those storms. Unlike recessions, terrorist attacks, and other modern crises, Covid affected all of us. Just as war forces extremely fast social and political evolution, so do pandemics. Inflation and insecurity caused by Trump's trade war will only add to that.

So back to the question: is Canada broken? Certainly, it's challenged. Canada was always a hard project. It defied geography. North American regions like the Appalachians, the Great Lakes basin, the Great Plains, and the Western mountain ranges run north to south. There have always been language fault lines, especially between Quebec and the rest of Canada. Each region is different, and our federal state evolved to give very limited powers to the national government. Earlier challenges like the conscription crises in the world wars, the pain of the Great Depression, and the threats of Quebec separatism hurt the country, but they did not break it. Politicians, including Justin Trudeau and Pierre Poilievre, have exploited class, gender, and racial cleavages in society.[37] The Conservative leader has exaggerated them in ways that he thinks will help his party. Let's get into some more of them.

WORKING PEOPLE HAVE been miserable, especially in the United States, after thirty years of neo-liberal economic policies that transferred wealth from the middle class to the super rich. Canada, already dealing with declines in its resource sector (outside of oil) and manufacturing, saw 40 percent of its investment capital flow into real estate rather than into job-creating factories, mills, mines, or research and development. By the end of the pandemic, real estate—the buying and selling of buildings—accounted for 20 percent of Canada's gross domestic product.[38] These are not signs of a healthy economy or an innovative and competitive nation. Poilievre had nothing to say about that other than to repeat his "build the houses" slogan.

Even before Covid, living standards had fallen for most people, except the very rich. Life expectancy was declining (although by

2023, Canadians would still, on average, live four years longer than Americans). Trump had promised to bring American jobs back. He started that process by launching a trade war with Canada, hoping our manufacturers, especially car companies and parts makers, would move to the United States. Covid became political when Poilievre and the Tories opposed financial help for people who'd lost their incomes and then supported the anti-vax movement. After life returned to a form of normal—though with an inflation that most family finances couldn't cope with—the feeling of malaise, uncertainty, and stress never left most Canadians. They looked around and saw people like Richard living on the street and thought drugs were out of control. His tent reminded them of the housing crisis. And when they watched the news, there was a good chance Pierre Poilievre, that quotable young man, was there to tell them the government was taxing them into poverty, the system was corrupt, and the country was falling apart. Repeat this enough, and people start to believe it.

The Trudeau government never seemed capable of defending itself. Its communications were, to be kind, amateurish. Chrystia Freeland's claim of "vibecession"—that people were mistaken when they felt the economy was worse—was patronizing.[39] Poilievre easily turned this gaslighting against her, posting on Instagram: "Trudeau Liberals say it's a 'vibecession' and you're just imagining that the economy sucks, while food inflation grows bigger than people's wages. They're out of touch. You're out of money."[40] The next day, he stood in the House of Commons and said, "Mr Speaker, this is from a minister who, after finding out that the economy is entering its sixth consecutive quarter of shrinking per-capita GDP while the American income per person is up, and after learning that there are two million people lined up at food banks, 38% more chronic homelessness and 1,400 homeless encampments in Ontario after nine years of their government, says that we are not in a recession. We are in a vibecession, she says.

"What is the minister's message to people who are hungry and homeless after nine years of her government? Do they just need to get with the vibe?"[41]

Not many people took comfort in government statistics that showed that the country's overall gross domestic product was rising. With more than two million new people in the country since the end of Covid restrictions, the economic gains were a slightly bigger pie shared between a lot more people, as Poilievre pointed out with his "vibecession" comment. Canadians have been sinking deeper into debt for more than thirty years. By 2024, Canadians were, on average, deeper in debt than people in any other G7 country, owing almost two years of their gross income.[42] The Liberals made the same mistake that the Democrats did in the spring of 2024 when they rallied around an obviously unfit Joe Biden: they told people not to believe what they could see with their own eyes.[43]

But is Canada really broken, or is it just changing so fast that a large part of the population wants someone to put on the brakes? Maybe "vibecession" was a stupid thing to say, but then again, maybe the right's claims of national economic demise are greatly exaggerated. David Olive, who had written for the *Toronto Star*'s business pages for years, reported in the summer of 2024 that Rebecca Young, a Scotiabank economist, worried that Canadians might "talk ourselves into decline" and thought that we needed to do a "sentiment check." Olive hooked his column on a study of the economy that Young had just released.

Pessimism, Young said, works against "sweeping transformations [that] are necessary—such as overhauls in tax and transfer systems, extensive reforms in health and education, rightsizing governments, or a revitalization of co-operative federalism." The never-ending bitching and arguing of political partisans and doomsaying academics, business leaders, and media commentators stops the political class and the nation's people from finding and agreeing on solutions.

Young found Canadian household net worth exceeds pre-pandemic levels by more than 25 percent, partly because of the increase in real estate values, and partly because of a better economy. But that increase in net worth was limited only to homeowners: the Bank of Canada said about 35 percent of Canadians were likely to carry big credit card balances and fall into arrears.[44] Renters were piling on this high-income debt much faster than homeowners.

Yet the Liberals could claim at least some people were doing better than they had been. Olive reported that Young found the net wealth of the poorest 20 percent of Canadian households was 50 percent higher than it had been at the start of the pandemic. Again, much of this increase was from real estate. It was wealth that could be borrowed against but not collected and spent unless the homeowner moved into a cheaper place.[45] The numbers for the 20 percent above them on the economic ladder—what she called "the next quintile"—were almost as good.[46] Canada was second only to the US as a preferred destination for direct foreign investment. Investors like Canada's social and political stability and economic prospects. This, supposedly, meant new jobs. But this was no comfort to Canadians who were making higher mortgage and car payments and no longer had room on their credit card for the week or two they used spend in cheap resorts in Cuba or the Dominican Republic to beat the winter blahs.

Investment consultant and former Harper cabinet minister Garth Turner looked to different economists. Turner, who left the Harper government on bad terms and crossed the floor to join the Liberals, suggested that the unemployed were having an increasingly difficult time finding work in 2024. This was something new: when the economy bounced back in 2021 and 2022 after the Covid pandemic, there had been plenty of jobs. That happy time (for employees, not employers) was now over, in part because abnormally high immigration meant more people were chasing the same employment opportunities.

The national unemployment rate was at 6.4 per cent, but people between the ages of fifteen and twenty-four were more than twice as likely to be jobless. There was finger-pointing at the temporary foreign workers program, which allowed fast-food franchises to bring in foreign workers to do jobs that used to be open to young people and retirees. High school students who thought they could work evenings or weekends in a burger joint or coffee shop were now often out of luck. So were many Canadian kids who wanted a summer job.

Wage hikes, the former Tory minister of national revenue wrote, had managed to keep up with the rate of inflation, but that didn't matter if you didn't have a job.[47] It also didn't mean much if you were employed but had just renewed your mortgage at a higher interest rate or needed to borrow money to replace your car.

All these readings of economic chicken guts and predictions for the rest of the 2020s were made before Trump was elected. Presumably, Young, the Bank of Canada's researchers, and Turner started over again after January 20, 2025—and then tore up those research notes when Trump started his war against the Canadian economy two weeks later.

IN MID-JULY 2024, the International Monetary Fund predicted that in 2025 Canada would have the fastest-growing economy of the G7 group of industrialized nations.[48] This fact was reported in the *Financial Post*, but if anyone read it in the newsroom of its parent company, the right-wing Postmedia newspaper chain, they ignored it in their political coverage. Frank Graves, president of EKOS polling, surveyed Canadians and found a country riddled with distrust fuelled by disinformation. The number of Canadians who thought the economy would be healthy in the medium-term had reached an all-time low. A clear majority believed the country was in a recession, even though GDP was growing. Many of them were right: wealth inequality is worse than ever. The $200 billion increase in Elon Musk's personal fortune in 2024 was, as far as GDP is concerned, a net gain for the American economy even if nothing changed except a few numbers on paper. The economy is to a certain extent in the eye of the beholder, and an economy can grow and still leave a lot of people behind.

Whatever people saw and felt in the real world, they were getting a steady drumbeat of bad news and pessimism via social media. Fringe internet news sites, whether published by the far left or, much more likely, the right, said the wheels were coming off Canada and the other liberal democracies. Pollsters and politicians knocking on constituents' doors found millions of young Canadians who were convinced they'd never own a home or afford their parents' lifestyle. They were more pessimistic than even young millennials and Gen-Xers had been decades before. This funk hadn't set in during the pandemic: Graves' numbers spiked as the American presidential election campaign started peaking at the end of 2023 and the Trudeau government sank in the polls.

Graves blamed pandemic fatigue, disinformation, the affordability crisis, and a more dangerous external world for this malaise. Anger was increasingly directed at the Trudeau government and at immigrants. Opposition to immigration had not been this high since polling began in the 1930s. More than 60 percent of Canadians thought too many immigrants were coming into Canada. This was a four-fold increase since 2020. People living in cities and getting their news from professional sources were far more likely to support immigration and multiculturalism than rural Canadians and people who got their news exclusively from social media. There were ugly racial connotations to much of this: the number of people who believed Canada was letting in too many Brown and Black people was spiking upward. Canadians were wary of globalization, distrusting of China but surprisingly tolerant of Russia, which was in the third year of its invasion of Ukraine.

By the end of the pandemic, all the country's problems—unemployment, the influx of foreign students and temporary foreign workers, inflation, economic displacement, rising personal and government debt, "woke" culture, the doctor shortage, waiting lists for surgery, the housing shortage, lousy public transit, photo radar—had a one-word synonym: Trudeau.

Poilievre had made that happen. In the winter of 2022, the whirlwind sown at Poilievre's speaking events, in the country's conservative-dominated print media, on YouTube, in social media, in secret extremist chatrooms and in pseudo-news sites, started moving toward Ottawa.[49]

IN 2025, THE answer to the question "Is Canada broken?" is, frustratingly, "It depends." Each Canadian makes up their own mind. It depends on what part of the country you live in and whether you live in a city where homelessness and addiction are problems. It depends on whether you have a job and/or own a house. It depends on your age. Are you trying to start a career? Are you doing it in a city where it's impossible to find shelter for less than $2,000 a month? Are you a senior without savings or a decent pension? It depends on whether or not you have a trade or skill that's in demand, and on how much time you spend on the internet. The pandemic caused financial and emotional trauma that many Canadians still struggle with. Poilievre's talk of a broken Canada and his slogans for fixing it, combined with public distaste for a prime minister who stayed in power too long, gave the Conservatives a lead in national polls that the world's media believed unassailable. But he's offered no solutions, only slogans.

Nor has he shown, in more than twenty years as an MP, cabinet minister, and leader of the opposition, any ability to deal seriously with domestic problems or foreign threats.

Nationally, there are obvious problems: a housing bubble, a doctor shortage, an opioids crisis, greater public and private debt. Partisans on all sides could have fun in 2024 using cherry-picked figures to prove "vibecession," recession, and lots of other economic claims. But that was way back in 2024, when "axe the tax," "stop the crime," "build the houses," and "defund the CBC" were still issues that fired up the Tories and their supporters. Since Donald Trump's return to the White House and his launch of an economic war against our economy and sovereignty, the question of whether Canada is broken has become somewhat moot, since Canada, as we knew it up until the end of 2024, likely won't exist again.[50]

Now, rather, Canadians are faced with the very real possibility of an existential threat: of our country being absorbed into some kind of union with the United States, very much against the will of most Canadians, or our government capitulating over and over again and simply giving the Trump administration whatever it wants short of handing over sovereignty.[51] Even more likely is that the country will struggle with a brutal recession that will cause terrible hardship to the working people that Poilievre and the right have worked so hard to woo. The systemic problems of health care, housing, the cost of living, the decline of cities... all of those will still exist and probably worsen as Canada's national and provincial governments and many of the country's major cities struggle to cope with the threats and actions of the Trump administration. And if Trump doesn't finish his term, it's likely J.D. Vance, the vice-president, will continue his trade and expansionist policies.

Canada is not ready for a big recession. Its governments are broke. Infrastructure—things like housing, hospitals, schools, roads, even the electrical grid—were already desperately in need of money and work that governments across the country were not willing, or could not afford, to give. On January 20, 2025, a seismic shift brought many Canadians together but hurt many thousands of decent people who were just trying to get by. In 2024, many of these chose a side in the coming election, believing a party could make things better. In February 2025, when the first Trump tariffs were announced (and abandoned), much of that hope turned to anger and fear directed at

America, rather than other Canadians. In a sad way, it was, at least temporarily, a moment for Canadian weavers. Trump brought Canadians together. We might not like each other all the time, and we do fight over our country's issues, but almost every Canadian believes the country—or at least their part of it—is worth fighting for. This shifted the ground from under Poilievre, who was bleeding support after Trudeau's resignation. "Canada First" replaced the "Axe the Tax" sign on his portable podium.

On Canada Day 2024, just seven months before Trump started his trade war threats, 78 percent of young Canadians thought the country was broken, and one-third of them were embarrassed by Canada.[52] Just a few months later, in the weeks following Trump's inauguration, very few Canadians, except perhaps those on the fringes of the political spectrum, would say that out loud.

But a united front against a foreign threat won't get Richard out of his pup tent on Parliament Hill or improve (or save) the lives of the thousands of Canadians who live like him. Many more Canadians might join the addicted and mentally ill on the streets and in the urban woodlands if Trump crushes the Canadian economy. Those people, during the post-pandemic debate over the health of the nation, never suspected they'd lose their jobs in an unnecessary, cruel trade war with a country they thought of as an ally. Governments will try to help those people, but long-standing problems will, again, be ignored. Slogans won't feed families or keep them warm.

Pierre Poilievre is a pro-American libertarian who moralizes the sufferings of the marginalized, insists the free market has inherent genius, drives wedges between the regions of the country, and exploits class envy. By the early winter of 2025, the political gears of the country changed. The political fight in Canada quickly became about who was best to face the external threat and whose ideas were best to help Canadian families and businesses at a time of real danger.

10
THE CONVOY

"Canada is free and freedom is its nationality." That's why I'm running for Prime Minister—to put you back in control of your life, and make Canada the freest country on earth.

PIERRE POILIEVRE, TWITTER, JUNE 18, 2022

I THOUGHT THERE were a lot of trucks in the self-styled Freedom Convoy that plugged the streets of downtown Ottawa for three weeks in the winter of 2022 until I did some driving in the hellish suburban landscape near Canadian Pacific's huge Bolton railway yard, north of Toronto. Go on Google Earth and look at the countryside between Bolton and Brampton. The railway unloads thousands of shipping containers at its giant terminal. These containers are loaded onto trucks and shipped to warehouses, factories, and stores in the Greater Toronto Area (GTA). Fifty years ago, the Bolton yard was in the country and was much smaller. Now it's a hub of the ground-transportation system. Railway spur lines running into factory zones and big warehouses are long gone. Big trucks take the stuff from Bolton, bring it to the place where the container is opened and sorted—for imported consumer stuff, that's likely to be one of the GTA's giant Amazon or Walmart warehouses. Amazon gets orders out to customers with "last mile" trucking, which might not involve a truck at all. This is the most expensive and labour-intensive part of the process.

Around Bolton and Brampton, within a few kilometres of the rail yard, are thousands upon thousands of trucks covering hundreds of acres of truck parking lots. There are places that sell trucks, outfits that fix them.

Then swing over to Toronto's Pearson International Airport. Zoom into the area just west of it, across Etobicoke Creek, where you'll see hundreds of trucks and trailers that take freight from the airport and deliver it in southern Ontario. And then put "Pierre Trudeau International Airport" into the search bar. Google's satellite eye will take you to Dorval, a western Montreal suburb. Same landscape of truck yards, north and south of the airport, with acres and acres of trucks and trailers packed tightly. Same thing around the big rail yard at Cote St. Luc, closer to downtown. Montreal has one of the country's last big seaports. Lots of transport trucks around there, too. And in Halifax, Winnipeg, Windsor, Kitchener, Calgary, Kamloops, Vancouver, and Yellowknife.

Those are just the trucks that are sitting idle. Anyone who drives in Canada knows the highways are full of big transports. And there are garbage trucks, dump trucks, and delivery trucks all over the city streets.

I grew up believing truckers were the knights of the road. Like other kids in Craigleith, outside Collingwood, Ontario, I'd make a "toot toot" hand sign when a truck approached, hoping the driver would respond with a blast of the horn. When I was seventeen and living north of Lake Superior, I binged on trucker albums as an antidote to disco. Two summers working on the Canadian Pacific Railway's main line between Sudbury and Thunder Bay shifted my fan attention to three-kilometre freight trains pulled by five massive engines. Still, I never lost my respect for truckers, especially when I saw how hard one of my friends worked, and the grotesque affect on his health when he did quick trips from Texas to Toronto with loads of fruit and vegetables.

Some 77 percent of the things that are transported in Canada are loaded into the 120,000 semi-trailers licensed in this country. Rail, more efficient but less connected to communities and individual customers, lags far behind, at 22 percent. (Rail is mostly used for bulk freight, like wheat and oil, and for containers moving from seaports to central hubs where this freight still ends up on trucks.) Nearly 72 percent of the trade between Canada and the United States crosses the border on trucks. Trucking creates a lot of jobs: 3.6 percent of working Canadians are either drivers or work in businesses that keep trucks moving, like repair and sales. More than 95 percent of the drivers are men.

But there are problems. Big, systemic problems. Despite a serious shortage of truckers, wages have not kept up with the cost of living. Years ago, Canadian railway engineers and brakemen decertified their unions and signed up to the Teamsters. That union was formed to represent truckers, but it lost ground with the trade and branched out to other industries. Now it represents lawyers, zoo workers, newspaper reporters, and a lot of other people who've never driven a tractor-trailer.[1] Employers have managed to beat down truckers' wages in Canada and keep unions out.

Most truckers are older, white men: more than a third are over fifty-five. Only 3.5 percent are under twenty-five. To keep the trucks on the road, Canada's brought in so many immigrant drivers that at least 27 percent of drivers are new to Canada. That percentage is rising fast and is likely much higher on the 400-series highways in southern Ontario. Some of the old truck-stop restaurants along those highways offer separate menus of Indian cuisine.

Trucking HR Canada, which helps the industry recruit and train drivers, says Canada needs to train thousands of drivers right now. Few Canadians, especially women, want to be on the road. Transport-truck driving is hard on the body: sitting in a seat all day and night under a lot of stress; driving down boring highways, knowing that one human or mechanical error can leave you dead or crippled; being away from home for days at a time; eating truck-stop food for pretty low wages. The average long-haul trucker, the guys who are the top earners in the business, made $972 a week in 2024.[2] A railway locomotive engineer averages $120,000 a year, and since most are unionized, they have decent benefits, paid holidays, and pensions.[3] Truckers are paid by the mile, not the hour, so bathroom breaks are a luxury. Piss jugs litter the shoulders of Canada's major highways.

Women need a lot of persuasion to be talked into this life, and no longer are enough men drawn to it. While the older guys are hanging on until they've had enough, they blow a heart valve, or their doctor tells them to quit, many of the newbies don't stay long because the stress and exhaustion aren't well-compensated. It's a case study of an industry where a labour shortage doesn't translate into better wages.

You probably didn't buy or borrow this book to read about the trucking business. Still, if you haven't skipped over the numbers and the description of the tough working conditions and lousy money, you now know more about truckers than reporters and MPs did when the Freedom Convoy showed up on the national radar, heading eastbound.

Between the low pay and the tedious work, truckers had plenty of reasons to be unhappy. The right had already tried to harness their anger. Tamara Lich, who was an office worker, fitness instructor, singer in a band, advocate for Western separatism, and right-wing activist but who has never driven a transport truck, organized Yellow Vest protests that were supposed to cause the kind of trouble that dogged France in 2018–19 after the French government jacked up the tax on diesel fuel. Lich and her followers tried to cast a wide net by being anti-immigration. They also gave their movement an Alberta accent, tossing in support of that province's oil industry. Their United We Roll protest of 175 trucks, organized by Chris Barber, arrived in Ottawa in the early winter of 2019, and by then, almost all the gripes were about the carbon levy and the supposed need for more pipelines to carry Alberta crude. Ottawa city cops and the RCMP made them park their rigs on empty land and along what was then called the Sir John A. Macdonald Parkway, away from Parliament Hill and the city's downtown.

The protesters who showed up on the Hill were welcomed by the usual Tory suspects, including Poilievre, who showed up on that cold day wearing a trendy Canada Goose parka. "I'm here to tell you that the people of Ontario and the people of Ottawa strongly support your right to build pipelines and get world prices for your world-class oil. Andrew Scheer is the only national leader who has actually announced a plan to clear the way for pipelines." Poilievre told United We Roll demonstrators that Ottawa would use its constitutional interprovincial trade and transportation powers to force provinces to accept pipelines. It would "ban foreign money from the process of approving resource products [sic]." Presumably, this was money spent by environmentalists, not oil and pipeline companies. The Tories, he said, would scrap the carbon tax and gut regulations to make sure pipelines were built and oil production was profitable.

While most Canadians supported the expansion of Canada's oil pipeline network, Poilievre said, "the prime minister is going to try to trick them in the next election and pretend that he's trying to get pipelines built. And we know what he will do: the day after the election, he will make up a thousand new excuses as to why they can't get done. So our job is to expose him for what he has done and what he is doing." As he spoke, a woman in the crowd kept screeching, "Kick the UN out of Canada!" Ezra Levant's Rebel News recorded the speech and posted it to YouTube.[4]

Conservative senator David Tkachuk told them to "roll over every Liberal in the country," but after two days of freezing in Ottawa's brutal February cold, they left. There was some harsh talk in the media about extremists, dirty money, and where the $140,000 raised in a GoFundMe campaign went. But none of that is unusual in Ottawa. In the early winter of 2022, no one expected things to be much different when another convoy started rolling to the nation's capital.

ON NOVEMBER 16, 2021, during the fifth wave of Covid, Brigitte Belton's transport truck was flagged for inspection when it rolled into the Canada Border Services Agency (CBSA) compound on the Windsor side of the Ambassador Bridge. Belton was warned for not wearing a mask. While she waited at customs, she made an emotional TikTok video denouncing the border service and its agents. "In Canada, we're no longer free.... I'm done. I'm done. I don't know what I'm going to do next, but I'm done," she freely and easily posted to the internet. Belton, just in from Detroit and close to her home in Amherstburg, Ontario, said she was worried about being arrested for making the video. That didn't happen.

Later, she told a public inquiry: "I thought that time was the time they were finally going to take a truck that they did not own, take a load that did not belong to them, take my dog and euthanize him, and take me to jail. I was done with CBSA. I was done with the crap that Canada was going through. And I was definitely done with the behaviour of Canadians."

No one killed her dog, took her freight, stole her truck, or took her to jail.

Three days after border guards in Windsor told Belton to wear a mask, the federal government changed border-crossing rules. After January 15, anyone who came into the country by land needed a Covid shot or they'd be quarantined for two weeks. The United States government was tougher: starting on January 20, 2022, foreigners entering the United States by land or ferry needed a Covid shot. There was no quarantine option.[5]

Four days before the Canadian vaccination rule took effect, Belton, Chris Barber, James Bauder (founder of something called Canada Unity), and some others spoke on a Facebook Live event to an audience of three thousand people. They agreed to another United We Roll–style convoy. Tamara Lich started a Facebook page and a GoFundMe account that shocked organizers by raising $3 million in a week, with more money flowing in. In all, they would raise at least $24 million. Some 120,000 donors gave Lich nearly $10.1 million before donations were suspended, a report compiled by the Public Order Emergency Commission said.[6] Nicholas St. Louis, an Ottawa supporter of the convoy, started fundraising at the end of January and raised $1.2 million in cryptocurrency for convoy protesters through Tallycoin, a crowdfunding platform. The HonkHonk Hodl campaign distributed about $800,000 in cryptocurrency during the occupation by handing out $8,000 of bitcoin to each recipient.

Greg Foss, one of the men behind the HonkHonk Hodl campaign, told a newspaper reporter that he spoke to Poilievre "somewhat frequently" and hoped Poilievre would consider him a friend. Foss said he had never seen Poilievre in person, but he coached Poilievre on investing. Foss said the two men agreed that cryptocurrency may be part of the answer to Canada's economic problems. "I have talked with Pierre over time with respect to sound money," Foss said. "He is a sound money enthusiast."[7] (In the real world, "sound money" is currency that holds its value, usually because it's backed by precious metals. Crypto, no matter what the cultists say, is backed by nothing more than two questionable claims: that there's a finite amount of each type, and that people will buy the stuff. It has fluctuated wildly in value through the years, much more than major national currencies.)

There was plenty of real money around downtown Ottawa, too. Hundreds of thousands of dollars in cash donations were taken to a downtown Ottawa hotel, where the money was counted and placed into numbered envelopes with $500 in each one. Convoy organization workers signed for the envelopes and distributed them to protesters, the commission report said. Still, because of provincial and federal government orders, most of the money was returned to donors, with several million dollars remaining in an escrow account to pay the legal fees of people charged or sued for their part in organizing and running the occupation.

BY THE TIME the convoy arrived in Ottawa, thirty-five thousand Canadians had died of Covid. Still, it was easier to find "truckers" who believed in QAnon lies about Covid vaccines than protesters who gave a damn about the elderly people, and the not-so-old, who were gasping their lives out on respirators.

For years, James Bauder, an actual Calgary truck driver and QAnon supporter, had been trying to find some cause that would whip people into a frenzy that might lead to a real insurrection. He and his wife joined the convoy in their recreational vehicle. On the road to Ottawa, he told some supporters that God had told him to do this. Along the way, the protest morphed from being a demonstration against Covid rules to a demand that Trudeau resign. Bauder had a crazy "memorandum of understanding," a sort of Freeman on the Land pseudo-legal contract, that demanded, in the name of freedom and human rights, that the governor general, as the queen's representative, and the unelected Senate overthrow the elected House of Commons.

The rest of their written stuff was just as wacky, so much so that the rest of the convoy people—hardly a collection of constitutional scholars—realized Bauder was making them look stupid and Lich was talking too much. Six months after the protest ended, Belton told a *Toronto Star* reporter she'd fallen out with Lich soon after the protest started. It was Lich's fault that the convoy had so much negative media coverage. Lich wasn't a trucker; she was an activist for the hard-right Alberta separatist Maverick Party.

"I had a plan when I started Convoy, a very simple plan: let's get people involved. There was no political... there was no agenda, there was nothing," Belton said. "It was just to drop the mandates. Once those were dropped, see you later Ottawa. I can go back to my life, everybody can go back to their lives.... But the minute [Lich] came in, there were issues."[8]

Real truckers also tried to put a lot of miles between themselves and the Ottawa show. The Canadian Trucking Association, which has about 120,000 members, said 90 percent of its members were vaccinated, and all of them were compliant with Canada's laws.[9] The association said the people in Ottawa didn't represent them. Some trucking companies started firing employees and contract truckers who took company trucks to Parliament Hill. Canada's spy agencies agreed. In a report, they said many of the people honking horns, sleeping in trucks and RVs, and using downtown Ottawa streets and doorways as their lavatories, had no connection to the trucking business. "Some developed a range of perceived and real grievances that have been motivated by a sense of loss, humiliation, anger and blame, due primarily to underlying factors (e.g. mental health, ideological beliefs and economic situation)."[10]

SOON AFTER THE weird MOU's details were reported in the media, the rest of the convoy leadership shunted Bauder aside. Despite not being at the centre of the action, he still ended up charged with mischief to obstruct property, disobeying a lawful court order, and obstructing/resisting a peace officer. Still, prosecutors were lenient: like the Trump supporters who stormed the American Capitol on January 6, 2021, Bauder and his accomplices got away with trying to overthrow the government.[11] To be fair, Bauder just used nonsense legalese while the Trumpists attacked cops and occupied the Capitol building. Bauder's buddies tried to hide behind the fact that they'd put up a bouncy castle for kids who should never have been at the protest and MacGyvered what had to be the grossest hot tub in Canada.

The Canadian government's Integrated Terrorism Assessment Centre (ITAC) is an organization that analyzes intelligence gathered by the Royal Canadian Mounted Police and the Canadian Security Intelligence Service. It also gets information from the Communication Security Establishment (which intercepts communication and breaks codes), the Canadian Forces, and smaller intelligence agencies in the Privy Council Office (which is under the prime minister), Corrections Canada, the transport department, and the Canada Revenue Agency. These intelligence analysts saw the convoy coming. ITAC sent reports to the Privy Council Office, which sent them on to cabinet. However, the unclassified report ITAC gave to Justice Paul Rouleau's Public Order Emergency Commission, which investigated the government's actions during the crisis, said nothing about warnings to the Ottawa city police or the Ontario Provincial Police.

But someone told the Ottawa cops something. Peter Sloly, who was Ottawa's chief of police through most of the convoy, later told the *Toronto Star* he had been warned by policing partners not to allow the truckers to park downtown. Cabinet minister Bill Blair, a former Toronto police chief (and former supervisor of Sloly), was horrified when he saw trucks parking on the streets around Parliament Hill and became the strongest advocate of a quick end to the protest.

Although Sloly asked the provincial government for 1,800 officers from other forces to help deal with the protest, he got very little support. Ottawa Police Service lawyer David Migicovsky later told the Rouleau commission the force had little time to prepare for the convoy. This was hard to believe: it had been in the news for a couple of weeks before it got to Ottawa. By the time the trucks arrived in the capital, the largest convoy was "forty kilometres long and thousands of vehicles. More convoys followed," he said. This was an exaggeration. Most of the "vehicles" were pickup trucks—almost eight hundred of them, and there were only 230 full-sized transports on Ottawa's streets, a number that would barely have filled a couple of Brampton-area truck yards.[12]

"What none of the intelligence predicted in the very brief period of time prior to the convoy's arrival was the level of community violence and social trauma that was inflicted upon the city and its residents," Migicovsky added. This was true: most of the office buildings in the downtown core were empty because public servants were still working from home, and people there were curious but not afraid. They assumed the convoy was just like the United We Roll protest: truckers would show up and be redirected away from the downtown to an out-of-the-way place that was still within walking distance of Parliament Hill. They'd protest for a day or two, get bored, freeze, and head home. No one had tried to occupy the lawn of Parliament Hill since the winter of 1996–97, when Indigenous protesters lived in a camp.[13] And no one had ever blocked the streets of the government district of the capital for more than a few hours.

On the first weekend, Ottawans weren't surprised by the convoy, the "Fuck Trudeau" banners, the screwballs carrying "Don't Tread on Me" flags from the American Revolution, Confederate flags, and the odd swastika. Demonstrators come and go all the time. They might tie up traffic and be offensive in some way, but respecting free-expression rights is part of the price of being a national capital, with all the jobs and taxpayer-paid amenities that come with that. But the convoy stayed and stayed, and no one knew when they would leave. Or if they would.

Although the convoy members and some journalists portrayed Ottawa as pampered and unaware of the harms caused by Covid rules—not the disease, which was at its peak during the convoy, but the measures taken to mitigate it—the pandemic had hurt people in the national capital as much as it hurt people in the supposed truckers' home towns. Businesses, universities, and schools were shut. Ottawa's bylaw and parking enforcement officers, the most efficient public servants in the city, handed out outrageous fines during the pandemic for trivial offences like walking dogs in closed parks. Ottawa and its Quebec twin city, Gatineau, had been separated for weeks when Quebec police closed the border. Like everyone, Ottawa residents hoped that their lives would get back to normal with vaccines or mythical "herd immunity." Now, people in Ottawa's downtown core were targeted by noisy, angry protesters, whether they had anything to do with the federal government or not. The pandemic was bad for Ottawa, but for many people in the city the protest was the worst part.[14]

Poilievre didn't see it that way.

"[T]he political class has had a wonderful two years," he said a couple of months after the occupation ended. "They have an unbelievable amount of power and a tremendous amount of comfort. All of their homes have gone up by 50% in value and their stock portfolios up until recently have been inflated. And so they're, they're sort of looking down at the working class and saying, oh, what, what are you complaining about? Isn't it, you've never had it so good....

"And you know what? I think that the real backlash by the elites against the truckers was this idea that truckers have no business going to Ottawa and raising their voices. That's the idea that the elites were trying to push back against. They want, they think that the working classes should just shut up and pay up and let the experts just run things for us and, and the population should provide total deference to these institutional elites to just run our lives for us and do what we're told."[15]

But the people whose lives were disrupted by the Ottawa occupation were not the elites or members of the political class. Downtown Ottawa government offices were empty. Most people still in the city's core in the early months of 2022 were working people, mostly renters. A lot of them were seniors, students, small-business owners, and people who didn't work for the government, and those who did were usually low on the bureaucratic food chain. The policymakers at the top of the power pyramid and the media heavyweights can afford to live in trendy neighbourhoods, which downtown Ottawa, with its grim high-rises, certainly is not. If the convoy had occupied old-money Rockcliffe, trendy (for Ottawa) New Edinburgh (where the prime minister lives), upscale Westboro, or lawyer-infested Ottawa South, things would have been very different.

The truly powerful, in their lovely neighbourhoods, and people like Poilievre who lived in the capital's ugly suburbs, might as well have been in another city. Poilievre went downtown for photo ops, then drove home for quiet evenings with his wife and kids. Cabinet ministers and senior bureaucrats avoided the downtown altogether.

CSIS analysts picked up things about the convoy crowd that Ottawa people would only learn from hard experience and most Canadian media would never report. After the protest was over, they submitted a report to the Rouleau commission. In it, CSIS agents said: "The COVID-19 pandemic exacerbated xenophobic and anti-authority narratives. Some violent extremists view COVID-19 as a real but welcome crisis that could hasten the collapse of Western society. Many [extremist] threat actors have adopted conspiracy theories about the pandemic in an attempt to rationalize and justify violence. These narratives have contributed to efforts to undermine trust in the integrity of government and confidence in scientific expertise.

"While aspects of conspiracy theory rhetoric are a legitimate exercise in free expression, online rhetoric that is increasingly violent and calls for the arrest and execution of specific individuals is of concern," the report added. CSIS and the RCMP knew social media and the disruption caused by the pandemic "created an environment ripe for exploitation by influencers and extremists to commit serious acts of violence."[16]

Months later, Poilievre was still pushing his myth that the protesters went to Ottawa to save their jobs. First, even if the people who blocked Ottawa's streets and blast horns were really truckers, they were a very small part of the nation's haulers. Almost all truckers were on the job, making their livings hauling freight. Poilievre was selling a fantasy when he said the protesters refused to leave Ottawa after the first few days because "they had nowhere to go because the government had taken away their jobs. They weren't allowed to go back to their jobs. You can imagine if Trudeau had just said, 'We're going to lift the mandate on the truckers.' They would've fired up their machines and hit the road to go back to work. But he took away their jobs and their livelihoods. No wonder they stayed there for so long. And it was absolutely unscientific and malicious."[17]

That's nonsense. They stayed so long because they were paid to protest. No one needed proof of vaccination to drive a truck in Canada, unless a province made a rule against crossing their borders without one. Quebec's extremely conservative government closed its borders with other provinces to all but essential traffic on April 18, 2021. Police posted at border crossings had a lot of discretion to determine what was essential, though deliveries to Quebec were specifically exempted in the order. People who could show they were vaccinated were not exempted. No one protested.

By January 2022, unvaccinated people could drive anywhere in the country. The convoy protesters proved that when they drove across the country to get to Ottawa. The governments of the United States and Canada required proof of vaccination to cross the international border. That meant the Biden administration would have had to drop its mandate to allow unvaccinated truckers to cross the border. Traffic is always two ways: the truck that leaves Canada must return.

As for the people of downtown Ottawa—supposedly members of the political class who had had "a wonderful two years" during the pandemic—and whether they deserved the noise and disruption of the "trucker" occupation, let's give Pat King the last word. King was one the convoy's key strategists, a man who talked tough in media and YouTube videos. He was also the first main organizer to be convicted. At his sentencing hearing in January 2025, King told that judge, "I am extremely sorry for what happened to the City of Ottawa, and for that, I absolutely apologize for my actions." He said he could "relate" to downtown Ottawa residents who were angry and upset with the weeks of constant honking.[18]

—

THE CONVOY ORGANIZERS, with their weird list of demands for the governor general and their microbe-filled hot tub, were not the kind of people that a responsible politician wants any part of. Or, at least, they weren't until Pierre Poilievre made his move on the Conservative leadership. As the convoy was being put together, Poilievre claimed the government's vaccine policy was "emptying grocery shelves and ballooning food prices," leaving some Canadians to "go hungry." Poilievre said he wasn't against vaccinations, but he did oppose rules that required people to get shots. "We think the best way to get people vaccinated is through persuasion, not intimidation," Poilievre, tapping into his libertarian talking points, said before the convoy arrived. "We don't believe in robbing people's freedoms. We believe in convincing them through data, science, and logic."[19]

The party's transport critic, Toronto-area MP Melissa Lantsman, claimed the federal policy would result in the loss of thousands of jobs and "empty shelves in Canadian retail sectors." She didn't mention provincial rules, which, in some provinces, were more stringent or that the United States would not allow unvaccinated Canadian truckers in to pick up food or anything else.

These were the firebreathers. Their party's leader, Erin O'Toole, wanted Justin Trudeau to walk a line that might have been impossible for anyone to find: "Let's be crystal clear. We can advocate for vaccines but also advocate for people to not lose their ... home or their livelihood," he said. Canadians needed a "practical" alternative to a vaccine mandate.[20]

Two days before the trucks arrived, O'Toole said, "I've never seen the country more divided, and I've never seen a time when we need to come together more than now. After two years, Canadians are tired. They're tired because they followed the rules. They worked from home. Their kids have not been in school. We've shifted our life. Most Canadians got the jab. We've all been trying to follow the rules. And this year started out like last year, with lockdowns, with curfews...."

"I will always fight for the trucker, the essential worker, the Canadian who wants to work. And so will any member of the Conservative caucus." He asked why Trudeau wouldn't hear them out.[21] Then he answered his own question. "The convoy is becoming a symbol of the division and the fatigue that we are seeing in this country." He promised to meet the truckers the next day.

THE TRUCKERS REACHED Ottawa on January 26, 2022.

Poilievre stood on an overpass making a YouTube video as the convoy passed underneath. He made a video manifesto for them. This protest "was not just for truckers, but for the 60 percent of Canadians who say they worry they can't afford food." It was for "the sixty-year-old small businessman who has spent his entire adult life building up an enterprise and watching it get wiped out . . . the depressed fourteen-year-old who's been locked out of school," and "the families that can't take it anymore."

Now the convoy was for "the people who want to stand and speak for their freedoms" and "all those that our government and our media have insulted and left behind."

"Freedom, not fear," Poilievre ended with. "Truckers, not Trudeau."[22] The Great Alliterator was hard at work: slogans over substance; soundbites over sound policy.[23]

There would be plenty of fear in downtown Ottawa over the next three weeks as people who had endured the same inconveniences and stress as everyone else now had to cope with sleep deprivation from the constant horns and shouting, the yelling of obscenities, challenges to fight, and the real possibility of a riot. The noise and threats affected my children. I could watch on TV as "freedom" protesters menaced some of my friends in the media, at least two of whom lost their jobs within the next year because of the decay of journalism in Canada, and, possibly, for alienating right-wing politicians.

Ottawa police did not push the truckers through the downtown and to the parkway along the river as they had done with the United We Roll convoy. Drivers parked their rigs on Wellington Street, which runs in front of Parliament Hill, and on streets nearby. The conquerors of the core of the nation's capital got out of their rigs and began forming up on Parliament's lawn. Some headed into the rest of the downtown.

Early in the protest, some of these "truckers" invaded the Rideau Centre shopping mall in downtown Ottawa and hassled store staff about wearing masks. The mall, one of the biggest in the city, was shut down for the duration. The fear level in the city was jacked up when a false story of an arson was reported in the media. Some reporters lifted a Twitter thread posted by an Ottawa apartment dweller who claimed to have seen a couple of men set a fire in an old apartment building on the edge of the downtown and chain the doors shut. Around the same time, word came from the border community of Coutts, Alberta, that police had found a cache of guns and body armour at a parallel protest. Fifteen protesters were arrested and charged with weapons offences and conspiring to kill police officers. Rumours went around the city that the Ottawa "truckers" were armed, too. Pat King, one of the more vocal convoy leaders, a white supremacist who bragged in online videos that he wasn't afraid of the cops or jail, said on TikTok, "Trudeau, someone's going to make you catch a bullet." (He later hedged this at the Rouleau inquiry, saying he believed a person with mental health issues, not King himself, would do the shooting.[24] But King seemed big, mean, and unhinged.)

There were others in the crowd who were obviously, for lack of a better term, batshit crazy. Romana Didulo, who'd failed at a couple of businesses and now described herself as Queen of Canada, was living proof that anyone could start a cult if their message was strange enough. In late 2020, Q, the mysterious figure behind the QAnon conspiracy theory, went silent.[25] Didulo tried to take up that space and was able to gather some followers. Police saw her as a real threat, partly because of the cultish behavior of the self-styled monarch and partly because she's always been able to raise a lot of money. Using sovereign-citizen rhetoric—a bizarre belief that people can simply opt out of society and the rule of law—she convinced many of her followers to stop paying their bills, including the property taxes on their homes. In Ottawa, she swanned around the city, and young residents who would never have bothered to turn out for a real royal visit kept track of Queen Didulo sightings.

Whatever the threats, and whether the incessant talk of staying and fighting in Ottawa for "freedom" was hyperbole, no one could miss the honking and the blasting of truck horns that went on day and night. They pestered students, retirees, ordinary office workers, and the odd university professor. Some of the protesters showed up at one of the downtown's big shelters for homeless people and demanded food. Staff said the "truckers" menaced the manager and hit one of the clients. People in Ottawa started calling them the Clownvoy, a name that has stuck. They called Didulo "Queen Dildo" and taunted the protesters with the gay anthem "Ram Ranch," a 2012 song by Canadian country artist Grant MacDonald about an orgy of hot young cowboys.

Protesters wandered the core with "Fuck Trudeau" and "Pierre for Prime Minister" flags. Some genius was spotted near Parliament with a Nazi swastika, which earned a slap on the wrist tweet from Poilievre. "People flying evil confederate or Nazi flags or disrespecting monuments are individually responsible for reprehensible acts. They do not represent the thousands of lawful truckers who are actually part of the protest and are peacefully championing their livelihoods & freedoms."[26]

CSIS agents saw convoy organizers handing out directories with the names of all Ottawa city police officers. The Ottawa police were either too poorly led or their leaders believed they could not be trusted to enforce an order to clear the streets. Reporters cherry-picked video to find instances where the cops were nice to the protesters. And it's true that some were just a little too friendly, doing kind things like carrying gas for convoy generators.

When Liberal MPs criticized Poilievre for associating with a protest where some fringe activists carried swastikas, he tried to turn the criticism back on Justin Trudeau. "Just because the Prime Minister dressed up in racist costumes so many times, he can't remember them all," Poilievre said, "doesn't mean every single Liberal is a racist. Just because the Prime Minister had tried to help a corporation [SNC-Lavalin] avoid prosecution after it stole from some of Africa's poorest people, doesn't mean all Liberals are racist. Just because about a half-dozen Liberal MPs who are racial minorities complained about his treatment of them does not mean that all Liberals are racist. That is guilt by association. Why doesn't the Prime Minister opt instead for personal responsibility?"

And then, after Liberal house leader Mark Holland asked Poilievre to be civil, Poilievre blamed Justin Trudeau for teen suicides and destroying the finances of working people.

"They've shown no respect for the people," Poilievre said. "This country right now is like a raw nerve, and the Prime Minister is jumping up and down on it again and again with his inflammatory rhetoric. We are talking about people who have 14-year-old kids who are suicidal after two years of lockdowns. I just spoke to a waitress whose business was wiped out by lockdowns. I'm talking to truckers, who have been delivering foods to our plates throughout this. These are the very people, honest, hard-working and shirt-off-your-back types of people, that the Prime Minister keeps attacking."[27]

EVERYTHING WAS FALLING into place for Poilievre. The Conservative Party had just hired a new communications director, Sarah Fischer. O'Toole likely didn't know she was a Poilievre supporter. Within a couple of days of getting the job, Fischer, who had run for the party in 2019, was on the street in front of the Parliament buildings schmoozing with truckers and honking horns on their rigs. She had already sounded off about "globalists" and "the inception of a new world order," which were dog whistles for racists and conspiracy theorists.

As the truckers packed for their trips to Ottawa, Conservative MPs were at a retreat, trying to figure out how they'd beat Justin Trudeau. There was a solid core inside the party that wanted O'Toole out and believed the party should push to the right. As the lines of trucks on the Trans-Canada Highway grew, the far-right seized the full attention of the nation's media. Protesters who were the most outrageous were likely to get more airtime.

The anti-vaxxers among them ignored Poilievre's support for (completely voluntary) immunization and embraced him. Along with the "Fuck Trudeau" banners were many MAGA hats and Trump signs in the convoy, along with a few Confederate flags and picket signs with the word *Freedom*. Gary Mason, the *Globe and Mail*'s Western Canada columnist, said that the message had meanings that went far beyond the literal definition of the word. "For many, [freedom] is a word that has become code for white-identity politics and the far-right's weapon of choice in the culture wars."[28]

Fiona MacDonald, associate professor of political science at the University of Northern British Columbia, took that analysis even further. "Regardless of political rhetoric, it's overwhelmingly clear that this protest is not about truckers or vaccines," she wrote. "Rather it's about what American sociologist Michael Kimmel refers to as 'aggrieved entitlement'—a perception that the benefits and/or status you believe yourself entitled to have been wrongfully taken away from you by unforeseen forces. This perception can lead to feelings of humiliation and, in turn, violence.

"In a textbook-worthy example of 'aggrieved entitlement,' the organizers of the convoy protest, most of whom aren't employed in the trucking industry, seized on the trucker vaccine mandate to mobilize those Canadians already angry and mistrustful about the direction of our society. That's why it's not surprising the messaging goes far beyond vaccine mandates and includes overt symbols of racism such as swastikas and Confederate flags. It's also funded at least in part by what observers have labelled 'rage donating.'"[29]

O'Toole tried to connect with the convoy, but it was too late. As he had in the WE Charity hearings, Poilievre had put himself into the middle of the biggest story of the day, even before it had taken shape in Ottawa. On February 1, five days after the trucks arrived in Ottawa, Poilievre claimed "PierreforPM.ca" at the country's internet domain registry, though some trucks had arrived in Ottawa as early as January 28 with "Pierre Poilievre for PM" flags fluttering alongside their "Fuck Trudeau" and Confederate banners.[30] It's not clear who made these flags, and whether Poilievre was their man because he supported United We Roll or had secret connections among the convoy movement. It was Poilievre, not O'Toole, who welcomed the convoy and became their political advocate. Truck engines were still warm when Poilievre tweeted that the protesters were "bright, joyful and peaceful Canadians" and started taking selfies with them.

The convoy crowd loved Poilievre, and not just because he delivered coffee to them. (Poilievre is know around Ottawa as a coffee snob, but Tim Hortons was all right for the truckers.) They had a meeting of the minds on many of the main issues: vaccines, "lockdowns," and the supposedly sinister plans of the World Economic Forum (to which he's been a delegate). This was the "Great Reset," a 2021 American conspiracy theory of world domination by rich people who attend the WEF's annual meeting in Davos. Poilievre, alone among the people who have led the federal Conservative leaders, seemed to believe in it.

The WEF, he said, was a gathering of "global financial elites" attempting to "re-engineer economies and societies" to "empower the elites at the expense of the people." Freedom-loving people "must fight back against global elites" and "their power grab." In November

2020, during a lull in the hearings on the controversy over the federal student-grants plan, Poilievre loudly launched a petition that people were supposed to use to call on the government to "protect our freedom" and "end plans to impose the 'Great Reset.'"[31]

In April 2021, Poilievre had made his "gatekeepers" speech denouncing what he saw as the various elites that got in the way of entrepreneurial people. "They are the bureaucracies, lobbyists, the consulting class, the politicians, and the agencies who make their living by stopping other people and charging them excess tolls to do anything positive at all." The House of Commons was, as usual, nearly empty when Poilievre made the speech. But the speech wasn't for other MPs; it was aimed at the people who found it on social media and watched it on YouTube. So Poilievre had credibility with members of the convoy and their supporters long before they decided to come to Ottawa.

Political columnist Michael Harris is one of the best journalists in Canada. He broke the Mount Cashel Catholic boys' school sex abuse scandal in Newfoundland and the wrongful murder conviction of Mi'kmaq fisherman Donald Marshall, and his 2014 book *Party of One*, on Stephen Harper's years in power, was one of the few recent political books nominated for a Governor General's Award for literature. Harris watched events closely as they quickly developed.

He saw how a faction in the Conservative Party wagered that the "occupation could supercharge aggrievement across the country. They saw potential in the pandemic's persistent pain, recent chaos at the country's airports, a sputtering health-care system and brutal inflation. Just maybe the trucker's protest could distill all that frustration into one compelling and very useful spectacle." This was too much for Ontario premier Doug Ford. He might be a populist, but the economy of his province was threatened. "It's not a protest anymore. It's become an occupation," Ford said. "It's only hurting families. It's hurting businesses that these folks are supposed to be supporting, but it's hurting businesses in a big way."[32]

The Conservative Party "lurched to the populist right in the very first days of dysfunction in Ottawa, Harris wrote. "It abruptly changed leaders, championed the truckers, and came after Justin Trudeau personally. They were betting that with the help of evangelicals, angry blue-collar workers and the usual fatigue with any three-term government, the truckers would chauffeur them back into power. And no matter what he and his allies will say publicly, Poilievre's direction for the Conservatives clearly was inspired by Donald Trump's Make America Great Again movement."[33] O'Toole, who had tried to be a moderate in Eastern Canada and a hard-right Tory in Western Canada, had lost his balance and been pushed off the political stage. After seeing a video Poilievre made as the convoy entered Ottawa, Aaron Wherry, another bright pundit, told his CBC audience that the protest was the kickoff for the Conservative leadership race.[34] He was right: in less than a day, O'Toole would be out.

On February 2, 2022, six days after the first trucks arrived, Conservative MPs held a secret ballot on O'Toole's leadership. He hadn't expected this. The entire party was supposed to meet at a convention the next year to decide whether O'Toole should stay on. But on the weekend that the truckers arrived, thirty-five Tory MPs signed a letter to force an immediate leadership review, which would be decided only by members of the caucus of Tory MPs. The result wasn't even close: of the 118 ballots cast, 73 MPs voted to fire O'Toole. The Conservative leadership race was on. After the weeks of fawning media coverage in 2020 and 2021 when he was destroying WE Charity, and with his new momentum as chief political backer of the convoy, Poilievre was now the front-runner. One of his opponents anonymously posted a two-year-old video of Poilievre trashing Indigenous activists who'd blockaded a highway to protest the building of a pipeline across their land. "All hell is breaking loose," Poilievre told the host of CBC's *Power & Politics* early in 2020. "These blockaders are taking away the freedom of other people to move themselves and their goods where they want to go and that is wrong."[35] But this didn't stick: Poilievre and many in the modern right don't worry about inconsistency.

Protesters blockaded the approaches to the Ambassador Bridge, which links Windsor and Detroit, on February 7. This protest was a serious threat to the North American auto industry. Ford's plant in Windsor shut down, and parts suppliers for the city's big Chrysler plant also started closing. The next day, premier Doug Ford declared the Ambassador Bridge reopened, but it wasn't true: the crowd of men, women, and children held off police for another five days. Toyota's three Ontario assembly plants started running out of parts on February 10. This forced Ford's hand. On February 12, he invoked the province's *Emergencies Act*, and police forced demonstrators away from the bridge. (Windsor would claim its taxpayers were stiffed by Ottawa and Queen's Park for $7 million in extra policing costs.)

The day before the Ambassador Bridge was shut down, Poilievre announced he was running for leader. He used the word *freedom* or a variation of it nine times in his three-minute speech. He promised to make Canadians the "freest people on earth," with "freedom to make your own health and vaccine choices, freedom to speak without fear."[36]

POILIEVRE'S IDEOLOGICAL COLLEAGUES in the United States were watching, which made the whole thing even more thrilling to Canada's right and sent thrills through the reporters covering the protest. Nasty Trumpists, like Congress members Marjorie Taylor Greene and Jim Jordan, and Florida governor Ron DeSantis, praised the Freedom Convoy. Then Trump himself told one of his rallies, "We want the great Canadian truckers to know we are with them all the way," and called Trudeau a "far-left lunatic."[37]

His mouthpieces at Fox News, people like Tucker Carlson (who still had a job there), Sean Hannity, and Laura Ingraham, also lent their support to the convoy. So did future Martian Elon Musk, who tweeted "Canadian truckers rule" and "if the Canadian government is suppressing peaceful protests, that's where fascism lies." Musk also compared Trudeau to Hitler but took down that tweet.[38] (In January 2025, Musk made what looked like a fascist salute at a Trump rally, something he denied. A few weeks later, he told Alternative für Deutschland, the extreme-right German political party, that Germans should stop wallowing in Holocaust guilt.)[39]

After the protest, the National Observer, an online newspaper, tracked the social media support of the convoy by Russian media and that country's army of online sock puppets and bots and found clear evidence of foreign interference.[40] RT, the Russian state TV network that has been caught creating disinformation and been accused of espionage, sent reporters to encourage the "truckers" by asking them loaded questions and causing as much trouble as they could.

Poilievre kept using the truckers as a cudgel. The crisis was all Trudeau's fault.

"I'm proud of the truckers and I stand with them," Poilievre said in a newspaper interview. "They have reached a breaking point after two years of massive government overreach of a prime minister who insults and degrades anyone who disagrees with his heavy-handed approach. But let's be honest, if Canadians are being inconvenienced, or in any way suffering from these protests, it is because Justin Trudeau made these protests happen and his intransigence is keeping the protests going."

Poilievre accused Trudeau of imposing a vaccine mandate on truckers "as a vindictive wedge strategy to divide Canadians and demonize an apparently unpopular minority of unvaccinated people to his own political advantage. But now it's blown up in his face. So he's gotten himself into an impossible political situation. And unfortunately, the rest of the country is held hostage by his unwillingness to do the right thing, admit he was wrong, and lift these mandates."[41]

Many journalists claimed the Ottawa occupation would only end if Trudeau deployed the army.[42] (They'd clamoured for the imposition of the *Emergencies Act* in the spring of 2020, but the government didn't believe it needed these powers to fight Covid.) Some of these reporters later conveniently forgot their enthusiasm for the use of soldiers in the pandemic and in downtown Ottawa.

Chief Sloly was forced out when Ottawa cops didn't, or wouldn't, clear the streets. Some of the blame heaped on Sloly belonged to the mayor, a career politician named Jim Watson, who had made a deal with convoy leaders on February 13 that would have let them stay in the city if they moved their trucks off residential streets.[43] Sloly knew what was happening. "It would be very hard to believe that any individual could not understand that there was a level of unlawfulness and public danger and risk—heightened risk—at any point from January 29 onward," he testified months later. He might not have had enough cops and machinery to move the "truckers" out. Maybe he was right not to try: losing a fight to the protesters or having his cops embroiled in a riot in front of Parliament Hill would have caused unimaginable problems. As for Trudeau not coming out to meet them, what the prime minister said was correct: "It wasn't that they just wanted to be heard. They wanted to be obeyed."[44]

Fear ratcheted up even more on February 14, when the RCMP raided the protest encampment in Coutts, Alberta, and accused several protesters of possessing illegal firearms and plotting to kill police officers. (They would be convicted on the gun charges, acquitted for conspiracy.) That day, the federal cabinet said it would invoke the *Emergencies Act* to clear downtown Ottawa and end any blockades that might spring up in other parts of the country. The law gave police new powers to protect critical infrastructure, including downtown Ottawa.[45] Crowds were to be dispersed, tow trucks commandeered to move trucks, bank accounts frozen, truck insurance policies cancelled.[46]

POILIEVRE, UNAWARE OF or not caring about the irony, accused Prime Minister Justin Trudeau and his cabinet of engineering the crisis for political gain. "They have attempted to amplify and take advantage of every pain, every fear, every tragedy that has struck throughout this pandemic in order to divide one person against another and replace the people's freedom with the government's power." The *Emergencies Act*, he said, was the "latest and greatest example of attacks on our freedom."[47] He posted a petition on his Facebook page, saying the *Emergencies Act* was an attack "on the innocent."[48]

Ottawa police, with a new chief and backed by cops from forces across Ontario, Quebec, and some from other parts of the country, did their duty professionally and with a minimal amount of violence. Very few truckers had their insurance cancelled or faced any other punishment. It took less than two days to clear Ottawa's downtown, and another week or two to clean up the mess, including human waste, in the city core.

In the end, the convoy goons got away with a lot. Police never charged most of the people who committed petty crime and threatened people living in the downtown core.[49] Some of those who were serious about overthrowing the government left Ottawa with clean records or were charged with less serious crimes and were almost always freed on bail. So far, the cost of the convoy—$62 million for fire, police, paramedics, transit, roads, and other city services—along with losses to hundreds of private businesses, has been paid by Ottawa taxpayers and merchants. As of winter 2025, a serious class-action lawsuit for losses and suffering of people living in the downtown core is grinding through the court system. The people who are suing want the millions of dollars frozen in GiveSendGo and GoFundMe accounts. Hacks of the crowdfunding sites show most of this money, supposedly more than $10 million, came from American donors, though CSIS didn't try to track them because it would have needed three different approvals by two oversight agencies.

Poilievre and the convoy crowd claimed to speak for ordinary Canadians, but pollsters found this wasn't true. A survey taken by Leger near the height of the protest found only 32 percent of

Canadians supported the convoy. Nearly two-thirds of the country's people thought the convoy represented a small minority of selfish Canadians.[50]

I VISITED THE Antrim Truck Stop outside Ottawa in October 2024. My wife and I were starting out on a six-hour drive across central Ontario, and the Antrim Truck Stop says it has "the best cuisine on the 417." The place offers a meatloaf breakfast, we were running late, it was lunch time, so this seemed to be the right kind of thing to start the day with. And, being a truck stop, the meatloaf did not disappoint. It came with a generous serving of gravy that was put to use on the big pile of home fries. The place was busy with truckers and local people. The manager came around to ask how things were going; the waitress was there with coffee but didn't pester us with demands that we praise the food. On the way out, we stopped at the truck stop's bakery to load up for the long trip through the forest between Renfrew and Orillia, and we spent some time in the tuck shop, which sells interesting and clever things that truckers use.

I also grabbed a copy of *Today's Trucking* magazine. It seemed like a good way to learn a bit about the people I'm writing about. I come from a family of railroaders: my grandfather and my dad worked as teenage bellhops on Canadian Pacific's Great Lakes passenger ships to make money for their boarding school expenses and their vices. My two sisters and I worked for CP Rail, as did my brothers-in-law and their families. My nephew is a railway engineer. So trains, we get. Trucks, not so much. I had a friend who was a long-haul trucker, doing sleepless runs across the United States until he began puking blood. He had a lot of stories, some of them true. But that was a long time ago.

Today's Trucking calls itself "the business magazine of Canadian truckers." That seems like a reasonable claim. It's published in Toronto, and its features focus on the trends in the industry. There were other trucker publications around, but these magazines were sales listings for trucks and heavy equipment. A tiny logo on the masthead of *Today's Trucking* shows it gets money from the Canadian Periodical Fund, which is normal for trade magazines. There were no government ads for green-energy programs, nothing to suggest *Today's Trucking* does anything but cater to the interests of its readers, who are the people who run the trucking companies and the folks who drive the rigs.

Today's Trucking's readers' letters to the editor were about two issues: the need for better safety practices enforced without a lot more paperwork, and temporary foreign workers. Canada's truck companies seem to want more foreign workers to help ease the shortage of drivers in some parts of the country, and they worry that these new truckers are being put onto the highways without enough training. The Trudeau government had just announced cuts in the number of temporary foreign workers in the trucking industry.

Truckers' lives depend on safe vehicles and careful drivers. One *Today's Trucking* article warned that there are truck drivers on the highway with measurable levels of THC in their bloodstream. These are people on domestic runs. Truckers who cross the border are more careful to stay away from cannabis until it's out of their system. There was a handy article on making trucks safe for winter roads.

Truck company owners fear a recession and are getting ready for it. They see new technology as a money-maker, and they want to keep costs down to be able to compete with American haulers. How could they do that? With green technology like hydrogen fuel. There was a story in that issue of *Today's Trucking* about garbage trucks in Edmonton testing hydrogen fuel technology. Another story warned truckers that their customers would ask them about their efforts to reduce greenhouse gas emissions. They'd need telematic technology to measure that. But electric trucks were still up in the air. The truckers want them, but they need to be able to drive long distances without stopping for a long time to charge truck batteries.

Trucks now have a range of 400 kilometres (about 250 miles) on new batteries. That's up by 30 percent in the previous two years, so the technology seems to have potential. Long-haul truckers drive more than 400 kilometres in one shot. It's 370 kilometres from Toronto to Windsor (the busiest truck route in Canada), but traffic's an issue. And Toronto to Montreal is too far. The big warehouses in Cornwall, Ontario, are just barely out of range. But clearly, something's coming. Just as computers were coming in the 1980s. No one quoted in *Today's Trucking* saw this as a bad thing.[51]

There was no pissing and moaning in *Today's Trucking*. The conversation about temporary foreign workers focused on the needs of the industry, not the countries of origin of the foreign workers. Articles on green-energy conversion were discussions of technical feasibility and the costs of the new technology. They weren't attacks on carbon taxes and climate change science. There were stories about truck shows and drivers of the year. These were proud businesspeople who seemed confident of the future and self-assured of their ability to deal with change. It was a sharp contrast to the "victims" who showed up in Ottawa's downtown in 2022. I suspect the readers of *Today's Trucking* and the haulers that appear in its pages were on the highways that winter, not shitting in doorways near Parliament Hill and badgering Rideau Centre store clerks about wearing masks. Like the meatloaf, *Today's Trucking* made me feel very happy inside.

11
TOP DOG

If we have one takeaway from the past eight months, it's that a lot of Canadians are angry, angrier than most of us realized. They are mad about the pandemic, mad about taxes, mad about the high cost of living. They signed up in droves to make their voice heard, just like they descended on Ottawa to yell at the prime minister. They are like a hive of bees, ready to explode.

CONSERVATIVE STRATEGIST AND LOBBYIST
TASHA KHEIRIDDIN[1]

THE CONVOY CAME for Trudeau but ended up finishing Erin O'Toole's career as leader of the federal Conservatives. Knives were already out for O'Toole before the protest. Since the election, Conservative politicians and pundits argued over O'Toole's strategy of trying to attract centrist votes. The conservatives hadn't tapped into working-class anger to win more seats in eastern Canada. In Nova Scotia, voters rejected a Liberal government in a post-Covid election and elected a Conservative majority. Conservatives Doug Ford and François Legault had won re-election in Ontario and Quebec by running as Trumpists with a pinch of Canadian kindness. In 2021, O'Toole won more votes than Trudeau, but the People's Party of Canada led by former Tory leadership candidate Maxime Bernier siphoned off eight hundred thousand right-wing votes.[2]

In the fall of 2020, Senator Denise Batters tried to circulate a petition for a leadership review. The party's executive stood with O'Toole, and Batters was kicked out of the Conservative caucus. O'Toole should have been helped by a consultant's report that blamed professional campaign staff for the 2021 election loss. They had over-managed the candidate, and voters thought he'd been marketed and muzzled. Canadians knew that whoever O'Toole was, the one on the hustings was a fake. After the hearings on the WE Charity contract and smaller scandals—some real, some not—the Tories had expected to win the 2021 election. Someone had to be blamed.

The party was shifting to the right, with its loudest voices sounding more and more like Trumpists. Although hard-right Tories had been trying to drive O'Toole out since late summer 2021, the caucus vote that finished him off, his political assassin claimed, was triggered by an issue dear to the most extreme social conservatives. Despite serious opposition in his caucus, O'Toole supported the Trudeau government's amendments to the Criminal Code that banned the forced mental health "treatment" of trans and gay people, sometimes called "conversion therapy." Poilievre had also voted for this legislation. Conversion therapy and other LGBTQ+ issues were loudly fought over in the United States. Trump-supporting politicians enthusiastically supported conversion therapy, despite their claims that they fought for personal freedom.[3]

After news broke that MPs on the right wing of his party planned a challenge to his leadership, O'Toole turned to the power of poetry, using Robert Frost's "The Road Not Taken." Ahead, he said, lay two roads. Down one road was a party that would be "angry, negative, and extreme." Down the other was a party of "inclusion, optimism, ideas and hope." Choosing the former would take the Conservatives to a dead end. They would become the NDP of the right, a protest party with no chance of winning power. Voters would not believe the Conservatives could be a real alternative to the Liberals. O'Toole told his caucus that positive, inclusive Conservatism would ensure the party "better reflects the Canada of 2022." It was a clear warning to the old Reform wing that they stood to lose the gains they'd made in urban ridings, especially in Ontario, after the merger of the Canadian Alternative and Progressive Conservative parties.

In the end, the party turned right, with 73 out of 119 Tory MPs voting to push O'Toole out. One abstained.

O'Toole probably saw it coming. He had already recorded a video attacking his critics as shallow, saying: "This country needs a Conservative Party that is both an intellectual force and a governing force . . . Ideology without power is vanity. Seeking power without ideology is hubris."[4]

O'Toole's ouster was seen by Ottawa-based pundits as the victory of Western social conservatives over eastern Tories who tended to be socially liberal but wanted balanced budgets and less government meddling in the economy.[5] O'Toole was one of those eastern Conservatives, people who supported the centrist "Big Blue Machine" governments that ran Ontario from the Second World War until the mid-1980s. The pundits were wrong: there was no chasm between west and east. In the next few months Poilievre would prove conservatives across Canada had moved to the hard right. "Progressive" conservatism was, at least for now, a spent force in Canadian politics. In 2025, Chrystia Freeland and Mark Carney would try to incorporate its survivors into a more centrist Liberal Party.

IN 2024, O'TOOLE claimed foreign interference may have led to his removal. In an interview with lawyers working for the Foreign Interference Commission, O'Toole said he was suspicious about the motives of the person behind the petition that called for a leadership review following the 2021 election.

There's other evidence of meddling and dirty politics in O'Toole's ouster and in the early weeks of the leadership race. At the end of March 2022, Melanie Paradis, who had worked on O'Toole's parliamentary staff, told her Twitter followers that dirty money, probably foreign, was being used in the race. She'd been contacted about a $120 donation she never made. Laurence Toth, spokesman for Charest's campaign, said anonymous people made several false donation pledges to the former Quebec premier using the real names of party members and an internet account with a Ukrainian IP address. The money, which Charest was counting on, never arrived. The donation promises, he said, were an "obvious attempt to create chaos" for his campaign.[6]

Patrick Brown claimed memberships sold by his campaign simply disappeared from the party's records.

Poilievre's team was also targeted. On April 12, Poilievre said he suspected people using pre-paid credit cards to buy party memberships were manipulating the leadership election. The credit cards weren't handed out because memberships were expensive: it cost just $15 to join the Tories. More likely, they were used to buy memberships under fake names. After lawyers for the Poilievre campaign complained to the party's headquarters, the Conservatives stopped accepting membership payments from those cards.[7]

On July 5, 2022, the party disqualified Brown from the race. Debbie Jodoin, a staffer on Brown's campaign, claimed Brown broke the financial rules of the *Elections Act* by paying her through a third-party company.[8] Despite a concerted campaign against him by some provincial and federal conservative operatives, Brown was easily re-elected mayor of Brampton in the fall of 2022. A year later, when the *Toronto Star* uncovered a $37,000 payment to Jodoin's lawyer paid by the Poilievre campaign, Poilievre said it wasn't poof of sleaze. He supported whistle-blowers.

Whether foreigners had any serious role in O'Toole's defeat or used dark money or dirty tricks to try to manipulate the outcome, the nature of Canadian politics had changed. In all the major parties, leadership races are hardball campaigns. Friends who share political beliefs often turn against each other when they join opposing campaigns and never make up. Politicians running for a party leadership and candidates from outside politics pick apart the party's policies, insult the people who created them, and claim they can do a better job than the previous leader's team.

That rancour can last for years. In January 2025, O'Toole, now out of politics, thanked Liberal cabinet minister Anita Anand when she announced she wasn't running again. "I saw the dedication [Anand] brought to National Defence at a time it was desperately needed," O'Toole, who'd been a military officer before practising law and going into politics, wrote on Twitter. "She cared deeply about the CAF [the Canadian Armed Forces], their families and the need for Canada to do more. I wish her fair winds and following seas." Jenni Byrne, who'd run Poilievre's leadership campaign, shot back on the same Twitter thread with, "For anyone unsure why Erin is no longer leader of the Conservative Party... [Anand] supported DEI [diversity, equity and inclusion] policies like name, rank and pronouns. Tampons in men's rooms, etc."

O'Toole's 2020 leadership campaign co-chair, lawyer Walied Soliman, was one of the many people who criticized that comment as toxic, writing "to all the young people involved in [the Conservative Party] and politics in Canada generally, this is exactly how not to behave in those inevitably fleeting moments when you feel you are on top. Be humble in leadership."[9] In many parties, that kind of hard feelings hurts the chances of winning national elections. Paul Martin's career ended when many Jean Chrétien loyalists found other things to do during the 2004 and 2006 campaigns. But with national polls showing leads over the Liberals of 20 to 25 percent in the days before Trump was sworn in and the Liberal leadership campaign ramped up, Poilievre insiders believed they had power to burn.

—

AS SOON AS O'Toole was forced out, the Conservatives elected MP Candice Bergen their interim leader, with the leadership convention set for September 10. There would be no floor vote: starting in early July, ballots were mailed to party members. The September session would announce the winner.

Because of his name recognition, Poilievre was the only Conservative with wide support. Things had changed since 2019, when he'd floated a trial balloon in the *Toronto Star* saying he was putting together a campaign. He'd only been able to attract John Baird and Jenni Byrne to the Poilievre-for-leader team. That year, the party was looking for a centrist. After he won the leadership, O'Toole pushed Poilievre out of his high-profile critic job, but Poilievre was able to do an end-run around the leader by taking down Morneau and ruining WE Charity in Canada, then became the most vocal backer of the Ottawa occupation. The convoy showed two things: there were a lot of angry people who could be recruited to support the Conservatives if they lurched to the hard right, and Poilievre was the only leadership candidate who had the support of the kind of conservatives who, in the United States, were Donald Trump's base.

Because they didn't have Poilievre's name recognition, political team, and money, two candidates who were even further on the political right weren't in Poilievre's league. Social conservative Leslyn Lewis ran on causes dear to the religious right: repeal of the ban on conversion therapy for transexual people and funding cuts to pro-choice non-government organizations. Roman Baber, an independent member of the Ontario legislature, became a leadership candidate after he was booted from Doug Ford's caucus for saying in an open letter that "the lockdown is deadlier than COVID."

Journalists and pollsters tried to turn the 2022 leadership contest into something of a race. Jean Charest, ex-Mulroney cabinet minister, one of the two Progressive Conservatives who won a seat in the brutal Chrétien sweep of 1993, and former Liberal Premier of

Quebec, was built up as Poilievre's main competitor. The problem: there were too many "formers," and all of them came with baggage.

Charest had worked for years as a consultant and lobbyist. Huawei, the Chinese telecom giant punished by the Trump administration in 2018 for allegedly evading sanctions against Iran, was one of his law clients. That company's chief financial officer, Meng Wanzhou, was arrested in December 2018 and was out on bail, living in one of her Vancouver mansions. In retaliation, the Chinese government arrested Michael Spavor and Michael Kovrig, two Canadians working in China.

Charest's team had some respectable members, people like Tasha Kheiriddin, who had tested the leadership waters herself before deciding to help manage Charest's campaign. Early in the race, polls showed Charest ahead of Poilievre in Ontario. If those numbers were solid, and he sold enough party memberships there and in Quebec, he might have had a chance. The same poll, taken by the Angus Reid Institute between March 10 and March 15, 2022, also found people who'd voted Liberal were more open to changing their vote to Charest than they were to supporting Poilievre and the other people in the race. This was supposed to show Tory party members that Charest could beat Trudeau in a general election. But this was not a time for centrists.

Randy Besco, a professor of political science at the University of Toronto, told a CBC reporter, "Poilievre is more credible than [far-right leadership rivals] Roman Baber, Leslyn Lewis...because he's a high-profile former cabinet member and he seems more conservative than Jean Charest, who literally campaigned on being a moderate. Generally, the candidate that is the more conservative and also credible wins."

Another poli-sci prof, Barry Cooper at the University of Calgary, was even more harsh. "[Charest] is not yesterday's man. He's the day before yesterday's man." A Charest-led party would lose support in Western Canada, Cooper added. The professor didn't say which party could benefit from this lack of enthusiasm. Certainly, it wouldn't be the Liberals or New Democrats.[10]

POILIEVRE DIDN'T JUST enter the race a month earlier than his main opponents. He was miles ahead in his media strategy. Jean Charest and, while he was in the race, Patrick Brown campaigned as though it were the 1990s, when coverage by television networks and daily newspapers still mattered. In 2022, anyone expecting to get their message out by having the parliamentary press gallery and local journalists report their campaign trips and policy announcements might as well have given speeches in ghost towns. Poilievre and his team knew how to use new media to recruit hard-right internet trolls, conspiracy theorists, and angry people as well as "ordinary" Canadians. Mainstream media and popular culture mavens are wrong when they portray the internet as a medium for the young. Maybe grandmothers and middle-aged mill workers weren't on TikTok or making Pornhub videos—though a frightening number of grannies were—but they were on Facebook and Twitter. So were many long-time members of the Conservative Party.

While Twitter was, before it was bought by Elon Musk, the favoured medium of politicians and journalists—academics and the media dubbed the 2011 federal campaign the "Twitter Election"—YouTube was the big draw for actual voters. Many Canadians have cut their TV cables, tuned out network TV, and just watch streaming services and YouTube. During the 2022 leadership campaign, Poilievre had more than two hundred thousand YouTube subscribers—far more than any other Canadian politician.[11] Conservative MP Michelle Rempel Garner, who wasn't in the race, had forty-four thousand. Leslyn Lewis, who was a candidate, had about three thousand subscribers, while Roman Baber, a long-shot candidate, had just over one thousand.

Poilievre posted about 130 videos in the first three months of that campaign. Jean Charest, his only serious competitor, didn't make any, despite having some of the country's most high-profile political strategists and communications experts on his team. And there were dozens more YouTube videos uploaded by news outlets and the Canadian Public Affairs Channel (CPAC), the parliamentary news channel carried by all cable TV companies. In all of them, Poilievre rattled off his short, pithy, and often nasty slogans, nicknames, and insults.

Aengus Bridgman is a researcher at the Media Ecosystem Observatory, a joint project of McGill University and the University of Toronto. In May 2022, he told a *Hill Times* reporter, "When Poilievre is on YouTube...he's not looking for that same kind of [traditional] media presence" his competitors, like Charest and Brown, were "seeking...on platforms like Twitter. He's trying to speak directly to his constituents, and that's a very different type of approach."[12]

The most popular video on Poilievre's YouTube page was, and still is, a few minutes of footage from a 2022 House of Commons debate that Poilievre headlined. It's titled "Here is the clip the CBC didn't want you to see." It has been viewed five million times. Poilievre asked then deputy prime minister Chrystia Freeland if intelligence agencies had given the government an early warning about the new coronavirus. Poilievre pressed Freeland to say how many people had been allowed into Canada from China's Hubei province—where Covid supposedly originated—after cabinet ministers knew about the virus. Freeland either didn't know or wouldn't answer, but she said the government created quarantine rules when it learned of the Covid threat. Poilievre claims two thousand people were let into Canada from Hubei after the threat was known. "Were these two thousand people quarantined? Yes or no?" Freeland's answer: Travellers from afflicted areas "were very clearly told to self-isolate." Poilievre's response: "Told to self-isolate but not required to self-isolate, so this government let thousands of people into Canada from the affected regions even though there were briefings the government had explaining the danger of doing just that."

Unlike most of Poilievre's videos, it's not a clip that generates much emotion. There's no ominous music. Poilievre is low-key compared to some of his outbursts in the House of Commons during the convoy and after he became leader. But the video does push a hot button: Poilievre's insistence that the government, in its incompetence, had, as usual, allowed trouble to cross the border. Poilievre starts with several premises that he takes for granted, including his assumption that Covid, like the SARS virus that panicked Toronto in the spring of 2003, came directly from China. Epidemiologists believe Covid entered Canada from the United States or the Middle East.[13] And, despite its eye-catching title, there's no evidence that the CBC (or anyone else) didn't want Canadians to see the clip. Maybe CBC's staff thought the loaded questions, which went out across Canada on the CPAC parliamentary channel, were just boring.

But even on Twitter, where his opponents staked out some online media turf, Poilievre was beating Charest. Poilievre had more than a quarter-million followers. Charest had about twenty-five thousand, about the same as a typical backbench MP or a journalist with a bit of a national profile.

Ben Woodfinden, a conservative commentator who was a PhD student at McGill University in 2022, said Poilievre, unlike his opponents, has an "influencer vibe" and knows better than to suck up to the often unread deep-thinkers. "In this new media environment, whatever you want to call it, that we find ourselves in.... I suspect he's not too interested in having approving op-eds in the *Globe and Mail*."[14]

Nor did he try to get his own think-pieces into print newspapers. Even if the eyeballs and Tory votes were there, the opinion editors of the country's emaciated big-city dailies would never have let him use his dopamine-generating angry language, like this one from a YouTube video posted during the campaign: "Every time Trudeau kills a Canadian energy project, the dirty dictators like Venezuela's Maduro or Russia's Putin do a victory dance." He made that claim in a video posted early in the campaign that was watched by more than 130,000 people in its first few days on YouTube. Poilievre posted that video on his Facebook page, where he had 511,000 followers.[15] But Poilievre's big subscriber/follower counts don't tell the whole story. Again, unlike his competitors, the conservative internet pseudo-media, websites that pose as news outlets but shape their content so that it resonates with conservatives and drives them further to the right, amplified Poilievre's message. No one else got that kind of support.

Poilievre made the same pro-oil patch pitch in a piece posted on the webpage of the Post Millennial, a Montreal-based website founded in 2017 that publishes national and local news along with conservative opinion pieces. Human Events Media Group, the parent company of the American right-wing website Human Events, bought Post Millennial in 2022.[16] At the beginning of that year, the Post Millennial ranked twenty-third among Canadian media outlets by audience size, with an average of 1,968,000 unique web visits every month. Almost all the Post Millennial readers were Tory voters whom Poilievre might be able to sign up as party members to vote for him in the leadership election.[17]

Two days later, True North, a conservative media news and opinion website founded by former *Toronto Sun* columnist Candice Malcolm, ran Poilievre's piece under the headline "Canadian natural gas is the solution to Europe's Russian energy crisis." Canada Proud, a Conservative Party-linked Facebook group that has over 394,000 followers and influences public opinion by using "news" torqued to generate rage, posted a link to the True North piece.

And Poilievre's team used secret ways to manipulate YouTube to get his content in front of the most extreme potential voters. Between 2018 and 2020, Poilievre's YouTube videos had a hidden tag, MGTOW, which stands for "Men going their own way," used by a misogynistic online movement. The tag, like many others used by webpage makers to game search engines, is part of what tech bros call "search engine optimization." MGTOW had been hidden in Poilievre's videos' computer code since 2018. When Global News found the tags in 2022, they were quickly removed and Poilievre's staff denied knowing about them.[18]

Whether they found the videos because of secret tags or not, Poilievre's videos resonated with many Canadians. "I really like Pierre. It seems like he honestly just wants to fix this shit," a YouTube viewer wrote on the comment section of a video where Poilievre complained abut spending $123.74 to fill his car. Another, seemingly unaware of how gasoline works, wrote, "I love how Pierre used the cheapest grade of fuel just like the common man." This young man, who'd never had a full-time, permanent private-sector job, who had been a political staffer and politician his entire his life, and who now earned nearly $200,000 a year, had made himself relatable to people who had no idea what life was like in the Ottawa bubble. When right-wing pseudo-news sites like the Post Millennial, True North, and Rebel News gave blanket coverage to the convoy, Poilievre was almost always at the centre of their stories. The Canada Proud Facebook page sent out social media posts and email blitzes during and after the convoy. In one post, Poilievre stood in front of a convoy protest sign that said, "Stocked shelves, thank a trucker. Empty shelves, thank Trudeau."

Canada Proud also turned its guns on the three other Tory leadership candidates who were still in the race. The site posted a picture of a Sony Walkman, a brightly coloured ski jacket, and Jean Charest under the heading: "Things that belong in the '90s."

Jordan Peterson, who'd left academia to become a right-wing guru to disaffected young men, has far more Twitter followers than any Canadian media outlet.[19] He used that platform to hype Poilievre, saying he "is a Canadian politician who appears both courageous and articulate."[20] He also made a ninety-minute podcast with Poilievre in May while it was still possible for his fans to buy a Tory membership.

Charest's camp hoped sensible Conservatives would see their man as the kind of leader who didn't scare centrist voters and could attract more than just nutty truckers and those who hung truck nuts off their trailer hitches. But this is not what the party's membership thought was needed in 2022. Nor did they have any gratitude for a man who had survived the near wipeout of the Progressive Conservatives in 1993 and led that party back from the edge of the political cliff. Poilievre was ahead of him almost everywhere, even in Red Tory ridings in Ontario and Quebec. Again, as they had in the Harper years, Reform Party veterans who now ran the Conservatives had anticipated voter anger and Trumpist messaging, even before Trump was a candidate. In 2022, it seemed unlikely the man mocked as Mango Mussolini could make a comeback after he and his thugs had tried to steal the previous election in 2021 by attacking the US Capitol. In 2024, Trump was re-elected, and the Poilievre-led Conservatives were ahead in the polls by more than 20 percent.

Pollster Shachi Kurl did not understand where Canadian conservatism was heading. She thought voters would pick the mature politician, not the attack dog.

"Pierre Poilievre has massive amounts of appeal among the existing Conservative base but also among past People's Party voters. Poilievre is really the spirit guide of right-leaning and hard right-leaning voters in this country," Kurl, president of the Angus Reid Institute, told John Paul Tasker of CBC News. "For Jean Charest, what he's getting is side-eye and a second look not only from a majority of past Conservative voters but we also see that two-fifths of past Liberal voters are saying, 'Yeah that guy appeals to me.' So Charest has more potential, more of a path to growth."

But maybe Charest should have held out for the Liberal leadership, since the Angus Reid poll also showed 54 percent of people who voted Conservative in the 2021 federal election wanted Poilievre. Only 15 percent preferred Charest. "The question for Poilievre is, can he withstand the narrative that the party has more potential to win under Charest?" Kurl asked Tasker. "And can the Charest campaign survive the attacks that he's a faux Conservative and that he's not the real deal?"

The Angus Reid poll found solid majorities in BC (65 percent), Ontario (61 percent), Quebec (68 percent) and Atlantic Canada (61 percent) wanted the Conservatives to moderate the party's position on social issues. However, voters in Alberta, Saskatchewan, and Manitoba, wanted things to stay the same.[21]

There was a time when Charest could have led a national conservative party to power. He'd revived the Progressive Conservatives in the 1997 election, but that was a generation ago. And if the Tories wanted a likeable, somewhat moderate if pliable leader who might be able to attract non-partisan Liberal voters, they could have kept O'Toole. As for winning Quebec, François Legault was running a populist, hard-right provincial government that had great poll numbers. His only serious opponents were the left-leaning separatist Parti Quebecois and the Marxist Quebec Solidaire. Charest's old party, the Quebec Liberals, was barely alive, kept from extinction by voters in anglophone enclaves.[22] So, despite being a Quebecois, Charest had a tough time selling Tories the idea that he could bring a lot of the province's seventy-seven seats with him.

Poilievre was twenty years younger than Charest. He was bilingual and not because he'd grown up in Quebec.[23] Poilievre had learned French the hard way, as an adult, taking tedious lessons offered, at taxpayers' expense, by the House of Commons. Both men had been elected to Parliament when they were very young. But Poilievre had had a much less complicated career than his opponent. Jenni Byrne was one of the Poilievre supporters who used Charest's experience against him. Charest, she said, was a "Liberal who campaigned against Stephen Harper" while Quebec premier. "He supported the long gun registry, raised taxes, brought in a carbon tax and worked for Huawei while the Chinese (government) detained kidnapped Canadians."[24]

Leo Housakos, who worked on Charest's Tory leadership campaign in 1993, when Charest lost to Kim Campbell, described his former friend as an artifact of a different political era. "I think that every politician has their own time and place," said Housakos, who was co-chair of

Poilievre's campaign. "In public life, the country needs to look forward and not return to the past and to some of the divisive wars within the Conservative Party that is part of the legacy of Jean Charest back in the '90s when he was leader of the Progressive Conservatives."[25]

Charest and his people tried to portray Charest as a weaver. Yan Plante, a Quebec lobbyist and Conservative strategist, told *National Post* reporter Catherine Lévesque, "Canada has never been so divided since the [Quebec separatism] referendum in 1995." Charest has "experience in saving the country" and "he will do it again. He'll want to stress that Canada is not in a good place and that it takes someone with grey hair, someone with experience and with finesse to make sure the country will bounce back."[26] But no one wanted to make "saving the country" from Quebec separatism an issue in this campaign. Nor, just months after the convoy and the Covid restrictions, were Conservative party members looking for a meeting of the minds with people who disagreed with them.

Charest kicked off his campaign in Calgary and lined up the support of many MPs, senators, and party organizers, but nowhere near the numbers that Poilievre attracted. Poilievre had been ready when the race started. He declared his candidacy three days after O'Toole was ousted, more than a month earlier than Charest and Brown, the only two candidates who had any chance of beating him. Poilievre ran as the squeaky-clean enemy of gatekeepers, reminding party members that Charest's Quebec government had been accused of corruption.[27] In a lot of ways, the 2022 Conservative leadership race was a fight between old conservatism—which was one of careful and gradual social change, deference to the business elite, and restrained government action—and whatever conservatism can be called these days. No longer a big-tent movement, it is an anger-fed ideology that combines class warfare with Depression-era Republican economic sloganeering. It targets various "enemies" and attacks "elites" and experts. It accepts no one who disagrees with its often unhinged, illogical, and undefendable worldview.

Patrick Brown, former leader of the Ontario provincial Progressive Conservatives, who'd lost his job after a bogus sex scandal, now mayor of Brampton, was screwed again by his own party.[28] If he'd been allowed to finish the race, he might have been more of a spoiler for Charest than Poilievre. The other candidates, right-wing firebreathers, had some twisted entertainment value but were not serious contenders.

Poilievre wanted to axe the carbon "tax." He echoed Ezra Levant's Ethical Oil claim that the world was going to keep burning fossil fuels, and it was better for the planet and the people living on it if their oil and gas came from Canada. They'd get that fuel through the Northern Gateway and Energy East pipelines. The latter, which would have brought diluted oil sands bitumen from Alberta to New Brunswick and the United States, was cancelled in 2017 by the Trudeau government because of opposition from Ontario communities along the route. (Alberta's NDP government supported the pipeline). Northern Gateway, which would have carried oil to Kitimat, a port just south of BC's border with the Alaskan panhandle, was cancelled the year before because First Nations didn't want it crossing their land, and environmentalists worried about spills from the ships that were used to export the oil. Poilievre said he'd approve both pipelines. "If our policies simply increase pollution into the global atmosphere, but from other countries, then we're actually cutting off our nose to spite our face," Poilievre said in a policy paper released during the leadership campaign. Replacing foreign oil would "show the world we can produce this energy in the cleanest, greenest manner anywhere on earth." Charest said he believes in climate change and wanted Canada to meet its greenhouse-gas reduction targets in 2050, presumably long after he's out of office. But he and the long-shot challengers also wanted more oil and gas pipelines.

It was an ugly campaign that left scars in the party. Jenni Byrne and Tasha Kheiriddin were invited onto Evan Solomon's CTV show in early April, and the session turned into a vicious fight. The two women talked over each other and traded insults. "When you start scorched earth, eventually you're going to get it back," Kheiriddin said near the end of the interview.[29]

Even when Brown was still in the race, Poilievre was the only candidate who had any momentum. Charest, now seen by Poilievre's campaign and those who reported on it as the only credible challenger, came across as a guy running for something... again. After giving the matter some thought. And testing the water. Poilievre didn't pretend to weigh whether the Tory leadership was something worth campaigning for, or if he were the right person for the job. He'd been on the television news for months in 2020 and 2021, badgering witnesses at the two hearings into the awarding of the student grant contract to WE Charity. Then, after O'Toole took away Poilievre's finance critic job and trapped him in the political wilderness for more than a year, he'd hit paydirt again with the "truckers." Now he wanted "freedom." The convoy crowd believed in him.

Since very few potential supporters are too extreme for Poilievre, and the convoy people made such great news copy, Poilievre had backed the "truckers" unequivocally. Now, they and the Canadians who supported them were filling big halls across the country to hear Poilievre speak.[30] They signed up for party membership and gave what they could. A CBC analysis showed Canadians who donated to the Ottawa convoy protest contributed more than $460,000 to Conservative leadership candidates, and many of them were donating to a federal political party for the first time. Poilievre got 70 percent of that money.[31]

Charest said Poilievre's support of the convoy and the trouble it caused should have disqualified him from running for party leader. "The choice is this—either we do American-style politics, the politics of attack and of division, or we do politics the way we do it in Canada," Charest said in French while appearing on Radio-Canada's popular

Quebec show *Tout le Monde en Parle*. "Mr Poilievre, who is by the way a legislator ... supported a blockade that had very direct consequences on the Canadian economy and which was illegal. Laws are not like a buffet where we choose what we like and what we don't."[32]

NO MATTER WHAT dirty deeds, foreign or domestic, were going on behind the scenes, it's likely they had no effect on the outcome of the leadership race. Poilievre was always miles ahead, which was clear to anyone who followed Canadian politics. He held big rallies across the country, avoided mainstream media reporters until after he won, and, in the last weeks of the campaign, stopped showing up for nationally televised all candidates debates.

There were five of these debates. (Something called the Independent Press Gallery, an association of conservative content-makers marginalized by professional journalists, tried to hold a sixth debate but couldn't attract enough candidates.) Every candidate had to show up for debates. If they didn't, they faced a minimum fine of $50,000, paid to the Conservative Party.

Charest said he could stand up to Poilievre's nasty talk. "I'm not a wallflower either. If I'm going to be attacked, I'm going to answer. Maybe Mr Poilievre was not used to that. If there's going to be a debate. I'm not going to back down from defending myself."[33]

These debates could not have been fun for Charest, who was not used to an opponent who showed no respect and used half-truths, exaggeration, and insult to attack him.

Poilievre put on a good show at the first debate, hosted by the Canada Strong and Free Network (the old Manning Institute) in Ottawa. He came out strong in his defence of the people who had tormented downtown Ottawa and, presumably, the "trucker" leaders who were charged and out on bail.[34]

"Now, Mr Charest learned about the convoy on the CBC, just like other Liberals, and he misrepresented them. He believes I should be censored. He believes I should be cancelled from this leadership race and be 'disqualified,' in his word, because I don't share his Liberal viewpoint. That is the kind of cancel culture and censorship you would expect from Justin Trudeau, but instead we're getting it from this Liberal on this stage."[35] As Poilievre spoke Charest laughed, but it seemed forced and fake. "And frankly, Mr Charest, for you to talk about law and order is a little bit rich, considering that your party, your Liberal party, took a half million dollars of illegal donations when you were the head of that party. The average trucker has more integrity in his pinky finger than you had in your entire scandal-plagued Liberal cabinet."

Charest tried to answer. "This mess on the Hill is the fault of Mr Trudeau, but Mr Poilievre during that period supported an illegal blockade. You cannot make laws and break laws and then make laws for other people." By the second sentence, the crowd was booing, a moderator was interrupting, and Charest was mad as hell. "That is a question of basic foundational principles," he hollered as everyone in the hall tried to drown him out.

Any time Charest tried to speak, Poilievre interrupted him with short phases like "How much?" and "What's the number?" that rattled Charest and made journalists' soundbites about Poilievre, not Charest.

But the debate in Edmonton on May 12 made Poilievre so angry that he refused to show up to more. It was hosted by CTV journalist Tom Clark. The moderator was close to the end of his career as star of the afternoon political show that Mike Duffy had hosted before he was appointed to the Senate. Clark knew a bunch of politicians talking over each other did not make good television, and he wanted to prevent the bullying that marred the Ottawa debate, so candidates had to raise a ping-pong paddle if they wanted to say something, and they had to keep their mouths shut until Clark let them speak. This rule gave Charest and Brown a clearer shot at the front-runner.

Clark asked questions that might have been designed to show insight into the thinking of the competitors. Instead, Poilievre and many political pundits thought the questions were lame. What person inspired the candidates? Who was their favourite prime minister? What books were they reading? (Poilievre's answer: "Well, um, uh, uh, Jordan Peterson's *12 Rules*? Great book! And a lot of good lessons. We all need to, uh, improve ourselves, and I think he has a lot of good wisdom in that book that could help anybody.") They had to keep their answers short. If they went on too long, Clark made weird "womp! womp!" or "sad trombone" noises. He also docked Poilievre some answering time when one of his supporters in the audience booed Charest.

Each candidate did manage to get some of the message out. Charest, seeming to believe he'd returned to the early 1990s, said he would fight against creeping separatism. Poilievre, walking back his enthusiasm for cryptocurrency now that it was on one of its cyclical downturns (crypto is, at best, a Ponzi scheme requiring the recruitment of more drug lords and suckers to keep the party going), still said he'd keep his promise to fire the governor of the Bank of Canada. Charest said the threat to the central bank's independence was irresponsible. Brown, still in the race, claimed Poilievre helped ruin the Conservatives' chances of winning the 2015 election by supporting the niqab ban and the barbaric cultural practices tipline.[36]

"I know it was a weird little journey to go on, but I think it was interesting," Clark said when the segment was over. It was a minority opinion. (Poilievre got his revenge by attacking Clark after the broadcaster was appointed Canadian consul in New York. The foreign affairs department sold the consulate's Manhattan apartment for $13 million and replaced it with a $9 million co-op. Poilievre's front bench said this was all too rich for a Canadian diplomat. The Tory leader warned Clark to keep his bags packed and be ready to be fired as soon as he became prime minister.)

"This is a tremendously horrible debate format, maybe the worst I've ever seen," political scientist Royce Koop wrote on Twitter. "No one wants to hear these little mini-speeches with the moderator interrupting and lecturing the candidates. I can barely comprehend the topic they're on before they move on." Face-to-face exchanges in the second half of the debate provided a bit more drama but not much more information.

Poilievre probably won the debate. If he did lose, it wasn't by much. He hit all his major talking points and slogans. "People feel like they've lost control of their lives," he said, making his "freedom" pitch. He targeted the "gatekeepers," saying he would fire them. He'd got in his frequent description of the Bank of Canada as the Trudeau government's ATM machine.

In July, Jenni Byrne said Poilievre would boycott the last two debates. (One of the original five was cancelled.) And it was all Tom Clark's fault. The Edmonton debate "was widely recognized as an embarrassment," she wrote in a statement posted on Twitter.

Byrne said it was bad enough that the May debates cut into Poilievre's time to sell memberships. The summer debate fell into the time when the Poilievre team was doing "get out the vote" work on members who'd received their mail-in-ballots. (Presumably, there was never a good time for a debate.)

"The Party's third debate is smack dab in the middle of the get out the vote period," Byrne wrote. "As we have stated publicly, Pierre's campaign sold 311,958 new memberships. The sole objective now is to get new members and existing members to fill out their ballots and submit them before the September deadline. Pierre will be on the road again, without interruption, to help make that happen."

Clearly, Byrne and Poilievre did not think he had anything to gain by debating, even if he won. They made no connection between Poilievre's debate performance, any good publicity it might generate, and success in the election.

"Thousands and thousands of Canadians have come to our campaign events. Our largest event had 7,000 people attend. Jean Charest has had a hard time getting even a couple dozen people to his campaign events. This is why he wants another debate—to use Pierre's popularity with the members to bring out an audience he can't get on his own. No one is interested in a scandal-plagued, tax and spend, carbon tax-loving, defeated Liberal premier."

There would be no kindness in this campaign, no attempts to heal the party's wounds afterwards.

GARRY KELLER, A Calgarian and senior Tory staffer in the Harper years who's respected by people in all the national political parties for his quick mind and humour, said Poilievre's campaign showed that something was happening in Canada. It looked a lot like the lead up to the 2015 federal election, only this time the momentum was with a Tory. "[Trudeau] was getting mega-crowds for Canadian politics with a moment's notice," Keller said. "You can't fake that. I'm seeing a lot of similarities with Pierre's campaign."[37]

During the campaign, polls had portrayed this thing as a race. They should have been surveying the people who'd bought party memberships and planned to vote. Pollsters quoted "Canadians'" views, but Canadians who weren't members of the Conservative Party didn't have a say in the outcome.

In June 2022, Charest's campaign sent out a press release saying they'd signed up enough new Conservative Party members to win the leadership. That turned out to be a bad joke. On the first ballot, Poilievre, who was endorsed by the old Reform heavyweights in the party including Stephen Harper, won nearly 71 percent of the votes (68 percent of the points, under rules that gave weight to both individual votes cast and riding support). This was solid proof that the Conservative Party was united under his leadership. Stephen Harper had been the last Conservative leader who'd taken the prize on the first ballot. That mandate gave Poilievre the power to stifle any doubters in his caucus or the party at large who might make trouble by organizing against him or leaking to the media. Charest got less than 12 percent, barely beating out Leslyn Lewis, a strange politician who ran even farther to the right than Poilievre. Roman Baber won a little over 5 percent of the votes.

Charest's decision to run turned out to be a blessing for Poilievre. Rather than run against a handful of no-hopers, Poilievre went head-to-head against a seasoned, respected politician and cleaned his clock. If this had been the 1993 Progressive Conservative leadership election, Charest's blows would have landed. He could have convinced delegates to a twentieth-century Tory convention—lawyers, small business owners, farmers—that Poilievre was a fringe actor. But this was a Tory party in the time of Trump, Covid, Twitter, and "trucker" occupations. In the debates, Charest ended up playing a sort of straight man to a smirking Poilievre, who made the older politician a symbol of the brokerage politics of the past. By beating Charest on the campaign trail and in the vote, Poilievre showed he had the organizational skills, the stamina, and the confidence to fight a national general election campaign. Charest did himself no favours by running, but his candidacy was the best favour he could have done for Poilievre. After it was over, Charest was no longer a force in politics.

Speaking in the Ottawa convention centre after the vote result was announced, Poilievre said, "Tonight begins the journey to replace an old government that costs you more and delivers you less, with a new government that puts you first, your paycheque, your retirement, your home, your country." Queen Elizabeth II had died the day before. "I feel a small catch in my throat when I utter the words that no leader has stated in this country for over seven decades, God Save the King," he said, thrilling people who wanted to, as one of Poilievre's slogans said, "take back Canada" to a time when "Britishness" was one quality required by Canadian voters.[38]

There was a shout out to the losing candidates. "To supporters of all of these fine candidates I open up my arms to you. Now, today, we are one party serving one country," Poilievre said. But none of them would be anywhere near the centre of power, and most simply disappeared from politics.

"There are people in this country who are just hanging on by a thread.... They don't need a government to run their lives, they need a government that can run a passport office," Poilievre said to cheers. "They need a prime minister who hears them, and offers them hope that they can again afford to buy a home, a car, pay their bills, afford food, have a secure retirement, and God forbid even achieve their dreams if they work hard. They need a prime minister who will restore that hope, and I will be that prime minister."

The leadership race was over, but the campaigning didn't stop. Between that late summer day when Poilievre took control of the party and the next federal election, Poilievre never stopped running. Being a candidate wasn't a job or a task. It was what Poilievre was, every minute, every day, anywhere someone could see and hear him.

12
TROLLING (FOR) THE WORKING CLASS

> *I'm very much in the trenches, and I don't live in the lap of luxury. I come from a working-class military family. We watch the news and read the paper and vote, so there's always something to be upset about. I always have a certain amount of angst in my back pocket.*
>
> PINK

ALGOMA STEEL WAS founded in the early years of the twentieth century to make Sault Ste. Marie, Ontario, a manufacturing hub. Iron comes down the St. Mary's River from Lake Superior. Limestone is mined just south of "the Soo." Coal comes in from the United States by ship, but that's about to change. The smelters are switching over to electricity. That's an important part of this story.

The steel mill, Canada's second largest, had gone broke twice and was on the verge of bankruptcy again in this century, but good corporate leadership along with a rebound in steel prices put the company in the black before it was bought in 2008 by the Indian steel conglomerate Essar Group. About 2,700 people work for it.

Prime Minister Justin Trudeau was in Sault Ste. Marie on the

Friday before the Labour Day weekend of 2024, meeting workers coming out of Algoma Steel. After offering them doughnuts "right over there," he made eye contact with an obvious non-fan who asked, "Can I bring some for my kids?" Right away, Trudeau reminded the steelworker of the government's recent move to protect Canada's steel makers. "The twenty-five percent tariffs we just brought in [on Chinese steel] is going to help you out.... That's going to keep your job," said Trudeau. "I'm going to invest in you and your job."

"What about the forty percent taxes I am paying and I don't have a doctor?" the thirty-seven-year-old steelworker asked.

Trudeau mentioned the $420 million the federal government is investing as part of its strategy for meeting international climate targets. The money went toward a new electric smelting system. Algoma's project is expected to reduce CO_2 emissions by three million tonnes annually, or 70 percent. That equates to more than a tenth of Canada's 2030 goal under the Paris Agreement.

That didn't seem to matter. Talking over the prime minister, the steelworker said, "I think you are only here for another year, we won't see you around in another year because—"

"That's what elections are for," Trudeau answered, realizing his words were not changing the worker's mind. "Basic choice, we're going to invest in you and your job."

"I don't believe you for a second," the steelworker said, even though construction workers were busy inside his workplace, on the taxpayer's dime.

"Dental care? You know anyone who got dental care?" Trudeau asked, giving a Bill Clinton–style thumbs up. Then he stuck his hands in the pockets of his blue jeans.

"Yeah, I pay for it myself. And we're, like, three years behind. Every time we go for a dental visit, it has cost me about fifty dollars out of my pocket per person. Why? I have a good job, but you're not really doing anything for us," he said.

"Actually," Trudeau said, "we've invested so that half a million people could go to the dentist over the past year."

"Probably like my neighbour who doesn't go to work because she's lazy," the steelworker said. "She doesn't have to go to work, and she lives the same life I do."

"You know what? Most Canadians try to stick up for each other, and that's what we've got to keep doing," Trudeau said as he wished the man luck. The prime minister tried to shake his hand. "No. Have a nice day," the man said as he walked away.

The exchange was posted on YouTube and on news sites all over the world. Right-wing outlets described it as a humiliation of the prime minister. On social media, Trudeau's supporters floated the idea that the worker was a Tory plant. Some even said it was Jeff Ballingall, the eminence grise of Canadian right-wing Twitter. But the guy who shunned Trudeau really did work at Algoma.

Not a single journalist reported on the investment Trudeau mentioned, so no one was told about the $420 million spent to modernize the Algoma Steel plant and bring it up to environmental standard. (It took me about fifteen seconds to find it with a Google search). And, of course, no one asked Pierre Poilievre if a Conservative government would have made that investment in green tech.

Not many people, whether on social media or in the mainstream, mentioned that the man's inability to find a doctor was a failing of Ontario's Progressive Conservative provincial government, not the feds.[1] Nor did they notice some of the holes in the worker's story. He claimed to be in a 40 percent tax bracket and yet couldn't, or wouldn't, spend the $200 co-pay to take his family to the dentist. (Besides, the co-pay is a fee agreed on by the company and its benefits provider. The federal dental care program was never supposed to cover that, so it was irrelevant to the issue at hand.)

Various commentators of the professional and less-professional variety speculated about this worker's pay and whether he actually paid 40 percent of his wages in taxes. They could have looked his salary up online and made some quick calculations. The August 2022 collective agreement between Algoma Steel and Local 2251 of the United Steelworkers shows that the mill pays pretty well, especially since decent suburban houses in the Soo were selling for about $450,000 in the summer of 2024.[2] Rentals were in the $1,300 to $2,500 range.[3]

Depending on the job, Algoma Steel unionized employees earn between $35 and $40 an hour when they start, with a maximum pay of between $50 and $55, not including shift differentials, overtime, and extra pay for any statutory holidays that they work. For a thirty-five-hour week, that's a base pay of $63,700. At the top end of the skills and seniority list, the base pay is $100,100. The average salary for a Canadian with a job is about $55,000 a year. The federal tax rate on the highest-paid workers at Algoma Steel start at 15 percent of a taxable income of $55,687, and 20.5% of any income between $55,687 and $111,733, plus Canada Pension and Employment Insurance check-offs. So nowhere near 40 percent.

Being a unionized employee of Algoma Steel pays off in other ways too. Union members with nine to fifteen years' service get four weeks of paid vacation, six weeks off after twenty years, and another week after twenty-five years. If they're off on long-term disability for a health problem that isn't workplace-related, they get thirteen weeks of full pay. After twenty-five years, that doubles. If they're off because of a workplace injury, all employees' provincial compensation benefits are topped up to bring them to their full pay for one year.[4]

Postmedia pundit John Ivison, whose Google skills need work, estimated the angry steelworker paid no more than 29 percent of his income in federal taxes.[5] In fact, the 29 percent federal rate applies *only* to earnings between $173,000 and $246,000. If the steelworker made that much money, which the union contract shows he didn't, he'd pay a lower percentage on all the money he made below $173,000. (These kinds of eye-splitting, brain-freezing calculations are one reason tax accountants do so well.)

So what we seem to have here is a guy who makes a decent buck, but not a fortune, in a hard job. He's a member of a union, so he has decent pay and good benefits. If he sticks around long enough, he gets 14 percent of his salary in vacation pay every year, which means he can take most of the summer off. He qualifies for a pension. His dental plan, if he's telling the truth about the $50 co-payment, is not as good as the one that the federal government negotiated for its workers. But he shouldn't be a candidate for a food bank, nor does he deserve to be. He's a Canadian working in what used to be a typical manufacturing plant in an affordable city. And's he's so pissed off that he snubbed the prime minister of Canada.

There were a couple of other things worth noting in the video. The rest of the Algoma workers were, at least, polite. Some were even friendly. But the media and Trudeau's opponents seized on the words of one angry, rude man. The working man's angry tirade and Trudeau's ineffective response got the headlines and made the video go viral. It showed up on news sites in India and on right-wing webpages in the United States.

Trudeau said Canadians look after each other. No one seemed to take note of this at all. In fact, a lot of Canadians don't take care of one another. The Covid pandemic proved that, when older Canadians were dying by the score in nursing homes and many younger people took their last breaths from hospital ventilators. The most extreme fringe of this group encouraged Tory MPs to drive Erin O'Toole out of the Conservative leadership and helped install Pierre Poilievre. The Algoma Steel worker seems to have bought into this rage, even though he's benefitted from federal government trade and protection policy, a big federal handout that should make his employer more competitive, and a union that negotiated a wages and benefit deal that's far better than workers get in most non-union shops. If he and the rest of Canada's working-class vote for Pierre Poilievre, how will he be better off? Axing the carbon tax would save him a few dollars. Gutting climate change mitigation would cost him his job. Gatekeepers? Not a problem for him. Housing? He can afford the Soo's prices.

But Donald Trump's tariff on steel may finally kill the mill, the mines, the railway and the ships that feed it, and the steelworker's job. If it doesn't, the threat of US protectionism always hangs over this steel mill. And no matter what its workers think of whoever's prime minister, this mill and the mines that sell to it and the railroads it relies on exist only because the federal government want them to. If the mill does close, it would be hard for its workers to find a job in that part of the country, let alone one at a comparable wage. The closest Canadian steel mills are in Hamilton, and they don't need nearly three thousand new employees.

Nor can they find good jobs in Northern Ontario in some other resource industry or factory. Every mine and paper mill in Ontario became endangered when Trump took office. And the region has been declining for years. US tariffs on lumber killed most of the sawmills. The big lumber and pulp mill at Terrace Bay, on Lake Superior's north shore, which had a billion dollars' worth of upgrades (in today's money) in the late 1970s, was sold earlier this century to an Indian company that broke the unions and cut wages. It closed for good in January 2024. The lumber and pulp mill in Marathon, the next town to the east on Lake Superior, shut down in 2009. Red Rock, west of Terrace Bay, lost its mill in 2006.[6] Mining is the last resource industry left in the region, and it's not doing that well.[7]

A reporter for *Soo Today* found the Algoma Steel worker about a month after his encounter with Trudeau.

"I did not see that coming in the slightest," he told the reporter. "Even to this day it still hasn't really hit me how this [the conversation with Trudeau] actually could have happened.... I think honest conversation is really the only way to resolve issues and conflict but unfortunately the world we live in is extremely sensitive to that," he added. "I've realized that most people seem to side with me on this subject, however I've noticed that some people have very negative intent with the things that I say." The *Toronto Sun* called him "Man of Steel" in a front-page headline. People across the country offered him cases of beer.[8]

A LOT OF academics, political strategists, and journalists are trying to understand the lure of the new right. It often doesn't make economic sense. Buying into a campaign by British Tories and right-wing agitator Nigel Farage, Brexit-supporting workers in the United Kingdom voted themselves out of 330,000 jobs and plunged their country into stagnation.[9] The right made big gains in the Netherlands and France in recent parliamentary elections. In the summer of 2024, neo-fascists made major gains in German states that used to be part of East Germany, then helped topple the federal government. A far-right politician was sworn in as chancellor of Austria. Donald Trump's political career would have been stillborn if he hadn't won the support of a lot of working people. In the 2024 election, Trump won the Rust Belt—those industrial states south of the Great Lakes—and took counties that had solidly voted for Barack Obama in 2008 and 2012. Then Trump began menacing the auto industry, so important to that region, with tariffs.[10]

And in Canada, workers at some of the best-paying unionized manufacturing plants in the country drive around with "Fuck Trudeau" and "Poilievre for PM" flags on their cars and trucks. Why would they vote for a man who's always tried to destroy their unions so they can bargain individually with the corporation that employs them? Would they really hand the country over to a right-wing politician over a relatively minor carbon tax? How is Poilievre, despite his sheltered upbringing and life as a professional politician, somehow relatable, able to get his message through, and make them as angry as he is?

Some of the less-bright conservative pundits tell readers that Poilievre will win the working-class vote because the conservatives truly care. Shannon Proudfoot, who grew up in a working-class family in the Soo, wrote a piece in the *Globe and Mail* about Poilievre's visit to her hometown in the summer of 2023. He drew a respectable crowd of about four hundred people to his rally. Poilievre described how a waitress came up to him before the show, threw her arms around him, and ordered him to "Get him out, get in there and fix this." By "this," she meant the mess that Justin Trudeau's supposed to have made.

Then things got weird.

"I don't know her personal story," Poilievre said about his eager fan. "But let's say that she has three kids. And let's say that she earns sixty thousand dollars, twenty-five bucks an hour," he said. He didn't notice people react with shock and what Proudfoot artfully described as "strangled noises of surprise." Unlike Poilievre, they had some idea of what a waitress in the Soo earns. It's not $60,000 a year. Some big-city wait staff make that kind of money in high-end restaurants, but it's not the kind of money that Soo waitresses pull down. Proudfoot told *Globe* readers the median income of all workers in Sault Ste. Marie— the Algoma steelworkers, the lawyers, the doctors, the teachers, and people in the service industry jobs—was $40,800 in 2020. The average annual income of people working in the food service industry across Canada was $21,175 in 2022. The silliness of this first claim should have made rallygoers question the rest of the story, yet they didn't laugh at Poilievre.

Nor did working people abandon Poilievre when he said a well-kept wartime house in Niagara was a "shack." Lots of people live in those little 1940s houses. Entire communities of these homes were built in northern resource towns after the Second World War, and they're often starter, retiree, and lifelong homes for Canadians in working-class cities across the country. And a few months before that, Poilievre posted a video showing how out of touch he really is. "I just had a great weekend, meeting with the common people, listening to their common sense," he patronized. "I just want to remind everyone politics is supposed to be a blue-collar job. Check out these boots." The camera, slightly out of focus, was aimed at his feet. Although you couldn't see them clearly, let's accept his claim that his shoes were muddy. "That's what it's like to be out with the people, in the rain, attending their festivals, listening to their stories, hearing their dreams." This all seemed new to him. Hanging with the ordinary folks was some kind of exercise in anthropology. Poilievre has never held a job that required work boots.[11]

PATRICK MUTTART, ONE of the key architects of Stephen Harper's rise to power, developed strategies to bring working people into the Conservative fold. It was a challenge: for generations, conservatism was the ideology of the rich and the old, people who were skeptical of change, especially when it threatened the class system and the relationship of workers and capital. Muttart found that historically working-class voters supported centre-left governments. This was no surprise. But partly because of Muttart's strategy, the working class became the core vote for Harper and what people started calling the Tory "base." The success of Ronald Reagan and Margaret Thatcher in the 1980s offered signposts of the future. Newt Gingrich had been a pioneer in a congressional movement that left East Coast country-club conservatives far behind and laid the foundation for the Tea Party. Donald Trump built on that, but Harper had done the same thing and departed the scene long before Trump arrived to basically copy him.

Muttart found that academics, journalists, and political strategists were wrong when they wrote or campaigned believing working-class voters fit neatly on the traditional left-right continuum. What the working poor and the lower middle class wanted, above all else, was reduced government spending and lower taxes. Even though their own tax burden, in dollars, seemed low to some, they themselves believed that they had no money to spare. Nor did they connect the taxes they did pay to the services provided by government: this left them ripe for conversion.

Blue-collar people, likely with some justification, believed trade deals like the North American Free Trade Agreement (beginning with the 1988 Canada–US Free Trade Agreement) and China's rejoining of the General Agreement on Tariffs and Trade at the end of the 1980s took their jobs.[12] They were also suspicious of big business and believed many large companies were getting too many government handouts (this was after the 2008 financial crisis). They didn't want demographic or social change and believed immigrants threatened both their class rank and their jobs. Many of these working-class people were open-minded about mainstream sex issues, nonchalant about LGBTQ+ people, as long as they were somewhere else, and not in your face. They were patriotic. They supported the military but weren't big on foreign wars. Working people did not seek class mobility or want to become members of an elite, even if they did buy lottery tickets.[13] Rather, they wanted a job, a paycheque that supported what they saw as a decent lifestyle—a house, a car, a charter flight to an all-inclusive resort in the Dominican Republic or Cuba once in a while—security in their employment and retirement, and as little stress as possible: a decent, predictable life without much worry, and governments that didn't bother them or ask for much.

Muttart developed fictional voters—single young people trying to get an economic foothold, suburban parents, widows—and tailored policies and promises to fit each. He also dealt with the issue of Harper himself, who was a man who had spent all his life either in politics or working for conservative advocacy groups. Harper's attractive kids and his dynamic wife were understood to be assets, and Harper, at least, didn't seem particularly strange to people who didn't know him well.

Dealing with the past was a bigger challenge. Harper became prime minister without ever being a minister or even an important member of Parliament. In contrast, Poilievre has been in the House of Commons for more than twenty years. He was a cabinet minister. Poilievre likes to say he's spoken to more local unions than he has to corporate business crowds. His populism glorifies small business and lumps in big corporations (except oil and gas companies) with other gatekeepers.[14] Poilievre sends a mixed message to unions: he whipped all his MPs, including long-time union bashers like Andrew Scheer, into supporting the Trudeau government's bill banning federally regulated workplaces from using replacement workers during strikes or lockouts, yet over and over, he's denounced "union bosses" in the House of Commons. Before he voted for the anti-scab law, Poilievre backed every anti-union bill passed during the Harper years.

In 2022, he began holding Trump-style rallies in legions and shabby halls, hunting for support from the same kind of angry working-class people who are Trump's base and who came to Ottawa in their trucks. He also stopped antagonizing rank-and-file union members. As well as supporting the Trudeau government's anti-scab law, Poilievre stopped the Tory habit of calling on the government to use back-to-work legislation to end major strikes, like the one that shut down WestJet in the summer of 2024 and a short public servants' strike earlier that year.[15] When Canadian Pacific train crews went on strike at about the same time, Poilievre wouldn't say whether he favoured a back-to-work order, and his MPs were forbidden from talking about the dispute.[16] Railway workers were bitter about being forced to give up their strike. All their anger was directed at Trudeau. But unionized workers should look carefully at Poilievre's record and what he says now: even in the debate over the federal anti-scab bill, Poilievre said it's up to government, not unions, to put more money in workers' pockets. He would do that by cutting taxes, not by increasing wages.

This kind of talk would have been a much bigger problem for Poilievre fifty years ago, when private sector unions could make or break candidates. But, again, Poilievre's timing has been lucky. He became a contender when industrial unions were on the ropes, and dues-paying workers started to believe the people who ran their unions care more about race, gender, and foreign policy issues than they do for shift differentials and seniority rules. Union executives, whether they like Poilievre or not, can't deliver the votes of rank-and-file members anymore.[17]

Sometimes he sounded like some kind of strange hybrid of Margaret Thatcher and Vladimir Lenin. "You represent the wage earners and the future pensioners," Poilievre told a big union meeting in Gatineau, Quebec, in 2024. "Wages and pensions have lost purchasing power. Meanwhile, big government and big business and big capital has gotten rich by the inflationary policies of government. It is a transfer of wealth from the have-nots to the have-yachts." He was right about the widening wealth disparity, but he didn't explain why it's happening or why taxation and economic regulation couldn't fix that problem. And no one mentioned the fat ticket prices of Poilievre's fundraising events with Canada's business leaders in some of the most elegant halls in the country. In those very private places, there was no pandering to people who wanted better wages.[18]

Poilievre and his party have two sources of money: wealthy Canadian business owners and high-income people who want low taxes and less government regulation, and hundreds of thousands of working people who make small donations. The language of his populism, which generates those small contributions, reflects the anti-Toronto, anti-Montreal talk of Western socialism during the Great Depression. He's also seized on the concept of *Laurentian elites*. That's a wedge term that carelessly lumps the Quebec and Ontario business communities, academia, non-government organizations like environmental groups and charities, with the federal government and the rest of the people living south and east of the Canadian Shield. *Laurentian elites* includes the media, which, again, is a sloppy stereotype. Canada's media is made up of organizations ranging from the CBC (itself a Frankenstein's monster of Indigenous, French, and English radio, television, podcasts, and internet text news, along with music and video streaming); the *Toronto Sun* and its chain of right-wing tabloids; the conservative *National Post*, founded by Conrad Black and now in the Postmedia chain of papers, every one of which has endorsed the Conservative Party in every recent election; the *Toronto Star*, which has swung to the right since it was sold to a private investor during the pandemic; and the *Globe and Mail*, where the term was first popularized.

Laurentian elites, really a code phrase for "eastern liberals," plays well with people who have not lived in different parts of Canada. This tired concept, which goes back to the days of CPR bashing—Canadian Pacific was blamed for decades by Western populists for what they saw as exploitive freight rates—"others" people in the rest of Canada the same way separatist discourse in Quebec isolates francophone Quebecois from the rest of the nation. Those who use the term offer no serious solutions to the problems they've invented. Move the federal government to Winnipeg so it's out of the Laurentian region, or get rid of it altogether and be a group of thirteen weak jurisdictions bordering an increasingly dysfunctional superpower? Dismantle eastern industry, built on cheap, abundant electricity? Scatter Toronto's financial community, one of the most important in the world? Throwing the divisive term around wins votes and donations from low-information Western voters. It fosters a mentality that makes governing a united Canada impossible. And it threatens the very survival of the nation in the face of regional separatist movements and foreign threats.

In his first year leading the Conservatives, Poilievre told Toronto business leaders, "I almost never speak to crowds in downtown Toronto or even close to Bay Street."[19] That didn't stop him from starring at about fifty fundraisers at private venues between his leadership victory in September 2022 and May 2024. A CBC investigation of his big-ticket private events found they drew dozens of registered federal government lobbyists, who paid up to $1,725 each to get in. Bay Street was also represented: the reporters found that a billionaire oil tycoon, an airline executive, and a vice-president at AtkinsRéalis, formerly called SNC-Lavalin, paid to hear Poilievre speak at private mansions and expensive clubs.[20]

Poilievre also tells his rallies that his door is closed to lobbyists, although his political partner Jenni Byrne runs an Ottawa lobbying company, and lobbyists have hosted dozens of big fundraising events for the Tories—the CBC investigation found that more than twenty-five active federal lobbyists attended Poilievre fundraisers in his first twenty months as leader. The reporters also found the names of one hundred inactive (but still registered) federal lobbyists on the lists of attendees at Poilievre events. Poilievre publicly rails against business lobbyists not because they're influence peddlers but for talking to the wrong people. "The only area where any business lobby has borne fruit has been the rotten fruit of undue handouts, privileges, and protections by the state," he wrote in a *National Post* opinion piece in May 2024. "Want to stop the latest tax hike? Or get bureaucracy out of the way to build homes, mines, factories, pipelines and more? Then cancel your lunch meeting at the Rideau Club. Fire your lobbyist. And go to the people."[21]

Muttart and Poilievre did not invent this strategy. Paul Wells, writing in the summer of 2024 about the Trump campaign's wooing of unionized voters, said with some wisdom: "Now, at the Republican convention in Milwaukee, we saw Trump's vice-presidential pick, J.D. Vance, proclaiming: 'We're done, ladies and gentlemen, catering to Wall Street. We'll commit to the working man.'" Why? Because "Wall Street barons crashed the economy." America, Vance said, needs "a leader who's not in the pocket of big business, but answers to the working man, union and non-union alike. A leader who won't sell out to multinational corporations, but will stand up for American companies and American industry."[22]

This talk must be hard for old-school Tories, who brought us most of our foreign trade deals, gladly went to World Economic

Forum sessions, enjoyed the delights of Toronto's Albany Club, and tapped Rosedale millionaires to pay for Tory campaigns. These people made up the core of the old Progressive Conservative Party for generations. Now, they had no say in the party that claimed to be the voice of small government and free enterprise.

More and more, conservatism combined nationalism with the economic theories of Milton Friedman. Then it added the class warfare messages of Vladimir Lenin and the early Nazi party. Oren Cass, chief economist of the Washington-based conservative think tank American Compass, advocates shifting the right's attention from blind faith in free markets to "focus on workers, their families and communities, and the national interest."

In a *New York Times* op-ed piece that ran in the first week of July 2024, Cass made the case that post–Cold War America had been a difficult time for the working class. Bad things were happening to wage-earning families in the American heartland. Their problems were ignored or patronized by media (presumably including the pretentious *Times*), and their votes were taken for granted by politicians.

The statistics he offered provided solid evidence of the stress and struggle endured by a class of people who, as Muttart found, like neither. Paycheques didn't provide security. Young people weren't successfully launching their careers and families. Many who couldn't cope because of the economic environment or some personal setback were using drugs that were extremely addictive and, too often, killed kids.

"Opioid deaths are more than a terrible tragedy," Cass wrote in the *Times*. "They are also a telltale sign of national decay and desperation." Polls in Canada and the United States showed young people believed they'd never be as well-off as their parents. In his stump speech, Poilievre told a story of a person in his riding who had the same job, even the same desk, that his retired mother had. The man said he'd never be able to buy his mother's house or afford any other home in the Ottawa area. The story is believable. Cass's think tank found a wide gap between the way that mass media portray the lifestyles of young people and the reality of people who were just starting out on their own. Only one in five young people moved easily from high school to college to career, and women were more likely to succeed. In real terms, men in their twenties earned less than people in that age group were paid in the early 1970s. More adult Americans under thirty-four were living with their parents than with a significant other.[23]

More than a third of American men between the ages of eighteen and twenty-four have no sex life at all, even with themselves. This suggests an epidemic of clinical depression among the young. And, not surprisingly, a survey of people in their late twenties and early thirties showed men with jobs had a better chance of having a sex life.[24]

Women are more likely to want to apply for bachelor of arts programs in Canada.[25] Women were almost twice as likely to graduate from a health science program and more likely to get into law school. In 2024, 55 percent of the University of Toronto law school's first-year students were women. At the University of Windsor, women had 70 percent of those spots. Women were also the majority in Canada's medical schools (58 percent to 42 percent).[26]

Since the Covid pandemic, the public service, at all three levels of government, has been the largest source of new white-collar jobs. In the fall of 2024, the Trudeau government imposed a hiring freeze on the federal bureaucracy.

In 2024, a poll showed 40 percent of people in their twenties living in Toronto—a group of 430,000 voting-age people, of whom 68 percent aged twenty to twenty-four were racialized—struggle with housing costs.[27] And 45 percent of them said their mental health was fair or poor. People in their thirties were doing a bit better, but not much: 22 percent were concerned about the cost of their rent or mortgage, and 33 percent reported fair or poor mental health. Between 2019 and 2023, the number of people in their twenties who got help from Toronto's Daily Bread Food Bank increased six-fold.

That was twice the increase of other age groups. The writers of the survey recommended managers find ways to hire and mentor young people and try to get more face-to-face contact and networking between them, even if it seemed this was just for fun.[28]

Jobs and careers have never been easy for young people—youth unemployment through the 1980s often hovered at 20 percent, and people entering the job market in the early 1980s sometimes never got a shot at a decent career—but most generations could count on patience and hard work paying off. Not now. It's as bad as the 1980s, but for different reasons. It's hard to find a job with a future in a world where permanent jobs are replaced with gig work, and technology disrupts entire manufacturing and service industries. In most places, it's almost impossible to find a decent and affordable place to live. Pairing up to have a family while having some job security? The math simply doesn't work. This is political dynamite that destroys incumbent governments.

People aren't stupid. They know their manufacturing jobs were exported by corporations, with the approval of politicians. In 1988, the federal Liberals under John Turner opposed the first North American Free Trade Agreement, as did the New Democratic Party. After that, Liberals and Tories, whether in government or opposition, have always supported trade deals, while the NDP haven't effectively opposed them. (This was in lockstep with the United States, where Bill Clinton's government was almost as pro-free trade as the Reagan and Bush administrations that preceded it.)

By the 2010s, the loudest criticisms of trade agreements and the globalization of manufacturing was coming from the right: Nigel Farage and the United Kingdom Independence Party, Donald Trump in rhetoric if not in action, Maxime Bernier and the People's Party of Canada. So it's not really a surprise that by the summer of 2024, Pierre Poilievre had started calling for tough tariffs (but only on China, which now supplies most of the things sold in stores).[29] Cass's think tank found 90 percent of Americans wanted a stronger manufacturing sector. (It would be interesting to know what the other 10 percent thought). Poorer Americans were willing to pay higher prices if that would strengthen local manufacturing. They were far less willing to pay to fight climate change. Wealthier Americans had an opposite view.

The struggles of young men affect the way they see politics and politicians. In the 2021 federal election, the Liberals and Tories evenly split the votes of young men. Two years later, the Liberals were thirty points behind the Tories with this group. In Britain, young men were the core group of voters for the right-wing populist Reform UK party, led by Nigel Farage, the most right-wing national party on offer. In France, Marine Le Pen's party pulled the votes of this demographic away from President Emmanuel Macron and his parliamentary supporters, who, themselves, came to power as outsiders in 2018 because French voters wanted to punish the previous government for a nepotism scandal. Young American voters put Joe Biden into the White House in 2020, but four years later many of them either shifted their vote to Trump or stayed home.[30]

Tasha Kheiriddin, a Conservative strategist, lobbyist, and *National Post* political columnist—Canadian media doesn't blink anymore at people being all three at the same time—said after Labour Day 2024 that Poilievre has labour's vote in the bag. She admitted, "Pierre Poilievre's record on workers' rights isn't exactly stellar." He voted for Bill C-377, a Harper-era law that required unions to disclose how they spend their money. Poilievre voted against the repeal of that law in 2017. He also campaigned for American-style "right to work" laws. And he wanted an end to the Rand Formula, which requires employees in federally-regulated workplaces to pay union dues, even if they don't want to be members of the union.

"But ever since the Freedom Convoy, the working class has become the Tories' new best friend," Kheiriddin wrote. "Many blue-collar workers were negatively impacted by Covid, suffering financial losses as construction sites shut down, retail stores and restaurants closed, and physical distance mandates made in-person work impossible. Meanwhile, white-collar workers retreated to their home offices with their laptops and kept working."[31]

By saying that white-collar workers got off easy during the pandemic, Kheiriddin worked a vein that the right has mined for years: the stereotype of effete urban leftists who care more about Palestinian and transexual rights than workers' paycheques. These are, supposedly, the people who drink ten-dollar lattes and have jobs that are so undemanding that they need to go to the gym after work to burn off energy, the kind of people who whine about the lack of bike lanes. With their academic, arts, or unionized public-sector jobs, they're not sliding into debt. Their kids go to good French immersion schools where drag queens read weird books to them. Those kids will grow up to get government jobs. The right's urban elite stereotype matches the one they've created about Trudeau and his insiders: out of touch, rich, smug, privileged. Their jobs won't be taken by immigrants who work for less money. They don't see the crime and the drugs. (Anyone who's visited Ottawa or any other major city recently would be quickly disabused of that idea.) They prefer Volvos, BMWs, and Mercedes to cars made in Canada.

Many years ago, Ontario premier Bill Davis, who had a solid grounding in small-town Ontario, eviscerated provincial Liberal leader Stuart Smith. The opposition leader was a Montreal-born psychiatrist living in Ottawa who vaguely resembled Pierre Trudeau—about as culturally and physically removed from working-class Ontarians as a politician can get.

"What kind of car do you drive?" Davis once asked him during a debate in the legislature.

"A Peugeot," Smith replied.

"A Pooo-joe?" Davis said, pulling hard on the word. "None of my neighbours make Poooooo-joes."

Exploiting this divide gets people elected.

NOW, LET'S LOOK at the Liberals. Too often, the Trudeau government couldn't or wouldn't explain themselves and their policies. Even senior Liberals say Trudeau's staff was terrible at communications after 2021. Simple requests from journalists weren't answered or even acknowledged. No one was ever available for an interview unless the journalist was among a few favoured members of the press gallery or a friend of the communications staff, even for sound-hungry radio and for TV, which needs visuals. Answers from the government, when they came at all, were boring boilerplate written by a committee and sent by email. When answers did arrive, they were usually too late to be useful. This was a government that never clearly explained. It let conservatives entrench ideas such as the feds overreached on Covid into Canadians' consciousness. There was constant assurance that people weren't really seeing what they were seeing. Until Trudeau resigned, there was rarely any real pushback against Poilievre and his nasty talk. When it did come, like in the summer of 2024 when Poilievre posted an over-the-top graphic of Karl Marx on Twitter under the heading "Sign here to have a Prime Minister who doesn't admire basic communist dictatorships," and Trudeau responded, "I think this guy needs to touch grass," Liberals were pleasantly surprised.

Ministers in Trudeau's government could have taken on Poilievre, people like Mark Holland, Marc Miller, and Nate Erskine-Smith, but it was clear they were not allowed to talk. The Trudeau team made the same mistake as Harper's: by trying to control the message, they had made everything about the leader. This only works if the prime minister can speak about every issue to any journalist who needs an answer or interview. This simply can't happen in a twenty-four-hour day, and if it did, it still made cabinet ministers feel like nobodies. Trudeau did not call out bullshit or clearly warn that Canada could go Trumpist. Instead, he gave little homilies and pep talks. Once the leadership race began, leading Liberals slipped free of the Prime Minister's Office's yoke.

There are so many reasons why a farmer, factory worker, waitress, or retiree should take a cold, hard look at Poilievre and his party before deciding they'd make a better government than the people we have now. But they haven't heard those reasons from the Liberals. The government's inability to defend itself should be blamed on Trudeau and his communications staff, but there were systemic problems. Some Liberals have won fights with Poilievre in Question Period, but it's been a long time since most Canadians tuned into it. The Liberal failure starts on the shop floor, extending into riding associations that have no real say in the party, up to the offices of MPs and ministers who have no freedom to speak, and into a Prime Minister's Office dominated by young, pretty, recent grads from good universities who have no clue of how to talk to Canadians. Too often, they don't even have basic manners, let alone knowledge of Canada's insanely complicated government and respect for the people who make democracy work.

As for the NDP, they've been disconnected from the shop floor for a very long time. Power and influence in Canada's union movement has shifted from industrial trade unions to organizations representing public-sector unions. People in the private sector who benefit from unionization want higher wages and job protection but either ignore or oppose the movement's social agenda and its stand on international issues. The NDP and Liberals have lost almost all their seats in Canada's manufacturing towns since the 1980s—something that did not need to happen—and the right has turned the debate into a one-way conversation. It will take years for the union movement to win back its own membership and expand into more factories and service businesses—if it happens at all.

13
THE MEDIA AND THE MESSAGE

Don't believe everything you read on the internet.

ALBERT EINSTEIN,
PRINCETON UNIVERSITY, 1958

IN DECEMBER 2024, Pierre Poilievre posted a chart showing the slowdown of growth in the Canadian economy. To make his point that the economy started to lag when Trudeau was elected, the chart makers suggested Trudeau took office in late 2014, not in November 2015. That way, the chart hid the fact that Canada took a serious hit when world oil prices dropped 60 percent between June 2014 and January 2015.[1]

National Observer columnist Max Fawcett caught the chart's manipulation and wrote, "The idea that Justin Trudeau's election in late 2015 is somehow responsible for the economic impact of the massive collapse in oil prices that happened a year earlier—and was driven by a decision made in Saudi Arabia—is a pretty obvious example of spurious correlation, and one Conservatives have been trading in for years now. But sharing a chart that falsely indicates Trudeau was elected in late 2014, as Poilievre did, is a whole different level of deceit. The fact that he did it more than once, despite being called out for the obvious falsehood, shows just how little he cares about the truth."[2]

Fawcett hit on something that's common to modern right-wing politicians: their willingness to ignore or twist the truth. Conservatives claim a higher moral ground than liberals. Many of them, like Benjamin Netanyahu and Donald Trump, claim their conservatism exists on a religious foundation. Trump, in his 2025 inauguration speech, credited God for his political comeback. He must believe in a God who believes the ends justify the means, that truth can be sacrificed for a greater good.

Poilievre's critics often accuse him of fact manipulation and outright lying. The record shows this smart, plain-speaking politician has serious failures when he speaks to Canadian voters. Politicians are not obliged to tell the whole truth and nothing but the truth or to keep their promises.[3] People expect them to put their best foot forward. But no one likes to be lied to.

When a reporter asked Poilievre if his slogan "jail not bail" meant an end to the legal presumption that a person is innocent until proven guilty, Poilievre dodged the question by saying, "In Vancouver, they had to arrest the same forty offenders six thousand times in one year. On average, an offender would have been arrested a hundred fifty times a year. Many of them would have had a hundred arrests, and they're newly arrested for a serious violent offence and literally released within hours."[4] Earlier, Poilievre told the House of Commons during a March 2024 Question Period that the arrests are "a direct result of the prime minister's easy bail system."

Were forty "offenders" arrested for violent crimes? No. Poilievre's staff plucked the numbers from a British Columbia report on property crime. Were they arrested six thousand times? No. Poilievre's numbers were not arrests but what police call "negative contacts" with officers. Every interaction with the police is noted and put into databases. Ottawa criminal defence lawyer Michael Spratt tried to track Poilievre's numbers down and talked to prosecutors, police, and defence lawyers in Vancouver. He found Poilievre's numbers were absurd. The police had identified "super chronic offenders," people convicted of five break-and-enters in the past decade, and ten "negative police contacts" in 2021, the year the BC crime report was written.[5]

The claim that the Liberals are soft on crime is central to Poilievre's stump speeches and slogans. There's an entire section on his YouTube page of videos accusing the Liberals of being not just incompetent at catching and prosecuting criminals but, for reasons unknown, pro-crime and friendly to criminals.

Poilievre has also misrepresented the Trudeau government's pharmacare, introduced after they made a deal with the New Democrats to keep the Liberals in power after the 2021 election. In an interview with Tory-friendly pundit Rob Snow, Poilievre said the law would prevent Canadians from buying extra insurance for drugs not covered by the federal plan.

"The pharmacare bill Trudeau's brought forward would ban that and require you move over to a federal government plan, not a workplace plan, a federal government plan," Poilievre told Snow, who did nothing to correct him. "I will not be supporting any plan like the one in the Liberal government's bill that would ban you from having a workplace drug coverage."[6]

Health minister Mark Holland called Poilievre's comments "nonsense fearmongering," saying, "It's bad enough that Pierre Poilievre wants to block women from getting access to universal contraceptives or stop diabetes patients from getting the medication they need. That's fine if you want to vote against that. But spreading what are out and out lies and misinformation is reckless and totally irresponsible."[7]

Drugs were also on Poilievre's mind when he talked about crime in British Columbia and the fentanyl pandemic that struck North America's cities starting in 2011, when the much-prescribed painkiller started to be synthesized by criminals and sold to opioid addicts. Because the drug is so potent, it's easy for clandestine drug labs to make batches that are far stronger than expected.

In one tweet, Poilievre said, "Trudeau's wacko drug policies have killed 42,000 Canadians." Trudeau had agreed to a 2022 request from British Columbia to legalize the possession of small amounts of drugs so addicts would buy and carry safe drugs with prescriptions, rather than buy opioids from street dealers.

In the summer of 2024, Poilievre posted a YouTube video of himself telling voters Canada "has the fastest-shrinking economy in the G7."[8] In fact, the International Monetary Fund had just predicted Canada would have the fastest-growing economy in the Group of Seven major economic powers in 2025.[9] Canada's GDP growth was second highest of the G7 countries in 2023 and 2024.[10] And, while the United States' GDP is higher than other developed countries and growing faster, that money flows to a very small group of insanely wealthy people. GDP does not factor in income disparity or quality of life, where Canadians are far ahead of Americans.[11]

In a black-and-white video with an ominous soundtrack, Poilievre used clips of Trudeau talking about his government's policy of trying to ensure addicts had safe artificial opiates. In the first nine months of 2024, more than 1,700 people died from overdoses of opioids, mostly fentanyl bought on the street, in British Columbia alone. The province was losing about six people a day.[12]

Meanwhile, the Liberals are safe from armed rebellion because the government plans to take their guns. Or at least that's what Poilievre tells his rallies. "Trudeau & the NDP will ban all hunting rifles if they are re-elected," Poilievre posted on Twitter. That's not true. Their gun-control bills limited access to handguns, which have been restricted to vetted owners with a legitimate reason to own them since 1892. After Gabriel Wortman went on a killing spree in Nova Scotia in April 2020, the Trudeau government banned AR15s, the rifle of choice for American school shooters and extreme-right survivalists, and other "assault-style" weapons. But the Trudeau government did not change the status of the 30-06 Springfield rifle, the most popular hunting rifle in Canada.[13] At worst, the Liberals bungled the introduction of their new gun-control regime—by including some popular hunting guns on an initial restricted list, for example. But, after an outcry, they amended their plans and passed a bill with strong public support—a law that Poilievre swears to replace.

What about the Liberals and the NDP? How are they handling Poilievre's often over-the-top and truth-challenged messaging?

Like the Democrats in the United States, the Liberals have never been able to figure out ways to debunk the lies and half-truths of their right-wing opponents. Trudeau has a natural sense of fun that voters stopped seeing long before he quit politics. He was also a scrapper. He understood what was going on. He called out Poilievre and his movement as authoritarian, anti-democratic, even fascistic, but he didn't do it often enough, and it cost him. Trudeau's handlers let him down. They were very selective about the journalists he talked to, and Trudeau never connected with editors and writers who don't work for big media or weren't seen as hip and friendly. He did nothing to cultivate journalists in the hinterland. Shoe-leather reporters covering the federal government didn't count. This was a gross misreading of how media works and a failure to understand that new reporters will, in a few years, be running their bureaus or working at more important places. The Prime Minister's office's appallingly bad communications managers ordered staffers to contact reporters and "tell" them to write a story on certain issues. That's a great way to embarrass junior staff and alienate reporters. Reporters became so angry with the Trudeau government that it became hard for the Trudeau comms people to get anything into the media.

The prime minister's press handlers were nowhere in the league of Jenni Byrne, who's very good at using a carrot-and-stick approach with the media. After Poilievre won the leadership and the Tories began polling so well that conventional wisdom said they couldn't lose the next election, Byrne made it very clear to senior and junior political journalists that any of them who were "Liberal-friendly" would be shut out by the inevitable Poilievre prime minister's office. This, too, helps explain the parliamentary press gallery's normalization of Pierre Poilievre. The media, with some rare exceptions, just lets this stuff go by, as though lies are just part of modern political marketing. Political reporters and pundits see themselves as part of a marketing game, rather than as fact-checkers with an obligation to try to protect the public.[14]

THERE'S A LOVELY media myth of a happy time when journalists were objective, fair, professional, mature, and obsessed with facts. Community-minded publishers left newsrooms alone, satisfied with the 15 percent on investment that they made by selling ads and copies of their newspapers. Journalists worked on beats and became experts on the subjects they covered. They called things as they saw them and wrote without fear of favour. Their editors bravely printed the truth, even if threatened by advertisers, politicians, or some other powerful people.

I always hate to smother a fantasy. It's fun to compare modern media to this golden age. It makes life easier. But, outside of the CBC and provincial public broadcasters, media was owned by people who were up to their chins in politics. Editors knew their careers depended on keeping their employers happy and stayed within a narrow ideological range.

There's a disconnect between the people and the media. Many journalists think news needs some kind of sponsor, someone speaking through the journalist. Almost all "news" is created, not found. Often, newspapers and newscasts are filled with artificial events, official announcements, trial balloons, and planted stories. (The fact that we read and see these things on computer screens doesn't change that.) Most reporters, especially those covering politics, spend little or no time looking for new facts and issues. What's packaged as "news" comes to them from the "communications" people working for political parties, government departments, and lobbying groups who, in Ottawa, outnumber journalists by at least ten to one. Conservative historian Daniel J. Boorstin wrote about media and advertising "pseudo-events" in the early 1960s. Modern conservatives have twisted his ideas and exaggerated them to brand professional journalism "fake news." They're creating their own coverage, in their own media, of their own rallies, using their online platforms and allies in professional and pseudo-media to exaggerate crime rates, hype stories about gender transition, and create their own funhouse-mirror versions of reality.

During the Harper years, and distressingly so under Trudeau as well, journalists were increasingly prevented by the "centre"—the prime minister and his senior staff—from informing people about the huge, complex government of Canada. (Anyone who wants to know how this started and why it happens should read my 2015 book *Kill the Messengers: Stephen Harper's Attack on Your Right to Know*.)[15] They were stuck with writing about official news, speculation, and fake outrage from Poilievre and other opposition politicians. Pundits wrote about politics as though they were gossiping in a high school cafeteria. Who's cute and who's not? Who's popular? Who's shit-talking other people?

Instead of fact-checked stories, we now are too often served videos and still photos of politicians walking down parliamentary hallways, posed in obviously faked photo ops, trading banalities with other world leaders, standing behind a lectern by the doors of the House of Commons reading from a script. Usually, they talk about things that few people care about. (This includes most journalists, who rarely read newspapers or books). And they see so much spin they've become cynical, though maybe not quite as world-weary as Hill reporters. If fifty boys on your street are crying wolf every day, wolf stories quickly become boring.

Poilievre has figured this out. His Trump-style rallies are visually more interesting than anything on Parliament Hill. In media coverage, whether created by the Tories or their allies in the internet "news" sites supported by right-wing donors and the professional media, the energy of these rallies contrasted sharply with visuals of Justin Trudeau or Chrystia Freeland trying to explain a complex tax change in ten seconds while posed in a fake kitchen.[16] These rallies imitate Donald Trump's and have the same purpose: to shout down opponents and dominate a media that craves visual effects.

Rally coverage, showing worked-up crowds responding almost on demand to Poilievre's fired-off slogans, implies popularity, enthusiasm, and political momentum. Here, voters believe they are insiders. In the rest of the coverage of politics, voters are outsiders, important only because they get a ballot. It's not just the voters who feel empowered: without the people cheering him on in person or watching the slick videos produced by his party, Poilievre would be just another dorky right-wing YouTuber pushing tax cuts and petroleum, just as Trump would be another New York huckster.

City newspapers used to send reporters to Ottawa to cover MPS and cabinet ministers from their region. Papers in Vancouver, Calgary, Edmonton, Winnipeg, Windsor, London, Montreal, Quebec City, Fredericton, and Halifax had reporters in the parliamentary press gallery in the nineteenth and twentieth centuries. Now, none of them do.[17] These reporters and people working for chains of small-town newspapers used to ask questions about issues important to their readers and their region. They helped build the reputations of powerful ministers. Now, the Toronto-centred "national" media—the CBC, the Canadian Press wire service, and the three Toronto dailies that make up, by far, the bulk of the Parliamentary Press Gallery—focuses almost exclusively on party leaders instead of ministers, legislation, and the bureaucracy. That's why, for the first time in this country's history, we have a major party leader who says he's running for prime minister. Our parliamentary system is ignored. Poilievre is campaigning to be Canada's president. So far, Canada's political system doesn't work that way.

Like Trump, Poilievre gets a lot of free media coverage. And, like Trump, it's worth a lot. By 2023, reporters and pundits in Canada reached a consensus that Justin Trudeau had to go. By mid-2024, Pierre Poilievre's election victory was portrayed in all media—professional or partisan—as a given. Suggesting any other outcome generated eyerolling. No one's studied the value of Poilievre's media coverage, but experts have quantified Trump's. Seven months before the 2016 presidential election, when Trump was winning his first primary, the *New York Times* used long-term academic studies to estimate Trump had already received $US2 billion worth of "earned media" from TV, radio, newspaper, and internet outlets. A Harvard study released in May 2017 found "Trump's coverage during his first 100 days was negative even by the standards of today's hyper-critical press." So Trump benefitted twice: once from the publicity that kept him front of mind and inspired people to talk about him, and again when he told his rallies the media was against him. Another study by the same Harvard team looked at stories on CNN—hardly a Trump-friendly network. The profs and grad students found the phrases *Crooked Hillary* and *lock her up* were repeated three thousand times during the campaign on that network alone. Stories about Trump's tweets are a good example of how Trump and the right use outrageous behavior to fire up the free advertising machine.[18] Poilievre says Canada's media is against him and his party, yet in the 2021 federal election, the *Toronto Star* was the only large newspaper in Canada that endorsed the Liberals. Poilievre and his fans talked about "Justin's Journos," yet by January 2025, editorial writers and opinion columnists in every media outlet in Canada said it was time for Trudeau to go.[19]

Like other former prime ministers and pensioned-off American presidents, we probably won't hear much more from Trudeau. Trump bucked that trend, constantly campaigning after he left Washington in disgrace in 2021. He kept feeding the media goat. Watching American late-night talk shows in 2023 and 2024, it was hard to imagine what Stephen Colbert, Seth Meyers, Jon Stewart, Jimmy Kimmel, and the rest would joke about if Trump lost and stopped talking. Fortunately for them, they got a reprieve in 2024.

The numbers tell an essential story about Trump's value to the American media's bottom line: during the first Trump campaign and his 2017–2021 presidency, the *New York Times*' digital circulation grew from two million to more than seven million. The *Washington Post* saw its digital subscriptions increase at least fivefold. Cable news subscriptions, which had been moribund before Trump's candidacy, more than doubled between early 2016 and 2020. Audiences for all the big American news networks—Fox, CNN, and MSNBC—took off. Even little NPR made bank on Trump: when Trump's secretary of state attacked the public broadcaster live on air, falsely claiming one of its journalists had broken the ground rules of his interview, the national office and member stations were flooded with donations.[20]

Canada has no late-night talk shows. A person could be in the witness program and be safe hosting a Canadian cable news show. Still, the Canadian media drummed it into voters' heads that Prime Minister Poilievre was inevitable. The *National Post* ran headlines like "What Poilievre's shift from underdog to front-runner means for his strategy in 2024." On the day Trudeau quit, January 6, 2025, the *New York Times* told its readers, "Meet the Combative Populist on a Path to Become Canada's Next Leader: Pierre Poilievre, the Conservative leader, enjoys a commanding lead in the polls as Canadians look to the next general election."[21] Australia's Sky News posted a YouTube video the next day with the headline "Pierre Poilievre emerges as front-runner to become next prime minister after Trudeau exit." Even the *Catholic Register* published, "9 Things to Know About Pierre Poilievre, Canada's Likely Next Prime Minister." It's very difficult to find a mainstream media article published before Trump's inauguration that suggested the 2025 campaign might be a race decided by voters, after a national campaign.

WHEN POILIEVRE DOESN'T get the media deference he thinks he deserves, he tries to bully reporters and editors. Poilievre was cheered on by right-wingers in Canada and the United States in 2023 when a video of him causally eating an apple while humiliating a reporter went viral.

Don Urquhart, editor of the *Times Chronicle*, the local paper for the southern part of British Columbia's Okanagan Valley, was Poilievre's target. He gets caught up in Poilievre's circular logic and lets the Tory leader question him. Urquhart was back-footed and didn't remind Poilievre that the apple-eater was the only person in the conversation who was running to become prime minister.

"You're obviously taking the populist pathway," Urquhart says in the video.

"What does that mean?" Poilievre asks.

"Certainly you tap very strong ideological language quite frequently," Urquhart says.

"Like what?" Poilievre asks.

"Left wing, you know, this and that, right wing," Urquhart replies.

Poilievre said he "never really" talks about the left or right. "I don't really believe in that," he says.

"A lot of people would say that you're simply taking a page out of the Donald Trump book," says Urquhart.

"A lot of people? Like which people would say that?" Poilievre asked as he bit down again.

The Trumpist media in Canada and the US loved the video. *National Post* columnist Colby Cosh put down his pom-poms to type the "takedown is now being studied as an example of political jiu-jitsu worldwide." Fox News described it as Poilievre "batting down [a] reporter's questions." On her Sirius Radio show, Megyn Kelly asked, "Can we get him in our country?"

London's *Daily Mail* said the video showed Poilievre "calmly tearing apart a reporter." On Twitter, Elon Musk implied Poilievre had made the big time. He'd "never heard of him before, but this interview is [fire emoji]." Ben Shapiro's Daily Wire had the best headline "Canadian Conservative Appears to be Eating an Apple; He's Actually Chewing Up This Lefty Journalist."

Fred DeLorey, who was Erin O'Toole's co-campaign manager in the 2021 federal election before joining a lobbying firm, had a clearer idea of the video's political value. "He is a darling of the right in many regards," he said. The video "put him on the map" and signalled that the leader would fight the media. "As a conservative, a lot of times we feel we're asked to apologize for being conservative and he just takes on these questions with a lot of strength. Those who like him love the video. Those who don't like him don't like the video," DeLorey said.

But would it change any voters' minds? It might, DeLorey believes, if they are looking for a strong leader. "He feels like a no-nonsense politician, which I think a lot of people are interested in right now." But then DeLorey lost the plot. He said, "It just shows that you can be a strong statesman." Anyone familiar with real statesmen would see the video as the trick that it is. There were two easy ways for Urquhart to have avoided the bullying: show up with written material to back up his claim (have receipts), or simply tell Poilievre that he's the politician so he should answer the question without trying to deflect. And don't let him lead the way down the rabbit hole.

And Andrew Lawton, Poilievre's supportive biographer and now a Tory candidate in southwestern Ontario, liked the exchange so much there's a transcript of it on the back cover of his book.[22]

POILIEVRE TALKS OF "Justin Journos." He knows better. Outside the CBC, professional media is dominated by conservative journalists and corporate owners, most of whom have supported his candidacy since before he became the party leader. Besides, most of the reporters who vexed Harper have already lost their jobs. The last avowed progressive newspaper, the *Toronto Star*, was sold to a conservative investor in 2020 for less money than it had in the bank.[23] Postmedia bought all of the important newspapers in Atlantic Canada, giving its American hedge-fund owners a monopoly in cities outside the southern Ontario Golden Horseshoe (with the notable exceptions of Winnipeg, Montreal, and Quebec City). The two private English-language networks with Hill bureaus, CTV and Global, lean hard to the right. The so-called news-radio stations on the AM dial in Vancouver, Toronto, Ottawa, and Montreal haven't had a reporter on Parliament Hill in years, but they feed red meat to their elderly conservative listeners by hunting on the webpages of the right-wing press and conservative internet sites.

So he's lying when he says the press is biased against him, his party, and their values. He's more accurate when he claims mainstream journalism is unimportant then offers up instead partisan conservative online outlets as alternatives. Poilievre has used the media since high school, and we would have never heard of him if he hadn't mastered the modern soundbite. But just when media power was fracturing and partisans on both ends of the political spectrum were herding their supporters into echo-chamber online news and social-media outlets, Poilievre's mythology got a boost. The Liberal federal government started giving money to newspapers. Now he could say journalists were on the payroll. Canada's big newspaper companies pried hundreds of millions of dollars out of the Trudeau government, claiming they'd be dead without public money. Some of the money came as direct subsidies and some when the government created the Local Journalism Initiative to pay part of the cost of some reporters' salaries.[24] Subscriptions became tax deductible, though the refund is not nearly as high as you get from a political donation.[25] Even though almost all the country's major papers are owned by Trump-connected hedge funds or conservative Canadian investors, Poilievre can say negative things about them and claim any negative questions and articles are motivated by media fears of being driven away from the public trough.

And the newspapers rarely fought back. The most articulate defence of the bailout came from the editor of a small newspaper in Niagara-on-the-Lake, Ontario, who took apart Poilievre's lies about the media. When Poilievre was in the Niagara region for a rally, Richard Harley asked him what his party would do to support local journalism. Poilievre answered, "Free speech. I am going to repeal the censorship laws, make it possible for Canadian news to be visible again on Facebook, Instagram, and all other social media platforms. And get rid of the terrible censorship laws that have taken those news stories down from the internet and deprived independent local media to have a voice."

In an editorial that went viral on social media, Harley pointed out there are no censorship laws in Canada. He assumed Poilievre was referring to the *Online News Act*, which requires internet platforms to compensate news organizations for content used or made available on their sites, material that's made these companies billions of dollars in Canada and, arguably, brought readers to news websites. Meta (the company that owns Facebook and Instagram) blocked news links rather than pay media companies. That, Harley pointed out, is the only "censorship" that's happened because of this law.

"So recap: Poilievre calls Bill C-18 a censorship law, which it absolutely is not. He's being blatantly misleading. And to the average, uninformed voter who doesn't understand it, it could seem true. We mean this with as little offence as possible, but he's relying on his voter base to not be smart enough to know the difference," Harley wrote.

When Poilievre was asked a question about the future of the Local Journalism Initiative, he answered, "It is terrible how...local journalism has done under nine years of Trudeau. He's tried to take it over and basically wants everyone to work for the government so that he can have regurgitated propaganda paid for by taxpayers."

Harley said this is false. "The Trudeau government has funded the Local Journalism Initiative, yes. But let's digest this, too. As editors of a journalism organization, we can simply say it's not 'terrible' how local journalism has done under nine years of Trudeau. In fact, the LJI program is one of the reasons local journalism can thrive in small communities, often called 'news deserts' because they have no local coverage. They don't have a big newspaper and often issues go uncovered because of a lack of reporters covering the area.

"Secondly, the notion that Trudeau wants everyone to work for the government and has 'propaganda' placed in newspapers is simply ridiculous. . . . LJI reporters don't work for the government. They work for the news organizations that receive the funding. The only person who ever tells reporters what to write about is their editor. Notably, several conservative-leaning news outlets receive the same funding."[26]

CONSERVATIVES TEND TO be remarkably thin-skinned, even for politicians. Harper mentor Tom Flanagan once told the *Hill Times* how Harper's hatred of the press was fixed in stone when the then-opposition leader was hammered in a news conference over an outrageous press release from the Conservative campaign that very strongly suggested Paul Martin tolerated, and maybe even supported, child pornography. On its live broadcast of the scrum, CBC Newsworld showed newspaper reporters huddled together, sharing a voice recording of the Conservative leader's reaction to the uproar. To Harper, Flanagan said, the reporters looked like hungry sharks or wolves. "There's no question, just as a historical comment, that that episode, the child-porn fiasco, represented a turning point for Harper," Flanagan said.[27] The idea that journalists would be shocked and scandalized when a major political party falsely accused a prime minister of coddling child pornographers, and that they would see this as low-blow politics, doesn't seem to have crossed Harper's and Flanagan's minds. Though these days, after years of over-the-top allegations by the right, including accusations of pedophilia flung around at Justin Trudeau by internet trolls and constant charges of corruption levelled by Poilievre, perhaps reporters wouldn't be scandalized by any claims anymore. CNN employs a full-time fact-checker to call out politicians' lies. He's a small voice in a mob. And, ironically, he's a Canadian, Daniel Dale, who made his name covering the insane antics of Toronto's crack-smoking mayor, Rob Ford, for the *Toronto Star*.[28] Canadian media's policing of truth and lies is haphazard at best.

Harper said the media was biased, he couldn't get a fair shake from them, and they had to learn their place. Trump has said that the media are enemies of the people. Poilievre says to anyone he can that they're bought and paid for by the Liberals. His hundreds of thousands of social media followers seem to agree. As I predicted in *Kill the Messengers,* conservatives have worked hard, and spent a lot of money, to replace the old media with a partisan version that looks like professional commercial websites.[29]

Ezra Levant, who co-wrote opinion pieces in the *Calgary Herald* with Poilievre, worked for Preston Manning and Stockwell Day on the Hill, and anchored the defunct Sun News Network in the Harper years, runs an online media outlet called Rebel News that regularly platforms members of the extreme right. Levant uses his fundraising talents to develop ginned-up grievance campaigns that create a steady flow of cash for his organization. What seems like bad news for other outlets is good news for Levant: every lawsuit, every denial by some official of press credentials, every arrest of a Rebel staffer, is cause for another fundraising drive.

Levant is also one of the few Canadian authors who makes decent money from books. He's written bestsellers about human rights agencies and the moral superiority of Alberta's oil over Persian Gulf, Nigerian, and Venezuelan crude.[30] McClelland & Stewart published *Ethical Oil* when the University of Toronto was the controlling shareholder of the legendary Canadian publisher. It won the prestigious National Business Book Award, and its ideas are now part of the Alberta public school curriculum.[31] Just as Poilievre shilled for Levant in the 2002 Calgary Southwest byelection, Levant and his team are all-in for Poilievre.

In the fall of 2023, when Poilievre went after traditionally centre-right CTV News, Levant used his large Twitter platform to praise Poilievre's attacks on traditional media.

"I can't tell you how reassuring I find Pierre Poilievre's attack on CTV. It's frankly more important than any given policy in the Conservative platform," Levant told his half-million followers. "By publicly and brutally disparaging CTV (and the CBC, and Global, and Canadian Press, etc.,) Poilievre is showing he's not afraid of the greatest power in Ottawa: peer pressure from the left-wing press gallery. Andrew Scheer and Erin O'Toole were terrified of the Media Party. And they actually thought they could win them over by being personally charming. That made them especially vulnerable to pressure, because they were always trying to ingratiate themselves ... Poilievre really doesn't care if reporters are his "friends" or not—in fact, he has a bit of fun mocking them. (Which ordinary Canadians looooove.) Any politician can lie to you, and Conservative politicians usually lie by claiming they'll be conservative, but failing to follow through once in power. And they always give the same excuse: the media. Poilievre is showing the character trait necessary to resist that siren song. Very few can pull it off. Attacking journalists is my favourite thing about Poilievre."[32]

The Post Millennial—an anti-liberal, pro-Poilievre news site founded by Matthew Azrieli, grandson of a billionaire Israeli property owner; cryptocurrency developer Ali Taghva; and Madison Hofmeester, an expert in developing ways to push websites to the top of Google—was created in alliance with Jeff Ballingall. He was the creator of Ontario Proud, an "astroturf"—fake grass roots—company that helped elect Doug Ford's government in Ontario. It sent out mass emails and social media posts that inflamed liberals and centrists with exaggerated and sometimes weird stories that villainized mainstream politicians and media. These companies are independently owned, but they appear to share resources between them. It's not clear if they make any money from journalism, but their material is valuable because it's often shared by conservatives on social media.

True North, the third major Canadian online pseudo-news site, offers ample evidence that good intentions can have unintended consequences. After Stephen Harper sicced the Canada Revenue Agency on charities that he believed too progressive, Justin Trudeau promised to fix the *Income Tax Act* to give charities more political freedom. He kept that promise in his first term, despite warnings that he risked creating the same kind of political action committees (PACs) that have used their money to warp American politics. Charities can now educate people on important policy issues and use organizations with charitable status to do it. Conservatives jumped on this and used the new rules to start tax-exempt think tanks and pseudo-media.

The Canada Revenue Agency gave charitable status to the Independent Immigration Aid Association in 1994 to help immigrants from the United Kingdom settle in British Columbia. A new board took over in 2017, after the *Income Tax Act* amendments came into effect, and changed the organization's name to True North. It now runs a partisan news site under that name and says, in its CRA filings, that it does "public policy research on issues related to immigration, integration and national security." True North's four-member board of directors includes Kaz Nejatian, a former staffer for Jason Kenney in Alberta, and now chief operating officer of the online retail behemoth Shopify. He's married to Candice Malcolm, another former Kenney aide and author of compelling books like *Losing True North: Justin Trudeau's Assault on Canadian Citizenship* and the bizarre *Generation Screwed*.

Andrew Lawton was one of True North's hosts until he won the Conservative nomination in a riding near London, Ontario. Sue-Ann Levy, a former *Toronto Sun* columnist whom the National

NewsMedia Council scolded for falsely reporting that refugee claimants were slaughtering goats in the bathroom of a suburban Toronto hotel, is a regular True North contributor. So is Lindsay Shepherd, a former grad student who was at the centre of a controversy after she showed her undergrad tutorial class a video of Jordan Peterson criticizing the Trudeau government for adding gender identity and expression as grounds for protection under the *Canadian Human Rights Act*. The predictable student complaints, university overreaction, lawsuits, and publicity ensued, and Shepherd became a darling of Canada's far right.

Many of these outlets base their stories on data produced by right-wing think tanks. These mimic American outfits like the libertarian Cato Institute and the Heritage Foundation, which wrote Project 2025, a blueprint for the Christian authoritarian takeover of the US government. The Fraser Institute has become one of the Canada's most successful think tanks, and its research—often of inconsistent quality and almost always agenda-driven—is used without much questioning by most of the Canadian media. The Fraser Institute has copied Florida businessman Dallas Hostetler's Tax Freedom Day and picked up on many other American crusades. At the same time, it has attacked the Canadian medicare system for its wait times, with the suggestion that a mixed or, even better, private health-care system would be more effective. The Fraser Institute has also pressured the provinces to return to back-to-basics education, using headline-grabbing school rankings.

Tasha Kheiriddin and Poilievre's long-time friend Adam Daifallah are proponents of the think tank system because they employ credentialed experts and have access to much of the media. These think tanks have worked to change the language of politics, and, in doing so, the way people think. Years ago, Kheiriddin, a lawyer, gave them some suggestions: "For the Liberal terms 'medicare' and 'public health care,' substitute 'state health care monopoly'; for the Liberal 'social services,' substitute 'government programs'; for the Liberal 'investing tax dollars,' substitute 'spending taxpayers' money'; for the Liberal 'budget surplus,' substitute 'amount Canadians were overtaxed.'"[33] We've already seen how "tar sands," used until this century to describe bitumen-rich subsoils in Alberta and Quebec, has been replaced with "oil sands." As conservative pundit Colby Cosh pointed out in *Maclean's* in 2012, "To refer to them as the Athabasca 'tar sands' has become a signal of opposition to their uninhibited exploitation. Calling them the 'oil sands,' the industry-approved phrase, indicates that one is comfortable with digging them up and selling them to the highest bidder, whether Chinese or Chicagoan." In the United States, conservatives have reframed inheritance taxes as "death tax."[34] This parallels the language-editing done by government experts and progressives. The disease dubbed monkey pox by media has been renamed Mpox, presumably to remove the stigma from our primate relatives.

Canadian journalists have also joined their colleagues in accepting and spreading the far-right's redefinition of the word *woke*. It was first used by African American folk singer Lead Belly in a song about the Scottsboro Boys, nine Black men wrongly convicted of raping two white women in the American South in 1931. He told his listeners to "stay woke, keep their eyes open." In 2008, the word was revived in Erykah Badu's song "Master Teacher" and was used by Black people again during the protests following the police killings of Michael Brown in Missouri in 2014 and George Floyd in Minnesota in 2020.

The far-right, including Trump and Fox News, redefined it to mean absurd demands for gender and racial justice. After cherry-picking and torquing news about protests to make them seem completely ridiculous and far outside the mainstream, they went on to cast environmentalism, criticism of the death penalty and mass incarceration, and demands for humane treatment of immigrants and refugees as "woke." Poilievre used the word once in Parliament in 2022 and again in 2023 before making it a mainstay of his slogans. Now he uses "woke" to denigrate anyone who seeks race and gender inclusivity in school curriculums and workplace hiring practices. People who want fairness for women and minorities in Canada's military are "woke." So are animal-rights activists, the country's telecommunications regulator, the bail system, and provincial and federal safe-drug-supply policies. People who want less plastic in the environment and advocate for reusable grocery bags and paper straws are "woke." So are people who believe in man-made climate change.

In 2023, a Liberal MP asked Poilievre to define the word.

"It has plenty of pretexts but only one purpose: control. It is designed to divide people by race, gender, ethnicity, religion, vaccine status and any other way one can divide people into groups. Why? It is because then one can justify having a government to control all those groups," Poilievre told the House. "No more woke. We need freedom."[35]

Like "axe the tax," which Australia's centre-right Liberal Party utilized to win their country's 2013 federal election, Poilievre's use of *woke* is not original. It's part of the language of right-wing politicians in Western countries. Media and politicians in the United Kingdom—where the press doesn't pretend to be objective—have taken sides in the "war on woke" while right-wing and neo-fascist politicians in France (and Quebec) claim "le wokisme" threatens national values.[36]

POILIEVRE FEEDS THE right-wing pseudo-media with succinct quotes and carefully crafted simplistic takes on complex issues. "I'm a believer in using simple Anglo-Saxon words that strike right at the meaning that I'm trying to convey," he said on a 2024 podcast hosted by Jordan Peterson. "And so I say things that people say, 'Yeah, that actually makes sense.'"[37]

Pollster Frank Graves and respected pundit Stephen Maher, writing in *The Walrus* magazine in 2022, quoted political scientist

Pippa Norris saying Poilievre's style "allows leaders to appeal to diverse groups with heterogeneous grievances."[38]

By the time he became leader, Poilievre had stopped giving one-on-one interviews with most journalists from major media outlets and now only talks with partisan journalists or celebrity influencers like Peterson who don't ask tough questions, and never, ever fact-check him. In December 2023, he gave year-end interviews to nearly a dozen right-wing journalists and respectful editors of small publications aimed at audiences of new Canadians. Conservative talk-radio hosts and extreme right-wing pundits, like Brian Lilley of the Sun newspaper chain and Rex Murphy of Postmedia, also got time with Poilievre. All other requests for traditional year-end interviews were turned down.[39] This is the culmination of a strategy that began under Harper: replace professional media with something that looks like print and TV news, run by conservative partisans. Canadians are not media literate, but political strategists are. The internet has allowed partisans, almost always on the right, to develop a separate media universe where news and opinion consumers are never exposed to opposing ideas, and "facts" are shaped to fit a narrative. This mockery of journalism is creeping into mainstream media, where people like Marc Kielburger and others who worked for WE Charity endured the malpractice of a media pack that started each assignment with a pre-determined story and did not let facts get in the way.

After Trump's re-election, Sean Speer, editor of The Hub, a conservative opinion site, told his readers that the de-legitimization of professional mainstream media—"legacy media" in New Right lingo—was complete in the United States and Canada. A majority of voters either did not believe established media or were disconnected from the diminished news outlets that used to have so much power.

Speer described how more than fifty journalists had shown up to a big Tory event in Mississauga in 2011 to be briefed on the soon-to-be-released Conservative platform. Four years later, when

Harper was still in power and his party had a fair chance of winning re-election, fewer than twenty journalists came to the same kind of event. It was a lesson for the Conservatives. There are far fewer reporters now, newspapers (and their websites) are thin, and the new generation of journalists is poorly trained and badly supervised. The big-city dailies and local TV stations have very little political clout, since most people ignore them. If Canadian conservatives hadn't learned this lesson before the 2024 American election, they know it now. Speer quoted a television executive who said just before Trump's re-election, "If half the country has decided that Trump is qualified to be president, that means they're not reading any of this media, and we've lost this audience completely."[40]

Take a subway, an LRT (when it's running), or a bus, and you'll likely see no one reading a newspaper or a book. It's hard to know if many of the people looking at their phones are on a newspaper's webpage, reading news behind a paywall. Subscription numbers and website-visit statistics show mainstream media is just one part of the online wall of sound.

As for traditional screen-watching, 95.6 percent of Canadians who still watch TV do not tune in to CBC's English language prime-time programming outside of hockey games. Local and national newscasts used to draw huge numbers. Now, just twenty thousand people watch CBC's supper-hour newscast in Calgary.[41] National news anchors like Peter Mansbridge used to be household names. Now, few people can name them.[42] CBC doesn't divulge the audience numbers for its newscasts but says more than a million people tuned in for a special report on the convoy in 2022. That leaves about thirty-nine million who didn't.[43]

THE INTERNET IS addictive, triggering powerful dopamine reactions in the brain. As it's become wired in to the brains of voters in democracies, domestic and foreign bad actors have waged a disinformation war on our society. For hostile foreign governments, disinformation is a cheap and deniable way to wage asymmetrical war against democracies. Countries have used propaganda for centuries but never with this kind of sophistication.

Earlier in the book, I talked about a survey by the Ottawa polling firm EKOS that showed the vast gulf in political views of informed and disinformed people. In 2024, Carleton University gave Frank Graves, EKOS's president, an honorary doctorate. In his convocation speech, which must have been something of a buzzkill to graduating students and their parents, Graves warned that he has "never seen our country in such a dark and divided state.

"Whether looking at confidence in national direction, outlook on the future, fears of the external world or even basic attachment to our country and public institutions, I am recording unprecedented record low scores on key barometers of social cohesion. If anything, these nadirs are even lower amongst younger Canadians and notably the incidence of those who see a university education as a sound investment has plummeted from eighty-five to forty-five percent over the past twenty years (lower still amongst young men)."

The pollster told grads how political discourse was riddled with lies.

"We live in an era which sees a crisis of both trust and truth," he said. "A growing number believe that climate change is a hoax and forest fires are a product of arsonists. Nearly a third believe that governments have intentionally concealed the real number of deaths from vaccines. The web of designed deceit is broadening and deepening and we are losing this contest for the future. Disinformation is polarizing our society in ways that we have never seen. At best we can take some comfort in knowing that these forces are by no means unique to Canada, but gripping most advanced Western democracies."[44]

Investigations of foreign interference in the politics of Western countries have been going on for a decade. (Before that, democracies were more concerned with recruitment propaganda from Islamic extremists.) When alleged meddling and propaganda became a political issue in Canada, the Tories tried to portray the Liberals as naive and soft on hostile countries, even though the Harper government signed a secret trade deal with China. In August 2010, when Poilievre was a backbencher, he hosted a banquet for the China National Tourism Administration and issued a press release praising China for issuing a decree that allowed its citizens to easily travel to Canada on big guided tours and see Canadian tourism ads.[45] At the time, the event was normal and fit with Canadian policy. Today, politicians in all the parties are editing their memories of events with Chinese men in black suits. (Canada was stricken from the list of China's acceptable tourism destinations in 2023 because this country hurt dictator Xi Jinping's feelings. The United States and Australia made the cut.)

Despite Xi's obvious hatred of Trudeau, which seems mutual, Poilievre insisted Trudeau's government ignored Chinese meddling in Canadian affairs. In 2023, the federal government created a committee to study foreign interference. It turned into a carnival, with vague accusations about unnamed politicians, most of them supposedly ethnic Chinese. Stories about meddling in riding nominations did expose a problem that none of the political parties want to fix: candidates are chosen in a process that practically begs for fraud. Kids can vote in these party meetings. Non-citizens can vote, too. The people who pick local candidates don't have to live in the riding. They can be bussed in from God-knows-where, and their votes are as good as people who've been decades-long members, donors, and volunteers of a local association. It is a system that rewards people willing to pull any trick and pay any price to scrape up people for a few hours. But an investigation by Marie-Josée Hogue, a judge on the Quebec Court of Appeal, found attempts by foreign governments to interfere in Canadian politics produced minimal results. While some MPs may have been friendly with foreign diplomats, none of them were traitors. The biggest threat to Canadian democracy, she said, was from disinformation spread by foreign and domestic actors.[46] Russia is a pro when all the other world powers' interference campaigns are minor league. For many years, the Putin regime has been waging an effective campaign against democratic institutions, social cohesion in Western countries, and politicians who do not support Putin. The American right has moved from being anti-Soviet to pro-Russia, as that unfortunate country has fallen into the hands of a fascist. Putin's propagandists supported Trump in his three runs for the presidency and he has reciprocated since re-taking office.

Russia's Social Design Agency (SDA) creates and spreads Putin's propaganda. FBI files describe it as "a public relations company, specializing in election campaigns, with deep ties to the Russian government." Journalists, using material from a data leak, said SDA's bot army, dubbed the Russian Digital Army, generated 33.9 million social media comments. SDA claimed it produced 39,899 "content units" on social media, including 4,641 videos and 2,516 memes and graphics. SDA was given quotas: in a project targeting Germany and France, it had to produce: "Cartoons—60 units. Memes—180 units. Article comments—400."[47]

Russian propagandists are accused of funnelling money through the RT, the state-controlled media company, to right-wing YouTube influencers in Canada and the United States. Putin's propaganda system went nuclear in the lead up to Russia's 2022 invasion of Ukraine. RT's English webpage, which employs Brits, Americans, and at least one Canadian, is a shrine for Trump and a hellscape for Western progressives. After the invasion, the Canadian Radio-television and Telecommunications Commission (CRTC) ordered Canada's satellite and cable companies to drop RT, but they were playing a twenty-first-century game with twentieth-century strategy. People who want RT's programs can get them off the internet. (Canada also sanctioned RT and its parent company, for what that was worth.)

So far, though, most of the disinformation—whatever its original source—comes to Canada through American-owned social media companies. Twitter is now a right-wing echo chamber that reinforces the myths of Trumpism. Now that it's no longer a virtual "town square," it may have run its course as a medium that can change voters' minds.

The House of Commons had its own foreign interference hearings, which raised the question of Indian meddling in the 2020 Conservative leadership race. Supposedly, Poilievre was the preferred candidate because he opposed Sikh separatists who want their own independent nation. Some of this dirt stuck to Poilievre, especially after he refused to get a security clearance to see the committee's secret documents. Poilievre's decision generated suspicion and rumour, but he stuck to it.

AUDIO, VIDEO, AND digital photos—podcasts, TikTok, Instagram, and YouTube—are more potent, and have more potential, than Twitter and Facebook's text-heavy platforms. Poilievre was the first, and has so far been the only, Canadian politician to master YouTube. Even when Erin O'Toole led the Conservatives, Poilievre made YouTube videos pushing his pet policies and attacking his political opponents. He could never have gotten away with that during the Harper years. But in opposition and nowhere near returning to power, Conservative leaders had little control over caucus members, though O'Toole did demote Poilievre from his job as finance critic.

Poilievre has about five hundred thousand YouTube followers who see his videos every time they go onto the platform. He'd posted three thousand videos as of the end of 2024.

In late February 2021, Poilievre shared a video about the Ukraine crisis to the more than 211,000 followers that he had on YouTube at that time. It had been just days since Vladimir Putin ordered Russian troops across the border. Over a montage of video clips appearing to be from the invasion, Poilievre blamed what was happening on Trudeau's climate change policies.

"Every time Trudeau kills a Canadian energy project, the dirty dictators like Venezuela's Maduro or Russia's Putin do a victory dance," Poilievre said in the video, which has now been viewed more than two hundred thousand times. Elect me, Poilievre promised to his 511,000 followers on Facebook, where he reposted the video, and it would be Canadian oil and gas producers doing the dancing. "As prime minister I will reject Trudeau's anti-energy laws," he said.[48]

Of course, Putin's decision to invade Russia's neighbour had nothing to do with the oil sands or pipelines. But Poilievre seized his chance, using the winds of war to bear aloft his domestic political message.

The Poilievre videos are usually well-made, well-written, focused, and short. He highlights these videos on Twitter, where he has more than a million followers. Since Poilievre won the leadership, his MPs have been told to hire staffers who know how to make, edit, and post videos. These clips will be on the site during the next election campaign. Sharing them on social media will allow the Conservatives to use a popular, potent form of advertising that already exists and isn't covered by election spending rules.

BY EARLY 2025, Poilievre had 530,000 YouTube subscribers. His clips are well-organized by topic, and some of them are in French. Justin Trudeau's Prime Minister of Canada account had just one thousand videos and seventy-two thousand subscribers when he resigned in January 2025, and many of them are boring clips of him speaking in generalities and platitudes.[49] (That's still better than the three main contenders for Trudeau's job. Karina Gould was the only candidate with her own YouTube channel when the race started, even though Mark Carney and Chrystia Freeland were supposedly laying the groundwork for their campaigns since at least 2021.)

Sometimes, Poilievre's video makers screw up. In mid-August 2024, they posted a three-minute YouTube video of Poilievre's speech at that summer's Calgary Stampede. The Tories had a month to work on the short film, but they saved time by combing through stock footage on the internet. The images, with Poilievre's voice-over, were a call to rural white Canadians to support the leader and his values. If the man in the tight white T-shirt and the white Stetson was elected, he'd make Canada into a fantasy place where farmers were appreciated. They could be sure their kids would get a good, non-woke education free of left-wing censorship. They'd be able to celebrate a relative's long-term sobriety with a family get-together and feel safe knowing a strong military protected them.

But there were a few problems. The internet is a worldwide thing. It's one place that needs more Canada, especially if you're looking for stock images that you can use without paying. The ad shows happy people doing nice things, like grandparents walking in a park with a toddler. That turned out to be Richmond Park, London (not the London in Ontario, either).

"It's easy to forget what home and hope look like," Poilievre says in the video. If viewers hoped to be reminded, they would have been smart to go elsewhere. A neatly dressed little ginger kid sitting at his school desk was filmed in Serbia. A more adult ginger-blond student glowing with pride (or something) was filmed at Kyiv Polytechnic Institute. The polytechnic is not in Kiev, Saskatchewan, which, unfortunately, is now a ghost town.

This young (Ukrainian) man looks adoringly at the sky. The next shot shows two fighter planes. "And he looks up, and what does he see? He sees a brand-new fighter jet. They're doing a training mission in the sky to defend our home and native land," Poilievre says. The pilots may well have been defending their home and native land, but if that appreciative young man saw them on a mission, it would have been against Russians. As Daniel Minden, spokesman for defence minister Bill Blair pointed out, the jets were Russian. "Shockingly,

Mr. Poilievre's dream for Canada includes Russian fighter jets flying over our glorious prairies on a 'training mission,'" Minden said.

In fact, the Tory leader and the Liberal spokesman might have both been wrong. The Su-27 is a fighter that the Soviets deployed forty years ago and stopped making in 2010. However, the Chinese have been making them under licence, and the stock footage was taken from such a long distance that its markings can't be made out. It may have been a Chinese air force plane. The Su-17 is an even older plane. The Russians stopped building them in 1990. They're still in the arsenal of Poland, Vietnam, Syria, and Iran's Revolutionary Guards.

That means they're not much of a threat to the house builders celebrated in Poilievre's ad. Sharp-eyed Twitter users, able to read the data embedded in the images, found these happy carpenters were working safely in Slovenia, a gorgeous country with no known enemies, partly because few people have heard of it and or can find it on a map. Poilievre said in the video that the builders were using Canadian lumber. Anything's possible.

The video of a truck driving down a suburban street was shot somewhere in the United States. Contented cattle were grazing on a hill in California when the camera crew showed up. The man in the truck is supposed to have dropped his kid off at school. In the next shot, he's at a gas station, tanking up on reasonably priced non-carbon-taxed Canadian gas. It's nighttime. Daylight returns as he drives past what Poilievre describes as a combine. It's really a tractor pulling a wagon of rolls of straw in North Dakota.

The entire extended family shows up at the end of the day, Poilievre tells the Stampede crowd and the YouTube viewers, to celebrate the tenth year of sobriety of one of its members, who was addicted to drugs. Something seems off. Sentient Canadians are unlikely to organize a sobriety dinner where everyone's holding a big glass of wine. Prairie families, if they were insensitive to the problems of the addicted, are more likely to have a few beers and maybe some whisky. But dinner wine is normal to Tuscan families like the one in the video.

The Stampeders were asked by the Conservative leader to look west to the foothills (shot in Indonesia) and the Rockies (the round mountains in the ad are in Utah). The only scene filmed in Canada was shot at the Kawartha Montessori School near Peterborough. That's a long trip for a Calgary kid to make every day.

After the stock imagery was exposed, the Tories took the video off YouTube, but several copies were posted by people who wanted it immortalized. "The video was removed—mistakes happen, as you can see here," Conservative party spokeswoman Sarah Fischer told reporters. Then she added a stock Conservative responsibility dodge: she said a Liberal ad from 2011 was scrutinized over *its* use of stock images.

But the Poilievre YouTube video was amateur hour compared to what Donald Trump's people were doing. The day Poilievre and his ad people were mocked on social media for making a video showing Californian cows protected by outdated Soviet fighters, Donald Trump's campaign was putting out an artificial-intelligence (AI) ad showing a digitally created Taylor Swift endorsing Trump. The video also featured cute Swifties happily wearing Trump merch.

In Canada, the Tory screw-up generated some mirth. In the United States, the fake Taylor Swift created real fear and demands from artists, tech experts, and politicians for laws to prevent that level of fakery. The Poilievre team's cut-and-paste Canada was laughable. Trump's computer-generated "Taylor Swift and the Swifties" endorsement and the number of people fooled by it was proof that fakery has become dangerously believable.[50]

POILIEVRE POSTS ON Twitter with the blunt, harsh style that earns clicks and generates the anger that pushes posts on the site's algorithm. Twitter and Facebook are programed to generate anger and division: responses that show anger get more value in the mathematic models of social-media sites than those that show joy or approval. Social media does not reward traditional PR happy talk and bureaucratic-speak. While Trudeau's tweets got the government's message out, they weren't likely to reach or resonate with working-class voters because they were boring and free of emotion. Justin Trudeau has more than six million followers, but his posts don't generate engagement. Most of them are nice talk about programs, and he rarely pushed back on Poilievre's mythology.

The Liberals don't have partisan "news" websites. When the left-of-centre new media shows blatant partisanship, it's towards the NDP. That party has its own media outlet, PressProgress, which is owned by the Broadbent Institute. Its impact, compared to Tory media, is minimal. All the left-of-centre online media, whether party-affiliated or not, attacked the Trudeau government as hard as the right-wing outlets.

THERE'S STILL ONE giant left. The Canadian Broadcasting Corporation (CBC), the nation's public broadcaster, is in trouble, which should scare anyone who cares about politics, books, arts, amateur sports, Indigenous issues, LGBTQ+ news, and the country's regions. Why do so many Poilievre supporters hate the CBC? You can look at its news coverage and their programming. It's easy to see that coverage of rural Canada, small towns, and the West, places where Poilievre's base lives, are not a CBC priority. Programming, when it notices anything outside of downtown Toronto, tends to pander.[51] The network accepts man-made climate change as fact and doesn't treat trans people like freaks. Poilievre has always accused the CBC of favouring Liberals, with no recognition that much of the CBC's 2020s-era journalism has been hostile to Justin Trudeau and his government. For awhile, the CBC carried opinion columns on its website edited by Robin Urback, who'd come from the *National Post* and would go on to the *Globe and Mail*. Urback platformed some of the most conservative columnists in Canada. No one, on the left or right, asked why CBC resources were going into the one thing that there's no shortage of in this country: unresearched partisan opinion pieces. Maybe no one made the CBC opinion columns an issue because most people didn't know they existed. (CBC managers quietly snuffed out the experiment in 2024.)

Poilievre has his own reasons to dislike the CBC. In 2010, CBC comedian Rick Mercer made fun of Poilievre for recently qualifying for a parliamentary pension at the age of thirty-one. While the original broadcast is moving through outer space at the speed of light—it passed the edge of the Oort Cloud and the heliopause by 2012—the segment is available on Earth by visiting YouTube, where more than 450,000 people have seen it. CBC's *This Hour Has 22 Minutes* has a Poilievre impersonator who plays off Poilievre's speeches and YouTube clips. They're spoofed Poilievre videos. In 2024, they made a parody ad of Poilievre explaining, in a Poilievre-imitator's voice-over of material from Poilievre's own YouTube clips, why he's not "wacko."[52] That one's been seen sixty-five thousand times on YouTube. The comedy show has also sent cast members to Poilievre rallies, where the Conservative leader has called them "government comedians" and told them they're not funny. And they posted a video on February 1, 2025, with the heading "You can't look so nerdy and still have to copy someone else's homework." Host Mark Critch mocked Poilievre for echoing Trump's statement that there are only two genders and that all illegal immigrants and non-citizens who commit crimes should be deported, and for making up insulting nicknames to use on opponents.[53] (To be fair to Poilievre, the Conservative leader was doing that long before Trump went into politics.)

While I was researching this book, Conservatives and some journalists told me Poilievre only intends to "defund" CBC's largely unwatched English television network. That's not what he said. Time after time, he's talked about taking $1 billion from the CBC's budget, which would only leave enough for its French services. Poilievre has never said he would keep CBC Radio, CBC's news and entertainment webpages, its podcasts, music stations, or Gem (the broadcaster's internet video service).

One of the things I've wanted show in this book is that Poilievre is consistent in his beliefs and will keep his promises unless they cause him serious harm. Many of the same people who think Poilievre is not serious about core promises like defunding the CBC parsed Trump the same way, saying he'd never do the things he blathered on about. They conveniently forgot Trump's past and picked through his threats and promises to remove the ones they didn't like. This explains why Amer Ghalib, the Democratic mayor of Hamtramck, Michigan, an enclave of Detroit with a lot of Muslims, endorsed Trump in 2024. Somehow, Ghalib forgot Trump's ban of Muslim immigrants in the 2017–21 term and convinced himself Trump's stand on Israel's bombardment of Gaza would be tougher than Joe Biden's. Within days of the election, Trump was promising more military aid to the Netanyahu government. In the second week of his new term, Trump said his plan for Gaza is "to clean out the whole thing" and turn the place into a resort. He wanted Gazans shipped off to refugee camps in other Arab countries.[54] When people like Poilievre and Trump tell you who they are, listen to them.

14
ON SHIFTING GROUND

It is difficult to free fools from the chains they revere.
                                              VOLTAIRE

TWO DAYS AFTER winning the leadership, Poilievre held a Conservative caucus meeting. Hill journalists were allowed to watch for a moment as Poilievre made a speech specifically for them, not for his own Tory MPs and senators. "Canadians are hurting and it is our job to transform that hurt into hope, and that is my mission," Poilievre declared. He blamed the Trudeau government's taxes, especially the carbon levy, for higher grocery prices that made life tougher for Canadians.

"If you really understand the suffering of Canadians, Mr Prime Minister, if you understand that people can't gas their cars, feed their families or afford homes for themselves, if you really care, commit today that there will be no new tax increases on workers and on seniors. None."[1] There was no magnanimity, no olive branch in Poilievre's speech. He said he was speaking to "the prime minister, and to his radical, woke coalition with the NDP."

"Here's my commitment," Poilievre told the cameras. "We as Conservatives are always happy to work with any party to collaborate and extend and advance the interests of Canadians. We are. But there will be no compromise on this point: Conservatives will not support any new tax increases, and we will fight tooth and nail to stop the coalition from introducing any."

The prime minister was not in the room. He wasn't even in Ottawa. Trudeau was on a three-day caucus retreat in New Brunswick, working on strategy for that fall's session of Parliament. Trudeau held a press conference of his own, congratulating Poilievre on his leadership win before attacking the new Tory leader's economic policies and portraying him as mean.

"We've been making every effort to work with all parliamentarians, and we will continue to do so," he said in his most earnest Trudeau tone. "But this doesn't mean that we're not going to be calling out highly questionable, reckless economic ideas. What Canadians need is responsible leadership."

Take Poilievre's ill-advised hyping of cryptocurrency, Trudeau said. It was at the time losing value—again. "Telling people they can 'opt out of inflation' by investing their savings in volatile cryptocurrencies is not responsible leadership," Trudeau said.[2] (Poilievre made the claim in March 2022 during a leadership campaign stop at a shawarma restaurant in London, Ontario.)[3] "When Conservative politicians say we should fight inflation with more pollution, this team will remind them that climate change is real, and that real people are affected by the floods and wildfires that it aggravates."

Poilievre uses "buzzwords, dog whistles and careless attacks," which, the prime minister said, "don't add up to a plan for Canadians." Attacking the institutions that make our society fair, safe and free is not responsible leadership. Fighting against vaccines that saved millions of lives? That's not responsible leadership. Opposing the support and investments that have helped save jobs, businesses and families during the pandemic? That's not responsible leadership," Trudeau continued.

Poilievre had attacked the Liberals for spending billions to bail out Canadians during the Covid pandemic, but "it was the smart thing to do."[4]

That day, Alain Rayes, a Quebec MP who supported Jean Charest in the leadership race, quit the Tory caucus to sit in the House of Commons as an independent. He told his colleagues and the media that the party's path under Poilievre was incompatible with his "political ideals, values, and convictions." Then, strange things started to happen. An anonymous text message started landing on phones in his riding that claimed Rayes decided not to fight inflation with Poilievre's team. Constituents (and anyone else who got it) were urged to call the MP's office and tell him to resign. The sender was thoughtful enough to include the number. Rayes saw the text message campaign as a strategy to intimidate him and to make any other doubter in the Tory caucus reconsider a similar protest against the new leader.[5]

The 2025 election campaign was on, or seemed to be. Poilievre would take on Justin Trudeau on taxes, housing, crime, and voters' desire for change. He would, conventional wisdom in Ottawa's back rooms and media corps thought, ride the right-wing wave sweeping Western democracies into the prime minister's office. Within a year, Poilievre's poll numbers were fantastic.

POILIEVRE AND TRUDEAU, who still planned to run again, campaigned in 2024 on two very different ideas of Canada. Poilievre portrayed the country and its people as broken by big governments and out-of-touch socialist urban elites who want, or don't care about, high taxes, crime, drugs, and a housing shortage. The Liberals talked about a Canada that wants to be part of a new economy. Theirs is a brokerage party that tries to build a national coalition by advocating equality for minorities; national unity; cultural diversity; French–English bilingualism in national institutions; mitigation of historic wrongs, especially to Indigenous Canadians; anti-racism; and multilateralism. The Tories had adopted, with some Canadian tweaks, the rigid policies advocated by members of the International

Democracy Union, a worldwide organization of right-wing political parties led by Stephen Harper.

Poilievre and Trudeau accused each other of sowing division, and to an extent, they're right: both leaders staked out positions on culture war issues and used those to build (or, in Trudeau's case, try to hold) their followings. Trudeau was poor at reaching out to, or even listening to, people who held strong feelings on issues he disagreed with. Rather than debate, he tended to demean those he believed conned by Trumpist ideology. He may have thought he was taking the political high road, but he came across as patronizing and snobbish. This gave Poilievre an opening. He went to marginalized parts of the country and talked to people. This represented a huge change in Conservative strategy: before the 1980s Reform/Progressive Conservative split, the party's leaders had been the voice of big business. Except for John Diefenbaker, they didn't give barnburner speeches at small halls in little towns and hang around afterwards to talk to people who came up to them. The NDP's leaders used to do that. So had Jean Chrétien. The Trudeau-era Liberal party, supposedly the umbrella for centre and left-of-centre voters and strategists, hid behind a wall while Poilievre was on the road with his Trump-like message.

SINCE TRUDEAU'S RESIGNATION, Poilievre and the pundits who amplify his message have tried to frame all Liberals as clones of Trudeau. For their part, the Liberals paint a picture of Poilievre as an angry, dishonest, deliberately uninformed Trump imitator who would say anything to get himself and his front bench into government.

Poilievre had settled on a simple chant: "Axe the tax, build the homes, fix the budget, stop the crime." The shots at the carbon tax were the centre of his non-stop campaign. The "axe the tax" slogan isn't original. Poilievre swiped the entire anti-carbon tax campaign, including the slogan, from Tony Abbott, prime minister of Australia from 2013 to 2015.[6] Carbon pricing had been in Harper's platform in 2008. At that time, environment minister and Poilievre ally John Baird called it a key part of the country's strategy to fight man-made climate change. In the end, though, the Harper government didn't bring in carbon pricing. They stopped talking about it after Baird was shuffled out of the energy portfolio, then dropped it from their platform for the 2011 election. In the 2021 election, party leader Erin O'Toole backed a carbon tax. Some provinces have already brought them in. All these leaders, to some extent, have at least pretended they believed man-made climate change is real. The present leader does not. A Poilievre government would accompany a Trump regime that will not allow climate change to be mentioned on government webpages and has a policy of purging all climate change research and mitigation programs from the United States government.

As for crime, Poilievre has argued that he will use the Constitution's notwithstanding clause to push through tough-on-crime bills. This has never been done before, and it's not clear the federal government could use that constitutional escape hatch. And if these tougher laws can't be reviewed by the courts, does it mean crime rates will tumble? Crime rates have been going down for years as Canada's population ages, but this is merely an inconvenient fact that Canadian media rarely mentions. Tough-on-crime laws are based on the idea that people calculate the length of their crime's potential jail term against the perceived benefits of committing the crime before deciding to break the law. This implies a level of analysis that might work in the calculations of a politician but likely doesn't exist in the mind of a meth addict. If Poilievre believes increased policing is the answer to Canada's so-called crime problem, he might want to talk to the country's mayors and the premiers of the provinces that have provincial police forces. They've been fattening police budgets for decades, to mixed effect.[7] As for court cases being thrown out because they've dragged on too long, court houses, court staff, Crown prosecutors, and the judges who remand cases are provincial employees. The federal government only appoints the judges who conduct the trials of the most serious cases. So it will be very difficult for a Poilievre government to radically alter the way crime is treated or punished in this country.

No one can argue that Canada doesn't have an opioid and methamphetamine crisis that affects both rural Canada and all its big cities. Poilievre suggests the current federal government and the police don't care about the problem, which is an insult to the police and border agents who hunt smugglers, drug makers, and wholesalers. Canadian cops have the same frustrations as their American colleagues: synthetic opioids and meth are made here, unlike cocaine. The chemicals for these very addictive drugs are easy to smuggle into Canada and the United States from China, and fentanyl is easy to make. (Hillbillies have been making meth in the United States for years. You don't have to be Walter White, the anti-hero of *Breaking Bad*, to brew it.[8]) America's demand for the stuff fuels the drug trade. The Drug Enforcement Administration, Federal Bureau of Investigation, and local cops haven't been able shut down this trade, nor have any politicians come up with a realistic plan to end the addiction crisis. It is starting to look like the situation in nineteenth-century China when Britain was foisting Indian opium on that country.

If Poilievre has an effective drug-fighting plan, the world is waiting to hear it. He has mentioned increasing treatment for addicts, which might help, but yet again, Canada's wonky federalism comes into play: health care is a provincial jurisdiction. A Poilievre government might part with the money to pay for this treatment. The provinces might agree to build a lot more hospital and clinic rooms. But where will the medical staff come from at a time when so many Canadians don't even have a family doctor? And how will anyone convince or force addicts to get treatment and stay clean? Courts can send people to jail, but making them take medical treatment is much more difficult and involves an expensive legal process. It would take mental gymnastics of the first order for a Poilievre government to argue that an addict must submit to intensive psychiatric treatment while saying truckers should have the right to refuse vaccines.

As for housing, it is a mess that every government in North America and most of Europe is dealing with. Canadian houses are too expensive to build or buy. Many houses and apartments have been taken off the market and listed as short-term rentals through companies like Airbnb and VRBO. This has put pressure on rent, especially in provinces with no rent controls. It would take a lot of coercion to force landlords to put their profitable short-term rentals back on the local long-term housing market, so it's hard to believe a free-market libertarian like Poilievre, or the right-wing premiers who hold office in most of Canada's provinces, will tackle that.

And that's without tariffs.

Housing costs are affected by land prices, the cost of city levies and approvals, availability of labour, and the profit expectations of builders.[9] They are also greatly affected by people's expectations, which Poilievre has done nothing to change, referring to the wartime single-dwelling homes that have maintained generations of families in this country as shacks. People now too often want and expect houses that are bigger than the Victorian homes that were built for wealthy families with five or ten kids. They expect a level of fixtures and finishing that can't be called palatial because palaces never had marble bathrooms and quartzite countertops. Will his government's housing initiative work to convince Canadians to be satisfied with smaller townhouses, or to try to make homes in the tiny, expensive condo units that are a glut on the Toronto real estate market? And how easy is it to square his claim of concern about housing with the 2024 edicts to his own MPs to refuse to help communities in their ridings get federal money for housing projects? In November 2024, one anonymous Tory MP told Radio-Canada, "If by any chance I attended a municipal housing announcement funded by a Liberal initiative, I would be in a lot of trouble."[10] Partisanship, again, trumped measures that might help Canadians, even when delivered by members of Poilievre's caucus.

In 2023, Poilievre played one of his housing games, talking about a Toronto couple who'd sold their house and bought a castle in France. Now, he said, they couldn't afford to unload the castle and come back to Canada. They were stuck living as aristocrats in France.[11] In fact, the castle-buyers were from the small Ontario town of Fergus. They'd bought a large manor house, not a castle. Sara Cole and her husband told *Toronto Life* they knew they were making a bad financial decision: old houses aren't rare in France, and many French people see them as white elephants.

And, as real estate agents like to say, "location, location, location." The European countryside has been emptying as populations age and farms consolidate. In Italy, some governments have been selling ancient houses in half-empty old walled towns for a euro. The Coles bought the chateau because they are history buffs, not to make money. "Buying a château like this is an objectively bad financial decision," Sara told the *Toronto Life* journalist. "You don't get the same returns you'd expect on a property in Canada because it's a heritage building and needs constant upkeep by specialized artisans." The building is also a fire trap. It took a lot of money and sweat to make it the gorgeous, quirky house that it is now. And the Coles aren't trapped. They don't want to come back.[12] No one in the Canadian media fact-checked Poilievre's claims about the Coles and their French home, nor did any of his political opponents.

Politicians say they would love to get people into homes they can afford. At the same time, homeowners who are relying on the equity in their homes to support them when they retire could become very loud if politicians pop the housing bubble. Two-thirds of Canadians own houses, and almost all of them have seen their equity grow. If prices come down, a third of the population might have a better chance to buy a home, but two-thirds of Canadians will see themselves as poorer. And some of those people are counting on their homes to finance their retirements.

—

THE SHADOW OF Donald Trump looms over Canada's politics. At first, politicians and pundits said his musings about waging economic warfare to make Canada the fifty-first state was just a running joke. But he kept doubling down on it, including in a speech to the World Economic Forum in January 2025. Delegates to that conference gasped when he talked about annexing Canada. Then he began using tariffs as a weapon. It didn't matter to Trump that the free trade agreement between Canada, the United States, and Mexico doesn't expire until 2026. He and his advisers made it clear they want all of Canada's auto plants to move to the United States, and he'd use tariffs to make them do it.

Canadian political conversation changed in January from "axe the tax" to "who will be the best leader to defend Canada?" Trashing Trudeau and the carbon tax during the first thirty months of Poilievre's non-stop campaign became irrelevant news by late January, as Canadian political leaders shuttled between Ottawa, the provincial capitals, and Washington to try to defuse Trump's threats. And Trudeau had quit, making a lot of truck flags redundant.

After Trump became president and continued his threats against Canada, polls that had long shown a nearly insurmountable lead for Poilievre and the Conservatives started shifting. Polls reported Poilievre with a lead of as much as 27 percent over the Liberals in late 2024. The governing party was at risk of falling back to third place, in worse shape than it was when Justin Trudeau won its leadership. Twitter trolls attacked Frank Graves in January 2025, when his polling company, EKOS, was the first to show a big shift. The Liberals were just five points behind the Conservatives after Trump made his first tariff threat.

But the Trump revolution, despite his rhetoric, is not about trade. Republicans, much like Poilievre, believe a strong leader operating without boundaries and regulations provides efficient government and keeps leftist dissenters in their place. British writer George Monbiot believes this New Right revolution is "a deliberate means of changing the nature of power."

Trump and the rest of the authoritarian right, Monbiot argues, use populism to win elections so they can use political power "to take the last restraints off capitalism."[13] Any success results from their policies. Failure happens because people are weak. This is the essence of the libertarianism of Trump, J.D. Vance, and Pierre Poilievre.

"Never mind that your school has lost its playing field or you are living in a food desert," political scientist Richard Crockett wrote in 1995. "[I]f your kid is fat, it's because you're a bad parent. The blame for systemic failure is individuated. We absorb the philosophy until we become our own persecutors. Perhaps it's no coincidence that we've seen a rising epidemic of self-harm and other forms of distress, of loneliness, alienation and mental illness."[14]

POILIEVRE IS THE best campaigner in Canada, the most effective since Jean Chrétien. Whether this revolution comes to Canada depends on Canadian voters. Poilievre has money, mainstream media companies, conservative online media, many provincial politicians, conservative think tanks, and most of the major pollsters on his side.[15] Whether he's heard of it or not, Poilievre has tried hard to follow the maxim of Napoleonic War–era Prussian general Carl von Clausewitz, who said wars are won or lost in the minds of soldiers before they even start. By the end of 2024, he'd convinced journalists and many voters that he could not be stopped.

Incumbency used to be a political advantage. It isn't now. In this decade, it's a rare national government that's survived an election: leaders have been turfed out in the United States, the Netherlands, and Italy, among other places. Voters are throwing the bums out, and it doesn't matter if the incumbents are on the right or the left. The Conservatives in the United Kingdom suffered a far worse humiliation than the Democrats did in the United States. Emergency Covid hospitals in Brazil were just shutting down in 2023 when President Jair Bolsonaro, who makes Trump look like Jimmy Carter, was chucked out. France swung sharply to the right, and even if President Emmanuel Macron didn't suffer the fate of most of his allies in 2024 (he isn't up for re-election until 2027), his party took a beating in parliamentary elections.

Poilievre's strategy has been to bypass professional media when it asks for intelligent policy. His party has, as Hungary's Victor Orbán advises, created its own media environment.[16] Voters are expected and are being trained to count on The Leader to make decisions that will make things right. Poilievre is portrayed in his own media, and in the legacy press, as someone who has the ear of the common man and cares only about making them happy. So why would he need to explain how he would do it? That would shift the conversation to his ideas, which are weak at best. Poilievre acted as though his success was assured if he could keep the public's focus on Justin Trudeau, convince people the Liberals were sticking with all his policies that "broke" Canada, and maintain the consensus of the inevitability of his victory. After early February 2025, when Trump was threatening Canada and Trudeau was being shuffled off the stage, that became a much more difficult task.

While there was a consensus among opinion-makers and many politicians in 2024 that Poilievre had the 2025 election in the bag, there has been no sign that the Conservatives have been working on the policies that they'd use in government. Simcoe North MP Adam Chambers, a bright, personable man who'd worked in Toronto's financial district and for finance minister Jim Flaherty, was supposed to be developing an economic plan. That would be a tough project in normal times. But, in early 2025, there was no serious energy policy, nothing on climate change mitigation, no substantial housing plan. Conservative provincial politicians like Doug Ford have simply refused to issue election platforms and have won. Before the 2024 election, Trump portrayed Project 2025, a manual for a radical makeover of the American government, as a theoretical plan that he hadn't even read, then began to implement it the day he was sworn in.[17]

Like Trump, Poilievre is always campaigning. And, like the American president, he channels his own anger to inflame the anger and anxiety of the people who go to his rallies. Both politicians are mean, and as is the case with Trump, there's no boundary on what Poilievre will say or the crowd he'll talk to. In the spring of 2024, he turned up at a camp of tax protesters near the New Brunswick-Nova Scotia border. He went into a trailer that had a handwritten logo of the extremist group Diagolon next to its door. These are people who want to accelerate the fascist revolution they believe is coming and have a member who once made an online threat to rape Anaida Poilievre.[18] The Conservative leader told the campers, who described themselves as a convoy (though they never went anywhere), that the prime minister lied about "everything." He described their "convoy" as "a good old-fashioned tax revolt" and told them to "keep it up."

"Everyone hates the tax because everyone's been screwed over," Poilievre told them, giving credence to their gripes. As he walked among the trucks with their "Axe the Tax" and "Fuck Trudeau" flags, one of the protesters asked for a selfie. The Tory leader suggested they move a bit to keep a "Fuck Trudeau" flag out of the photo.[19]

This was one of the few times Trudeau fought back, accusing Pierre Poilievre of welcoming "the support of conspiracy theorists and extremists."

"Every politician has to make choices about what kind of leader they want to be," Trudeau told reporters. "Are they the kind of leader that is going to exacerbate divisions, fears, and polarization in our country, make personal attacks, and welcome the support of conspiracy theorists and extremists? Because that's exactly what Pierre Poilievre continues to do, not just when you see him engaging with members of Diagolon but also when he refuses to condemn and reject the endorsement of Alex Jones."[20]

Jones, who'd been sued into bankruptcy after saying the 2012 school massacre at Sandy Hook was faked, was a hero to the extreme right but a pariah to decent people. "[T]he fact that one of the world's most notorious liars says he's on Team Poilievre should give us all pause," law professor and author Timothy Caulfield wrote in *The Walrus* magazine. Jones made his endorsement after one of Poilievre's rants about the World Economic Forum. "When Jones sounds off about something—be it Hillary Clinton's demonic sex trafficking ring, how the chemicals the US government is adding to water are turning frogs gay, or how the Sandy Hook shooting was staged—it is safe to assume he's *spectacularly wrong*. That's the default. But this time, Jones is on to something. A merging of the Jones and Poilievre world views."[21]

Billionaire Elon Musk had glommed onto Trump during the 2024 presidential election. Since then, Musk had been couch-surfing wherever Trump was living. Speaking in December 2024 from Mar-a-Lago, Trump's Florida hangout, Musk came out for Poilievre and kept hyping him afterwards. "[Poilievre] is extremely impressive. He should be Canada's next leader. The sooner the better," he posted on Twitter. Poilievre "perfectly articulated" his anti-inflation message, Musk said. He reposted Poilievre's tweets and links to his videos. But as public opinion began to turn against Musk, some Canadian political analysts wondered whether Musk was helping or hindering Poilievre's chances of winning.[22]

THERE'S NO BLOW too low, no overreach that Poilievre hasn't been willing to make. When an anti-NATO street fight broke out in Montreal while Trudeau was taking his daughter to a Taylor Swift concert in Toronto, Poilievre pounced. Although the Montreal police easily stopped the riot, and there was no need for federal involvement, Poilievre said Trudeau should have taken charge. That would have meant walking out of the concert, with or without his young daughter. "I have no problem with him taking his kids to a concert. That's everyone's right," Poilievre said. "But part of the job of being prime minister is you get called away from important family and other functions to do your job."[23]

It was also Trudeau's fault that Hindus and Sikhs fought in Brampton. "So he uses and incites divisions here at home. These divisions are the result of him," Poilievre said in the House of Commons. "Now we see sectarian riots on the streets of Brampton. This never happened before this prime minister. Does he take ownership for the divisions he's caused and the violence that has resulted?"

Later, on Twitter, Poilievre wrote, "I will unite our people and end the chaos."[24] Yet it's difficult, maybe impossible, to find a time in his adult life where he brought people together. The number of times when he has "othered" people who have different views on the economy, the role of government, the environment, social issues, health, crime reduction, Indigenous issues, and so many other things that Canadians debate, are uncountable.

When members of the Parliamentary committee studying foreign interference in Canadian politics said a hostile government meddled in the 2022 Conservative leadership race, Poilievre deflected the criticism to Trudeau, claiming the prime minister had a secret list of traitors sitting in the House of Commons. Presumably, these foreign agents were Liberals, New Democrats, or members of the Bloc Quebecois. "We've got nothing to hide, so name the names, Mr Trudeau," he said. It was, he declared, Liberal MPs "who are compromised." The Tory leader claimed the Chinese helped elect Trudeau in the last two elections, and said, "This is a man who had a track record of lying about everything."[25]

Yet, in at least one YouTube video, Poilievre spreads the false rumour that there's a baby picture of Justin Trudeau in the new passports. And he never corrects anyone who says batshit-crazy things about his opponents. During the 2022 leadership campaign, Pierre and Anaida Poilievre were questioned by a woman who came out to one of his rallies. She demanded to know if Poilievre had confronted Trudeau about the fortune that conspiracy theorists believe the prime minister accrued from owning stocks in pharmacy companies that made Covid vaccines. A man, standing behind the woman, piped up: "Seventy million dollars in two years." Poilievre didn't stand up for the integrity of Canadian politicians. Instead, he simply said no, he hadn't spoken to him. Then, turning to Anaida Poilievre, the woman said she'd heard the same thing about the Tory leader. Anaida denied owning pharmaceutical stock: "I do not, darling," Anaida said. "I really do not. And I am honest, and I promise you."

The people at the rally cheered and clapped. "I hope to God that's true," the woman says. "I hope you guys are who we think you are."[26]

Poilievre, Jenni Byrne, deputy Tory leader Melissa Lantsman, and other people on the Conservative team seem determined to purge any remaining civility from Canadian politics. After Jenni Byrne posted a vicious tweet about former Tory leader Erin O'Toole, *Globe and Mail* columnist Shannon Proudfoot put her finger on a key problem for Canadian democracy. "Think about what we end up with if Canadian politics slides fully into that mood in a bar when a patron has had too much to drink and the air around them vibrates as they scan the room, begging for eye contact so they can punch someone in the face," she wrote. "The United States is currently in an advanced stage of this, and each week feels like another sentence in a future history textbook about how one of the world's extinct giants toppled into the sea. Who would run for public office, for any party, if this is what it means? The best and the brightest will stay far, far away from such an asinine thunderdome. Eventually, the only people who volunteer would be spineless toadies, hyperpartisan whack jobs or anger addicts, left to run the country like a 'roided-out island of misfit toys."[27]

This is the environment that Lantsman thrives in. A former communication staffer in the Harper government and a corporate lobbyist, Lantsman leads with her elbows. On the last Saturday of January 2025, Lantsman set up a podium on Danforth Avenue in Toronto's Greektown, across the street from where local Liberal MP Nate Erskine-Smith was holding an event for Liberal leadership candidate Mark Carney. She described her sidewalk speech as a news conference. Although she had often demanded Justin Trudeau's resignation, she now accused Trudeau of leaving Canada leaderless while the country faced Donald Trump's tariff threats. But she saved her nastiest talk for Erskine-Smith, whom she accused of being paid by Carney for his support. The MP, a likely leadership contender someday, was, Lantsman said, "a radical drug advocate." (Erskine-Smith supported prescribed safe drugs for opioid addicts, but Lantsman didn't explain that.)

Poilievre, who was once tossed from the House of Commons for refusing to apologize for calling the prime minister a "wacko," tried to tag Mark Carney with the nickname "Carbon Tax Carney," saying the Liberal leadership candidate had won the endorsement of "Crazy Carbon Tax Guilbeault" (environment minister Steven Guilbeault).[28] It all sounds a lot like Trump's "Crooked Hillary" Clinton and "Sleepy Joe" Biden. Poilievre's staff set up a webpage at justlikejustin.ca before the Liberal leadership race started. When potential candidates declined to run, the word OUT in big red letters was stamped over their pictures. An old picture of Trudeau was superimposed over photos of Carney and Freeland. Aside from being an attack ad, the site was also what marketers call a "data scraping" webpage. People clicking photos of Liberal leadership candidates were asked for their contact information, which, supposedly, would help Poilievre "call for a carbon tax election now."

UNIVERSITY OF OTTAWA social sciences professor Patrick Fafard says the new generation of populist politicians engage in "short-term, chase-the-news-cycle" partisan rhetoric. This erodes public trust in government and leaves voters open to misinformation. "I think I can say quite confidently that I'm more concerned now than I would have been, say, ten or twenty years ago," Fafard said in early 2024. "There's a constant challenge that politicians are tempted to engage in sloganeering and simple solutions, but problems are complex.

The current controversy over foreign interference is a wonderful example of that."[29]

Political polarization has raised the risk to the physical safety of politicians. "I wasn't hurt by the attacks and the nickname Poilievre gave me," one former Liberal minister told me. "I was scared when he said I was killing people's jobs. What if some guy got it into his head that it was my fault that he'd lost his job? What if he showed up at my house?" Trudeau's ministers couldn't walk down the streets of Ottawa and their hometowns without people yelling insults out of car windows. During the pandemic, an armed man showed up near Trudeau's home, telling the cops who tackled him that he was just there to "talk" to the prime minister. In the summer of 2024, two Alberta men were charged with threatening the lives of Trudeau, finance minister Chrystia Freeland, and NDP leader Jagmeet Singh. This came five months after a Montreal man was arrested for threatening to kill Trudeau.[30]

By the fall of 2024, the people in charge of protecting the governor general, prime minister, cabinet, and Parliament Hill said they didn't have enough staff and money to do their jobs.[31] The head of security of the House of Commons said harassment of MPs in and around the parliamentary precinct had increased by 800 percent since 2018, and in that time twice as many MPs have asked for police protection. NDP MP Charlie Angus said politics was becoming dangerous, posting on Facebook: "I received a death threat this afternoon after calling out Pierre Poilievre for harassing a medical doctor. Dr. Andrea Sereda is on the front lines trying to keep people alive during the opioid epidemic. But Poilievre is trying to demonize her for the benefit of his fund-raising machine. Conservative MPs are ganging up to trash her expertise claiming that she is a liar, a radical and calling for her license to be revoked. I called out Poilievre for his disgraceful behaviour. Lo and behold I was sent a death threat."[32]

Poilievre, whose wife had already been targeted with a rape threat from a right-wing extremist, said he had asked for increased protection for himself and family, but he wouldn't ease up on his nasty attacks. After the July 2024 assassination attempt on Donald Trump, Poilievre refused to dial down his rhetoric. "Let's be very clear," he told a Toronto AM radio talk-show host. "My criticisms of the prime minister are entirely reasonable and focused on his policy agenda. We are not going to self-censor ourselves now. We are not going to allow the shooter to shut down our debate."[33]

When a journalist confronted Poilievre about the fears of violence in downtown Ottawa during the "convoy," Poilievre simply said MPs came and went from Parliament Hill without any trouble.

Poilievre said his criticism of Trudeau's governing agenda "will continue. That is my job.... The worst thing that could happen is that we become a country, like the dictatorial countries where no one's allowed to criticize the leadership, and we're not going to do that."[34] When *Montreal Gazette* reporter Aaron Derfel pushed Poilievre about his lack of civility, the Tory leader replied, "I think when politesse is in conflict with the truth, I choose the truth. I think we've been too polite for too long with our political class."[35]

But criticism won't be a problem for Poilievre or any other Canadian leader in a country where there's not much professional, Canadian-owned media. His promise to "defund" the CBC, cutting all its government support, except for the French service, draws more cheers at his rallies than any other of his slogans. He's never promised to fix Canada's broken freedom-of-information system, nor do anything about the disinformation that threatens Canada's political discourse. His vision of this country is one where he can say what he wants, bully his opponents, attack enemies of his choosing, and not be faced with criticism. We can look south to see what happens when this becomes normalized.

Canada's media has special protection in law and privileges that the rest of us don't have. It needs to professionalize, with a real accreditation system, rules of practice, and a disciplinary body to deal with bad actors. It also needs money. The best way to keep it alive would be through public support. If you want media outlets to survive, subscribe to them. Solving media financial problems and fostering start-ups may take government action, through an arm's-length agency set up to finance professional journalism. Federal and provincial governments could offer 100 percent tax credits to media subscribers, which would allow the public to decide which outlets get financial support. And we also need a national public broadcaster, one that provides information on all the major platforms to every part of the country. People may not like everything on the CBC, but it serves large areas of the country and diverse groups of Canadians who would be ignored by whatever's left of private media. It's one of the few truly national institutions left in this country.

POLLSTER FRANK GRAVES did a survey just before the 2022 Tory leadership vote and found that many Canadians were angry. Some embraced the same populist ideas as Donald Trump, Orbán in Hungary, Silvio Berlusconi in Italy, Jair Bolsonaro in Brazil, and Narendra Modi in India. People in all these nations were convinced that they were tumbling into poverty while "elites" ran their countries into the ground. The populist right promised to crush these corrupt elites and to turn back the clock to better days.[36] Like the rest of those politicians, Poilievre promises a return to a mythical better time when governments were smaller and taxes were lower. He doesn't, however, specify when those good times were. Donald Trump does: he points to the Gilded Age, those years before the First World War, when wealth disparity was almost as bad as it is now.[37] In the Gilded Age, the poor and the working class lived hard lives. Those who had jobs usually worked six-day weeks, often in unregulated, unsafe workplaces. Attempts to unionize and strike for better pay and safer workplaces were put down with state violence. It wasn't just a golden age for the rich; it was the time when most of the famous union martyrs were made. Working people had large families because so many children died in childbirth or in their first years of life. Hospitals were funded by charity, doctors sometimes had to accept barter from their poorer patients or simply turn them away, and untaxed millionaires built mansions on New York's Fifth Avenue, Long Island, or in the Thousand Islands. The Gilded Age was a great time to be rich. But it was a miserable time to be poor. Or Black. Or Indigenous—these were the years of genocide on the Great Plains. Or gay.

For decades, the American right harkened back to the great prosperity of the post-war years. You may have noticed they've stopped doing that. During Dwight Eisenhower's presidency (1953–1961), the marginal tax rate applied on income over $400,000 was 91 percent. (A $400,000 income had the buying power of more than $4 million in today's money.) It was also the beginning of the civil rights era, when a Republican president sent troops to the South to desegregate schools, and the Supreme Court struck down Jim Crow laws that made Black people second-class citizens in their own country.

In Britain, the Reform Party and some other Conservatives harken back to the days before immigration changed the colour of British cities. In Germany and Austria, far-right parties conjure up the ghost of Nazism as much as the law will allow.[38] Poilievre talks of a Canadian past whose story has been edited by leftist historians. "This business of deleting our past must end," he told one rally. "And this is a matter on which English Canada must learn from Quebec. Quebecers—and I'm saying this in English deliberately—do not apologize for their culture, language, or history. They celebrate it. All Canadians should do the same."[39] Poilievre is saying he'd turn the clock back to a time when many Canadians were outsiders. That goes a lot farther than deflating Trudeau's version of history, which damned many historic figures using modern and post-modern values.

This is not the traditional conservatism of Mulroney or Clark or even Reagan and Thatcher. It's a type of populism that some political scientists and historians call fascist. Robert Paxton, a leading American historian, had doubts about that label but changed his mind after Trump's supporters attacked the US Capitol on January 6, 2021.[40] University of California, Berkeley historian John Connelly, one of the most respected scholars of modern European history, said in September 2024 that the right's attitudes today resemble those of people living in that continent in the aftermath of the First World War. Like then, "there's kind of a disdain for democracy. There's a willingness to think of going beyond the technicalities of a democratic system in order to solve problems. There's a longing—there's a respect for strong leadership that many believe is lacking in a standard liberal democracy."[41]

The problem with the word *fascism* is that historians and political scientists have no clear definition of the ideology, partly because of the differences between the regimes that have been given that label. They have the same problem with communism: regimes that call themselves communist have never followed Karl Marx's philosophy, nor do they act consistently. The communism of China during Mao Zedong's Cultural Revolution (1966–1976) is a far different thing from the state-controlled capitalism of Xi Jinping's regime. To save time, I turned to Grok, the artificial intelligence program on Elon Musk's X.[42] Its definition of fascism isn't too bad.

"Historical Context: Fascism, as seen in 20th-century Italy under Mussolini, involves authoritarianism, nationalism, dictatorial power, suppression of opposition, and often a form of totalitarian control over society," Grok told me. "Scholarly Definitions: Modern scholarship might define fascism with traits like extreme nationalism, rejection of democratic norms in favor of autocratic power, control over media, and often, but not always, racial or ethnic supremacy."

But then Grok went off the rails. When asked if Trump is a fascist, Grok said the term might not fit the president because, among other very debatable things, "Trump was elected through democratic processes, which contrasts with the typical fascist seizure of power through force or coup." But Hitler, Mussolini, Hungary's Miklós Horthy, Kurt von Schuschnigg of Austria, and António de Oliveira

Salazar of Portugal, among other fascists, didn't seize power through coups or by force. They became chief ministers of their countries constitutionally.[43] If you're trying to determine if a leader is a fascist, don't just look at the election that brought them to power. It's the next one, if any, that's the real test.

Whatever this movement is called—and someone needs to come up with a name that sticks—Poilievre and its adherents in the US, France, Italy, Hungary, Germany, and Britain use variations of a political program that appeals to nihilists and people who have lost faith in anyone except tech bros and corporations. It ignores conservative ideas of community, honour, respect for tradition, and belief in the need for the rule of law. Though it claims to be founded in Christian ethics, it makes a mockery of the Christian virtues of charity and honesty, exalting the wealthy and insulting the meek.

Even *Globe and Mail* columnist John Ibbitson, who rarely criticizes Poilievre and his party, admits minorities have a lot to worry about under a Poilievre regime. "The Liberal agenda of promoting diversity within the public service—gone. Protections for gender-diverse youth—gone. Efforts to combat discrimination in the criminal justice system—gone. Pretty much every major element of the Liberal environmental, social and justice agenda—gone."[44] Poilievre rarely talks about immigrants or immigration, but has said, "The radical, out-of-control NDP-Liberal government has destroyed our [immigration] system. We have to have a smaller population growth."[45] Which seems fine, until you look to the US and see how far anti-immigrant policies can go, or if you try to pin Conservatives down on the question of how much immigration is needed by this country. Poilievre is much more progressive on LGBTQ+ issues than members of his own party and the pseudo-media that feeds them. As for the problems of Indigenous Canadians and righting the wrongs of colonialism, marginalization, and historical policies that were used to try to destroy their cultures, Poilievre's record is, to be generous, mixed. He's backed by a movement that denies the abuse of residential school victims and the inter-generational trauma caused by those institutions.[46]

Some traditional conservatives are very worried about what a Poilievre regime might mean for the country. Kim Campbell, who led the Progressive Conservatives in 1993 and was Canada's first female prime minister, has called Poilievre a "liar and hate-monger." She told listeners of the *Beyond a Ballot* podcast in 2024 that she likely wouldn't vote for the Tories in the next election. Campbell, who worked as a diplomat and Harvard lecturer and chaired the steering committee of the World Movement for Democracy from 2008 to 2015, warned about Russian expansionism and said, "People who want to play footsie with Donald Trump...don't get it....I think there might be some quite good people in the Conservative party. I have problems with their leader." Poilievre spokesperson Sebastian Skamski counterattacked by implying winning counts more than truth: "Ms. Campbell's own political record speaks for itself."[47]

Later that year, Joe Clark used the forty-fifth anniversary of his election as Canada's sixteenth prime minister to beg politicians for "cooperation across our differences" and to "counter the negativism that characterizes public debate today." Again and again, he returned to "the divisions arising in Canada today" and political campaigning that "concentrates on what we want rather than what the country needs."

Lester Pearson, Robert Stanfield, and Nelson Mandela were, Clark said, political leaders who healed the divisions of their times, and brought people together. "That spirit is not present today," he said.[48] They were weavers, not rippers.

ACKNOWLEDGEMENTS

I'D LIKE TO thank the people in the political sphere—people involved in all the major parties—who helped me with facts and opinions. Many of these people did not know I was working on this book until later in the process. I am leaving out a lot of names, but I will try to express my gratitude to you individually.

I would like to single out Marc Kielburger, who was very generous with his time, for a special thanks. I am also grateful to friends in the military who gave me details about the options that were open to the government during the "Freedom Convoy."

As well, I owe a heavy debt to journalists and academics whose work I've used and cited. I have tried very hard to credit the people who have recorded Poilievre's life since his teenage years and people who have devoted their careers to analyzing the state of media and politics. We've got to fight hard to save journalism, and the citations in this book show why. Dozens of skilled and talented people created a massive public record that would not exist without mainstream media and online publishing. I would especially like to thank Marc

Edge for his books and his insights. Thanks to the Ottawa Public Library and Library and Archives Canada for their help. I'd like to single out a few people who were especially supportive: Constance Backhouse and Adam Dodek at the University of Ottawa, and authors Elaine Dewar, Michael Harris, Lawrence Martin, Stephen Maher, Paul Wells, John Ibbitson, Frank Graves, Ben Perrin, Brian "Chip" Martin, Charlotte Gray, Carol Off, Nahlah Ayed, and Nate Hendley.

I also want to credit Andrew Lawton for his book *Pierre Poilievre: A Political Life*. At the time of writing, it was the only biography of Poilievre, and it provides insights into aspects of his life that no one would have known without Lawton's insider perspective and contacts. This book is not an attempt to duplicate it. Rather, I want to explain Poilievre's political career and the environment that allowed him to cut himself out of the very large pack of conservative politicians and become one of just two real Tory contenders in more than thirty years.

I'd like to thank Janice Zawerbny, Patrick Crean, and Linda Pruessen, friends in publishing who didn't work on this book but were supportive and helpful. I have known Janice and Linda since the late 1990s, when they worked at KeyPorter, and they've become great friends who have offered me a lot of useful advice. Same goes for Anna Porter and her kind husband, Julian. Speaking of defamation lawyers, I'd also like to thank Will McDowell, who literally wrote the book on libel. And I want to give credit to people I know through social media, who pointed me to some interesting material, as well as sending me down a few dead ends.

Special thanks to Dan Wells, Vanessa Stauffer, John Metcalf and the rest of the good people at Biblioasis, and to my agent, John Pearce at Westwood Creative Artists. They did their own jobs well and kept me going when I thought this book might never be finished and published. This book simply wouldn't exist without the emotional support of my family and friends. That's not just boilerplate. I wasn't much fun to be around in 2024.

Any errors of fact and faulty opinions in the book are mine. I apologize in advance for them and will try to correct them in later editions.

I'd also like to thank my friends at Ottawa's Perfect Books, and the booksellers across Canada who have embraced my earlier books. Perfect Books was the source of the new books that I mined for up-to-date political information and its staff gave me good advice about what people look for in political writing. Black Squirrel, Ottawa's biggest used bookseller, was the source of many of the older books that I drew material from.

I am especially grateful to the Ontario Arts Council for support from its Recommender Grants for Writers program.

ENDNOTES

INTRODUCTION: **PIERRE POILIEVRE AND THE NEW POLITICS**

1. This brilliant journalist and historian sometimes gets social media abuse from Canadians who think she's a minister in Justin Trudeau's government.
2. There were two in Russia: the somewhat democratic revolution of 1990 and Putin's seizure of absolute power. China's had several, though they were less obvious: the end of Maoism, a sort of liberalization in which presidents' power was limited, and the authoritarian coup of Xi Jinping, who consolidated the major positions of the Communist Party and the Chinese state and effectively made himself president for life.
3. Ellie Quinlan Houghtaling, "Here's the Net Worth of Trump's Inauguration Day Entourage," *New Republic*, January 20, 2025. Annual Financial Report of the Government of Canada Fiscal Year 2023–2024 at https://www.canada.ca/en/department-finance/services/publications/annual-financial-report/2024.html. I've converted the Canadian dollar debt figures to us dollars.
4. Arguably, until the Industrial Revolution, war was the great provider of opportunity for class mobility. Almost all the noble families of the world start with someone who was successful in battle and could organize a fighting force for people higher up the pyramid. Religious institutions, whether those of the Abrahamic religions, Buddhism, Hinduism, or Confucianism, also offered social mobility. In Indigenous North American cultures, some leaders came from an old nobility likely founded by proven military commanders, or, as in the Iroquoian nations, from men with the ability and credibility to organize and lead military expeditions. Now, real power comes from the ability to organize capital (banking) or from wealth generated from intellectual property rights and corporate ownership (among the wealthiest, this is usually co-mingled).

5 Max Cantor, the actor who played him, had worse luck: he died of a heroin overdose when he was thirty-two.
6 For an interesting examination of that aspect of modern politics, see Corina Knoll, Elizabeth Dias, Orlando Mayorquin, and Dana Goldstein, "Behind the Election Anger May Be Something Else: Lingering Covid Grief," *New York Times*, Nov. 4, 2024 (the day before the 2024 US election).
7 Robert Reich, an American professor, author, lawyer, and political commentator who worked in the administrations of presidents Gerald Ford and Jimmy Carter and served as secretary of labor from 1993 to 1997 in the cabinet of President Bill Clinton, started calling Trump a fascist in 2024. By that year's election, Kamala Harris also called Trump a fascist, as did writers in some centrists and leftist media. As will be described later in the book, there's no accepted definition of fascism, which differed in the various countries where fascists held power in the twentieth century.
8 Leaders of fascist countries have no problem with victimizing foreign fascist regimes. The fascist leanings of governments in some countries that were victimized by Hitler are rarely written about because they make the story of the origins of the Second World War much more complicated.
9 I know the word "fascist" will hit a nerve, but what are the substantial political and operational differences between Donald Trump and Benito Mussolini? Victor Orbán and Francisco Franco? It seems to me that people are hung up on aesthetics, that fascists need to be in uniform. The world of the 1920s and 1930s was one of uniforms. Even the prime minister of Canada had one, the Windsor Court uniform. William Lyon Mackenzie King wore one to royal events. In the 1920s, when Mussolini came to power, European leaders were expected to be in uniforms. Even democracies like France and Britain were much more militarized than they are now, and many people, from railway stationmasters to letter carriers, wore military-style uniforms. Leaders don't need to wear medals or set up death camps to be fascists.
10 In the early 1990s, when machinery was being packed and shipped to Georgio, I called that state's labour department to see what rights the new workers on these assembly lines would have. I got a recorded message of what rights workers *didn't* have, things that would be normal to Canadian workers, whether they were unionized or not.
11 I caught Covid after getting some vaccination shots and, for better or worse, am still here.
12 It was a good time to buy.
13 Andrzej Strzelecki, "The Plunder of Victims and Their Corpses," in *Anatomy of the Auschwitz Death Camp*, eds. Michael Berenbaum and Yisrael Gutman (Bloomington, IN: Indiana University Press, 2008), 250–51. See also "The Holocaust Explained" at https://www.theholocaustexplained.org/kanada/
14 With some exceptions like the Long Depression (1873–99), the short depression after the First World War, the Great Depression of 1929–39, and the recession of the early 1980s, Canada has had a labour shortage since the first permanent European settlement in 1608. During the Long Depression, the federal government built the first transcontinental railway and opened Prairie farmland for agriculture. Immigration policies have tended to mirror the need for labour, though until the late 1960s, Liberal and Conservative governments made policies and rules to bar or deter people of colour from coming to Canada.
15 Andrew Griffith, "Diversity in the public service's executive ranks," *Policy Options*, Oct. 16, 2017.

16 My own take: Canadian men face two big career challenges. Our country has always had a serious nepotism problem. After people are past the age of forty, entrenched ageism makes it very difficult to find a job. Both things affect women, too, though white women have benefitted more than any other group from DEI. Men have also been set back because they accept mass culture's stereotypes of readers and thinkers as unpopular "nerds" with no chance of having sex.

17 Some of the frustration is, as I hinted at in the section on Quebec, rooted in racism as Canada's complexion becomes darker. I'm not going to show any sympathy to racists, but there are enough of them to be a (usually) quiet factor in Canadian politics. Leftist parties have also been accused of being too "woke," overly sensitive to the demands and needs of LGBTQ+ people. People like Jordan Peterson beat that gong. That backlash motivates reactionary elements of Canadian society, but it's still more of a gripe than a voting issue. Justin Trudeau was "woke" in 2015 but had no problem getting elected.

18 This happened even after the imposition of sanctions on Russia because the UK is one of the few jurisdictions that will let people buy real estate anonymously, through numbered companies.

19 Reform elected an MP in Manitoba and one in Ontario. In the latter province, they split the vote with the Progressive Conservatives, allowing dozens of Liberals to be elected in ridings that were usually safe Tory ridings. Ed Harper of Barrie was the sole Reform MP from Ontario, who beat the popular mayor of Barrie, Janice Laking, by 193 votes. In 1997, Harper went back to Barrie to run his tire business. The Parliament elected in 1993 had three Harpers: Stephen, Ed, and Elijah Harper, an Oji-Cree activist who, as a Manitoba MLA, helped kill the Meech Lake Accord.

20 Committees and debates on bills usually don't generate the kind of soundbites that TV and radio need. Now, broadcast reporters want quotes that are less than ten seconds long. Some committees do get coverage, like the 2020 WE Charity hearings and the meetings of the House of Commons committee that investigated foreign interference in Canadian politics in 2024.

21 Christine Anderson of Germany's Alternative für Deutschland (AfD) is one exception, though Poilievre did not criticize the three Conservative MPs who met her when she toured Canada in 2023. See Alistair Steele, "Poilievre condemns 'vile' views of German politician seen lunching with Conservative MPs," CBC News, Feb. 24, 2023.

22 There's a lot of debate about whether this new movement is fascism. Economist Robert Reich, a member of Bill Clinton's cabinet, insists that it is. Other political scientists are split. Part of the problem lies with the lack of an accepted definition of fascism. As well, the fascism of Mussolini's Italy was different from Hitler's National Socialism. The militarism of the first half of the twentieth century gives us the impression that fascists tend to be in uniforms. In fact, a substantial element of the military classes of Germany and Italy were important opponents of fascism. Fascism does not require an expansionist element. Smaller pre-war fascist states in Europe—Hungary, Austria, Poland—had relatively little interest in seriously changing their borders except to recover areas with substantial numbers of their people.

23 No one should have idealized visions of early Canadian politics. Violence was a normal part of campaigns, especially on voting days, when men—women couldn't vote—had to show up at polling places and vote in public. The murder of the Donnelly family in 1880 was partly caused by politics, as was the ineffective prosecution of their killers. (The Donnelleys were Conservatives in an Irish Catholic community that supported the Liberals, though this was just one small factor in

their neighbours' decision to murder them. The prosecution was ineffective and the Liberal judge should have moved the trial out of Middlesex County.)

24 Anyone who wants to understand modern populism at the federal level should read George Grant's *Lament for a Nation*, which is not just an examination of the collapse of Diefenbaker's nationalist crusade but also a guidebook for any centrist or left-wing populist who wants to take on the Canadian version of twenty-first-century neofascism. Diefenbaker opposed regionalism, along with military and economic integration with the United States. He opposed a national oil pipeline and the American militarization of the Canadian Arctic and the deployment of American nuclear weapons in Canada, all of which the Liberals supported. Diefenbaker also opposed trade policies that would make Canada dependent on the United States, and he tried to maintain our trade with the United Kingdom and Europe. (The British government betrayed him by dropping Commonwealth trade preferences to get into the European Common Market.) He was, for his time, anti-racist. Diefenbaker was able to expand his party's support outside its southern Ontario stronghold, winning seats in Quebec and Western Canada after years of his party being in the wilderness in those regions. The modern analogy shouldn't be stretched too far, but there are lessons. Diefenbaker is, sadly, remembered more for his spite than his policies.

CHAPTER 1: **A MAN OF HIS TIME AND PLACE**

1 Andrew Perez, "Pierre Poilievre's unique family story could be an ace up his sleeve," *Globe and Mail*, Oct. 24, 2022.
2 Online trolls have used this against Poilievre. It seems like a small dig. Poilievre certainly never identified as Jeff or Jeff Farrell, and it's not his real name. Andrew Lawton says he knew about the name, and his friends used it as a nickname in high school. See Andrew Lawton, *Pierre Poilievre: A Political Life* (Toronto: Sutherland House, 2024), 3.
3 The show was carried on small-town radio stations across the country into the 1980s.
4 Jason Kenney would realize many Muslims, Sikhs, Hindus, Buddhists, and Jews shared the social conservatism of Christian evangelicals and reached out to these groups when he was a member of Stephen Harper's cabinet. Now, a conservative movement that was, like much of the left in the first half of the twentieth century, anti-foreigner and anti-Semitic, has become Zionist and more open to immigration if those immigrants are not anti-capitalist and anti-Western.
5 Although the Laurier government banned immigration of Black people into Canada, a substantial number of Black cowboys came to Canada between the US Civil War and the First World War to work in Alberta. Most arrived during Sir John A. Macdonald's administration. Some of their descendants are still there.
6 Until the federal government passed the *Divorce Act* in 1968, men wanting a divorce had to prove their wives committed adultery. Women had a tougher time. They had to petition a senior court and provide evidence of some kind of misconduct: incestuous adultery, rape, sodomy, bestiality, bigamy, or adultery coupled with cruelty or desertion. If they had the means and connections, they could have an MP or senator sponsor a private bill that, if passed by Parliament, legislated an end to the marriage. Both avenues were unaffordable to most Canadians.
7 Jordan Peterson podcast, Spotify, May 16, 2022.
8 This went back to the days when Alberta was bought from the Hudson's Bay

9 "In the '70s and '80s, some wanted Alberta to separate from Canada," CBC News, Oct. 24, 2019.
10 I was at a Stuart Smith rally in Blenheim, Ontario, during that campaign and saw the lack of interest of local farmers in some of the best farmland in Canada. Now, many farmers in that region lease some of their land for the many wind turbines between London and Windsor. Ethanol was first used as automobile fuel during the Second World War but was uneconomical during the cheap oil years that followed. It's now used in almost all gasoline blends as fuel and a way of increasing octane. Since it gums up four-stroke and two-stroke engines, only use premium fuel in your small engines and add a carburetor cleaner to the gas.
11 This includes the Trudeau government's multi-billion-dollar purchase and construction of the TransMountain pipeline from Alberta to the Pacific coast and the Liberal government of Louis St. Laurent's construction of the TransCanada natural gas pipeline in 1956. The Conservatives and CCF opposed that pipeline, and St. Laurent was voted out of office the following year.
12 In fact, oil supply is not a problem if you're willing to pay the financial and ecological price. In the 1970s and 1980s, oil sands production seemed to be an exotic alterative to imports, but extraction from oil shales was something far off on the horizon. Now, most of Canada's oil is produced from the sands in Alberta. Fracking of oil shale deposits has turned the United States from an oil importer to an exporter.
13 The offshore oil fields in Atlantic Canada now produce about 5 percent of the country's oil. Southern Quebec and southern Ontario have oil deposits (in upper Ordovician shales) that could be exploited by fracking. Quebec seriously considered fracking the vast, oil-rich Lorraine Shale of the St. Lawrence Valley in the early years of this century but decided not to. It has stopped granting exploration permits on Anticosti Island in the Gulf of St. Lawrence.
14 In 2018, nearly half of the oil refined in Canada—mostly in Sarnia and the Montreal area—was imported, with Quebec being the largest user of OPEC oil. See Statistics Canada data at https://www.cer-rec.gc.ca/en/data-analysis/energy-commodities/crude-oil-petroleum-products/report/archive/2019-gasoline/index.html Alberta imports refined petroleum products from the US that are needed to extract oil from the tar sands. See Statistics Canada data at https://www.cer-rec.gc.ca/en/data-analysis/energy-markets/market-snapshots/2023/market-snapshot-refined-petroleum-products-imports-rose-5-percent-2022.html.
15 Both governments later sold their oil company holdings.
16 Even now, Western Canadian oil refined in eastern Canada travels through pipelines that run across the United States. Building oil pipelines through the Canadian Shield of Northern Ontario would be insanely expensive and environmentally risky.
17 A fun fact about Canada: British Columbians see themselves as Western Canadians but not in the same way as Manitobans, Saskatchewanians, and Albertans. People in northwestern Ontario also believe they live in the West, and describe Toronto as "down east." I believed Western Canada could be described as the part of the country where you can buy Old Dutch potato chips until the company made a deal to sell their stuff in Ontario (they're not as good).
18 After Confederation, Nova Scotia's separatists were important provincial and national political players. Hence the use of "modern."

19 All oil prices are in US dollars. Factoring in six years of inflation. In simple cash, the fall was just over 50 percent.
20 See Re/Max blog "Purpose-Built Rental Top Asset Class in Calgary Commercial Real Estate Market" at https://blog.remax.ca/purpose-built-rental-top-asset-class-in-calgary-commercial-real-estate-market. Like many other cities, Calgary's downtown is being transformed. Office buildings are converted to apartments as white-collar staff follow the continent-wide shift to "work from home." Now renamed Suncor Energy Centre, the buildings are owned by the House of Arenburg and the Toronto-based real estate company Brookfield Management.
21 Shannon Proudfoot, "Why is Pierre Poilievre So Angry?" *Maclean's*, Mar. 10, 2022. To be fair to Albertans, people in central Canada blamed the federal government for their economic problems. The whole country tossed out the Trudeau government in September 1984, giving Brian Mulroney's Progressive Conservatives one of the largest majorities in Canadian history.
22 Jordan Peterson podcast, Spotify, May 16, 2022.
23 The influence of Friedman on Poilievre's political thinking is discussed later in the chapter.
24 If they'd been able to hang on to the rental properties through the recession, they would have made a lot of money. At the time, the math was against them: high interest rates pushed debt payments to levels that made it impossible for rents to cover them. In Ontario, this caused the collapse of several large investment schemes, including one involving 10 percent of Toronto's high-rise apartment buildings and hundreds of smaller properties across the province. Two over-leveraged trust companies collapsed, and the principals in the scheme went to prison.
25 Jordan Peterson podcast, Spotify, May 16, 2022.
26 They lost everything above the Federal Deposit Insurance Corporation's limit of $100,000.
27 The number is even worse when you consider that only about 60 percent of the people are in the work force.
28 Jordan Peterson podcast, Spotify, May 16, 2022.
29 The record is vague about how old Pierre was when this happened, but it's clear that, whether he lived with his wife or not, Donald Poilievre stayed active in his son's life. Its unlikely the full story of what happened in that home will ever come out, but it appears Marlene and Donald Poilievre put aside whatever animosity they had and worked out a good co-parenting plan.
30 Jordan Peterson podcast, Spotify, May 16, 2022.
31 Hansard, Apr. 15, 2005.
32 Andrew Lawton, *Pierre Poilievre: A Political Life* (Toronto: Sutherland House, 2024), 5.
33 Jordan Peterson podcast, Spotify, May 16, 2022. See also Campbell Clark, "The Conservative Leader has preached small government since his teenage years. Now people are embracing the message—and the messenger," *Globe and Mail*, Sept. 16, 2022.
34 Jordan Peterson podcast, Spotify, May 16, 2022.
35 Chloe Fedio, "The Minister of Nepean–Carleton," *Ottawa Citizen*, Oct. 25, 2012.
36 Divorce is not a grounds for excommunication, but the Roman Catholic Church does not recognize civil divorce. Marlene would need an annulment if she wanted to be, in the Church's view, shed of her marriage.
37 Interestingly, many modern conservatives make this claim about the Islamic world.
38 It turns out the jury is still out about whether political tyranny stifles creativity as well as individual freedom, though it doesn't look all that good for police states.

Hitler's Third Reich pushed rocketry and aircraft propulsion ahead, but wars are great stimulators of invention. Arts and letters under the Nazi regime were dismal. As for China, the development of its intellectual life has been far less impressive than the expansion of its manufacturing.

39 Campbell Clark, "The Conservative Leader has preached small government since his teenage years. Now people are embracing the message—and the messenger," *Globe and Mail*, Sept. 16, 2022. Brian Mulroney, who became prime minister in 1984, when Poilievre was five years old, paid lip service to Friedman's ideas but, other than a few cuts to social benefits and environmental regulation, didn't make substantial changes to the way the federal government worked.

40 Jordan Peterson podcast, May 16, 2022.

CHAPTER 2: **LARVAL POLITICIAN**

1 Western conservatives tend to ignore British Columbia when talking about the West, but this prediction includes BC and its very un-Calgarian metropolis of Vancouver.

2 For a deep dive on this, see Stevie Cameron's *On The Take: Crime, Corruption and Greed in the Mulroney Years* (Toronto: Macfarlane Walter & Ross, 1994) and Mary Janigan, *Let the Eastern Bastards Freeze in the Dark: The West Versus The Rest Since Confederation* (Toronto: Knopf Canada, 2012).

3 Chloe Fedio, "The Minister of Nepean–Carleton," *Ottawa Citizen*, Oct. 25, 2012.

4 Brenda Bouw, "Reform youth attracted by Manning's stand on deficit," *Vancouver Sun*, June 8, 1996.

5 Poilievre is referencing the brief blowback endured by the Chrétien government when it broke its promise to end the GST. It culminated in Deputy Prime Minister Sheila Copps resigning her seat and asking voters in her riding to give her a new mandate. They obliged.

6 Pierre Poilievre, "A great deal of our future earnings were spent before we young Canadians were old enough to know what a six-billion-dollar debt was ripping off young people.," *Calgary Herald*, Apr. 27, 1997.

7 Chloe Fedio, "The Minister of Nepean–Carleton," *Ottawa Citizen*, Oct. 25, 2012. People who claim Poilievre never had a job in the private sector either don't know about, or don't bother mentioning, this call-centre job. It's interesting that almost all the jobs Poilievre had in private and political workplaces in those years involved telemarketing.

8 Chloe Fedio, "The Minister of Nepean–Carleton," *Ottawa Citizen*, Oct. 25, 2012.

9 This success caused a problem familiar to anyone who read George Orwell's *Animal Farm*. Preston Manning once said he'd turn Stornoway, the Ottawa mansion that's one of the perks of the opposition leader, into a bingo hall. (The place isn't big enough, but it sounded good.) When he qualified to get Stornoway, Manning moved in. Manning was also taking lessons to deal with his grating voice and improved his wardrobe and hairstyle. Poilievre, still a kid in Calgary, had nothing to do with any of these decisions, but there would come a time when Manning—who, like Stockwell Day, had spent part of his privileged youth in Ottawa—would be taken down by Poilievre and other ambitious Calgarians for succumbing to the lure of Ottawa's perks, along with the belief Manning had taken the party as far as he could.

10 Jordan Peterson podcast, Spotify, May 16, 2022.

11 I sympathize with nerds and geeks and hope to see a day when movies show young men with intellectual interests get laid. I blame the way smart kids are portrayed in mass culture for the general decline in men's reading and the decline of voter

intelligence. I also think bright kids suffer a lot from the disdain of mass-culture leaders. They have enough problems without that humiliation. As for the stereotype, it ignores the fact that there are smart women who are clever enough to see through media framings and are quite happy to have sex with bright men.
12 Jordan Peterson podcast, Spotify, May 16, 2022.
13 Perrin later became a law professor and broke with his party's tough-on-crime policies, believing they caused more problems than they fixed.
14 Chloe Fedio, "The Minister of Nepean–Carleton," *Ottawa Citizen*, Oct. 25, 2012.
15 Tom Arnold, "Private Schools Shut Out," *Edmonton Journal*, Oct. 26, 1997.
16 *Calgary Herald*, Aug. 29, 2002.
17 Peter Zimonjic, "Pierre Poilievre and the anti-elite populism that won the day," CBC News, Sept. 9, 2022.
18 Campbell Clark, "The Conservative Leader has preached small government since his teenage years. Now people are embracing the message—and the messenger," *Globe and Mail*, Sept. 12, 2022.
19 Pierre Poilievre, "MacBeth making mistake," *Calgary Herald*, July 23, 1998.
20 After the election, I met Brown and Morton at the Chateau Laurier in Ottawa to interview them for a *Hill Times* piece. Both men would have made fine senators, which was the point their party was trying to make. Senate reform is such an inside-baseball topic, but there are solid arguments to be made for an appointed Senate with members who can scrutinize legislation, usually from the elected House of Commons, without having to worry about being punished by their party or voters. This falls apart when senators are chosen because of their work for the governing party. Strategists like Keith Davey, David Smith, and Marjory LeBreton were political to the bone. An elected Senate would be democratic. Would its members have a mandate to make the institution so powerful that it would add to legislative gridlock, especially when one party held a majority in the House of Commons and another dominated the Senate? Would prime ministers sit in the Senate? Would cabinet have members in both houses?
21 Unlike real exiles, Moriarty could go home anytime he wanted. He eventually became a Canadian citizen, living for awhile in Halifax and Toronto before settling in Vancouver. Quitting *Law and Order* effectively ended his career, which had been stellar.
22 Churchill was nowhere near the beaches of Dunkirk during the 1940 evacuation.
23 Monte Stewart, "Join the new Republicans, actor urges," *Calgary Herald*, Mar. 28, 1999. The story ran in other Canwest (later Postmedia) newspapers.
24 In 2024, Stronach was arrested and charged for historic sexual assaults that police alleged occurred in a time frame that overlaps with this contest.
25 Despite the political leanings of the judges, some liberals did well. Peter Loewen, who went on to head the Munk School for Global Affairs & Public Policy at the University of Toronto before becoming dean of arts at Cornell University, made the finals.
26 Campbell Clark, "The Conservative Leader has preached small government since his teenage years. Now people are embracing the message—and the messenger," *Globe and Mail*, Sept. 12, 2022.
27 In fact, R.B. Bennett's Conservative government doesn't get credit for Canada's version of the New Deal, which did help some Canadians cope with the Great Depression. Herbert Hoover, president of the United States when the Great Depression started, firmly believed governments should not meddle with economic forces but had also earned a reputation as a humanitarian. In World War I, Hoover ran a successful relief program that saved many Europeans from starvation. Democratic

president Harry Truman tapped Hoover, a Republican, to do similar work in Europe after the Nazis were overthrown. It is only recently that conservatives have become so disdainful of people in dire need. I believe their reinterpretation of Christianity and their rejection of its teachings of charity and embrace of the selfish ideology of people like Ayn Rand can be blamed.

28 Despite decades of Tory rule, people in the United Kingdom pay 40 percent on estates worth more than £325,000, excluding the value of a house worth less than £750,000 left to a spouse. See https://www.gov.uk/inheritance-tax. Some aristocrats have unloaded their palatial estates to the National Trust. That's why so many stately British homes are open to the public. While there is no federal inheritance tax in the US, most states collect between 15 and 20 percent of the value of an estate over a modest threshold. Canadians pay nothing, though some provinces collect small probate fees.

29 Two prime ministers, John Abbott and Mackenzie Bowell, sat in the Senate. Abbott was also mayor of Montreal. It's unlikely modern voters would put up with that. William Lyon Mackenzie King lost his seat in the 1925 election and held onto power for a short time, even though his party won fewer seats than the Conservatives.

30 The full essay is available at https://pastebin.com/hmxMtvve.

31 Stephanie Levitz, "Pierre Poilievre was twenty when he wrote about what he would do as prime minister. Here's what he said then—and what he says now," *Toronto Star*, June 22, 2024.

32 Nunavut was still part of the Northwest Territories until April 1999. The contest overlapped the splitting of the territory.

33 MacDonald turned down a request to be interviewed for this book.

34 Suzanne Wilton, "City student wins $10,000 for essay," *Calgary Herald*, Sept. 17, 1999.

35 Mike Scandiffio, "Reformers step up house tactics [Five parties try to catch the media's eye]," *Hill Times*, February 16, 1998.

36 Anne McIlroy, "Clark lauded for attack on rivals," *Globe and Mail*, May 13, 2000,

37 Frum, trained as a lawyer, was a member of an American conservative think tank and a columnist for the *Weekly Standard*. More important for Canadian politics, he was a protégé of Conrad Black and the press baron's media manager, Ken Whyte. Frum wrote for Black and Whyte when they ran *Saturday Night* magazine. A year after the London conference, Black launched the *National Post* with Whyte as its first editor and Frum as a day-one columnist. In 2001, Frum began a brief career as a speech writer for President George W. Bush.

38 Chandler was an Ontarian who was an early member of the Reform Party and a supporter of the moribund Social Credit movement. When he organized this conference, he led the oddly named Progressive Group for Independent Business.

39 Kheiriddin, a lawyer, got her start at *Canadian Lawyer* magazine under its brilliant editor Mike Fitz-James.

40 Jim Cunningham, "University Tories may bolt to UA," *Calgary Herald*, Oct. 19, 1999.

CHAPTER 3: **ON TO OTTAWA**

1 The latter may come back to haunt some of these people, since some embassies, like the Chinese, are very good at hosting popular events while their governments are not so good at keeping their noses out of the business of other nations.

2 Byrne briefly studied at the University of Ottawa and headed its Reform Party club but quickly went back to the Hill. Anyone who knows the University of Ottawa would understand it was a bad fit.

3. Pierre Poilievre, "Debt-free Alberta is a prize worth every cent of savings: Increase the speed of debt reduction," *Edmonton Journal*, Aug. 31, 2002. Poilievre doesn't square that plan with his support of Klein's oil royalties cut.
4. Norma Greenaway, "Lots of Backing for Day as Leader of New Party," *Ottawa Citizen*, May 7, 2000.
5. Andrew Lawton, *Pierre Poilievre: A Political Life* (Toronto: Sutherland House, 2024), 29.
6. Sheldon Alberts, "Manning plan puzzles party faithful," *National Post*, May 28, 1999.
7. Lawyers represent clients whose actions they deplore because they know a person will likely not be wrongly convicted if both the prosecution and defence do their job well. They are officers of the court, not co-defendants or advocates of their clients' lifestyles or beliefs.
8. Keep in mind there was no important social media or YouTube back then. Norma Greenaway, "Lots of backing for Day as leader of new party," *Ottawa Citizen*, Mar. 7, 2000.
9. "Day nets 10,000 visits on leadership Web site," *Calgary Herald*, Feb. 20, 2020.
10. Mark Bourrie, "UA race could cost $500,000 to $1m, Day worried about raising the cash needed," *Hill Times*, Feb. 21, 2000.
11. The polling company surveyed Alberta Reform members and Ontario provincial Progressive Conservatives.
12. Howard May, "Poll shows Day tops in Ontario," *Calgary Herald*, Mar. 10, 2020.
13. "Stockwell Day: Preaching politician," BBC News, Nov. 28, 2000.
14. Paul Tuns, *Jean Chrétien: A legacy of scandal* (Jordan, Ontario: Freedom Press, 2004), 89.
15. Some Canadian campaign workers were inspired by the 1993 documentary *The War Room* to embrace attack politics that followed a pattern of hyping a fact or statement made by an opponent and using the so-called gaffe to define the personality of their target. This fit well with a new type of political coverage dubbed "gotcha journalism." See George Bain, *Gotcha* (Toronto: Key Porter, 1994). Bain was a long-time *Globe and Mail* Ottawa journalist who despised the new style of ginning up "gaffes." While Bain's own generation committed its own sins, and the book seemed over-the-top when it came out, his thesis that political writers tend to ignore policy and immigration and are too focused on personality has stood the test of time.
16. The river flows north, from Lake Erie to Lake Ontario. (I had to check to be sure.)
17. Jack Boulware, "Breasts across British Columbia," *Salon*, Dec. 4, 2000.
18. He has made money since then from his political consulting business and house rentals, but this was the last time when he worked for a wage.
19. Canada did send a fighting force to Afghanistan.
20. Since there was absolutely no chance of the Liberals or NDP taking the riding in the by-election, Manning must have been trying to stop Levant.
21. Joe Paraskevas, "Manning's joint-party candidate plan panned: Alliance members denounce proposal to work with Tories," *Calgary Herald*, Nov. 22, 2001.
22. Prentice went on to a stellar career as a minister in Stephen Harper's government and briefly served as premier of Alberta, losing to the NDP's Rachel Notley in 2015. Prentice quit federal politics in 2010 to work for the Canadian Imperial Bank of Commerce, so he never sat at the cabinet table with the man who called him GST Jim.
23. Joe Paraskevas, "Harper looks for way to get into Commons," *Calgary Herald*, Mar. 23, 2002.

24 Chloe Fedio, "The Minister of Nepean–Carleton," *Ottawa Citizen*, Oct. 25, 2012.
25 This included the *Walrus*, which ran an excerpt as its cover story. The book was also hyped in the *Toronto Star* and on the CBC.
26 Glen McGregor was the best prankster. After a stint at *Frank*, he was hired by the *Ottawa Citizen* and wrote an important series of investigative articles that won him, his writing partner Stephen Maher, and their newspaper the most important newspaper awards. Conservatives never forgot the pranks, though they weren't just played on them. McGregor pretended to be a government official offering the governor-general appointment to various Canadian stuffed shirts. He tried this on Adrienne Clarkson who, unknown to McGregor, already had the job in the bag. Probably the funniest prank was played on a Health Canada scientist who ran an experiment that was about to end with the euthanizing of his test subjects, dozens of rhesus monkeys. McGregor conned the scientist into believing he was a Reform staffer who wanted to save the monkeys so they could be put to work picking fruit in BC. The angry scientist insisted he needed to kill the monkeys and study their brains.
27 Counting Gatineau, the Ottawa suburbs on the Quebec side of the Ottawa River.
28 About half of MPs' marriages break down in the first term. Affairs between MPs and staffers are still common, despite the risks. Proximity, loneliness, fame and power, long hours and compatibility—especially political—fuel many of these.
29 Any serious student of the culture that the first group of Reform MPs walked into should read Stevie Cameron's *Ottawa Inside Out*, published in 1989.
30 Political staffers are not members of the public service, though when Poilievre was a staffer, some had the right to move into public service jobs (Harper ended this practice). The NDP's political staff are unionized, which makes for some interesting labour disputes.
31 Chloe Fedio, "The Minister of Nepean–Carleton," *Ottawa Citizen*, Oct. 25, 2012.
32 Chloe Fedio, "The Minister of Nepean–Carleton," *Ottawa Citizen*, Oct. 25, 2012.
33 Twitter was especially good for connecting with journalists and monitoring their interests, since they were very enthusiastic early adopters. It worked well on Blackberries, which almost all journalists carried until the rollout of the iPhone.
34 Progressive Conservative always seemed like an oxymoron, but the party had made it work. It got its name when the Western populist Progressive Party and the century-old Conservative Party merged in 1942 to try to break Mackenzie King's lock on power. At first, the idea seemed to be a non-starter, but it paid off fourteen years later when John Diefenbaker, who was a fiscal conservative, a progressive in areas like criminal justice and Indigenous rights, and a Canadian nationalist, led his party out of their twenty-year trek in the political wilderness.
35 Some aspects of Harper's personality endeared themselves to me. When he was opposition leader, I'd see him on rainy or snowy weekends at Cosmic Adventures, the giant indoor kids' jungle gym and arcade. Once, he was sitting at the next table reading a biography of John Lennon. Later, when he was prime minister, I went to a party at 24 Sussex, where Harper tried to give me a cat. I explained my nasty old tomcat would not be thrilled, but Harper insisted Kitchissippi Willy would take his cat under his wing. But we had three kids and a small place, and I had to say no. I'm sure a lot of old cats were saved because people wanted a cat from the prime minister. Laureen, who was targeted with ugly rumours that sometimes made the newspapers (the *Globe and Mail* once printed a column of false claims about her private life), supported good causes in Ottawa and was much better company than

her husband. My kids met theirs when they were very young, and Harper's two children went to high school with my two oldest. Kids at Lisgar High School were possessive of the Harper children, who were well-brought-up teens.

36 In his comprehensive book on Stephen Harper, called *Stephen Harper*, journalist John Ibbitson quotes Harper saying Martin's decision to put off an election for a few months, rather than ambush the new Conservative leader, was the biggest mistake of Martin's political life. It's hard to see how Martin could have gone straight from a brutal internal fight with the Chrétien faction to a leadership race and then into a federal election campaign. Money and fatigue would have been big problems. Martin also led a party that was a mirror image of Harper's project: divided, undisciplined, and infested with Chrétien people who wanted Martin to fail, no matter the cost to their party and the country. Justin Trudeau, who both factions saw as a winner, was finally able to defuse some of the bitterness after two full-time leaders, and a strong interim leader couldn't do it. See John Ibbitson, *Stephen Harper* (Toronto: McClelland and Stewart, 2015), 185–87.

CHAPTER 4: **NEWBIE**

1 The riding's borders have shifted over the years, but it's always been an area outside of Ottawa, out of sight of Parliament Hill and culturally disconnected from the governing class.

2 Francis went on to represent Ottawa West and become speaker of the House of Commons.

3 In some forty-five years of following municipal politics, I've never seen mayors and councillors as mediocre as those in Ottawa. Being a successful municipal councillor in Ottawa is like being the smartest kid in summer school. In a city with so many political and public service opportunities, municipal politics isn't much of a draw.

4 I know this is another tangent, but it affects the political culture of Poilievre's riding. Ottawa has a serious structural problem. The locals were hornswoggled into hiring a French consultant, Jacques Gréber, in the 1940s to plan their pretty little city. Gréber combined the worst urban-planning ideas of his time with nineteenth-century European concepts that don't work here. Gréber designed a city for cars, not people, with sprawling suburbs and satellite cities. A greenbelt that's too close to the city adds a lot to the expense of transit and basic services: all of them have to cross miles of fields whose owner, the federal government, pays far less tax than these services cost. This means the suburban communities that Poilievre represents are disconnected from the cultural and business centre of the city and have inadequate transit. This problem is a big driver of local, provincial, and federal politics in the capital. Gréber's plans also caused the destruction of gorgeous old buildings in the core and the decision to move the train station to an inconvenient place away from the downtown. Gréber had a wacky plan for a "ceremonial way" like Paris's Champs Elysee and Berlin's Unter der Linden for the capital of a country that rarely parades its army through the city core. This idea was still alive in the 1990s, when the Chrétien government seriously considered tearing down some of the best surviving nineteenth-century buildings in the downtown to build this "ceremonial way" before locals managed to kill the project. The point of this: suburban Ottawa is far from the Parliament Hill bubble, culturally and physically, with its own local issues.

5 After Pratt was out of office, the city elected a mayor and council who cancelled the $600 million contract.

6 Andrew Lawton, *Pierre Poilievre: A Political Life* (Toronto: Sutherland House, 2024), 58.
7 Mahfouz took the loss badly. He ended up joining the Liberals and running against Poilievre in a later election but didn't come close to beating him.
8 It really makes a difference. Candidates never come to my downtown Ottawa home. I voted Progressive Conservative in the 2011 Ontario provincial election because the Tory candidate came up to me while I was having breakfast at the old Mayflower restaurant on Elgin Street. Since he seemed like a decent guy and was the only candidate to ask for my vote, I voted for him.
9 Note the clever use of the word *studied*, which does a lot of work here. Poilievre had not graduated. He finished later by correspondence.
10 People have a hard time wrapping their heads around this. Health is a provincial responsibility. The federal *Canada Health Act* enshrines medicare. The feds collect taxes and give provinces money to pay for health care. Some provinces use part pf this money to pay for highways and other things, citing their jurisdiction. When people can't find a doctor or complain about sitting in an emergency ward for ten hours, politicians at all levels point at each other. This is how federalism operates.
11 Many of the New Brunswickers who worked on the long-gun registry program were hired during Stephen Harper's term as prime minister to work on the Phoenix payroll system, which was a disaster. Many public servants were paid the wrong amount, missed being paid at all, or were paid double. For months, my wife collected her pay and her supervisors'. After that was straightened out, the managers of the system came back and said my wife had been overpaid and needed to pay that money back, too. This was not an unusual story in Ottawa in the last years of the Harper government and the first years of Justin Trudeau's tenure. There are still problems with the system.
12 Ken Gray, "Welcome to suburbia: They're well-educated, well-off and they vote in droves," *Ottawa Citizen,* May 19, 2004.
13 Paco Francoli, "Fifty ridings to watch," *Hill Times,* June 7, 2000.
14 Chloe Fedio, "The Minister of Nepean–Carleton," *Ottawa Citizen,* Oct. 25, 2012.
15 Daniel Tencer, Ken Gray, and Mohammed Adam, "Tory support for O-Train in question," *Ottawa Citizen,* June 19, 2004. When it was finally built, the problem-riddled north-south LRT ended up costing far more. It took a different route, connecting to Carleton University and the Ottawa airport instead of going to the suburb of Barrhaven.
16 Chloe Fedio, "The Minister of Nepean–Carleton," *Ottawa Citizen,* Oct. 25, 2012.
17 "Pratt facing a cliffhanger in Nepean–Carleton," *Hill Times,* June 14, 2000.
18 In print, including Garth Turner's book on life in the Tory caucus in the first months of the Harper government, Byrne was almost always described as Poilievre's spouse.
19 Chloe Fedio, "The Minister of Nepean–Carleton," *Ottawa Citizen,* Oct. 25, 2012.
20 Andrew Lawton, *Pierre Poilievre: A Political Life* (Toronto: Sutherland House, 2024), 158.
21 Hansard, Oct. 6, 2004.
22 Hansard, Oct. 12, 2004.
23 This plan died when Jack Layton and the NDP brought down the government in 2005.
24 Tonda MacCharles, "Justin Trudeau blames Conservative premiers for 'slow-walking' child-care rollout and taking their cues from Pierre Poilievre," *Toronto Star,* Mar. 28, 2024.

25 "Conservatives still seek acceptance in Ontario," *Edmonton Journal*, Mar. 16, 2005.
26 Ian Bailey, "Hot debate over youth wing," Canwest News, Mar. 16, 2005.
27 See CPAC's coverage at https://www.cpac.ca/articles/conventions/2005-cpc.
28 Pierre Poilievre, "In Ottawa, Tories Deliver for the Grassroots," *Ottawa Citizen*, Oct. 7, 2006. In fact, the portrait gallery, which never happened, was a suggested use for the empty building across from Parliament Hill that used to be the American embassy. Only the Tories made a big deal of it. The National Capital Commission is a major real estate agency of the federal government and has few friends in the federal government. Lobbyists didn't care about either of them. Lobbyists exist to make money for big business. In the later years of the Chrétien-Martin regime, copyright changes and military purchases were the bread and butter of lobbyists.
29 Harrison later went back to Saskatchewan and had a decent career as a Saskatchewan Party MLSA, even being considered leadership material (he lost to Scott Moe). Harrison's career hit a rock in the spring of 2024 when he was accused by the legislature's speaker of sending him "intimidating and harassing" text messages to try to make him rule in favour of his party. As strange, and maybe worse—though this was Saskatchewan—people found out about him bringing a rifle into the legislature building. He said he was going on a hunting trip after work, and he didn't want to leave the gun in his car. It cost him his cabinet job as government house leader. He admitted, "In retrospect, I should not have done this." Politicians do make comebacks from these kinds of mistakes.
30 Andrew Lawton, *Pierre Poilievre: A Political Life* (Toronto: Sutherland House, 2024), 61.
31 Speakers of the House of Commons get to choose a speaker's Scotch. Andrew Scheer picked a twelve-year-old Glenmorangie single malt. When Ontario's liquor board stopped selling that brand, Scheer switched to twelve-year-old Balvenie DoubleWood. As for "Tory Blue" and "Liberal Red," the colour label far predates Confederation, and even the Liberal and Conservative political parties themselves. Conservatives and Labour in the UK also use this colour scheme. Red is the colour of the left throughout the world. The American use of a reverse of the colour scheme can be traced back to the days when the Democrats were America's conservative party and the Republicans were mildly liberal. Republicans leaned toward the abolition of slavery while Confederates were Democrats. Republican president Teddy Roosevelt was an environmentalist and an opponent of corporate monopolies. The ground shifted in the First World War, and Franklin Roosevelt completed the flip. The South, caring more for its Civil War history than modern ideology, kept electing conservative southern Dixiecrats until Richard Nixon finished the realignment of the parties with his racist "southern strategy" in 1968. That's why the Americans use a colour scheme that requires translation.
32 Nigel Hannaford, "Tiny Tories," *Calgary Herald*, July 10, 2004.
33 He didn't finish the program.
34 Any pundit or academic who thinks party labels mean anything in Canada should clip that sentence and keep it in their wallet.
35 Campbell Clark, "The Conservative Leader has preached small government since his teenage years. Now people are embracing the message—and the messenger," *Globe and Mail*, Sept. 16, 2022.
36 Bea Vongdouangchanh, "Ballots in . . . Stronach, MacKay, Ambrose, Brison Best-Dressed: Conservative MP Belinda Stronach's chic, expensive suits, shoes dazzle political Hill staffers," *Hill Times*, Apr. 4, 2004.

37 Bea Vongdouangchanh, "Goodale, Cotler and Volpe most influential in Cabinet: survey," *Hill Times,* Apr. 10, 2005.
38 One, a brilliant young man named Sir John Thompson, can't be blamed for the Tory failure, as he dropped dead in 1894 while having lunch with Queen Victoria.
39 Whether this explains Justin Trudeau's determination to stay in office is open to debate. It is safe to say Canadian prime ministers stay too long. In the United States, it's rare for a party to hang on to the presidency after a member of their party has served two terms. This eight-year limit on a presidency is shorter than the terms served by Pierre Trudeau, Brian Mulroney, Jean Chrétien, Stephen Harper, and Justin Trudeau.
40 In 2006, the Ontario Court of Appeal agreed.
41 Pierre Poilievre, "Birth of a child shouldn't become healthcare roulette: exclusion of autism treatment from Canada's medicare," *Hill Times,* Mar. 21, 2005.
42 Dave Rogers, "Bloc MP refuses to give flags to veterans," Postmedia News, Nov. 6, 2004.
43 Standing Committee on Government Operations and Estimates, December 2, 2004, 11–12.
44 Hansard, Dec. 6, 2004.
45 Bill Curry, "Alcock defends familiarity in government appointments," *Ottawa Citizen,* Dec. 3, 2004, and Bill Curry, "Reg Alcock an anti-youth bigot," *Ottawa Citizen,* Dec. 7, 2004.

CHAPTER 5: **DIAL-A-QUOTE**

1 Hayley Mick, "Nepean–Carleton MP gets jump on campaign," *Ottawa Citizen,* Apr. 25, 2005.
2 "Feds Deny Boondoggle," Canwest News, Apr. 25, 2005.
3 Massicotte's company was awarded a fifteen-year contract worth $99-million, for a ten-storey office building in Gatineau in February 2002, before he became a senator. That should be the kind of contract that attracts attention. The real estate dealings of the federal government are well worth investigating, as is the renovation of the Centre Block of Parliament. That work is costing, in real terms, about as much money as the 1976 Montreal Olympics, and none of the governments in power—Tory or Liberal—has shown a coherent plan for the work.
4 Hansard, June 6, 2005. See also Jack Aubry, "Real estate corp, with Liberal ties, should be fined, Tory says," Postmedia News, June 7, 2005.
5 The riding contains a weird mix of trendy anglos from outside Quebec—descendants of English-speaking settlers in the Shawville area, where the Orange Lodge, an anti-Catholic fraternal organization, was politically powerful until late in the last century—and a French-Canadian majority. There are also two Indigenous territories and tiny Polish and German settlements. The district, with that odd mix, is a swing riding. It went Conservative in the 2006 election, NDP in 2011, and Liberal when Justin Trudeau won in 2015. Smith, elected in 2004, served just two years in the House of Commons, placing third in 2006.
6 Jack Aubry, "Watchdog probes contracts to firm controlled by Liberal MP's wife," Postmedia News, Nov. 16, 2005.
7 My mother was secretary of an NDP riding association before jumping the fence and becoming a conservative. The idea that the job came with any power or serious influence can be debunked very easily. The records did take up a lot of space in our house and we got a *lot* of political guff in the mail.

8 Grant Robertson, "Mounties included in federal whistleblower bill," Postmedia News, June 22, 2005.
9 Matthew Kupfer and Estelle Côté-Stroka, "Overwhelmed by workload, public sector integrity commissioner asks for more money," CBC News, Oct. 2024.
10 David Hutton, "Canada's whistleblowing system protects wrongdoers, not whistleblowers," Ottawa Citizen, Oct. 19, 2022.
11 Ottawa is divided into linguistic areas, with the eastern part of the downtown and the suburbs having a strong French presence while the western part of the city is predominantly English. In the rural areas, the farther west and north you go, the francophones are fewer and the amount of anti-French bigotry is greater.
12 Randall Denley, "Tory rally a poor showing: Descending into petty name-calling won't win over voters," Ottawa Citizen, Apr. 21, 2005. The daycare plan died when the NDP pulled the plug on the Martin government. Stephen Harper did come up with a plan to give a small cash subsidy for daycare, but it was not even close to being adequate for families who needed all-day child care. After years of being taunted by Quebec, which has heavily subsidized daycare (if you can find it), Justin Trudeau's government came up with a plan in its second minority term.
13 "MP Poilievre protests Public Works move to force tenants to follow language rules," Ottawa Citizen, Apr. 16, 2004.
14 Hansard, Apr. 19, 2005.
15 Campbell Clark, "The Conservative Leader has preached small government since his teenage years. Now people are embracing the message—and the messenger," Globe and Mail, Sept. 16, 2022.
16 Many of these stories are told by government staff who travelled with the vice-regal couple.
17 Vallières wrote a book with a title that uses an unspeakable word. Just saying the title of this work destroyed Wendy Mesley's career at CBC. I read the book when it was assigned in university and saw this work as proof that Vallières should have read and travelled more before taking up the hobby of writing political manifestos, rather than draft a xenophobic blueprint for a future Quebec based on skewed views of history.
18 Jean ended up being one of the best of the Canadian-born governors general, praised by leaders of all the political parties when her term ended. Stephen Harper backed her to head the Francophonie, the organization that includes countries with some element of French culture.
19 Jack Aubry and Mike De Souza, "Jean's husband defended FLQ sympathizer," Montreal Gazette, Aug. 13, 2005.
20 "Lafond's new film hits hot buttons," CBC News, Apr. 26, 2006.
21 L. Ian MacDonald, "Sometimes it's more like Porky's than Parliament," Montreal Gazette, Oct. 30, 2006.
22 Jane Taber, "The ten most irritating politicians of 2008," Globe and Mail, Dec. 17, 2009.
23 She was killed by Kevin Davis, a twenty-four-year-old pizza maker. It took almost two years for Ottawa police to catch him, even though, partway through the investigation, David ran naked down a suburban Ottawa street yelling, "I killed Jennifer Teague! I killed Jennifer Teague!" Police believed it was the magic mushrooms talking, and they took him to a psychiatric ward. It took another year for them to realize he was telling the truth and to get the evidence to convict him. Wood's killer was later caught by Sudbury police.

24 Andrew Duffy, "'A layer of innocence peeled away,'" *Ottawa Citizen*, Sept. 14, 2005.
25 Harris also tried to close the Montfort Hospital, which served the city's French community. He backed down after Ottawa francophones ran a superb campaign to keep it open.
26 An independence that is rather dubious, no matter whether the Tories or Liberals are in power. Since the government sets the NCC's budget and appoints its supporters to the NCC board, it has subtle and less-than-subtle ways of cracking the whip.
27 John Baird won that riding in the next election.
28 Mohammed Adam and Tony Lofaro, "Liberals reject $1 land rent for hospital," Postmedia News, Oct. 7, 2005.
29 Hillary Clinton faced a similar torpedo attack from FBI director James Comey, who told reporters during the 2016 presidential campaign that Clinton was being investigated for failing to protect secret government emails. Neither candidate was charged. Neither cop did well after their election adventures. Zaccardelli was out by the end of 2006. Comey wasn't sufficiently subservient to Donald Trump and was fired in 2017.
30 "Liberal apologizes for saying Harper day-care bucks may buy beer, popcorn," CBC News, Dec. 11, 2005.
31 Garth Turner, *Sheeple: Caucus Confidential in Stephen Harper's Ottawa* (Toronto: KeyPorter, 2009), 21.
32 Garth Turner, *Sheeple: Caucus Confidential in Stephen Harper's Ottawa* (Toronto: KeyPorter, 2009), 112. When Justin Trudeau became prime minister in 2015, the PMO continued Harper's policy of having his advisers hire and fire ministerial staff. One former senior minister in Trudeau's government told me they were horrified when they found out they couldn't pick their own advisers.
33 Michael Harris, *Party of One: Stephen Harper and Canada's Radical Makeover* (Toronto: Viking, 2014), 68.
34 Lawrence Martin, *Harperland: The Politics of Control* (Toronto: Viking, 2010), 64. This was a bit rich coming from Flanagan, who, after the WikiLeaks data dump, told CBC host Evan Solomon that Julian Assange, the man behind the expose, "should be assassinated," adding, "I'm feeling pretty manly today." Flanagan later retracted his call for Assange's murder. "Flanagan regrets WikiLeaks assassination remark," CBC News Dec. 1, 2010 .
35 Lawrence Martin, *Harperland: The Politics of Control* (Toronto: Viking, 2010), 64.
36 Stephanie Levitz, "There's a new book about Pierre Poilievre. Here are five things we learned about the Conservative leader," *Toronto Star*, May 24, 2024.
37 "Poilievre urged to step aside over Hill breach," CBC News, Oct. 8, 2010, and Richard Brenna, "Conservative MP blows by Hill security check," *Toronto Star*, Oct. 8, 2010.
38 F. Abbas Rana, "Conservatives won't say who will be the next public sector integrity commissioner," *Hill Times*, Apr. 10, 2006.
39 Jennifer Ditchburn, "Liberals, NDP want floor-crossing rules in Accountability Act," Canadian Press, June 6, 2006.
40 Ian Bron, "A former whistleblower explains the dangers of Canada's feeble whistleblowing laws," *Conversation*, Aug. 24, 2022. The Liberals didn't strengthen the law after they came to power. Bron is a senior fellow at the Centre for Free Expression Whistleblowing Initiative. The idea of paying whistle-blowers would haunt the Tories after they took power. See Tim Naumetz, "Whistleblower says Tories promised payment if they formed government," *Ottawa Citizen*, July 6, 2006.
41 Susan Riley column, *Ottawa Citizen*, June 13, 2006.

42 In the early days of internet advertising, this was a common embarrassment for advertisers. As for Poilievre's distaste for the parliamentary job and the situations he was put in, see Andrew Lawton, *Pierre Poilievre: A Political Life* (Toronto: Sutherland House, 2024), 86.
43 "Ottawa newspaper names MP the 'biggest gossip,'" Postmedia News, May 19, 2006.
44 This has been especially true since some Western First Nations began using ground-penetrating radar to look for lost graveyards near the schools. Tom Flanagan, Stephen Harper's mentor, is, with C.P. Champion, co-author of *Grave Error: How the Media Misled Us (and the Truth about Residential Schools)*, self-published, 2023.
45 "Conservative MP apologizes for 'hurtful' comments on aboriginal people," CBC News, June 12, 2008. ·
46 See "Tory MP defends use of term 'tar baby,'" CBC News, May 29, 2009; Glen McGregor, "House of Commons No Place for 'Tar Baby' Remark, MPs Say," *Ottawa Citizen*, May 30, 2009.
47 Geoffrey Simpson, "A pre-election flurry of self-promotion," *Guelph Mercury*, Feb. 28, 2011.
48 His father was in Joe Clark's Progressive Conservative Cabinet, his grandfather served in the Cabinet of Maurice Duplessis.
49 While the popular vote does not determine election success in Canada, Layton and his candidates got 2,515,288 in the 2008 federal election and 4,508,474 in 2011. This was enough to crush the Bloc Quebecois and pick up seats in the Greater Toronto and Vancouver areas at the expense of the Liberals.
50 In the 1990s, people working in the Centre Block of Parliament (the main building), noticed a very sharp uptick in prostate cancer cases among MPs, building employees, and even some media people. There was a lot of talk about whether the cases were simply a reflection of the fact that many MPs are men of the age when prostate cancer tends to be diagnosed or if their cases were found because they were among the class of people who get the best medical attention. There was also a suspicion that maybe the building had carcinogens. Some of the most famous federal politicians of the late 1900s and early 2000s were treated for the disease, almost always successfully, though Pierre Trudeau died of it. As far as I know, there was no epidemiological study of the phenomenon. In 2018, the building was closed for renovations that involved, among many other things, the removal of asbestos insulation.
51 Some of these young MPs, including former pub worker Ruth Ellen Brossard, became effective MPs. Most only lasted one term, but Brossard was re-elected in 2015 and earned a reputation as an effective constituency MP. Her last moment of fame came when Justin Trudeau accidentally stuck an elbow into one of her breasts during an argument on the floor of the House of Commons. Though she lost her seat in 2019, she had qualified for a parliamentary pension. When last heard of, she had become fluently bilingual and was happily married, living in her old riding.
52 In the previous government, Harper had appointed John Baird and Lawrence Cannon to the cabinet. Although Cannon was from Gatineau, the Quebec side of the Ottawa urban area, he could be sold as a Quebec minister, rather than someone from Ottawa. He left government in 2011 and was appointed ambassador to France the following year. That's a dream appointment for a Quebecois politician.
53 In 2013, Lebel accepted ministerial responsibility for the Lac-Mégantic rail disaster in rural Quebec and resigned from cabinet. He survived the Trudeau landslide of

2015 but left politics two years later when it became clear he'd never achieve his leadership ambition.
54 Ford would later find Hillier, a rural-property-rights advocate, to be too much for his government and pushed him out of his caucus. Hillier's constituents in Lanark County, part of the Ozarks of Ontario, sent him back to Queen's Park for one term as an Independent. He was still an MPP when he was charged with assaulting a Parliament Hill security officer during the 2022 "Freedom Convoy." Those charges were stayed in 2024 under the Jordan principle, which guarantees the right to a (relatively) speedy trial. Hillier lost his seat in the election of May 2022, when he was defeated by a candidate from Ford's party.
55 Tobi Cohen, "Long-gun registry set for scrap heap," *Vancouver Province*, Oct. 26, 2011.
56 The Lac-Mégantic disaster happened on a stretch of railway that had belonged to Canadian Pacific but had been sold to a short-line railway company. In the 1970s, the train would have had an engineman and a front-end brakeman, along with a conductor and tail-end brakeman in a caboose. Railways had succeeded in capturing the regulatory system under Liberal and Conservative governments so that, by 2013, a train like this could be operated by a single engineer. Lebel did not invent the system that allowed Lac-Mégantic to happen, he just had responsibility for it. This "demotion" did not force him from Cabinet. He stayed as intergovernmental affairs minister until the Tories lost power in 2015. Lebel left Parliament in 2017 to run the Quebec Forest Industry Council.

CHAPTER 6: **ELECTION SKULLDUGGERY**

1 Ed Broadbent, Frances Abele, Jonathan Sas, and Luke Savage, *Seeking Social Democracy: Seven Decades in the Fight for Equality* (Toronto: ECW Press), 221.
2 Unless they gave up "Indian" status, almost all Indigenous people were barred from voting in federal elections until 1960. Provincial governments were often slower to extend voting rights to women. They couldn't vote in Quebec until 1940, when their vote helped temporarily turf the fascistic government of Maurice Duplessis out of office. In New Brunswick, women could vote in 1919 but weren't allowed to seek a seat in the legislature until 1934.
3 Biggar was a fascinating man. Oliver Mowat, Ontario's first great premier, was his maternal grandfather. Biggar was judge advocate general in the First World War, started the fantastically named law firm Smart and Biggar during the Depression, and was head of the country's censorship system in the Second World War. He was a distant relative of author Farley Mowat.
4 Some Indigenous Canadians already had the right to vote if they had given up some of their aboriginal rights. This was especially true of First Nations people who received university educations and had become doctors, lawyers, and other professionals. They were accepted into "white" society, and the system served as a way of separating potential leaders from their communities.
5 Delcourt was robbed of the 2013 Shaughnessy Cohen Prize for Political Writing. The book was not even nominated. It was, however, shortlisted for the more lucrative and better-known Hilary Weston Writers' Trust Prize for Nonfiction. The next year, Michael Harris' wildly popular *Party of One* was also snubbed for a Cohen nomination, but it was one of the very few modern political books nominated for a Governor General's Award.

6 I knew this, on some level, but was shocked to see my twenty-nine-year-old daughter's Netflix account offered her movies and TV shows that I didn't even know were on the service. As I passed from middle-aged and my supposed peak earning years to "senior citizen," the ads offered to me switched. I stopped seeing pitches for expensive cars and exotic travel and now get ads for things like catheters and dating sites of older single and married women who liked to do nasty things with strangers. Years ago, people who thought their TVs were watching *them* were diagnosed as paranoid. Now they're right.
7 Susan Delacourt, *Shopping for Votes* (Vancouver: Douglas & McIntyre, 2013), 266.
8 Susan Delacourt, *Shopping for Votes* (Vancouver: Douglas & McIntyre, 2013), 266–69. Unless privacy laws change, this, along with tracking done by social media, internet-search companies and "cookies" quietly placed on your computer when you visit websites, is the future of all marketing, whether it's political parties trying to get your support or a company trying to sell you a snowblower.
9 See *McEwing v. Canada (Attorney General)*, 2013 FC 525 (CanLII), [2013] 4 FCR 63, paragraphs 244–46.
10 Campbell Clark, "Speaker rebukes Bev Oda over document in KAIROS case," *Globe and Mail*, Feb. 10, 2011.
11 I covered big tornados in Ontario in 1979 and 1985 and saw how Mennonites would show up at a flattened farm and work without breaks to rebuild it. It was inspiring.
12 Not at the same time but within living memory of some Canadian Mennonites, and Mennonites keep the memory of this oppression alive. Mennonite history is quite interesting. Time after time, regimes invited these pacifists to settle in their countries because they were good farmers and problem-free citizens. Almost every time, host nations turned against them when they refused to fight, even when their country was invaded. They also kept their German language and aspects of its culture. Mennonites started coming to North America in the 1700s, with big influxes after each persecution. Stalin added them to his long list of imaginary enemies, which generated the exodus of many thousands to North America before 1952.
13 "Mennonite magazine warned about 'political' articles," CBC News, Nov. 9, 2012.
14 *Credit Counselling Services of Atlantic Canada Inc v Minister of National Revenue*, 2016 FCA 193 [*Credit Counselling Services*] paragraph 185: "To satisfy the requirement that a purpose is for the relief of poverty, the person receiving the assistance must be a person who is then in poverty. Poverty is a relative term. Therefore, it is possible that in some situations providing assistance through counselling or by other means to individuals in serious financial trouble may be considered to be relieving poverty, even if the individuals are not then destitute."
15 For a book-length discussion of the Harper government's undermining of media and its strategy to control government information, see my book *Kill The Messengers: Stephen Harper's Attack on Your Right to Know* (Toronto: Harper Collins, 2015).
16 Marchand is my second cousin.
17 It turned out they were wrong, and Marchand lost the seat.
18 Bea Vongdouangchanh, "Conservatives confusing public on 'in and out' financing, says Prof. MacIvor," *Hill Times*, Apr. 21, 2008.
19 Les Whittington, "Liberals seek Tory ad probe; Conservatives accused of shuffling campaign funds between ridings, but party denies any wrongdoing," *Toronto Star*, Sept. 6, 2007.
20 On top of this skullduggery, near the end of the campaign, someone leaked a letter

from the head of the RCMP campaign that said finance minister Ralph Goodale was under investigation for allegedly leaking part of the last federal budget. Later, when the Liberals were out of power, Goodale was cleared, but the political damage was done. An official in the finance department was charged for leaking the changes to the tax regime for income trusts.

21 "Tories reject claims they broke election spending laws; Gov't wraps itself in free speech argument in election ad controversy," Postmedia News, Sept. 6, 2007.

22 Tim Naumetz and Glen MacGregor, "Liberals see potential fraud in Tory campaign spending dispute," *Ottawa Citizen*, Sept. 6, 2007.

23 Tim Naumetz, "Sponsorship figures stick to their stories; Guite and Pelletier deny lying to MPs," Postmedia News, June 7, 2007.

24 "Elections Canada chief won't back down on veiled voting," CBC News, Sept. 10, 2007.

25 Stephen Thorne, "Elections boss holds firm," Postmedia News, Sept. 14, 2007.

26 Tonda MacCharles, "Tories blast Elections Canada," *Toronto Star*, Apr. 30, 2008.

27 Frances Russell, "Conservative bullying undermines democracy," *Winnipeg Free Press*, May 14, 2008.

28 Tim Naumetz, "Tories' witnesses excluded in election-ad inquiry," *Globe and Mail*, July 17, 2008.

29 Steven Chase, "Tories dismiss election spending charges as 'accounting dispute,'" *Globe and Mail*, Feb. 26, 2011.

30 Hansard, May 8, 2008.

31 People for the American Way Foundation, "The New Face of Jim Crow: Voter Suppression in America," pfaw.org, Aug. 1, 2006.

32 Rachel E. Berry, "Democratic National Committee v. Edward J. Rollins: Politics as usual or Unusual Politics," *Race and Ethnic Ancestry Law Digest*, footnote 27, quoted in Chandler Davidson, Tanya Dunlap, Gale Kenny, and Benjamin Wise, "Republican Ballot Security Programs: Vote Protection or Minority Vote Suppression—or Both? A Report to the Center for Voting Rights and Protection at https://archives.library.rice.edu/repositories/2/archival_objects/77863 (Sept. 2004), 96.

33 Michael Harris, *Party of One* (Toronto: Viking, 2014), 80.

34 American Civil Liberties Union, "Block the Vote: How Politicians Are Trying to Block Voters from the Ballot Box," ACLUnews.org, Aug. 18, 2021.

35 Edward Lempinen, "Stacking the deck: How the GOP works to suppress minority voting," *UC Berkely News*, Sept. 29, 2020.

36 Steve Benen, "Conviction in GOP voter-suppression scheme," *Washington Monthly*, Dec. 7, 2011.

37 Stephen Chase and Daniel Leblanc, "Firm at centre of robocall storm unmasks mystery employee," *Globe and Mail*, Mar. 20, 2012.

38 To the great sadness of poutine lovers in Guelph, the place went out of business during the Covid pandemic.

39 McGregor worked for the *Citizen*, and Maher was the *Halifax Herald*'s one-man parliamentary bureau before joining the *Citizen*'s staff under the paper's scholarly young editor, Andrew Potter, who was trying to develop a career as a public intellectual. Their stories ran in any Postmedia paper that chose to use them Though the robocalls story became too complex to be understood by most readers, McGregor and Maher won all the major awards available to newspaper journalists. It's symptomatic of the state of this country's newspaper business that Maher and McGregor took buyouts from their employer. McGregor went on to a career in television news. Maher is a magazine writer and author.

40 Complaints about Tory calls began three days before polls opened. *The National*, Nov. 19, 2012.
41 Finley was never connected to the "robocalls" scandal but did admit to his role in the in-and-out finance scheme. Finley died in 2013.
42 Michael Harris, *Party of One* (Toronto: Viking, 2014), 67.
43 Michael Harris, *Party of One* (Toronto: Viking, 2014), 82.
44 *The National*, Aug. 24, 2012.
45 Alberta's United Conservative Party government brought in a similar law, even though elections officials had caught just five people cheating in provincial elections in the previous eleven years (three instances of people voting twice and two ineligible voters). Alexandra Ballos, Rachel Hwang, and Jared Wesley, "A Voter ID Law: Coming to an Election Near You?" *Policy Options*, Aug. 2024.
46 One of them was a writer for Toronto's NOW magazine, James DiFiore, who described how he obtained three ballots at Toronto polling stations in the 2008 federal election. Three years later, he was fined $250. See "Toronto writer fined $250 for vote-early-and-vote-often stunt," CBC.ca, Feb. 8, 2011.
47 See https://electionsanddemocracy.ca/canadas-elections/youth-voting-trends.
48 See https://bdp.parl.ca/sites/PublicWebsite/default/en_CA/ResearchPublications/2016104E#a5.
49 Pierre Poilievre, "Why the Fair Elections Act is, in fact, fair," *Globe and Mail*, Mar. 24, 2014.
50 Frank Graves and Stephen Maher, "Pierre Poilievre: The Secret to His Success," *Walrus*, Dec. 14, 2022.
51 Jeffrey Simpson, "The Fair Elections Act is ever so telling," *Globe and Mail*, Apr.16, 2014.
52 "Baloney Meter: Is Elections Canada biased in favour of Liberals, as Tory claims?" CityNews, June 14, 2019.

CHAPTER 7: **CONTENDER IN THE WILDERNESS**

1 Legally, the minimum length of a campaign is thirty-five days. Since 2015, a fifty-day limit has been imposed.
2 "Drowned Syrian migrant boy's father says he blames Canada for tragedy," *Globe and Mail*, Sept. 10, 2015.
3 Joe Friesen, "Prime Minister's Office ordered halt to refugee processing," *Globe and Mail*, Oct. 8, 2015.
4 In 2021, Trudeau and his government were quiet about the removal of a teacher from her classroom in Chelsea, Quebec, for wearing a hijab. The school is about eight kilometres from the prime minister's vacation home at Harrington Lake and fourteen kilometres from Parliament Hill. People in Chelsea protested the move by the local school board, which claimed to be following Quebec's "secular" laws and policies.
5 Tonda MacCharles, "Harper pitting country against Muslims, some Niqab wearers say," *Toronto Star*, Oct. 7, 2015.
6 "The Trudeau touch: 'Just watch me' note sells for $12K, chocolates go for $450," Oct.22, 2015.
7 Vanessa Friedman, "Justin Trudeau Takes an Image, and Wins With It," *New York Times*, Oct. 21, 2015.
8 Harper is twelve years older than Trudeau so had become prime minister when he was just three years older than Trudeau was in 2015. Neither person had run

anything larger than an opposition party's political office before they took power. Poilievre had cabinet experience when he became party leader but also had never run a large organization.

9   "'Old stock Canadians,' egg timer, creepy set top debate's odd moments, Moderator David Walmsley's Irish accent and a ringing bell get reaction on social media." CBC News, Sept. 17, 2015.
10 See *Zero Tolerance for Barbaric Cultural Practices Act*. PART 1, 2001, c. 27 and Ashley Csanady, "'Barbaric Cultural Practices' bill to criminalize forced marriage, tackle 'honour killings' passes final vote," *National Post*, June 17, 2015.
11 Tim Dowling, "Canada's Conservatives vow to create 'barbaric cultural practices' hotline," *Guardian,* Oct. 2, 2015.
12 Janice Dickson, "Poilievre's political fashion choice sparks criticism," iPolitics, July 20, 2015.
13 Jordan Press, "Elections watchdog says Poilievre's Tory golf shirt at child benefit event broke rule," iPolitics, July 21, 2017.
14 After New Democrat Emilie Taman, who lost her job as a federal government lawyer when she defied a public service rule and ran for a federal seat, won a lawsuit challenging that rule, thirty-five federal workers ran in 2015.
15 Blair Crawford, "Mission Impossible? Challengers aim to topple Pierre Poilievre in new riding of Carleton," *Ottawa Citizen,* Sept. 25, 2015.
16 Blair Crawford, "Mission Impossible? Challengers aim to topple Pierre Poilievre in new riding of Carleton," *Ottawa Citizen,* Sept. 25, 2015.
17 Nepean was the name of an Ottawa satellite town, built on the old Nepean Township. Carleton was the name of the county. In 2001, the Ontario government led by Mike Harris amalgamated all the communities and farmland in Carleton into the city of Ottawa.
18 *Party of One* was one of the few recent political books nominated for a Governor General's Award for literature.
19 Laura Payton, "Inside the battle for Ottawa's public-service vote," *Maclean's,* Oct. 6, 2015.
20 James Fitz-Morris, "Charter of Rights and the niqab collide in views on 'Canadian values,'" CBC News, Oct. 4, 2015.
21 "Former Conservative minister Pierre Poilievre re-elected in Ottawa riding," CBC News, Oct. 19, 2015.
22 Leslie MacKinnon, "Elections Canada drops plan for online voting due to cuts," CBC News, Oct. 1, 2013.
23 Andrew Lawton, *Pierre Poilievre: A Political Life* (Toronto: Sutherland House, 2024), 92–94.
24 When working on the Hill from 1994 to 2018 and while researching this book, I heard a lot of crazy talk about political wives and about the Trudeaus. In the late 1970s, while working in Toronto, I was told by some of the most famous journalists in Canada that Pierre Trudeau was a sort of Manchurian Candidate, a secret communist who had his wife impregnated by artificial insemination because he was gay and couldn't do it himself. Talk about Justin Trudeau is just as bad: supposedly, he's Fidel Castro's natural son and has done a lot of unnatural things to men and women. Political wives who had any profile and spoke out—Margaret Trudeau, Mila Mulroney, Laureen Harper, Anaida Poilievre—have been targeted by men and women in the Ottawa bubble with vile, sexist rumour. Gossips and their journalistic voice, *Frank Magazine,* tried to humiliate Kim Campbell, the country's only

female prime minister, by attacking her relationships. It's hard to know if any of this talk has hurt their husbands' careers, but it's worth noting how some well-known people on the left and right are willing to spread stories that are cruel and sexist about women who have few options for fighting back.

25 Tom Blackwell, "From immigrant background to two-person wedding, Anaida Poilievre a distinct Tory wife," *National Post*, Sept. 11, 2022.

26 People who claim the disability deduction on their income tax forms must go through a comprehensive medical exam and submit a thick medical record before CRA considers their application. Poilievre's bill was a good idea. It would have helped some high-income people, but these are outliers, and a ceiling could have been set on the tax break. The real problem is the low ODSP payments, which Poilievre couldn't do anything about, since they're provincial. This was an attempt to do something. I hope readers notice how Poilievre has tried to help autistic and disabled people. He started doing this advocacy before he and his wife had children. Since the early 2000s, Poilievre has advocated for more help for kids on the autism spectrum and their parents. In Ontario, where the couple lives, the provincial government still resists parental pressure for better services.

27 Hansard, Apr. 16, 2018. The bill, unlike so many of Poilievre's nasty soundbites, got no media coverage.

28 Kelly Carmichael, "What's the point of spending millions of dollars on consultations when the government ignores the findings?" *Policy Options*, Feb. 13, 2017. Gould is a survivor and a team player so she stayed on, holding important cabinet jobs and, as House leader after the 2021 election, quarterbacking the Liberals' legislative strategy in the House of Commons. She ran for Liberal leader in 2025. Proportional representation would have meant a change in the way governments are formed in Canada. For example, the Conservatives won more votes than the Liberals in 2019 and 2021 but nowhere enough to have a majority of seats. It's unlikely any other party would have supported them in a minority parliament. Likely, at least two parties would have had to form a real coalition, with ministers from all the parties that joined it. Canada has only had one true coalition government, formed after the 1917 election when Conservatives and some Liberals formed a "union" government until the First World War ended and the country adjusted to peace.

29 Trudeau forced Dion out of cabinet and made him ambassador to France. Coderre successfully ran for mayor of Montreal.

30 I'm one of the lawyers who represented Bernier in the resulting lawsuit.

31 Ryan Maloney, "Tory MP Pierre Poilievre Scolded Over 'Little Potato' Dig At Trudeau In House Of Commons," HuffPost, May 1, 2019.

32 Tu Thanh Ha, "Herron long-term care residents died of thirst, malnourishment, Quebec coroner's inquest told," *Globe and Mail*, Sept. 14, 2021.

CHAPTER 8: **WRECKING WE CHARITY**

1 In Canada, kids can work on family farms. Serious injuries are quite common.
2 Arguably, WE's leaders never made this comparison and might have defused accusations against them if they had done so in a clear way.
3 Which would be the right thing to do, if the corporations did not flee jurisdictions that seriously tax them. To make this work, every country on Earth would have to agree and enforce the rules.

4. "What WE Lost book review: What really happened to WE Charity," *Montreal Times*, undated.
5. Canadians did see big changes in domestic government operations in both world wars, but even though the government had plans drafted before the wars, they still didn't make economic and tax changes as quickly as they did in 2020, and they were able to do their work without the personal and workplace disruptions faced by every Canadian public servant in 2020.
6. As was Mark Carney's father, and, for that matter, mine.
7. CTV News interview, July 9, 2020.
8. Brown ran a series of podcasts attacking the Kielburgers and WE Charity during his 2019 Patreon drive and posted a second series in the fall of 2021. Krause is probably best known for her investigations into environmental groups that oppose oil industry practices.
9. Finance Committee transcript: https://openparliament.ca/committees/finance/43-1/43/pierre-poilievre-26/
10. Tonda MacCharles, "Bill Morneau resigns as Canada's finance minister," *Toronto Star*, Aug. 18, 2020.
11. The Liberals have something of a tradition of finance ministers stomping out, then coming back to lead the party.
12. In fact, to limit overall liability, many companies and organizations set up companies for one-off projects.
13. Peter Zimonjic and Kathleen Harris, "After 4-hour grilling by MPs, WE co-founders insist they had no financial motive in student grant deal," CBC News, July 28, 2020.
14. Testimony of Craig and Marc Kielburger at the House of Commons Finance Committee, July 28, 2020. https://www.ourcommons.ca/DocumentViewer/en/43-1/FINA/meeting-45/evidence beginning at 1 p.m.
15. Judith Timson, "Too polite or too rude? Summer's dog days provide a uniquely Canadian crisis," *Toronto Star*, July 30, 2020.
16. My book *Bush Runner: The Adventures of Pierre-Esprit Radisson* was visible on a shelf behind the prime minister. This created mixed emotions in my mother, who is no way a Trudeau supporter.
17. "Opposition Parties Decry Black Ink in WE Documents," *Toronto Star*, Aug. 18, 2020.
18. Kathleen Harris, "Conservatives claim 'coverup' after Trudeau shuts down Parliament," CBC News, Aug. 19, 2020.
19. Mia Rabson, "Tories say they want full truth of WE Charity scandal out before next election," Canadian Press, Aug. 19, 2020.
20. Personal conversation, January 16, 2025.
21. The *Toronto Telegram* had been a social enterprise in the first half of the twentieth century, with all its profits going to Toronto's Hospital for Sick Children. It was purchased by George McCullagh, owner of the *Globe and Mail*, in 1946. McCullagh used his political influence to thwart Atkinson's will. The provincial government passed a law preventing the transfer. Connaught Laboratories, founded by the University of Toronto to make and market insulin and, later, other drugs, was also a social enterprise that transferred all its profits to the university. I describe McCullagh's business and political dealings in my 2022 book, *Big Men Fear Me*.
22. Marco Chown Oved, "Before selling properties for an apparent loss, WE Charity shut down another bidder before he could offer a higher price," *Toronto Star*, Feb. 11, 2022.
23. The House of Commons had not jailed anyone in more than a century.

24 Sarah Turnbull, "Kielburgers blame 'political crossfire' for destroying WE Charity," CTV News, Mar. 15, 2021.
25 "Trudeau cleared of wrongdoing in WE Charity scandal by ethics watchdog," Canadian Press, May 13, 2021.
26 The judge's criticism of Canadaland's reporting and Brown's cruelty to this now elderly woman was scathing. See Kielburger v. Canadaland Inc., 2024 ONSC 2622 (CanLII), available at CANLII.org.
27 The provinces did impose some absurd rules. Twice, Quebec closed its borders with Ontario and New Brunswick and deployed cops to hunt down cars with out-of-province plates. Ontario, unlike the federal government, declared a state of emergency and tried to control some prices. The province banned people from using parks, basketball and tennis courts, off-leash dog parks, benches, skateboard and BMX parks, picnic areas, outdoor community gardens, park shelters, outdoor exercise equipment, condo parks and gardens, and other outdoor recreational amenities; closed all non-essential workplaces; and banned get-togethers with more than five people. No one protested these measures.
28 Tasha Kheiriddin, "Pierre Poilievre is plundering Jagmeet Singh's labour vote base," *National Post*, Sept. 3, 2024.
29 Aaron Derfel, "Records reveal chaos in the days before staff abandoned the Herron," *Montreal Gazette*, Apr. 17, 2020.
30 Bulgaria had the highest mortality rate in the world at 15000.6 deaths per million.
31 Kate McKenna, Harvey Cashore, and Mark Kelley, "Kielburger brothers say WE Charity controversy left them 'political roadkill,'" CBC News, Feb. 3, 2021.
32 Kate McKenna, Harvey Cashore, and Mark Kelley, "Kielburger brothers say WE Charity controversy left them 'political roadkill,'" CBC News, Feb. 3, 2021.

CHAPTER 9: **IS CANADA BROKEN?**

1 The provincial Tory governments of Mike Harris and Ernie Eves (1993–2003) slashed benefits to Ontario's most vulnerable people. The Liberal governments of Dalton McGuinty and Kathleen Wynne (2003–2018) did not restore them.
2 Josh Pringle, "Here's how much it costs to rent an apartment in Ottawa," CTV News, May 14, 2023.
3 The claim that rents are down a bit is anecdotal. All stats on rentals are speculative. Many landlords don't report their rents to anyone (including Canada Revenue Agency) and don't talk about their deals. Ontario ditched rent controls and a provincial rent registry years ago. One thing is clear: tenants in Ottawa and Toronto must jump through a lot of hoops to get a place, even when they can afford it. Credit checks, proof of employment, and the gut instincts of landlords are barriers to renting. And to be fair to landlords, provincial bureaucracy is so slow and cumbersome that it takes about a year to (legally) evict a deadbeat tenant. The failure of the landlord–tenant protection system has spawned a new type of fraudster who moves into rental houses and apartments with no intention of paying.
4 People might quibble with my belief that Bank Street is the city's main street, but it used to be an important commercial area. Now, the stretch closest to Parliament Hill is a mix of restaurants, tattoo parlours, weed and magic-mushroom shops, fake British and Irish pubs, empty storefronts, cheque-cashing joints, and a few surviving retail shops.
5 Perhaps the curse on the Maple Leafs somehow involves the failure to sign Richard. I should have asked him, as my own theories still need work.

6   I broke the ice by describing how my great-uncle Montcalm fell from the deck of an empty iron boat to the bottom of the ship and walked away with a few broken ribs. He did this by falling through an open hatch at the Soo locks after what the Brits used to call "a night of festivities." This was a downward trip of about forty feet onto steel. Had he been sober, he would certainly have died. This same great-uncle had an eye shot out by my grandfather with a homemade bow and arrow (yes, your mom was right; that kind of thing really happened). He also lost a couple of fingers hitting blasting caps with a hammer. These wounds and scars must have been challenging to a gay man who hit his peak earning and dating years in the Great Depression.

7   Erik White, "Ontario disability support rejections often overturned on appeal by provincially-funded legal clinics," CBC News, Feb. 25, 2019. The appeal process is far beyond the capabilities of people with serious mental disabilities and brain injuries, and of most other people, yet most appeals that make it through the system succeed. Community legal clinics employ lawyers doing the Lord's work, but a claimant has to be well enough to access the lawyers, have an address, and engage with the system.

8   People talk a lot about Ottawa's cold winters, but its summers are rotten, too. The city gets very hot and humid. It rained nearly every day in the summer of 2024. Fortunately, unlike many northern and western cities, biting insects are not a big problem.

9   It is the Centennial Flame, not the "eternal flame" that people mistake it for. The fire, fuelled by natural gas, goes out from time to time, usually because of high winds. People aren't really supposed to throw change into it. The money gets gross because it's so rarely collected. Years ago, some bright light in Parliament's administration decided to have staff use the fountain's blackened, rusty change in the tills of the House of Commons cafeteria. This did not last long.

10 A brief survey on Ottawa night life, taken from my three children, who are in their twenties, found young people are unimpressed with the bar scene, mainly a tired collection of fake Brit pubs, and believe they do not get value for money. One lives in Montreal, one is single and goes there a lot, and the oldest usually just visits friends. The "night mayor" has many challenges.

11 Twenty years ago, people hustled cash at the busier corners by "washing" windows with gross water and squeegees. In his "Common Sense Revolution," Ontario premier Mike Harris outlawed "squeegee kids." Now more people are walking through traffic, but they no longer pretend to offer a service.

12 Josh Pringle, "Here's a look at Ottawa's busiest red light cameras so far in 2024," CTV News, Apr. 2, 2024.

13 This latter problem, of big old houses that used to be divided into small apartments being turned back into mansions, might seem strange to urban readers, but, according to Robin Jones—former police officer, present mayor of Westport, Ontario, and chair of the Rural Ontario Municipalities Association—it's one of the main drivers of the rural housing crisis. People can sell an ordinary house in the Toronto area for more than a million dollars, buy a lovely old Victorian in a small town, evict the tenants and renovate, and still come out ahead. The movement of retirees from cities to rural communities in southern Ontario—arguably, a type of "white flight"—has driven up house prices and generated homelessness in places where people were never seen living on the streets, even in the dire recessions of the last two decades of the twentieth century.

14 Michael Buchanan, "A tent city next to Mayfair: Why cutting homelessness might be harder than before," BBC News, Sept. 8, 2024.

15 See Government of Canada, "Housing First," at https://housing-infrastructure.canada.ca/homelessness-sans-abri/resources-ressources/housing-first-logement-abord-eng.html
16 And though these events were traumatic to many Canadian families, especially those who lost relatives fighting overseas, the experience of Canadians in the Great Depression and the Second World War was nowhere near as awful as those of Europeans and East Asians.
17 Mike Crawley, "What Ontario's rising high school grades mean for university admissions," CBC News, June 20, 2023.
18 Janet Hurley, "99.5 per cent didn't get teen into the University of Waterloo but it got him to where he was meant to be," *Toronto Star*, Dec.26, 2024. I was offered admission to the University of Western Ontario, Trent University, and Ryerson's journalism school with a 66 percent average in grade thirteen. To be fair, I went to four high schools in four years and skipped the last six weeks of my last school year to work for the Canadian Pacific Railway. Like many other historians and people with ADD, my high school transcripts is a mix of A's and D's—great marks in history, geography, and some sciences, Ds in things involving numbers. In the 1970s, a B+ average in a BA program was enough to get into a good teachers' college, grad school, and even law school, if the applicant had a decent LSAT score. Now, A- averages are typical. Law school is an exception: a B+ average is still an achievement. And since everyone who gets into law school arrives with very high undergrad grades, the C's handed out by law professors can be traumatic. One of my friends, a former solicitor general of Ontario, was in an Osgoode Hall law school class (1963) that had no gold medallist because none of the students got honours.
19 The survey is available at https://vanierinstitute.ca/families-count-2024/young-adults-are-more-likely-to-live-with-parents/#:~:text=Men%20(64.6%25)%20and%20women,%25)%20and%20Ontario%20(53.3%25).
20 At the same time, Canadian wages were rising. The federal government's attempts to control wages and prices failed, and it took several years of slow growth to end the inflationary spiral.
21 Of course, the higher cost of housing—not just in dollars but also compared to the percentage of buyers' earnings spent on mortgage payments, taxes, insurance, and maintenance—now means an interest rate jump from 2 percent to 5 percent is a big financial hit in a country where half the people live paycheque to paycheque. Rising home equity provides some comfort, but the profit isn't realized until you sell. Unless you move to a cheaper place, that "wealth" is an abstract thing, though people are tempted to borrow against it. Variable-interest-rate lines of credit secured by home equity, often offered by banks at the time a house deal closes, have caused a lot of financial damage. As well, unlike in the interest rate crisis of the 1980s and the economic collapse of the oil patch in the low-price years, distressed homeowners can't hand their keys to the bank and walk away. They're stuck with any loss from the sale of their home, and banks will nuke their credit ratings and chase them for the money.
22 See Kelly Hill, "Canada's cultural economy in 2023: A broad view," Hill Strategies, Sept. 24, 2024, https://statsinsights.hillstrategies.com/p/canadas-cultural-economy-in-2023.
23 Lisa Hagen and Jude Joffe-Block, "Why right-wing influencers are blaming the California wildfires on diversity efforts," NPR, Jan. 10, 2025; Byron Brooks, "Misrepresented and misused: How The New York Times' attack on DEI is dangerous," *Michigan Daily*, Jan. 12, 2025; Wajahat Ali and Yusuf Zakir, "In defense of DEI," *Guardian*, Jan. 9, 2025.

24 "Costco shoppers speak out after company's DEI practices fall under scrutiny," Fox News, Jan. 30, 2025.
25 Elie Cantin-Nantel, "'It's all garbage,' Poilievre denounces equity and environmental ideologies," True North, Aug. 1, 2023.
26 See Ginny Roth, " 'Based' Pierre Poilievre is here to stay," *Hub*, Jan. 13, 2025. Presumably, he also wants to interfere in the priorities of the Canada Council, the federal arts funder. The agency was supposed to depend on a permanent endowment but now relies on Parliament for about $500 million in annual funding. The agency gets a lot of criticism for, among other things, refusing to fund mainstream non-fiction authors unless they write about themselves. Otherwise, the Canada Council does not consider non-fiction to be art.
27 Hansard, Dec. 1, 2023. The right has targeted provincial and federal human rights commissions a long time: Ezra Levant led a media campaign criticizing them and wrote a book in 2009 attacking them. My wife is corporate counsel to the Canadian Human Rights Commission, on medical leave at the time of writing.
28 As a lawyer, I find it hard to believe any government legal adviser would consider the treaties, especially those signed by chiefs in Northern Ontario and Western Canada as valid contracts.
29 In 2018, Doug Ford's government shut down the Ontario French-language commissioner's office and cancelled funding for the Université de l'Ontario français. Jason Kenney's government slashed the budget of Campus St-Jean. Danielle Smith didn't bother to appoint a minister responsible for francophone affairs. Quebec's CAQ government has rolled back the education and government services rights of the minority of Quebecers who speak English. Justin Trudeau's government's silence on these issues contrasts sharply with the minority-rights and national-unity polices of his father's administration.
30 Émilie Bergeron and Michel Saba, "Liberal officials say it's 'essential' their next party leader is bilingual," Canadian Press, Jan. 11, 2025.
31 Angus Reid study https://angusreid.org/new-west-western-identity/. Canada's early prime ministers usually weren't bilingual, and long-timers like John A. Macdonald and William Lyon Mackenzie King didn't even try. Now, a unilingual francophone or anglophone hasn't got a chance. And it's not just Quebec that demands complete fluency: Stéphane Dion was a brilliant intellectual who had both a speech impediment and a tin ear for languages. He worked very hard to learn English, but his failure to master it the way Brian Mulroney and Pierre Trudeau had cost him a lot of votes in English Canada.
32 Variations of this theory have white people being overwhelmed in numbers and marginalized. Modern demographics work against Caucasians, Japanese, Chinese and other industrialized, urban people, but that's hardly due to a conspiracy. Cities have always consumed more people than they produced.
33 Ontario has never had a government that wanted to make serious changes to the way the economy works, with the United Farmers–Labour one-term government of the post-First World War era the arguable exception.
34 Martin Loney, *The Pursuit of Division: Race, Gender, and Preferential Hiring in Canada* (Montreal and Kingston: McGill–Queen's University Press, 1999), xi.
35 I got a PhD at fifty-two and a law degree at sixty, and it sucked to know that people who yammer on about lifelong learning (professors) and the value of life experience (lawyers) were and are not going to hire anyone over forty. Age discrimination is normal in Canada, and a lot of talented people don't have a chance

to be productive. This goes to the top: in Ottawa, Justin Trudeau's people made it very clear when he took office in 2015 that this was a time of generational change among political staff and in central agencies like the Prime Minister's Office. This is a common gripe among Chrétien and Martin-era staffers whose resumes were ignored. There's a strong belief among older Liberals that Trudeau and his closest advisers wanted people who were young, bright, and attractive, and that Trudeau's team's lack of experience accounts for its gaffes over the years.

36 The ageism issue will generate more anger and frustration over the coming years. So-called Gen-X and the boomers make up the bulk of white Canadian workers. Those who want/need to work will find it much more difficult to find work in a country that does not take age discrimination seriously and refuses to value the skills and experience of older workers. The survey and a fairly substantial report on ageism in Canada can be found at https://www.canada.ca/en/employment-social-development/corporate/seniors-forum-federal-provincial-territorial/consultation-ageism/discussion-guide.html#h2.4.

37 Ironically, the New Democrats have toned down their rhetoric and are hardly the democratic social movement they were when their party was founded.

38 See Re/Max blog: https://blog.remax.ca/housing-nearly-40-of-all-of-canadas-gdp/.

39 Nojoud Al Mallees, "Freeland says the two-month GST holiday is meant to tackle the 'vibecession,'" Canadian Press, Nov. 25, 2024.

40 Pierre Poilievre, Instagram, Nov. 24, 2024.

41 Hansard, Nov. 25, 2024.

42 See James Gauthier and Carter McCormack, "Housing, wealth and debt: How are young Canadians adapting to current financial and housing pressures?" Statistics Canada, Mar. 27, 2024, at www150.statcan.gc.ca/n1/pub/36-28-0001/2024003/article/00004-eng.htm.

43 I'm sure people will argue about my take on Biden. He might have won the 2024 election, but there was no way he could have served effectively until January 2029 and dealt with an emergency as bad as 9/11. He was obviously in decline in the last years of his term, and he was quickly getting worse. That doesn't exempt Americans from blame for electing a fascist.

44 See Jia Qi Xiao, "The reliance of Canadians on credit card debt as a predictor of financial stress," Staff Analytical Note 2024-18 (English), Bank of Canada, July 2024, at www.bankofcanada.ca/2024/07/staff-analytical-note-2024-18/.

45 This was happening across Canada, especially in Ontario, where people in big cities sold houses at high prices and moved to small towns where they could buy similar houses at a lower price. This drove up small-town prices, making housing unaffordable for many low-income local people who'd previously been able to afford a decent place to live. This was going on while many houses were converted to short-term rentals and large old houses broken into apartments were turned back into big single-family homes. By the early 2020s, tourist towns in Ontario struggled with a labour shortage, since the low wages they paid weren't enough to cover the increased costs of housing. Poorer people moved away from places like Collingwood.

46 David Olive, "A broken Canada? No way. We're wealthier than before the pandemic — and the future looks bright," *Toronto Star*, Aug. 10, 2024.

47 Garth Turner, GreaterFool.com, July 6, 2024.

48 Jordan Gowling, "Canada set to be fastest growing economy in G7 in 2025, IMF forecasts," *Financial Post*, July 17, 2024.

49 He was a popular guest speaker at Tory riding meetings before he started holding his own rallies.
50 It's ironic that 2019 was portrayed in the North American media's 2019–2020 New Years coverage as a year worth forgetting. Then came 2020. As for the Trump trade war and its impact, see Murray Brewster, "Trump is starting a trade war," CBC News, Feb. 1, 2025.
51 This book was finished after the first tariff threat. By the time you read this, it's likely there will have been a second one in early March. No matter the result, Canadians know Trump can't be trusted, and he fantasizes about taking Canada over. No American president has talked like this since the War of 1812.
52 See IPSOS MEDIA RELEASE_Canada Day June 24 2024.

CHAPTER 10: **THE CONVOY**

1 See: https://teamster.org/about/who-are-teamsters/.
2 See https://ca.indeed.com/career/long-haul-driver/salaries.
3 Salary figure: https://www.payscale.com/research/CA/Job=Locomotive_Engineer/Salary. All the locomotive engineers on Canada's two main railways are unionized. Some short-line railways are non-union and pay less than the big corporations. The Montreal, Maine, and Atlantic Railway, whose negligence caused the wreck of a train carrying volatile petroleum in Lac-Mégantic that killed forty-seven people in 2013, was one of these non-union short lines. Trains on that line had just one crew member. The company went bankrupt after the disaster. It had formerly been CP Rail's link from Montreal to Portland, Maine.
4 See https://www.youtube.com/watch?v=wx0BBnuZmqs.
5 See DHS to Require Non-U.S. Individual Travelers Entering the United States at Land Ports of Entry and Ferry Terminals to be Fully Vaccinated Against COVID-19 at https://www.dhs.gov/news/2022/01/20/dhs-require-non-us-individual-travelers-entering-united-states-land-ports-entry-and. This rule lasted until May 12, 2023, when the Biden administration declared an end to the public health emergency. See DHS Statement on the Lifting of Title 19 Requirements at https://www.dhs.gov/news/2023/05/01/dhs-statement-lifting-title-19-requirements.
6 David Fraser, "Almost $8M of 'Freedom Convoy' donations still unaccounted for, documents show," CBC News, Apr. 7, 2022.
7 Grant LaFleche and Alex McKeen, "Why Pierre Poilievre has been embraced by Bitcoin believers—including one who's raising funds for the 'Freedom Convoy,'" *Toronto Star*, Feb. 10, 2022.
8 Tonda MacCharles, "Feuding politicians. Candid texts. A stunning inquiry. The behind-the-scenes story of how the 'Freedom Convoy' shook the foundations of Canadian politics," *Toronto Star*, Dec. 3, 2023. Unlike the major convoy organizers from Western Canada, Belton was not criminally charged. She ran for the Ontario Party in her home riding in the 2022 provincial election, winning 2.49 per cent of the vote.
9 Vaccinations weren't required for truckers if they stayed in Canada, so presumably the unvaccinated members of the CTA didn't cross the border.
10 *Canadian Security Intelligence Service (CSIS) and Integrated Terrorism Assessment Centre (ITAC) Institutional Report Prepared for the Public Order Emergency*, undated), 91–100.

11 In the end, Trump pardoned all the January 6 rioters, so after all the pre-trial "dead time" and the time served on prison sentences, the leaders of the Trump rioters spent more days behind bars. In the end, though, Trump's pardon erased their criminal records, while the convoy leaders' records will, at most, be stored separately from active records and kept from routine police and public access if the National Parole Board approves their applications for record suspensions, the most common type of clemency. A Canadian criminal record can still be dug out and used against someone who reoffends and may show up in databases used by foreign border agents. That keeps a lot of Canadians with old marijuana records from going to Florida without going through the process of applying to the Americans for a waiver.
12 Christopher Reynolds, "GoFundMe withholding $4.7 million from trucker convoy until plan presented," *Toronto Star*, Jan. 25, 2002.
13 Police made a deal with them to move to Victoria Island in the Ottawa River, where a few protesters held on for a few months. The protesters had to be moved because the Hill was about to be spruced up for a visit by the queen. In my experience in twenty-four years of working on the Hill, the best way to have all the construction scaffolds come down from the various holes was to schedule a visit by the queen or an American president. Time will tell whether a royal visit by Charles III would inspire a hop-to-it attitude among the people who dig holes and fill them in.
14 Quebec's right-wing government had some of the most extreme Covid rules in Canada while allowing epic fails to its regulatory system, such as the abandonment of the nursing home on the West Island of Montreal.
15 Jordan Peterson podcast, Spotify, May 16, 2022.
16 *Canadian Security Intelligence Service (CSIS) and Integrated Terrorism Assessment Centre (ITAC) Institutional Report Prepared for the Public Order Emergency Commission*, undated, 9–10.
17 Jordon Peterson podcast, Spotify, May 16, 2022.
18 King apologized during his sentencing hearing on mischief charges. The Crown prosecutor was asking for a ten-year sentence, though the judge immediately pushed back, saying this was too high. He reserved judgment. This book went to press before the judge in the case sentenced King. See David Fraser, "Pat King apologizes for role in Freedom Convoy, faces sentencing next month," CBC News, Jan. 17, 2025.
19 Aaron Wherry, "As the pandemic rages on, the political debate moves to the supermarket aisle," Radio-Canada International, Jan. 25, 2022.
20 John Paul Tasker, "Conservative MPs accuse Trudeau of pushing 'vaccine vendetta' as convoy protest heads to Ottawa," CBC News, Jan. 24, 2022.
21 The reader should try to imagine how such a meeting would have gone.
22 Aaron Wherry, "Conservatives hitch their wagons to the convoy protest without knowing where it's going," CBC News, Feb. 1, 2022.
23 Turns out it's easy to come up with that kind of stuff. I should have skipped grad school and gone into politics.
24 Carol Off, *At A Loss for Words* (Toronto: Radom House, 2024), 24. See also https://www.cbc.ca/player/play/video/1.6638673.
25 Google it. Life is too short.
26 Aaron Wherry, "Conservatives hitch their wagons to the convoy protest without knowing where it's going," CBC News, Feb. 1, 2022.
27 Hansard, Jan. 31, 2022.
28 Gary Mason, "How truck convoy supporters like Pierre Poilievre have weaponized 'freedom,'" *Globe and Mail*, Feb. 8, 2024.

29 Fiona MacDonald, "The 'freedom convoy' protesters are a textbook case of 'aggrieved entitlement,'" *Conversation*, Feb. 16, 2022.
30 This raises the question of whether Poilievre had let them know he was going to pull a coup on O'Toole. It takes several days, at least, to design and print a flag. Poilievre had considered running in the previous leadership campaign. The flags mighty have been printed at that time.
31 Aaron Wherry, "The 'Great Reset' reads like a globalist plot with some plot holes," CBC News, Nov. 27, 2020. The 2021 World Economic Forum was supposed to have the Great Reset as the theme of its annual conference, using the term to define a program that would fine-tune the liberal capitalist order to be more inclusive and sustainable. The meeting was postponed, and the next session had another topic.
32 Peter Zimonjic, "Cracks appear in Conservative caucus over anti-vaccine mandate protest," CBC News, Feb. 4, 2022.
33 Michael Harris, "Poilievre's Big Bet on Convoy-Loving Politics," *Tyee*, Apr. 5, 2023.
34 Aaron Wherry, "Conservatives hitch their wagons to the convoy protest without knowing where it's going," CBC News, Feb. 1, 2022.
35 Steve Burgess, "Pierre Poilievre's Drive to Power," *Tyee*, Feb. 4, 2022.
36 Gary Mason, "How truck convoy supporters like Pierre Poilievre have weaponized 'freedom,'" *Globe and Mail*, Feb. 8, 2024.
37 See https://www.youtube.com/watch?v=wo43dteBaAE.
38 Michael Harris, "Poilievre's Big Bet on Convoy-Loving Politics," *Tyee*, Apr. 5, 2023.
39 Freddie Clayton, "Elon Musk's call for Germany to 'move beyond' Nazi guilt is dangerous, Holocaust memorial chair says," NBC News, Jan. 26, 2025.
40 Sock puppets are accounts under fake names. Someone working in a disinformation operation can set up hundreds, even thousands, of fake accounts to make it look like a fringe idea has a lot of support.
41 Catherine Lévesque, "'I'm proud of the truckers,' says Poilievre in lambasting Justin Trudeau's response to protests," *National Post*, Feb. 11, 2022.
42 Senior government and military sources told me some people in cabinet wanted to use troops, but the generals had the good sense to dissuade them.
43 Ahmar Khan, "Watson's backdoor dealing with 'freedom convoy' is harmful, say some Ottawa residents," Global News, Feb. 25, 2022.
44 Julia Shapero, "Trudeau defends use of emergency powers to end trucker protest," *Hill*, Nov. 25, 2022.
45 Interestingly, the Ottawa media pack had loudly advocated for the use of the *Emergencies Act* early in the pandemic, a fact conveniently forgotten when a sizeable part of the public turned on Trudeau for using it against the "truckers."
46 Police earlier said local tow-truck owners had refused to help them because they were afraid of losing business and/or getting into fights with rig owners. Some in the military pointed out that the Canadian Forces had trucks in the city that were powerful enough to move tanks, but it was clear that the Trudeau government did not want any soldiers involved.
47 Christian Paas-Lang, "Party lines drawn ahead of key *Emergencies Act* vote on Monday," CBC News, Feb. 20, 2022.
48 Pierre Poilievre Facebook page, Feb. 22, 2022.
49 Including members of my family.
50 The Freedom Convoy and Federal Politics, Leger poll, Feb. 8, 2022, https://leger360.com/legers-north-american-tracker-february-8-2022/.
51 It will be interesting to see if governments continue to give free electricity to green

vehicles. If they do, the truckers' interest and limited enthusiasm for electric trucks is understandable, since they stand to save a fortune on fuel. Diesel, which used to be relatively cheap, cost more per litre than gasoline through most of the summer of 2024.

CHAPTER 11: **TOP DOG**

1 Tasha Kheiriddin, "I discovered firsthand the power of Poilievre. Liberals should be afraid," *National Post*, Sept. 12, 2022.
2 It was, in a way, revenge for the 2019 election, when the Tories paid to smear the People's Party and its leader, Maxime Bernier. I represented Bernier in the resulting lawsuit, believing politicians of all ideologies should be able to make their cases to the people in a political environment that's as clean as possible.
3 Mainstream Canadian Christian churches, including the United Church, the country's largest denomination, oppose conversion therapy. See "We oppose conversion therapy" at https://united-church.ca/social-action/justice-initiatives/conversion-therapy. Conversion therapy was debated as a medical issue, and thus under provincial jurisdiction, until the Trudeau government amended the Criminal Code to ban it. Despite this law, it's still happening. See Geoff McMaster, "Conversion practices continuing despite federal ban," *Folio*, Mar. 14, 2024, at https://www.ualberta.ca/en/folio/2024/03/conversion-practices-continuing-despite-federal-ban.html.
4 Dan Bilefsky and Ian Austen, "Canada's Conservative Leader Is Ousted," *New York Times*, Feb. 2, 2022.
5 Dan Bilefsky and Ian Austen, "Canada's Conservative Leader Is Ousted," *New York Times*, Feb. 2, 2022.
6 Rachel Aiello, "'Obvious attempt to create chaos,' Charest campaign says of fake donation pledges," CTV News, Mar. 31, 2022.
7 Alex Boutilier, "Conservatives ban pre-paid credit cards after Poilievre camp warns of membership 'fraud,'" Global News, Apr. 14, 2022.
8 Stephanie Levitz, "Pierre Poilievre's campaign paid legal bills of whistleblower who took down rival Patrick Brown," *Toronto Star*, July 20, 2023.
9 Kate McKenna, "Top Poilievre adviser targets former CPC leader for wishing departing Liberal well," CBC News, Jan. 13, 2025.
10 Peter Zimonjic, "Pierre Poilievre and the anti-elite populism that won the day," CBC News, Sept. 9, 2022.
11 His post-2022 YouTube and social media strategy are discussed in a later chapter.
12 Ian Campbell, "Poilievre's YouTube channel a way to talk directly to voters, but the platform may build 'deeper popularity in a smaller group," *Hill Times*, May 19, 2022.
13 Naizhuo Zhao, Ying Liu, Audrey Smargiassi, and Sasha Bernatsky, "Tracking the origin of early COVID-19 cases in Canada," *International Journal of Infectious Diseases* 96 (July 2020), 506–08.
14 Geoff Dembicki, "How Poilievre Is Reinventing Right-Wing Politicking," *Tyee*, Mar. 21, 2022.
15 I was blocked from Poilievre's Facebook page sometime in 2024 or early 2025, when word got around Ottawa that I was writing this book.
16 Under its old ownership, I did a very small amount of legal advising to the Post Millennial on an issue that does not relate to the content of this book.
17 A few might have been supporters of Maxime Bernier's People's Party of Canada, who were no friends of the Tories, especially after the 2019 federal election

campaign, when word leaked out that the Tories were paying a former Liberal operative to portray Bernier as a racist.

18 Alex Boutilier, "Pierre Poilievre's YouTube channel included hidden misogynistic tag to promote videos," Global News, Oct. 6, 2022.

19 Peterson had more than two million Twitter followers in early 2022. Now he has more than five million. The *Globe and Mail*, in the fall of 2024, had two million. Justin Trudeau had 6.5 million in late 2024. They were all weak beer compared to Talyor Swift's 94 million followers. (Don't expect her to follow you back. She doesn't follow anyone.) Elon Musk claimed to have more than 230 million in early 2025, which is patently absurd.

20 Geoff Dembicki, "How Poilievre Is Reinventing Right-Wing Politicking," *Tyee*, Mar. 22, 2022.

21 John Paul Tasker, "Charest has the edge in Ontario over Conservative leadership rival Poilievre, poll suggests," CBC News, Mar. 22, 2022.

22 Less than a month after the Tory leadership results were announced, Legault won another solid majority. Polls taken in late 2024 and early 2025 showed his government was in trouble. After Trump threatened to annex Canada by crippling our economy with tariffs, Legault's nationalist rhetoric was turned against the Americans.

23 Charest was born and raised in the Eastern Townships of Quebec, which has morphed from an English enclave with a sizeable French minority to a region dominated by French speakers. It would have been difficult to function in that region in the twentieth century without being bilingual. Now, people who can't speak English would have no problem living there.

24 Jenni Byrne, Twitter, Feb. 22, 2022.

25 Catherine Lévesque, "Poilievre vs. Charest—a Conservative leadership race where sparks could fly," *National Post*, Feb. 26, 2022.

26 Catherine Lévesque, "Poilievre vs. Charest—a Conservative leadership race where sparks could fly," *National Post*, Feb. 26, 2022.

27 Charest sued the Quebec government in 2020 for leaking the allegations. Charest was never charged, and it appears the lawsuit went nowhere. See "Former Quebec premier Jean Charest files lawsuit against province over corruption allegations," CBC News, Oct. 9, 2020.

28 The supposed scandal was based on CTV journalism when Brown seemed on the verge of becoming premier of Ontario in the winter of 2018. Brown was forced out of the party leadership. It was easily won by Doug Ford, who swept to power a few weeks later. Brown sued CTV and the journalists who reported the story. Just before entering the 2022 federal Conservative leadership race, CTV and Brown settled. No money changed hands, but CTV added a disclaimer to the web version of the stories, saying key details "were factually incorrect and required correction."

29 Don Martin, "The personal antipathy between Charest and Poilievre is damaging the Conservatives beyond repair," CTV News.ca, Apr. 12, 2022.

30 In fact, most donations to the convoy came from the United States, and a lot of them were also Trump donors. See Elizabeth Thompson, Roberto Rocha, and Albert Leung, "Hacked convoy data shows more than half of donations came from the U.S.," CBC News, Feb. 14, 2022.

31 Elizabeth Thompson and Christian Paas-Lang, "Convoy donors gave more than $460K to CPC leadership race—and many were first-time federal donors," CBC News, Sept. 16, 2022.

32 Catherine Cullen, "Big crowds turning out for Poilievre suggest a very different kind of Conservative leadership race," CBC News, Apr. 12, 2022.
33 Rick Bell, "Poilievre and Charest, the battle for Canadian conservatism rages," *Calgary Sun*, May 13, 2012.
34 "Jail not bail" slogans didn't apply to the people charged for committing mischief in downtown Ottawa.
35 Poilievre made air quotes with his fingers when he said *disqualified*.
36 Brown was mayor of Brampton, a southern Ontario city with hundreds of thousands of Muslim, Hindu and Sikh voters. The "hotline" had not gone over well in his town.
37 Catherine Cullen, "Big crowds turning out for Poilievre suggest a very different kind of Conservative leadership race," CBC News, Apr. 12, 2022.
38 I talk about this in my biography of twentieth-century newspaper mogul George McCullagh, *Big Men Fear Me* (Windsor, ON: Biblioasis, 2022).

CHAPTER 12: **TROLLING (FOR) THE WORKING CLASS**

1 It's amazing how little political and media effort has gone into understanding and explaining Canada's doctor shortage. There are several causes. In the 1990s, provincial premiers cut the number of medical school spaces in this country to deliberately reduce the number of physicians who can bill provincial medicare programs. Like some other professions, including law, medicine requires a period of on-the-job practical training. There are not enough of these positions. As well, doctors from many countries have a hard time having their credentials recognized in Canada. And, to make matters worse, the United States is happy to snap up Canadian medical professionals who want to work under their private system. Despite what candidates at various levels of government claim, fixing this will be very difficult and expensive.
2 Based on listings at local real estate website Houseful.ca in the summer of 2024.
3 Rental figures came from Sault Ste. Marie ON Houses for Rent at rentals.ca in the summer of 2024.
4 The collective agreement can be found at ASI 2251 Collective Agreement 2022 - Final.pdf (cdn-website.com).
5 John Ivison, "Irate Algoma Steel worker points to PM's predicament," *Sault Star*, Sept. 3, 2024.
6 Northwestern Ontario is an interesting case study for students of the Canadian housing bubble. In 2010, when the region was in recession because of lumber and pulp-mill layoffs and permanent job cuts on the CP Rail main line through the region, it was possible to buy a house in any of the towns on Highway 17, the southern Trans-Canada route, between the Soo and Thunder Bay—Wawa, White River, Marathon, Terrace Bay, Schreiber, Nipigon and Red Rock—for $25,000 or less. Real estate listings showed many houses with trucks parked in the driveway that were worth much more than the asking price of the house. In January 2025, two years after the Terrace Bay mill closed, sellers wanted $150,000 or more for the "wartime" houses built by the mill company in the 1940s that could be picked up fifteen years ago for $25,000.
7 Mining's fortunes ebb and flow with commodity prices. Marathon remains a regional centre because it is near major gold fields, though the big Hemlo deposit, the first one in the area to be exploited, appears to be exhausted. The Ring of Fire, several hundred miles northwest of Sault Ste Marie, has potential but, as of the

8   Kenneth Armstrong, "UPDATED: Local steelworker who wouldn't shake PM's hand says it wasn't 'for attention,'" SooToday.com, Oct. 7, 2024. In light of Trump's trade policies, it's ironic that Trudeau credited his tariffs on Chinese steel with saving the Algoma mill.
9   Dharshini David, "What impact has Brexit had on the UK economy?" BBC News, Jan. 31, 2023.
10 People can argue whether Trump's tariffs will "reindustrialize" the United States, but, until that happens, the auto industry in the Midwest relies on a free flow of parts between Canada and the US. When Trump started threatening a tariff on all Canadian products in early 2025, Michigan governor Gretchen Whitmer went on the talk show circuit to campaign against them. Whitmer has a good shot at winning the Democratic Party's presidential nomination in 2028.
11 Shannon Proudfoot, "The class tourist who didn't read the guidebook," *Globe and Mail*, Aug. 11, 2023.
12 China was a signatory to the original GATT in 1947. When the Communists took power, they ignored the treaty rather than refute it. In 1986, they began the process of adopting the terms of the treaty. That process still hasn't finished. Canada's Liberal Party opposed free trade in 1988, claiming it would gut Canadian manufacturing. When Jean Chrétien's government took power in 1993, it reversed its position and signed as many free-trade deals as it could. Stephen Harper did the same thing, including making a deal with China that has some secret terms.
13 Most lottery winners say they want the same lives but with nicer stuff. It's interesting how lottery ads talk about a life of adventure in exotic places, while so many winners say they just want to pay off their mortgage and give money to their kids.
14 For 2023's Small Business Week, the Tories put out a press release quoting Poilievre saying, "Small businesses employ nearly half of all private sector workers and make incredible contributions to our country from coast to coast to coast. The neighbourhood diner where families gather on Saturday morning. The construction company that sponsors the local hockey team. The innovative startup that brings powerful paycheques for hard-working young people. These are not 'just' businesses, but part of the fabric of our communities." See: https://www.conservative.ca/statement-from-conservative-leader-pierre-poilievre-on-small-business-week-3/.
15 Stephanie Taylor, "Labour leader urges unions to expose Poilievre's working-class overtures as 'fraud,'" Canadian Press, Apr. 18, 2024.
16 "Conservatives maintain silence as strife continues between union, railways," CBC News, Aug. 23, 2024.
17 Look at the shift in voting patterns in Windsor, Hamilton, and Oshawa since 1988, where the NDP has either been ousted or hangs on by a thread. Compare them to the core of Ottawa, where many voters belong to public sector unions. In the latter case, the unions can affect the outcome, as we've seen in Poilievre's near-death election of 2015. Public service workers tend to vote for people who don't promise to cut their jobs, 1993 and 1997 being notable exceptions.
18 Paul Wells, "Towards a working-class conservatism," Substack, July 19, 2024.
19 Pierre Poilievre YouTube video "8 years of Trudeau and the bill is coming due," at https://www.youtube.com/watch?v=xZqHMW2zbBY.
20 Ashley Burke, Kate McKenna, and Andrew Ryan, "Pierre Poilievre called lobbyists 'utterly useless,' but they're still attending his fundraisers," CBC News, May 7, 2024.

21 Pierre Poilievre, "Pierre Poilievre: Memo to corporate Canada—fire your lobbyist. Ignore politicians. Go to the people," *National Post*, May 3, 2024.
22 Paul Wells, "Towards a working-class conservatism: What do you get when you cross JD Vance with Pierre Poilievre?" Substack, July 19, 2024.
23 Oren Cass, "This is What Elite Failure Looks Like," *New York Times*, July 6, 2024.
24 "Nearly 1 in 3 young men in the US report having no sex, study finds," University of Indiana press release, June 15, 2020, https://news.iu.edu/live/news/26924-nearly-1-in-3-young-men-in-the-us-report-having-no.
25 See https://www150.statcan.gc.ca/n1/pub/36-28-0001/2021009/article/00004-eng.htm.
26 See https://pmc.ncbi.nlm.nih.gov/articles/PMC395806/#:~:text=The%20most%20recent%20Canadian%20medical,medical%20schools%20no%20longer%20exists.
27 This number seems high but is fairly close to the racial makeup of Torontonians of that age.
28 See https://torontofoundation.ca/wp-content/uploads/2024/08/TF-Perspectives-OnLifeInTheCity-Brief2024-Final-FINAL-ua.pdf.
29 Darren Major, "Conservative leader wants Canada to match U.S. tariffs on Chinese electric vehicles," CBC News, Aug. 9, 2024.
30 Campbell Clark, "When Liberals talk about Poilievre, Trudeau drowns out the sound," *Globe and Mail*, July 8, 2024.
31 Tasha Kheiriddin, "Pierre Poilievre is plundering Jagmeet Singh's labour vote base," *National Post*, Sept. 3, 2024.

CHAPTER 13: **THE MEDIA AND THE MESSAGE**

1 Center for International Relations and Sustained Development, "Oil Shock—Decoding the Causes and Consequences of the 2014 Oil Price Drop," *Horizons* no. 3 (Spring 2015), https://www.cirsd.org/en/horizons/horizons-spring-2015-issue-no3/oil-shock-%E2%80%94-decoding-the-causes-and-consequences-of-the-2014-oil-price-drop
2 Max Fawcett, "Pierre Poilievre's problem with the truth," National Observer, Dec. 4, 2024.
3 Brian Lewis, "Why Canada's Economy is Just Fine," *Maclean's*, Oct. 31, 2024.
4 Raisa Patel, "Pierre Poilievre claims 40 offenders were arrested 6,000 times in Vancouver in a year. Is that actually true?" *Toronto Star*, Feb. 11, 2024.
5 Raisa Patel, "Pierre Poilievre claims 40 offenders were arrested 6,000 times in Vancouver in a year. Is that actually true?" *Toronto Star*, Feb. 11, 2024.
6 Cormac MacSweeney and John Marchesan, "'Nonsense fearmongering:' Health minister slams Poilievre for 'lies' on pharmacare bill," CityNews, Apr. 18, 2024.
7 Cormac MacSweeney and John Marchesan, "'Nonsense fearmongering:' Health minister slams Poilievre for 'lies' on pharmacare bill," CityNews, Apr. 18, 2024.
8 Pierre Poilievre "Here's How Wackonomics Works, Or Doesn't," YouTube, www.youtube.com/watch?v=pkf80AJE8Gw.
9 Jordan Gowling, "Canada set to be fastest growing economy in G7 in 2025, IMF forecasts," *Financial Post*, July 17, 2024.
10 Vimal Sivakumar, "Canada has G7's 2nd highest projected real GDP growth in 2023 and 2024," cicnews.com, Apr. 25, 2023.
11 Brian Lewis, "Why Canada's Economy is Just Fine," *Maclean's*, Oct. 31, 2024.
12 Pierre Poilievre YouTube video, "Trudeau's Radical Experiment," https://www.youtube.com/watch?v=karFUOaL9mU. "More than 1,700 lives lost to drug

toxicity in first nine months of 2024," British Columbia Public Safety and Solicitor General press release, October 24, 2024, https://news.gov.bc.ca/releases/2024-PSSG0087-001567.
13. You can find the perfect hunting rifle on the Londero Sports website, for example. See also Eric Beer, "What Guns Are Legal in Canada (2023/2024): A Beginner's Guide," https://bcfirearmsacademy.ca.
14. For a good analysis of this problem, see Susan Riley, "Hey, Liberals! Why be shy? Isn't it time to refute the disinformation?" *Hill Times*, July 3, 2024.
15. Unavailable at fine stores everywhere. You can probably find it in a city library or get it on special order from an independent bookstore.
16. Freeland and Trudeau did this on November 21, 2024, in Newmarket, Ontario, when they announced a temporary moratorium on the collection of GST on some items and $250 cheques to low- and medium-income Canadians.
17. The French papers in Montreal still have staff in the press gallery. The *Winnipeg Free Press* was the last paper to close its bureau. A century ago, *Free Press* reporters were among the most important in Canada. John Dafoe and Grant Dexter were the eyes and ears of Western Canada, listened to as much by government leaders as by their readers. Big papers sent people to Ottawa year round. Smaller ones kept a reporter in Ottawa only when the House of Commons was in session. Until the 1930s, legislatures and parliament sat far less frequently.
18. Austin Yack, "Eighty Percent of Media Coverage on Trump is Negative," National Review, May 22, 2017.
19. Brian Lilley, "'Justin Journos' display little interest in carbon tax hike," *Toronto Sun*, Dec. 15, 2020.
20. Dan Kennedy, "For Five Years, Trump Outrage Has Fueled Media Profits. So Now What?" GBH News, Boston Public Radio, Jan. 27, 2021.
21. *New York Times*, Jan. 6, 2025.
22. Andrew Lawton, *Pierre Poilievre: A Political Life* (Toronto: Sutherland House, 2024)
23. The company, owned by a trust controlled by descendants of 1950s *Star* executives, was bleeding money. Its 2020 buyers probably made a profit after stripping the company's assets, but the paper's quality has noticeably suffered. It no longer dominates coverage in its own city. The *Star* is probably worthless and unsellable now.
24. This came with conditions, including the right of any other media in the country to use the work of these reporters without payment.
25. The deduction for political party donations starts at 75 percent for a small donation, which is why so many people write small cheques to the parties, especially when there's an issue that angers them. This is a much better percentage than taxpayers get from a donation to, say, cancer research or a children's hospital. Some opponents of media bailouts have suggested giving news media subscribers a 100 percent deduction. This would allow the public to determine which outlets get public money, rather than having the government or government-created organizations decide.
26. Richard Harley, "A local Niagara-on-the-Lake newspaper turned Pierre Poilievre's visit into a national conversation about the state of journalism in Canada," *Lake Report*, Aug. 14, 2024, republished at J-source.ca, Aug. 20, 2024, https://j-source.ca/a-local-niagara-on-the-lake-newspaper-turned-pierre-poilievres-visit-into-a-national-conversation-about-the-state-of-journalism-in-canada/.
27. Tim Naumetz, "Harper tactics powerful but disturbing," *Ottawa Citizen*, Mar. 12, 2007.

28 I hope all of Dale's immigration paperwork holds up to Trump administration scrutiny.
29 After the 2010s debacle of the Sun News Network, which had few viewers and almost no advertisers and chafed over CRTC oversight, conservatives gave up on cable news in Canada and migrated to the internet. The Fox News Network, carried on Canadian cable, is not a major player in Canada, partly because so many people have cancelled their cable subscriptions. Fox fans most likely watch its clips on YouTube.
30 My wife is corporate counsel to the Canadian Human Rights Commission. She joined the commission near the end of Levant's and other conservatives' fight over Section 13 of the *Canadian Human Rights Act*, which allowed people to complain about alleged racist speech, even if they were not targets of that expression, and collect damages. These complaints were heard by the Canadian Human Rights Tribunal, which is, administratively, separate from the commission. People who believed they were targeted by journalists because they were members of a category of people protected by human rights laws could complain to provincial tribunals. Mark Steyn and *Maclean's* magazine faced a long hearing in British Columbia over pieces Steyn wrote about Muslims. Levant wrote his book after being interviewed by an Alberta Human Rights Commission investigator over a complaint about Levant's decision to publish cartoons parodying Muslim prophet Mohammed. These cartoons are alleged to have resulted in a lethal attack on the French magazine *Charlie Hebdo*.
31 In 2010, about 10 percent of the oil imported into this country came from the US. Algeria was the largest single source of imports. Now the US accounts for about 72.5 percent of our imports., which were almost cut in half between 2010 and 2022. OPEC members Saudi Arabia and Nigeria each provide about 10 to 13 percent of our imports, all to eastern Canada. Imports from other OPEC countries are now negligible.
32 Ezra Levant X post, Sept. 29, 2023.
33 Adam Daifallah and Tasha Kheiriddin, *Rescuing Canada's Right: Blueprint for a Conservative Revolution* (Toronto: Wiley, 2005), 93–93.
34 Colby Cosh, "Don't call them 'tar sands.' The industry-approved lingo for Alberta's hydrocarbon gunk is 'oil sands,'" *Maclean's*, Apr. 3, 2012.
35 Raisa Patel, "How Pierre Poilievre successfully weaponized the word 'woke,'" *Toronto Star*, Jan. 25, 2025.
36 The Australian Liberals, who have shared a lot of their strategies with Canada's Conservative party, were also running against a carbon tax. As for the UK and French use of "woke" and how Poilievre's messaging fits into the new discourse, see Patrick McCurdy, Kaitlin Clarke, and Bart Cammaerts, "From Social Awareness to Authoritarian Other: The Conservative Weaponization of Woke in Canadian Parliamentary Discourse," *Journal of Language and Politics* open source at chrome-extension://efaidnbmnnnibpcajpcglclefindmkaj/https://ruor.uottawa.ca/server/api/core/bitstreams/f583acaa-674d-482d-91e8-68399fe91915/content.
37 Glen McGregor, "Poilievre faces backlash for comments on Jordan Peterson podcast," CTV News, May 22, 2022.
38 Frank Graves and Stephen Maher, "Pierre Poilievre: The Secret to His Success," *Walrus*, Dec. 14, 2022.
39 Adam Daifallah and Tasha Kheiriddin, *Rescuing Canada's Right: Blueprint for a Conservative Revolution* (Toronto: Wiley, 2005), 92–93.

40   Sean Speer, "A Trump victory means mainstream media is dead in its current form," *Hub*, Nov. 9, 2024.
41   "CBC English TV has lost its relevance. It's time to talk about that," editorial, *Globe and Mail*, May 20, 2023.
42   I can't.
43   See https://cbc.radio-canada.ca/en/impact-and-accountability/finance/annual-reports/ar-2021-2022/measuring-our-performance/performance-media-lines-cbc-highlights.
44   Carleton University convocation, June 21, 2024. Mr Graves gave me a copy of his speech.
45   "MP Pierre Poilievre Greets Chinese Tourism Officials in Ottawa," Marketwire, Aug. 23, 2010.
46   The two-volume report is available as a free PDF download at https://foreigninterferencecommission.ca/reports/final-report.
47   Martin Laine and Anastasiia Morozova, "Leaked Files from Putin's Troll Factory: How Russia Manipulated European Elections," *vsquare*, , Sept. 16, 2024.
48   Geoff Dembicki, "How Poilievre is Changing Right-Wing Politics," *Tyee*, March 21, 2022.
49   While Poilievre has a very respectable YouTube presence and is far ahead of competitors outside and inside his party, he's still not an A-list YouTuber, even in Canada. Neither Poilievre nor Trudeau come close to Canadian comedian Julie Nolke, who has more than a million subscribers. Nolke did a funny video with Trudeau in 2024 that got 160,000 views. Montreal movie critic Ryan George's "Pitch Meetings" video, which make fun of movie plot holes and bad film ideas, has 1.3 million subscribers. American YouTuber MrBeast (a.k.a Jimmy Donaldson), who makes slick videos of bizarre games, had 330 million subscribers in November 2024.
50   Irish Mae Silvestre, "Poilievre's Canadian dream ad deleted after visuals revealed to be non-Canadian," *Daily Hive*, Aug. 19, 2024. See also "Conservatives delete Pierre Poilievre video," Canadian Press, Aug. 19, 2024, and Rachel Looker, "Trump falsely implies Taylor Swift endorses him," BBC News, Aug. 19, 2024. This wasn't the first time the Tories had used foreign stock footage to make a point in Canada. In January 2022, newly elected Tory MP Melissa Lantsman, who went on to become a key Poilievre team member, posted images of empty store shelves in Britain and claimed the photos were from Canadian supermarkets. See Luke LeBrun, "Conservative MP's Photo of 'Empty Canadian Grocery Store' Actually Taken in Northern England, Not Canada," PressProgress, Jan. 24, 2022.
51   The only CBC television show set in Alberta was about people living on a ranch. It turned out to be one of the CBC's most popular shows. Its lead actress is from Ontario. In the 1960s and 1970s, the CBC broadcast two shows set in Northern Ontario, one in a ranger fort (such a thing never existed) and another in a lodge. Most people living in that part of the country live in one-industry resource towns, a setting that, on its own, doesn't make interesting television. *Little Mosque on the Prairie*, set in Saskatchewan, was filmed in Toronto, with some establishing shots from a real Saskatchewan village. CBC Radio One is, except for local morning and afternoon drive shows and a few highbrow shows like *Ideas*, somewhat Toronto-centric. There's a bizarre emphasis on American pop culture in its daytime morning broadcasts. These are my own gripes. I doubt most CBC haters have tuned into its TV or radio networks often enough to have detailed complaints.
52   See *This Hour Has 22 Minutes*' parody "Wackos: A Pierre Poilievre Production!" at www.youtube.com/watch?v=hAioPoEfkjQ. Other *This Hour Has 22 Minutes*

ENDNOTES 421

parodies of Poilievre can be found at www.youtube.com/results?search_query=Polievre+and+This+Hour+Has+22+Minutes. The "wacko" label came from the US presidential campaign, when Democratic Party vice-presidential candidate Tim Walz used it to describe Donald Trump and his supporters.

53 See "This Hour Has 22 Minutes" on YouTube at https://www.youtube.com/watch?-v=wrH3xzvwM3E&t=78s

54 Betsy Klein and Lex Harvey, "Trump suggests his plan for Gaza Strip is to 'clean out the whole thing,'" CNN, Jan. 26, 2025.

CHAPTER 14: **ON SHIFTING GROUND**

1 Since then, there's been an increase in the carbon levy, but in 2024 the Trudeau government raised the personal exemption for income tax and cut the tax rate in the second-lowest tax bracket. The government claimed twenty million middle-class Canadians saved, on average, more than $450 in 2024. Taxes on people with high incomes were increased.

2 Bitcoin, the main crypto currency, later went back to the region of $100,000. Still, a country needs a stable currency, not one that wildly swings in value and has no government backing. In effect, crypto is barter, and it invites criminality.

3 John Paul Tasker, "In a pitch to cryptocurrency investors, Poilievre says he wants Canada to be 'blockchain capital of the world,'" CBC News, Mar, 28, 2022.

4 Poilievre had opposed the Canadian Emergency Response Benefit and other Covid economic stimulus, calling the government's programs "freakonomics." See Kerri Breen, "Conservative finance critic says coronavirus programs amount to 'freakonomics,'" Global News, Apr. 26, 2020.; Alexandra Mae Jones, "Here's what Trudeau and Poilievre had to say about each other in speeches to caucus," CTV News, Sept. 13, 2022. The bracketed material came from the 2024 federal budget, available at https://www.budget.canada.ca/2024/report-rapport/chap8-en.html. See Sec. 8.1.

5 "Text message campaign targets Quebec MP Alain Rayes, who left Conservative party," Globe and Mail, Sept. 14, 2022.

6 In 2014, Australia was the first country in the world to repeal a carbon tax. Middle- and low-income Australians got half of all the revenue back as tax rebates, but they still voted for Abbott. See Carly Penrose, "Axe the Tax: Here's what happened after Australia killed its carbon pricing regime," Investigative Journalism Foundation, May 11, 2024.

7 Crime is one of those policy areas where politicians, academics, and cops cherry-pick figures to fit their biases. There are definitely changes in crime numbers. Obviously, marijuana-related arrests have pretty much ended since legalization, but various police forces deal with opioid possession and public drug use in different ways. There are more difficult things to measure. Some police forces have stopped investigating thefts of relatively inexpensive items like bikes. They'll record complaints that cars were broken into but won't do anything to find who did it. Serious crime does get investigated. As well, the aging of the population dampens down the crime rate, as young men are the most likely to commit crimes. All police forces take homicide seriously. Canada's homicide rate jumped from 1.5 murders per 100,000 in 2014 to 2.3 in 2022: a 53.4 percent increase. The homicide rate in the US was much higher, at 5.8 per 100,000 people in 2022. It increased 49.4 percent from 2014 to 2022. An examination of national statistics suggests 2022 was an unusual year, with big jumps in the number of murders in Vancouver, Calgary,

Winnipeg, Toronto, and Montreal. The numbers settled back to normal in the following two years.
8   But it helps. Meth lab explosions are common in rural America.
9   In a 2024 video, Poilievre said fees to governments made up a third of the cost to build a house. Fees vary from province to province and in different cities. Canada Mortgage and Housing Corporation says fees are about 20 percent, at the most. That's still a lot of money. See "Government Charges on Residential Development in Canada," Canada Mortgage and Housing Corporation, July 5, 2022, at www.cmhc-schl.gc.ca/blog/2022/government-charges-residential-development.
10 Christian Noël, "Conservative MPs frustrated after Poilievre bars them from promoting housing fund: sources," CBC News, Nov. 14, 2024.
11 Pierre Poilievre "More expensive than castle in France?" YouTube, Oct. 19, 2023.
12 Sara and Stephen Cole, as told to Maddy Mahoney, "We sold our house in Fergus, Ontario, and bought an 11-bedroom château in France," *Toronto Life*, Dec. 19, 2023.
13 George Monbiot and Peter Hutchison, *Invisible Doctrine: The Secret History of Neoliberalism* (London: Allen Lane, 2024), 2.
14 Richard Cockett, *Thinking the Unthinkable. Think-Tanks and the Economic Counter-Revolution, 1931–1983* (Fontana, 1995), 174–76.
15 By January 2025, the Tories had a war chest of almost $42 million, twice as much money as the Liberals and NDP combined. David Baxter, "Record-breaking Conservative fundraising for 2024 nearly double Liberal, NDP total," Canadian Press, Jan. 31, 2025.
16 In my 2015 book *Kill the Messengers*, I describe how conservatives in Canada had already started that process. Flora Garamvolgyi, "Viktor Orbán tells CPAC the path to power is to 'have your own media,'" *Guardian*, May 20, 2022.
17 Though Trump probably was telling the truth when he said he hadn't read it.
18 Richard Raycraft, "RCMP investigating rape threat against Pierre Poilievre's wife," CBC News, Sept. 26, 2022.
19 Catherine Tunney, "Poilievre visits convoy camp, claims Trudeau is lying about 'everything,'" CBC News, Apr. 24, 2024.
20 Catherine Tunney, "Poilievre visits convoy camp, claims Trudeau is lying about 'everything,'" CBC News, Apr. 24, 2024.
21 Timothy Caulfield, "Welcome to the Poilievre Conspiracy Theory Vortex." *Walrus*, Sept. 18, 2024.
22 Peter Zimonjic, "Elon Musk praises Poilievre, mocks Trudeau as he steps into Canadian politics," CBC News, Jan. 9, 2025; Jesse Cnockaert, "Musk's approval of Poilievre good for Conservatives, but may not sit well for others, say pollsters and strategists," *Hill Times*, Jan. 20, 2025.
23 Corné van Hoepen, "From 'Canada is lost' to 'Just a dad at a concert': Canadians react as Trudeau attends Taylor Swift's Eras Tour while riots shake Montreal," Yahoo News, Nov. 24, 2024.
24 Catherine Tunney, "GTA clashes led to arrests and triggered a public safety alert," CBC News, Nov. 5, 2024.
25 Catherine Tunney, "Poilievre visits convoy camp, claims Trudeau is lying about 'everything,'" CBC News, Apr. 24, 2024.
26 Frank Graves and Stephen Maher, "Pierre Poilievre: The Secret to His Success," *Walrus*, Dec. 14, 2022.
27 Shannon Proudfoot, "What you get when politics becomes about picking fights," *Globe and Mail*, Jan. 18, 2025.

28 Hansard, Apr. 24, 2004, and Pierre Poilievre, "The Carbon Tax Con Job," YouTube, Jan. 25, 2025.
29 Sirvan Karimi, "Populism and the quest for political power: the pitfalls to populist electoral success in Canada," *Humanities and Social Sciences Communication* 11, no. 1 (Feb. 2024).
30 "2 Alberta men charged with uttering threats against Trudeau online," CBC News, July 22, 2024.
31 Alex Ballingall, "Justin Trudeau's top security adviser warned of RCMP's struggles to meet demand as threats rise against politicians," *Toronto Star,* Nov. 25, 2024. The situation was made worse by an Iranian plan to kill former justice minister Irwin Cotler. He was given twenty-four-hour-a-day RCMP protection.
32 Charlie Angus/The Resistance.
33 Tonda MacCharles, "Pierre Poilievre worries about threats against his family—but says there's no need to tone down political criticism," *Toronto Star,* July 22, 2024.
34 Tonda MacCharles, "Pierre Poilievre worries about threats against his family—but says there's no need to tone down political criticism," *Toronto Star,* July 22, 2024.
35 Paul Wells, "Does Poilievre Represent a Threat to Canadian Identity?" *Walrus,* Sept. 18, 2024.
36 Frank Graves and Stephen Maher, "Pierre Poilievre: The Secret to His Success: How the Conservative leader is harnessing the growing tide of authoritarianism in Canada," *Walrus,* Dec. 14, 2022.
37 While poorer people are better off now than they were in the nineteenth century, no one in history has been as wealthy as today's financial elites. On paper, Elon Musk has a bigger fortune than John D. Rockefeller. William the Conqueror, in theory, owned all of England in 1066, but back then it wasn't much of a place. In today's money, it was worth about $100 billion. Marcus Licinus Crassus, banker to the Roman Empire, was worth about $20 billion in today's money. But back then, it didn't cost much to have someone killed or to raise an army. See https://www.businessinsider.com/richest-people-of-all-time-2011-1#1-john-d-rockefeller-20
38 Germany and Austria outlaw Nazi symbolism and makes pro-Nazi speech illegal.
39 Donald Wright, "Poilievre is wrong—no one is 'deleting' Canadian history," *Ottawa Citizen,* Sept. 19, 2023. Professor Wright was head of the Canadian Historical Association when he wrote this piece.
40 Elisabeth Zerofsky, "Is It Fascism? A Leading Historian Changes His Mind," *New York Times,* Oct. 23, 2024.
41 Edward Lempinem, "Fascism shattered Europe a century ago—and historians hear echoes today in the U.S.," *UC Berkeley News,* Sept. 9, 2024.
42 Through this book, I've used "Twitter," even after Musk re-named it X. I did this partly to be consistent, so people wouldn't think Twitter and X were different social media sites, and partly to frustrate Musk.
43 Hitler cobbled together a workable coalition in the Reichstag and was appointed chancellor of Germany. King Victor Emmanuel III named Mussolini prime minister of Italy, which was within in the king's legal power. Poland's Józef Piłsudski seized power in a coup, then held elections that he won. (It helped that the main opposition leaders had fled the country.) Francisco Franco led a popular movement that won the Spanish Cicil War.
44 John Ibbitson, "Pierre Poilievre makes his case for dismantling what the Trudeau government has built," *Globe and Mail,* June 29, 2024.

45 John Paul Tasker, "Poilievre says he would cut population growth after Liberals signal immigration changes coming," CBC News, Aug. 29, 2024.
46 For example, C.P. Champion, editor of the *Dorchester Review*, a mainstream right-wing journal, and Tim Flanagan, mentor and former chief of staff to then-prime minister Stephen Harper, self-published *Grave Error: How The Media Misled Us (and the Truth about Residential Schools)* in 2023. The book sold well on Amazon, often being a bestseller in various categories and earning, as of the beginning of February 2025, almost one thousand ratings, with an average score of 4.6 out of five. John S. Milloy's *A National Crime: The Canadian Government and Residential Schools*, published by the University of Manitoba Press in 2017, has a respectable 165 ratings and a score of 4.7 out of 5. *Canada's Residential Schools: The History, Part 1, Origins to 1939: The Final Report of the Truth and Reconciliation Commission of Canada, Volume 1*, issued in 2015, has seventeen Amazon ratings.
47 Alex Ballingall, "'He's a liar and a hate-monger': Former Prime Minister Kim Campbell slams Pierre Poilievre," *Toronto Star*, Mar. 8, 2024.
48 Douglas Roche, "Clark makes passionate plea for a return to 'co-operation across our differences' in politics today," *Hill Times*, May 27, 2024.

INDEX

Abbott, Tony, 357
Abdulrahman, Hassan, *See* Salahuddin, Dawud
Aberhart, William "Bible Bill", 26–27
Ablonczy, Diane, 79
abortion, 3, 14, 18, 26, 40, 43, 102, 168, 223, 280
Abotech Inc., 117
Accountability Act, 132–34
Adam, Mohammed, 392, 396
Agnew, Spiro, 11
Aiello, Rachel, 413
Air Canada, 43, 196
Alberts, Sheldon, 389
Alcock, Reg, 112–13
Alexander, Chris, 182–83
Al Mallee, Nojoud, 409
Amazon, 8, 231, 245–46
Ambassador Bridge, 250, 268
Ambrose, Rona, 109, 190
American Compass, 313
Amnesty International, 154
Anand, Anita, 1, 279
Anders, Rob, 45, 51, 96, 105
Anderson, Christine, 382

Angus, Charlie, 197, 208–09, 213, 219, 370
Angus Reid Institute, 281, 287–88
Antrim Truck Stop, 272
Arendt, Hannah, 5
Armageddon Factor, The, 83
Armstrong, Kenneth, 416
Arnold, Tom, 387
Artaxerxes, 51–52
Assadourian, Sarkis, 99
Atkinson Charitable Foundation, 213
Atkinson, Joseph, 213
Aubry, Jack, 394–95
Auschwitz, 13
Azrieli, Matthew, 336

Baber, Roman, 280–82, 297
Back to the Bible, 26–27
Badu, Erykah, 339
Bailey, Ian, 393
Bain, George, 389
Baird, John, 69, 87, 92–96, 98–99, 104, 119, 127–28, 130–34, 142, 187, 280, 358
Ballingall, Alex, 423–24
Ballingall, Jeff, 301, 336
Bance, Jerry, 177–78

Bank of Canada, 36, 221–22, 224, 230, 239–40, 294–95
Baraka Hospital, 200
"barbaric cultural practices" tip line, 182, 294
Barber, Chris, 248, 250
Barlow, Maude, 173
Barrhaven, 92, 105, 128
Batters, Denise, 276
Bauder, James, 250, 252–53
Bay Street, 89, 311–12
Belfield, David, *See* Salahudin, Dawud
Bell, Rick, 415
Belton, Brigitte, 250, 252
Benner, Dick, 153
Bennett, R.B., 4
Bergen, Candice, 143, 280
Bergeron, Émilie, 408
Berkshire Hathaway, 12
Berlusconi, Silvio, 372
Bernier, Maxime, 192, 276, 315
Besco, Randy, 281
Beyond a Ballot, 376
Biden, Joe, 219, 238, 258, 316, 353
Biggar, Oliver Mowat, 146
Bill of Rights, 64
bin Laden, Osama, 78, 154
Black, Conrad, 64–65, 71, 73, 98, 104, 311
Blackfoot, 27
Blackwell, Tom, 403
Blair, Bill, 254, 348
Blair, Tony, 86
Blatchford, Christie, 65
Bloc Quebecois, 45, 50, 63, 77, 110, 112, 129, 141, 155–56, 160–61, 180, 186, 191–92, 367
Blofeld, Ernst Stavro, 5
Bolsonaro, Jair, 50, 363, 372
Bond, James, 5
Boorstin, Daniel J., 326
Borden, Robert, 110
Bosch, Kevin, 177–78
Boucher, Jean-Christophe, 55
Boulware, Jack, 389
Boutilier, Alex, 413–14
Bouw, Brenda, 386
Brébeuf, Jean de, 5
Breen, Kerri, 421
Brewster, Murray, 410

Brexit, 15–16, 193, 305
Bridgman, Aengus, 283
Brison, Scott, 85, 116–17, 120
Bristol Aerospace, 44
British Columbia Court of Appeal, 52
British Empire, 91
Broadbent, Ed, 145
Broadbent Institute, 351
Bron, Ian, 396
Brooks, David, 9–11, 195
Brossard, Ruth Ellen, 397
Brown, Bert, 56
Brown, Jesse, 205, 217
Brown, Michael, 339
Brown, Patrick, 65, 78, 103, 278, 282–83, 289–91, 293–94
Bryan, William Jennings, 206
Buffett, Warren, 12
Bunner, Paul, 76
Burgess, Steve, 412
Burke, Ashley, 416
Bush, George H. W., 315
Bush, George W., 78, 86
Butts, Gerald, 17, 108, 192
Bynon, Arlene, 58
Byrne, Jenni, 46, 68, 81, 85, 87, 94, 98, 104–05, 128, 130–131, 167–68, 178, 180, 187, 195, 279–80, 288, 290–91, 295, 312, 324–25, 368

Calgary Herald, 55–56, 62, 66, 71, 73, 81, 104, 106, 335
Calgary School, 41, 55
Calgary Southeast (federal riding), 48
Calgary Southwest (federal riding), 45, 47, 77, 79, 81–82, 136, 336
Cambridge University, 139
Cameron, David, 89
Campbell, Kim, 57, 110, 288, 376
Canada Border Services (CBSA), 250
Canada Elections Act, 146, 159, 164, 168, 278
Canada Health Act, 392
Canada Life, 229
Canada Pension Plan, 47, 228, 302
Canada Post, 99, 112
Canada Proud, 285–86
Canada Reads, 107
Canada Revenue Agency (CRA), 153–54, 190, 254, 337

INDEX 427

Canada Service Corps, 202
Canada Strong and Free Network (formerly Manning Institute), 292
Canada Student Service Grant (CSSG), 202, 212
Canada–US Free Trade Agreement, 308
Canadair, 44
Canadaland, 217
Canada's Economic Action Plan, 137
Canada's Reform Party, 16
Canadian Alliance, 71, 76–77, 79, 81–82, 85–86, 89, 95, 98, 106, 149, 161, 165
Canadian Broadcasting Corporation (CBC), 351
Canadian Centre for Policy Alternatives, 154
Canadian Conference of Catholic Bishops, 152
Canadian Conservative Reform Alliance, 70
Canadian Emergency Response Benefit (CERB), 203, 421
Canadian Human Rights Act, 338, 419
Canadian Human Rights Commission, 232, 419
Canadian International Development Agency (CIDA), 151–52
Canadian Labour Code, 154
Canadian Mennonite, 153
Canadian Mennonite Publishing Service, 153
Canadian Pacific Railway, 13, 26, 30, 64, 246, 311
Canadian Periodical Fund, 273
Canadian Public Affairs Channel (CPAC), 283–84, 393
Canadian Security Intelligence Service (CSIS), 254
Canadian Trucking Association, 253
Cannon, Lawrence, 397
Cantin-Nantel, Elie, 408
Capitalism and Freedom, 40–41
Carleton (federal riding), 92, 138, 142
Carleton University, 343
Carlson, Tucker, 268
Carmichael, Kelly, 403
Carney, Mark, 20, 108, 277, 347, 369
Carter, Jimmy, 32, 364
Carville, James, 76

Cashore, Harvey, 405
Cass, Oren, 313, 315
Castonguay, Audrey, 78
Caulfield, Timothy, 366
CFRA (Ottawa radio station), 135
Chambers, Adam, 364
Champion, C.P., 397, 424
Chandler, Craig, 64
Charbonneau, Yvon, 99
Charest, Jean, 45, 63, 108, 278, 280–97, 356
Charlie Hebdo, 419
Charter rights, 52, 159
Chase, Stephen, 400
Chase, Steven, 400
Chávez, Hugo, 189
Chelsea, Quebec, 401
Chiarelli, Bob, 93
Chicago School, 41
Chown Oved, Marco, 404
Chrétien, Jean, 22, 46, 50, 54–56, 61–62, 65–66, 71, 74–89, 92, 99, 107, 109–11, 114–15, 124, 130, 143, 147, 158, 162, 177, 198, 234, 279–80, 357, 363
Christie, Doug, 34
Churchill, Winston, 57, 133
Citizens United, 151
Civil Marriage Act, 102
Clark, Campbell, 58, 109, 123
Clark, Catherine, 121
Clark, Joe, 26, 34, 63, 65–66, 70, 78, 81, 85, 89, 161, 376
Clark, Karl, 31
Clark, Tom, 293–95
Clarkson, Adrienne, 124
Clayton, Freddie, 412
Clement, Tony, 89, 102, 186
Clinton, Bill, 57, 76, 300, 315
Clinton, Hillary, 328, 366, 369
Cnockaert, Jesse, 422
Coast GasLink, 201
Coderre, Denis, 192
Cohen, Tobi, 398
Cohn, Roy, 11
Colbert, Stephen, 1, 329
Cole, Sara, 361
Communication Security Establishment (CSE), 254
Company of One Hundred Associates, 13
Conflict of Interest Act, 215

Connelly, John, 374
Constituent Information Management System (CIMS), 148–51, 173
conversion therapy, 276, 280
Cooper, Barry, 55, 281
Co-operative Commonwealth Federation (CCF), 108, 384
Copps, Sheila, 386
Cosh, Colby, 330, 339
Côté-Stroka, Estelle, 395
Cotler, Irwin, 166
Coutts, Alberta, 6, 261, 270
Covid, 3–4, 9–11, 193–96, 200–02, 205, 218–20, 230, 235–39, 250, 252, 255, 270, 275, 283–84, 297, 303, 314, 316, 318, 355, 363, 367. *See also* coronavirus
Coyne, Andrew, 23, 65
Coyne, Deborah, 184
coronavirus, 193–94, 283. *See also* Covid
Crawford, Blair, 402
Crawley, Mike, 407
Cree, 27, 42
Criminal Code, 110, 276
Crockatt, Joan, 58
Crockett, Richard, 363
Csanady, Ashley, 402
CTV News, 204, 290, 293, 332, 336
Cullen, Catherine, 415
Cunningham, Jim, 388
Curry, Bill, 394

Daifallah, Adam, 58, 78, 338
Daily Bread Food Bank, 314
Dale, Daniel, 335
Danson, Barney, 201
Darrow, Clarence, 206
Daviau, Debi, 185
David Suzuki Foundation, 154
Davis, Bill, 33, 317
Day, Logan, 76
Day, Stockwell, 23, 66, 70–76, 80–93, 161, 335
Décarie, Richard, 123
Delacourt, Susan, 147–48
DeLorey, Fred, 331
Dene, 42
Denis, Jonathan, 77, 82, 87–88, 93, 149
Denley, Randall, 395

Department of National Defence, 92, 279
Derfel, Aaron, 371, 405
DeSantis, Ron, 268
De Souza, Mike, 395
Diagolon, 365–66
Dickson, Janice, 402
Didulo, Romana, 261–62
Diefenbaker, John, 5, 23, 40, 89, 146, 357
Dion, Mario, 215–16
Dion, Stéphane, 138–40, 163, 192
disinformation, 220, 240–41, 269, 342–46, 371, 412, 418
Ditchburn, Jennifer, 396
diversity, equity, and inclusion (DEI), 15, 231–32, 234, 279, 382
Dowling, Tim, 402
Downie, Gord, 199
Drew, George, 5, 22, 92
Droege, Wolfgang, 34
Duffy, Mike, 58, 130, 179, 293
Duke of Aarschot, 35
Duke of Arenberg, 35
Duke of Meppen, 35
Dylan, Bob, 67

Easter, Wayne, 205–06, 208
Edmonton Journal, 69, 71
Eisenhower, Dwight, 5, 373
EKOS, 240, 343, 362
Elba, Idris, 199
Elections Canada, 20, 143, 147, 156–67, 169–76, 184, 187
Elections Modernization Act, 175
Emergencies Act (Canada), 270–71, 412
Emergencies Act (Ontario), 268
Emmanuel, Tristan, 86
Engelbert, Erik, 35
environmentalism, social and governance (ESG), 232
Erskine-Smith, Nate, 318, 368–69
ethanol, 31
Ethics Commissioner, 117–18, 204, 211, 215
Evangelical Lutheran Church, 152
Eves, Ernie, 405

Facebook, 15, 88, 231, 250–51, 271, 282, 285, 287, 333, 346–47, 350, 370
Fafard, Patrick, 370

Fair Elections Act, 169–70, 173–74, 176, 184, 188, 206
Faith and Politics, 51
False Claims Act, 132
Farage, Nigel, 16, 50, 305, 315–16
Farrell, Jacqueline, 25–26, 29
Fawcett, Max, 320–21
Federal Court of Appeal, 154
Federal Deposit Insurance Corporation, 37
Federal-Provincial Arrangements Act, 190
Federal Public Sector Labour Relations Act, 154
Feeney, Gordon, 99
Fenelon Falls, 46, 85, 94, 105
fentanyl, 322–23, 359
Ferry, Bryan, 98
Fifth Estate, The, 216–17
Financial Post, 130, 240, 409, 417
Finley, Doug, 130–31, 167
First World War, 5, 28, 110, 146, 372, 374
Fiscal Responsibility Act, 69
Fischer, Sarah, 263, 350
Fish Creek Provincial Park, 29
Fitz-Morris, James, 402
Flaherty, Jim, 365
Flanagan, Tom, 55, 131, 334
Fleming, Ian, 5
Fletcher, Steven, 142
Floyd, George, 206, 339
FLQ, 125
Ford, Doug, 142, 187, 266, 268, 275, 280, 336, 365
Ford, Rob, 335
Foss, Greg, 251
Fotheringham, Allan, 67
Foucault, Michel, 8
Fox News, 10, 217, 268, 329–30, 339
Fox, Terry, 141
Francis, Lloyd, 92
Francoli, Paco, 392
Frank magazine, 84, 105
Fraser, David, 410–11
Fraser Institute, 42, 338
Fraser, Sheila, 173
Free the Children, 198–99
Freeland, Chrystia, 20, 108, 237, 277, 283, 327, 347, 369–70
Friedman, Milton, 16, 36–37, 40–41, 83, 313

Friedman, Vanessa, 401
Friendly Dictator, The, 46, 115
Friesen, Joe, 401
Frontier Oilsands Mine, 201
Front Porch Strategies, 165
Frost, Robert, 276
Frum, David, 64
Furtado, Nelly, 199

Galindo, Anaida, *See* Poilievre, Anaida
gasohol, 31
Gauthier, James, 409
General Agreement on Tariffs and Trade, 308
General Motors, 26
Ghalib, Amer, 353
Giller Prize, 107
Gingrich, Newt, 307
Giorno, Guy, 187
GiveSendGo, 271
Global News (Canada), 285, 412–14, 421
Globe and Mail, 5, 46, 48, 58, 109, 115, 123, 127, 131, 138, 171, 174, 181, 205, 220, 264, 284, 306, 311, 351, 368, 375
Glorious Revolution, 6
GoFundMe, 249, 251, 271, 411
Goldwater, Barry, 6
Gomery, John, 114–15, 161
Gomez, Selena, 199
Goodale, Ralph, 129–30, 132, 162
Goodyear, Gary, 142, 161
Gould, Karina, 191–92, 347
Gowling, Jordan, 409, 417
Grant, George, 383
Grant, George Monro, 139
Graves, Frank, 240–41, 340, 343, 362, 372
Gray, Ken, 94–95
Great Depression, 13, 28, 59, 228, 236, 289, 310
"Great Reset," 265–66, 412
Green, Lowell, 68
Green Party, 95, 121, 166, 192
Greenaway, Norma, 73
Greene, Marjorie Taylor, 268
Grégoire Trudeau, Sophie, 11, 202
Grey, Deborah, 62
Griffith, Andrew, 380
Grok, 374

Guardian, 182
Guelph Mercury, 138
Guergis, Helena, 162
Guilbeault, Steven, 369
Guite, Chuck, 158

Ha, Tu Thanh, 403
Hagen, Lisa, 407
Haldeman, H.R., 131
Hall, Frank, 97
Hamilton, Lewis, 199
Hanger, Art, 49–50
Hannaford, Higel, 393
Hannity, Sean, 268
Harley, Richard, 333
Harper, Stephen
   2015 federal election, 176, 177–185, 187
   Calgary Southwest byelection, 79–82
   Elections Canada, 20, 143, 163, 167–69, 172–74
Harperland, 131, 396
Harris, Michael, 185, 266–67
Harris, Mike, 63, 71, 73, 88, 128, 234
Harrison, Jeremy, 58, 105
Hart Dungeon, 39
Hart House, 39
Hart, Bret, 39
Hart, Bruce, 39
Hart, Stu, 39
Harvard, John, 99
Hébert, Jacques, 201
Hefner, Hugh, 7
Heinz, 12
Henry Wise Wood High School, 39, 49
Hepburn, Mitchell, 22
Heritage Trust Fund, 69
Hess, Karl, 6–7
Hill, Grant, 79
Hill, Kelly, 407
Hill Times, 63, 95, 109, 135, 283, 334
Hillier, Randy, 142
Hitler, Adolf, 4–5, 17, 21, 269, 374
Hnatyshyn, Ray, 126
Hoeppner, Candice. *See* Bergen, Candice
Hofmeester, Madison, 336
Hogue, Marie-Josée, 344
Holland, Mark, 182, 263, 318, 322
Hollinshead Research Institute, 97
Holocaust, 34, 269

Holy Roman Empire, 153
HonkHonk Hodl, 251
Hope, Bob, 31
Horthy, Miklós, 374
Hostetler, Dallas, 338
Houghtaling, Ellie Quinlan, 380
Housakos, Leo, 288
Howe, C.D., 17
Huawei, 281, 288
Hubei, 283
Hudson, Jennifer, 199
Hudson's Bay Company, 13
Hughes, John, 83
Hunter, Paul, 75
Hurley, Janet, 407
Hurons, 5
Hutton, David, 395

Ibbitson, John, 89, 375, 391
Ignatieff, George, 139
Ignatieff, Michael, 137–41
Income Tax Act, 153, 337
Independent Immigration Aid Association, 337
Ingraham, Laura, 268
Instagram, 231, 237, 333, 346
Integrated Terrorism Assessment Centre (ITAC), 253–54,
Internal Revenue Service (IRS), 6
International Democratic Union, 165
iPolitics, 183
Iraq War, 78–79, 86, 111
Ishaq, Zunera, 180
Ivison, John, 105, 302

Jaffer, Rahim, 103, 105
James II, 6
Jean, Michaëlle, 123, 124–26
Jensen, Audrey, 116
Jim Crow laws, 373
Jinping, Xi, 9, 344, 374
Jodoin, Debbie, 278
Joffe-Block, Jude, 407
Jones, Alex, 365
Jones, Alexandra Mae, 420
Jones, Robin, 406
Jordan, Jim, 268
Justice Department (Canada), 176
KAIROS, 151–52

INDEX 431

Karimi, Sirvan, 423
Katimavik, 107, 201–02
Kay, Jonathan, 65
Keller, Garry, 99, 296
Kelley, Mark, 216
Kelly, Megyn, 330
Kennedy, Dan, 418
Kenney, Jason, 17, 46, 48–51, 69–71, 105, 134, 138, 152, 180, 337
Kent, Peter, 154
Kesler, Gordon, 34
Khan, Ahmar, 412
Kheiriddin, Tasha, 58, 65, 218, 275, 281, 290–91, 316–17, 338
Kielburger, Craig, 197–200, 202, 206, 208–209, 212–217
Kielburger, Marc, 199–200, 203–06, 208–09, 212–14, 216–17
Kielburger, Theresa, 197, 203, 205, 217
Kilrea, Terry, 119
Kimmel, Jimmy, 329
Kimmel, Michael, 264
King George III, 91
King, Pat, 258, 261
King, William Lyon Mackenzie, 110
Kingsley, Jean-Pierre, 172
Kipling, Rudyard, 38
Kishon Health Centre, 200
Klein, Ralph, 45–46, 55–56, 63, 66, 69, 72
Knopff, Rainer, 55
Koch brothers, 164
Koop, Royce, 295
Kovacevic, Michelle, 211–12
Kovrig, Michael, 281
KPMG, 117
Krause, Vivian, 205–06
Kupfer, Matthew, 395
Kurdi family, 179–80
Kurl, Shachi, 287
Kyoto Accord, 81, 102
Kyoto Joe, 81

Lac-Mégantic, 143, 397–98
LaFleche, Grant, 410
Lafond, Jean-Daniel, 124–27
Lantsman, Melissa, 259, 368–69, 420
Laporte, Pierre, 125
La Presse, 123
Larocque, Kc, 184

Laurentian elites, 84, 229, 231, 310–11
Laurier, Sir Wilfrid, 17, 27, 110, 190
Laval University, 191
Lawton, Andrew, 70, 134, 331, 337
Layton, Jack, 108, 129–30, 137, 140–42, 154, 181
Le Pen, Marine, 316
Lead Belly, 339
Lebel, Denis, 142–43
Leblanc, Daniel, 400
LeBlanc, Dominic, 157
LeBrun, Luke, 420
Legault, François, 275, 288
Leitch, Kellie, 182–83
Lenin, Vladimir, 310, 313
Leung, Sophia, 99
Levant, Ezra, 17, 56, 63–65, 74, 77, 79–82, 96, 104–05, 136, 173, 249, 290, 335–36
Lévesque, Catherine, 289
Lévesque, René, 30
Levitz, Stephanie, 388, 396, 413
Levy, Sue-Ann, 337
Lewis, Brian, 417
Lewis, Leslyn, 280–82, 297
libertarianism, 41, 50, 59, 244, 259 360
Library and Archives Canada, 116
Lich, Tamara, 248, 251–53
Lilley, Brian, 341
Lincoln, Abraham, 132
Local Journalism Initiative (LJI), 332–33
Loewen, Peter, 387
Loney, Martin, 234
Long, Huey, 11
Long, Tom, 71, 73
Lougheed, Peter, 35
Lovato, Demi, 199
Lukiwski, Tom, 160

MacCharles, Tonda, 392, 400, 401, 404, 410, 423
MacDonald, Cory, 61–62
MacDonald, Fiona, 264
MacDonald, Grant, 262
Macdonald, John A., 4, 22, 59, 64, 89, 92, 110, 145
MacDonald, L. Ian, 127
MacEachen, Allan, 17
MacKay, Peter, 85, 88–90, 101
Mackenzie, Alexander, 145

MacKinnon, Leslie, 402
Maclean's, 65, 127, 131, 339
MacLeod, Lisa, 94
Macron, Emmanuel, 316, 364
MacSweeney, Cormack, 417
Maduro, 284, 347
MAGA, 10–11, 264
Magna International, 58, 61–62, 68, 77
Maher, Stephen, 166–67, 172, 340
Mahfouz, Ed, 93, 121
Major, Darren, 417
Majumdar, Shuvaloy, 123
Malcolm, Candice, 285, 337
Maloney, Ryan, 403
Mandela, Nelson, 376
Manitoba Court of Appeal, 154
Manning Centre, 150
Manning, Ernest, 26
Manning Institute, 292
Manning, Preston, 41, 44–47, 51–53, 62–63, 66, 70–74, 79–80, 82, 88, 101, 103, 141, 168–69, 335
Manotick, 97, 119, 184
Mansbridge, Peter, 167, 342
Marchand, Jean-Paul, 155–56
Marchesan, John, 417
Marketplace, 177
Mark, Inky, 162
Marshall, Donald, 266
Marshall, Hamish, 82
Martin, Don, 414
Martin, Lawrence, 131
Martin, Pat, 98, 134
Martin, Paul, 38, 47, 66, 79, 88–90, 92–93, 95, 98–99, 102, 109–11, 114–116, 120–30, 138–39, 147, 156, 158, 162, 166, 178, 192, 279, 334
Marx, Karl, 57, 125, 288, 318, 374
Masih, Iqbal, 197–98
Maslanka, Jerzy, 80
Mason, Gary, 264
Massicotte, Paul, 117
Maverick Party, 252
May, Elizabeth, 192
May, Howard, 389
May, Kathryn, 19
Mayrand, Marc, 156, 159–60, 163, 169–70, 172–75
Mazankowski, Don, 17, 43

McCallum, John, 112
McCarthy, Joe, 11
McClelland & Stewart, 335
McCormack, Carter, 409
McCormick, Jessica, 173
McDonald, Marci, 83
McDowell, Will, 215
McGill University, 17, 141, 283–84
McGregor, Glen, 167
McGuinty, Dalton, 107, 111, 129,
McGuinty, David, 129, 132
McIlroy, Anne, 388
McKeen, Alex, 410
McKenna, Kate, 405, 413, 416,
McLachlan, Sarah, 199
McMaster, Geoff, 413
McQuaig, Linda, 65
McWhirter, Ross, 38
Media Ecosystem Observatory, 283
medicare, 75, 111, 338
Meech Lake Accord, 44
Meighen, Arthur, 110
Mennonite Central Committee, 152, 200
Mercer, Rick, 76, 352
Meta, 231, 333
Metis, 27
ME to WE, 200, 213
Mesley, Wendy, 395
Meyers, Seth, 329
MGTOW, 285
Mick, Hayley, 115
Migicovsky, Peter, 254–55
Milei, Javier Gerardo, 50
Milewski, Terry, 167
Miller, Marc, 17, 318
Milley, Mark, 6
Milliken, Peter, 153
Milloy, John S., 424
Minden, Daniel, 348–49
Modi, Narendra, 372
Monbiot, George, 362–63
Montreal Gazette, 127, 371
Montreal Mirror, 75
Moore, James, 135
Moriarty, Michael, 57
Morneau, Bill, 190, 202, 205–09, 215, 280
Morris, Jeffrey, 116
Morton, Ted, 55–56, 69
Mosaic law, 52

MSNBC, 10, 329
Muir, Robert, 44
Mulcair, Tom, 108, 178, 180–81
Mulroney, Ben, 199
Mulroney, Brian, 17, 22, 35, 43–44, 47, 85, 103, 106, 110, 126, 201, 280, 373
Munk School for Global Affairs & Public Policy, 107
Murphy, Rex, 341
Murray, Susan, 116
Musk, Elon, 11, 240, 268–69, 282, 331, 366, 374
Mussolini, Benito, 4, 21, 287, 374
Muttart, Patrick, 140, 154, 307–08, 312–13

Napoleon, 91
Napoleonic War, 363
National Arts Centre, 68
National Business Book Award, 335
National Capital Commission, 105, 128
National Energy Program (NEP), 29, 33–36, 43, 81
National Observer, 269, 320
National Post, 64, 71, 127, 173, 218, 289, 311–12, 316, 329–30, 351
National Press Club, 68
NATO, 366
Nehemiah, 51–52
Nejatian, Kaz, 337
Nepean, Ontario, 128
Nepean–Carleton (federal riding), 92, 95–96, 184
Netanyahu, Benjamin, 321, 353
New York Times, 9–10, 181, 313, 328, 329
Newman, Don, 74
NewsMedia Council, 338
Niagara Falls, 76, 86, 306, 333
Niagara-on-the-Lake, 333, 418
Nixon, Richard, 131
Noël, Christian, 422
Norris, Pippa, 340
North American Free Trade Agreement, 14, 308, 315, 362
Notley, Rachel, 389

Off, Carol, 411
Official Languages Act, 120
Olive, David, 238–39
Online News Act (Bill C-18), 333

Ontario Disability Support Program (ODSB), 222
Ontario Federation of Labour, 198
O'Regan, Seamus, 17
O'Toole, Erin, 55, 187, 259, 263–65, 267, 275–80, 288–91, 303, 331, 336, 346, 358, 368
Oda, Bev, 152–53
"Orange Crush," 181
Orbán, Viktor, 50, 364, 372
Orchard, David, 85
Organisation for Economic Cooperation and Development (OECD), 207
Organization of the Petroleum Exporting Countries (OPEC), 30, 33
Orwell, George, 40, 161
Ottawa Citizen, 19, 40, 64, 71, 94–95, 97, 105, 115, 117, 167
Ottawa Police Service, 254

Paas-Lang, Christian, 412, 414
pandemic, 4, 9–12, 23, 193, 195–96, 201–02, 206–07, 214, 218–19, 229–30, 235–36, 239, 241–44, 255–58, 266, 270–71, 275, 303, 311, 314, 317, 322, 355, 370
Paradis, Melanie, 278
Paraskevas, Joe, 389
Parliament of Canada Act, 117
Parliamentary Employees and Staff Relations Act, 154
Parliamentary Press Gallery, 157, 327
Parti Quebecois, 288
Party of One, 185, 266, 396, 398, 400–02
Paxton, Robert, 373
Pearson, Lester, 110, 376
Pelletier, Jean, 158
People's Liberation Army, 56
Perez, Andrew, 383
Perrin, Benjamin, 17, 54
Persian Empire, 51
Peterson, Jordan, 37–38, 286, 294, 338, 340
Petro-Canada, 33, 35, 43
Phillips, Tim, 164
Philpott, Jane, 192
"Pierre Poutine," 166–67
Plante, Yan, 289
Playboy, 7
Poilievre, Anaida, 188–89, 365, 368
Poilievre, Donald, 26–29, 38–39

Poilievre, Joseph, 27-28
Poilievre, Marlene, 26, 28-29, 38-40, 45, 47, 83
Poilievre, Patrick, 29
Poilievre, Paul, 28
Poilievre, Pierre
  early life, 25-29, 36-40
  education, 43-50, 53-56,
  elected Carleton riding MP, 183-187
  elected Nepean-Carleton riding MP, 93-98
  essay contest ("As Prime Minister, I Would..."), 58-62
  freedom convoy, 245, 249, 251, 256-71, 291-92, 371
  leadership race, 25, 189, 195, 220, 259, 267, 278-298
  media, 320-336, 339-341, 344, 346-353
  rallies, 60, 119, 292, 306-07, 309, 326-28, 333, 352, 373
  WE Charity, 203-16, 219-20
  YouTube, 242, 249, 260, 266, 282-83, 285-86, 301, 322-323, 329, 346-350, 352, 367
Policy Options magazine, 19
Pornhub, 282
Postmedia, 19, 167, 174, 240, 302, 311, 332, 341
Potter, Andrew, 400
Power & Politics, 267
Pratt, David, and family, 91-98, 127
Prentice, Jim, 81, 85
Presbyterian Church in Canada, 152
Press, Jordan, 402
Pretty and Smart, 189
Prince Harry, 199
Prince of Recklinghausen, 35
Pringle, Josh, 405, 406
Privy Council Office, 254
Professional Institute of the Public Service of Canada (PIPSC), 185
Proudfoot, Shannon, 306, 368
Public Order Emergency Commission (POEC), 254, 257, 261
Public Service Alliance of Canada (PSAC), 142, 155
Public Servants Disclosure Protection Act, 118
Putin, Vladimir, 9, 284, 345-47

QAnon, 252, 261
Quebec Court of Appeal, 344
Quebec Solidaire, 288
Queen's Park, 96, 104, 107, 268
Queensway Carleton Hospital, 94, 128

Rabson, Mia, 404
Radisson, Pierre-Esprit, 5
Rae, Bob, 138, 168, 234
Rana, F. Abbas, 396
Rand, Ayn, 3-4, 16, 83
Rand Formula, 142, 316
Raycraft, Richard, 422
Rayes, Alain, 356
Reagan, Ronald, 37, 41-42, 106, 307, 315, 373
Rebel News, 249, 286, 335
Red Tory, 78, 178, 287
Reform Party, 16-17, 19, 44-46, 48-50, 54, 56-58, 60, 62-63, 68, 70-71, 73, 133, 147, 287, 373, 388
Reform Party club, 19, 50, 54, 56, 63
Reform UK, 16, 316
Regan, Geoff, 193
Reich, Robert, 380, 382
Reid, Scott, 126, 130
Rempel Garner, Michelle, 282
Reno, Janet, 57
Report magazine, 76
Republican Party of Canada, 57
Research Council of Alberta, 31
residential schools, 42, 135-36, 206, 232, 376
Responsive Marketing Group, 149
Reynolds, Christopher, 411
Reynolds, John, 79, 81
Rideau Hall, 11, 126
Riel, Louis, 27
Riley, Susan, 396, 418
Ring of Fire, 415
Roberts, Stan, 44
Robertson, Grant, 395
robocalls, 134, 151, 165-70, 400, 401
Rocha, Roberto, 414
Roche, Douglas, 424
Rock, Allan, 99, 110
Rodgers, Chris, 184, 186, 193
Roman Empire, 2
Romanow, Roy, 168

Roosevelt, Theodore, 5, 59
Rose, Jacques, 125
Roth, Ginny, 408
Rouleau, Paul, 254
Royal Bank of Canada, 62
Royal Canadian Legion, 184
Royal Canadian Mounted Police (RCMP), 118, 129–30, 132, 160, 162, 182, 214, 249, 254, 257, 270
Roy Thomson Hall, 62
RT (Russian Television), 269, 345
Russell, Frances, 400
Russell, Todd, 136
Russian Digital Army, 345
Ryan, Andrew, 416

Saba, Michel, 408
Salahuddin, Dawud, 126–27
Salazar, António de Oliveira, 374–75
Salvation Army, 200, 225
same-sex marriage, 16, 18, 38, 75, 102, 121–23
Sanderson, Montague "Bugsy", 22
Satyarthi, Kailash, 198
Saul, John Ralston, 124
Saunders, Charles, 27
Sauvé, Jeanne, 126
Schartner, Louise, 28
Scheer, Andrew, 105, 187, 190, 192, 196, 212, 249, 309, 336
Scheer, Jill, 106
Schreyer, Ed, 126
Second World War, 2, 28, 34, 66, 146, 195–96, 228, 277, 306
Segal, Hugh, 169
Sereda, Dr. Andrea, 370
Severe Acute Respiratory Syndrome (SARS), 193–94, 284
Shapero, Julia, 412
Shapiro, Ben, 331
Shawinigate, 85
Shepherd, Lindsay, 338
Shepherds of Good Hope, 225
Shopping for Votes, 147–48, 399
Sifton, Clifford, 17, 27
Simms, Scott, 109
Simpson, Jeffrey, 46, 115, 174
Singh, Amitpal, 202
Singh, Jagmeet, 108, 192, 370

Singh, Lilly, 199
Sivakumar, Vimal, 417
Skamski, Sebastian, 376
Sloly, Peter, 254, 270
Smith, David, 117–18
Smith, Stuart, 31, 317
SNC-Lavalin, 176, 192, 263, 312
Snow, Rob, 322
Social Design Agency (SDA), 345
Solberg, Monte, 105
Soliman, Walied, 279
Solomon, Evan, 290
Sona, Michael, 168
Soo Today, 304
Spavor, Michael, 281
Speaker's Corner, 53
Speer, Sean, 341–42
sponsorship scandal, 85, 114, 116, 158–59, 161–62
Spratt, Michael, 321
St. Laurent, Louis, 110
St.Louis, Nicholas, 251
Stalin, Joseph, 153
Standing Committee on Government Operations and Estimates, 112
Stanfield, Robert, 89, 376
Stevens, Geoffrey, 138
Stewart, Jon, 329
Stewart, Monte, 387
Stewart-Olsen, Carolyn, 81
stock market crash, 1929, 28
Stoffer, Peter, 23, 111
Stronach, Belinda, 89–90, 133, 135
Stronach, Frank, 58, 62, 68, 77
Strong, Maurice, 35
Strzelecki, Andrzej, 381
Sun News Network, 141, 173, 335, 341
Suncor, 33
Supreme Court of Canada, 75, 111, 142, 233, 373
Sutherland House, 65
Swift, Taylor, 350, 367

Taber, Jane, 395
Taghva, Ali, 336
Taliban, 78, 153
Tallycoin, 251
Taman, Emilie, 402
Tasker, John Paul, 287

Tawney, R.H., 41
Taylor, Stephanie, 416
Tea Party, 44, 307
Teague, Jennifer, 128
Telford, Katie, 17, 107
Telus, 49, 77
Tencer, Daniel, 392
Teneycke, Kory, 68, 141
Thatcher, Margaret, 37, 41, 83, 106, 307, 310, 373
The House, 172
Thompson, Andy, 63
Thompson, Elizabeth, 412
Thompson Reuters, 108
Thorne, Stephen, 400
Tiananmen Square, 56
TikTok, 209, 261, 346
Timson, Judith, 209
Tkachuk, David, 249
Today's Trucking, 272–74
Toews, Vic, 143, 154
Toronto Life, 361
Toronto Star, 197, 209, 213, 238, 252, 254, 278, 280, 311, 328, 332, 335
Toth, Laurence, 278
Treasury Board, 131, 190
Trudeau, Alexandre, 202, 204
Trudeau, Justin,
  communication problems, 237–38, 318–19, 324,
  Covid response, 11, 201–02, 205, 218–19
  freedom convoy, 259–265, 267–70, 273
  new media, 181, 301, 318, 347, 350–51
  WE Charity, 199, 201–02, 204, 207–12, 215–17
Trudeau, Margaret, 202, 204
Trudeaumania, 29
Trump, Donald
  artificial intelligence, 350
  attack on Capitol, 6, 253, 374
  economic trade and tariff war on Canada, 229, 236–37, 240, 243–44, 304, 362–64, 369
  fascism, 4, 15, 269, 374
  media, 328–29, 335
  religion, 321
  second presidency, 231, 287, 341–42, 366
Tuns, Paul, 76
Turner, Garth, 130, 156, 239

Turner, John, 110, 315
Twitter, 11, 15, 49, 88, 181, 204, 261, 278–79, 282–85, 286, 295, 297, 301, 318, 323, 331, 336, 346–47, 349–50, 362, 366–67

United Alternative, 65–66, 70, 77–78
United Church of Canada, 152
United Conservative Party, 71
United Farmers of Alberta, 39
United Nations, 54, 182
United Steelworkers (union), 302
United We Roll, 248–49, 251, 255, 261, 265
University of Calgary, 17, 23, 41, 49–50, 54–55, 58, 63, 65, 69–70, 83, 94, 281
University of California, 374
University of Chicago, 41
University of Northern British Columbia, 264
University of Ottawa, 189, 225, 369
University of Toronto, 89, 107, 281, 283, 314, 335
University of Victoria, 72
University of Windsor, 314
Urback, Robin, 351
Urquhart, Don, 330–31

Valeriote, Frank, 166
Vallières, Pierre, 125
van Hoepen, Corné, 422
Vance, J.D., 11, 243, 312, 363
Vancouver Sun, 46
Vanier Institute of the Family, 229
Vaughan-King-Aurora (federal riding), 77
Viking, Alberta, 43
Voir, 125
von Clausewitz, Carl, 363
von Schuschnigg, Kurt, 374
Vongdouangchanh, Bea, 393, 394, 399

Wall Street Journal, 86
Walmsley, David, 181
Wanzhou, Meng, 281
War in Afghanistan, 78, 96, 110, 124, 182
Watson, Jim, 270
Wayne, Elsie, 45, 63
Weber, Max, 41
WE Charity, 11, 199–220
WE Day, 199–220

Wells, Paul, 65, 312
Wernick, Rachel, 202
Western Canada Concept Party, 34
Western Standard, 54
WestJet, 309
Westminster, 16, 84, 140
Weyrich, Paul, 164
Wherry, Aaron, 267
White, Erik, 406
White, Peter, 98
White, Randy, 73
Whittington, Les, 399
Whyte, Ken, 65
Wilde, Chloe, 199
Wilson-Raybould, Jody, 192
Wilton, Suzanne, 388
Winfrey, Oprah, 199
Winslet, Kate, 199
Wood, Ardeth, 128
Woodfinden, Ben, 284
World Economic Forum (WEF), 265, 362
Wortman, Gabriel, 323

Wright, Donald, 423
Wright, Nigel, 179
Wuhan, 10, 193–94

Xiao, Qi Jia, 409

Yellow Vest, 248
Yom Kippur War, 30
Young, Rebecca, 238–40
Youth for a Conservative Future, 78
YouTube, 49, 88, 175, 242, 249, 258, 260, 266, 282–83, 285–86, 301, 322–23, 327, 329, 345–52, 364, 367

Zaccardelli, Giuliano, 129–30
Zaharoff, Sir Basil, 5
Zedong, Mao, 374
Zero Tolerance for Barbaric Cultural Practices Act, 182
Zimonjic, Peter, 387, 404, 412, 413, 422
Zundel, Ernst, 34